Staging Creolization

NEW WORLD STUDIES

J. Michael Dash, *Editor*

Frank Moya Pons and
Sandra Pouchet Paquet,
Associate Editors

Staging Creolization

WOMEN'S THEATER AND
PERFORMANCE FROM THE
FRENCH CARIBBEAN

Emily Sahakian

University of Virginia Press
Charlottesville and London

THIS BOOK IS MADE POSSIBLE BY A COLLABORATIVE GRANT
FROM THE ANDREW W. MELLON FOUNDATION.

University of Virginia Press
© 2017 by the Rector and Visitors of the University of Virginia
All rights reserved
Printed in the United States of America on acid-free paper

First published 2017

ISBN 978-0-8139-4007-6 (cloth)
ISBN 978-0-8139-4008-3 (paperback)
ISBN 978-0-8139-4009-0 (e-book)

9 8 7 6 5 4 3 2 1

Library of Congress Cataloging-in-Publication Data is available from the Library of Congress.

For my family

Contents

	List of Illustrations	ix
	Acknowledgments	xi
	Introduction	1
1	Unsettling the Gendered Stereotypes of Plantation Culture: Ina Césaire's *Rosanie Soleil* and Maryse Condé's *Pension les Alizés*	23
2	Remixing Unity and Difference: Maryse Condé's *An tan revolisyon*, Ina Césaire's *Mémoires d'Isles*, and Gerty Dambury's *Lettres indiennes*	51
3	Syncretizing Performance and Moral Codes: Ina Césaire's *L'Enfant des passages* and Simone Schwarz-Bart's *Ton beau capitaine*	100
4	Diaspora Performances at Ubu Repertory Theater in New York	133
5	Recasting the Francophone Caribbean Couple at Ubu Repertory Theater	169
	Coda: Creolizing Knowledge in U.S. University Performances	205
	Notes	219
	Bibliography	249
	Index	265

Illustrations

1. Gilbert Laumord as Zéphyr in Maryse Condé's *An tan revolisyon*, Fort Fleur d'Epée, Guadeloupe, 1989 — 57
2. Anna Noverca as Solitude in Maryse Condé's *An tan revolisyon*, Fort Fleur d'Epée, Guadeloupe, 1989 — 60
3. Myrrha Donzenac as Aure and Mariann Mathéus as Hermance in Ina Césaire's *Mémoires d'Isles*, Bagneux, France, 1983 — 69
4. Myrrha Donzenac and Mariann Mathéus improvise a hair-braiding scene from Hermance's childhood in Ina Césaire's *Mémoires d'Isles*, Bagneux, France, 1983 — 70
5. The cast of Gerty Dambury's *Lettres indiennes*, Avignon, France, 1996 — 95
6. Ernestine Jackson as Hermance and Carmen de Lavallade as Aure in Ina Césaire's *Island Memories*, New York, 1991 — 139
7. Ernestine Jackson and Carmen de Lavallade as the she-devils of Ash Wednesday in Ina Césaire's *Island Memories*, New York, 1991 — 145
8. The cast of Ina Césaire's *Fire's Daughters*, New York, 1993 — 151
9. Mama Sun and Sister Smoke speak in code while Annarose hangs the laundry in Ina Césaire's *Fire's Daughters*, New York, 1993 — 152
10. Watoko Ueno's set of Ina Césaire's *Fire's Daughters*, New York, 1993 — 153

Illustrations

11. Kavitha Ladnier (née Ramachandran) performing Marie's dance in Gerty Dambury's *Crosscurrents*, New York, 1997 — 162
12. The cremation of Paul's father in Gerty Dambury's *Crosscurrents*, New York, 1997 — 164
13. Fructueuse at Paul's childhood home in Gerty Dambury's *Crosscurrents*, New York, 1997 — 165
14. Reg E. Cathey as Wilnor in Simone Schwarz-Bart's *Your Handsome Captain*, New York, 1989 — 179
15. Watoko Ueno's set of Maryse Condé's *The Tropical Breeze Hotel*, New York, 1995 — 190
16. Patrick Rameau as Ishmael and Jane White as Emma in Maryse Condé's *The Tropical Breeze Hotel*, New York, 1995 — 191
17. Jane White as Emma in Maryse Condé's *The Tropical Breeze Hotel*, New York, 1995 — 193
18. Emma and Ishmael dancing the merengue in Maryse Condé's *The Tropical Breeze Hotel*, New York, 1995 — 196

Acknowledgments

I've been thinking and writing about French Caribbean women's theater for nearly fourteen years, and this work has been shaped and guided by many mentors, colleagues, friends, and family members. It seems appropriate to acknowledge first the playwrights, since their plays have inspired and challenged me throughout the years. At the project's start, Jan Gross provided formative mentorship that has endured, and Daniel Lemahieu graciously agreed to supervise my *maîtrise* thesis on a then-anomalous topic at the Université de Paris III. In this early stage, I reached out to Judith Miller and Christiane Makward, two exemplary leaders in the field, whose generous support, insightful scholarship, and astute feedback continue to guide me.

At Northwestern University, I am grateful to Sandra Richards for her wisdom, conscientious feedback, and reminders to breathe. She sets a shining standard for meaningful scholarship in African diaspora theater and performance that I can only strive to emulate. Nicole Lapierre's wise counsel and discerning commentary strengthened the project, and Doris Garraway and Susan Manning provided key insights and suggestions. An unbeatable cohort of graduate students read drafts of my work and offered needed perspective. I continue to benefit from conversations with these fantastic friends and wish to thank, in particular, Katie Zien, Christina McMahon, and Daniel Smith for their precious advice, and Katia Gottin for facilitating my first research trip to Martinique.

At the University of Georgia I am fortunate to be surrounded by so many wonderful colleagues and friends in the Department of Theatre and Film Studies, the Department of Romance Languages, the Latin American and Caribbean Studies Institute, and beyond; I learn from my exchanges with these inspiring scholars and teachers every day. I am especially grateful to Doris Kadish, Jennifer Palmer, and Jonathan

Baillehache, who supported this project wholeheartedly and influenced my thinking in several ways. Rielle Navitski generously read two drafts of my entire manuscript. And Miriam Jacobson, Marla Carlson, Pilar Chamorro, Freda Scott Giles, and Cathy Jones offered constructive comments and professional advice.

This book has benefited tremendously from the indispensable research and support of Alvina Ruprecht and Stéphanie Bérard and my exchanges with these two terrific scholars. And it was recently reinvigorated by feedback from and discussions with Christian DuComb and Christine Mok. The American Society for Theatre Research has been an intellectual home away from home since my second year as a doctoral student, and I am proud to now be an associate member of Sylvie Chalaye's Scènes Francophones et Écritures de l'Altérité research laboratory.

My reconstructions of the performances would not have been possible without the help of the artists, translators, theater professionals, and scholars who graciously agreed to interviews and shared materials from their personal archives: Françoise Kourilsky, José Jernidier, Mariann Mathéus, Carol Ann Pelletier, Christiane Makward, Alvina Ruprecht, Judith Miller, Maryse Condé, Gerty Dambury, Catherine Temerson, Jonathan Slaff, Jasper McGruder, Sharon McGruder, Shauneille Perry, Saundra McClain, Kavi Ladnier, La Tonya Borsay, Watoku Ueno, Greg MacPherson, Tom Bishop, Stephanie Klapper, Philippa Wehle, Ronnie Scharfman, Chris Kapp, Susan Cohen, Richard Miller, Beth Turner, Dianne Kirksey-Floyd, Annick Justin-Joseph, Gilbert Laumord, Sonia Emmanuel, Jacques Martial, Ellen Bleier, Freda Scott Giles, Barbara Lewis, Syto Cavé, Alain Timar, and Aurélie Clément. (My apologies if I have inadvertently omitted anyone from this list.) I also thank Thom Stewart for restoring yellowed production photographs.

The theater archives at the Bibliothèque nationale de France, and particularly Ubu Repertory Theater's robust collections, were essential; there I owe a special debt to Alain Saccatti and Noëlle Giret. I also drew from research conducted at the Inathèque and the Fales Special Collections at New York University.

I wish to thank J. Michael Dash, Eric Brandt, and everyone at the University of Virginia Press, as well as Tim Roberts and the Modern Language Initiative, for guiding the project through its final stages. I am grateful to three anonymous readers for their constructive criticisms and shrewd assessments of the project's value, and to Judith Hoover for her meticulous edits and Marilyn Bliss for her work on the index.

Acknowledgments

Financial support for researching and writing this book was provided by the Willson Center for Humanities and Arts, the Office of the Provost, and the Office of Service-Learning at the University of Georgia, the American Society for Theatre Research's Targeted Areas Research Grant, the University of Cincinnati's Helen Weinberger Center, and Northwestern University's Paris Program in Critical Theory, French Interdisciplinary Group, Program in African American History, and Graduate School. Support from the Modern Language Initiative and Franklin College's First Book-Subvention Program at UGA assisted with indexing and image fees.

An earlier version of chapter 1 appeared as "Beyond the Marilisse and the Chestnut: Shattering Slavery's Sexual Stereotypes in the Drama of Ina Césaire and Maryse Condé," *Modern Drama* 57, no. 3 (2014): 385–408, and is reprinted with permission from University of Toronto Press (www.utpjournals.com). Previous research on *Mémoires d'Isles* and a few short selections from the analysis of this play in chapter 2 appeared in "Frameworks for Interpreting French Caribbean Women's Theatre: Ina Césaire's *Island Memories* at the Théâtre du Campagnol," *Theatre Survey* 50, no. 1 (2009): 67–90.

This book is dedicated to my family. My parents, David Sahakian and Wendy Zucker, instilled in me the values of compassion, listening, conscientiousness, and social justice that drive this and all of my work. They, along with Sam Sahakian and Brittany Alioto, provide me with unconditional, loving support. Ilya Winham, my love, grounds me, sees me clearly, and supports me fiercely. He gave me everything I needed to write this book, and his criticisms made it stronger. The arrival of our son, Leo Sahakian Winham, admittedly slowed the completion of the revised manuscript, but he gives me the *sweetest* smiles and hugs. I hope to one day teach him about learning from imbalance and the power of transformation.

Staging Creolization

Introduction

Onstage transformations pervade Martinican writer and ethnologist Ina Césaire's 1983 play *Mémoires d'Isles* (Island Memories). In front of the audience, the two women actors switch roles, sometimes with the aid of small costume pieces, but largely through their bodies, facial expressions, and voices. The play begins with a prologue in which the women, dressed as she-devils of Caribbean Carnival, perform a traditional dance and speak in riddles. At their makeup table, the actors then "transform themselves" from the she-devils into two grandmothers, the play's protagonists, Aure and Hermance.[1] The grandmothers traverse time, as the actresses embody their characters at several ages: the six-year-old child, the twenty-year-old bride, and the elderly woman nearing the end of her life. They also play roles from each other's life memories.

Mémoires d'Isles is based in ethnographic interviews with several generations of women from Martinique and Guadeloupe. Aure and Hermance were inspired by Césaire's own grandmothers. Through their divergent stories and the art of their performance, the two women embody the richness, multiplicity, and complexity of what it means to be a Caribbean woman. As they recall moments that marked their childhood, marriage, the births of their children, historical events, recipes, and dances, they transmit cultural memory. The play's content shows Caribbean women as loving, indomitable, and resourceful. In performance, it stresses their adaptability, fluidity, and capacity for transformation. Caribbean women cannot be fixed by exoticizing gazes—or by any gaze at all—because they will always reinvent themselves anew.

In 1991, eight years after the play's premiere, Césaire was invited by Ubu Repertory Theater for the occasion of the English-language premiere of *Mémoires d'Isles*. In New York, Césaire's Martinican grandmothers were played by two prominent black performers: Carmen De Lavallade, a dancer and choreographer, and Ernestine Jackson, who originated the role of Ruth Younger in Lorraine Hansberry's *Raisin in the Sun*. In a tribute to Ubu, Césaire praised the production for its convincing portrayal of Caribbean womanhood. Despite language barriers, she insists, the performers compellingly tapped into her beloved grandmothers, and even the author's own sense of self:

> A great emotional moment: my arrival in the simple room of a dance school where they are having the last rehearsal of my play, *Mémoires d'Isle*, which has become *Island Memories* for the occasion. . . . In this room where they are rehearsing my text in another language, I am welcomed with great warmth, a little like a sister they always knew. They are not discovering me, they are recovering me. These truly are my black American sisters, whom I am finally meeting. . . . The last rehearsal begins and it is immediately the magic of true theater: the two magnificent actresses are instantly transformed into old women, at once strong and broken (my own grandmothers, gone now). Despite my precarious English, I recognize each phrase, each expression, each gestural tic reminiscent of the dear old ladies to whom this text is dedicated, and tears come to my eyes.[2]

Though her play was rooted in the local stories and realities of the French Caribbean, Césaire saw a return to her play's core meanings when it was translated into English and performed by these actresses in New York. She claims her identity as a black woman, even though her other writings (for French and French Caribbean readers) expressly eschew racial essentialisms to embrace multiracial Creole identity. She describes experiencing a black sister connection as an affective sense of original belonging. Her choice of the term *recovering*, which she contrasts with *discovering*, evokes a return.

Why would her play's English translation, recasting, and New York restaging prompt this feeling of return? I believe that Césaire was not evoking a symbolic return to Africa, commonly associated with the Négritude movement, initiated by her father, Aimé Césaire, so much as a return to the process of transforming oneself across cultural space and chronological time that her two protagonists perform. This capacity for reinvention is what Césaire deems the "magic of true theater." It is also the crux of Caribbean womanhood, as Aure and Hermance perform it.

I use the term *creolization* to refer to this practice of cultural reinvention, this theatrical, cultural, and epistemological transformation through mixing, juxtaposition, contradiction, and conflict in the context of the legacies of slavery and colonialism. *Staging Creolization* traces how creolization is dramatized in late twentieth-century plays by French Caribbean women writers and enacted through these plays' international production and reception histories. Rather than a linguistic phenomenon, I locate creolization in performance: I theorize it as a practice of reinventing meaning and resisting the status quo that corresponds with the syncretic Caribbean performance practices of storytelling, music, dance, and ritual. Enslaved Africans combined and reshuffled performance practices, religions, and epistemologies in order to create new, hybrid belief systems and practices, which often involved strategic ambiguity, apparent contradictions, and interpretive tensions suited to the plantation. These syncretic performances enabled the enslaved to endure life on the plantation, to free themselves psychically from slavery's assaults on their sense of self, and to cultivate spiritual hope and strength under extreme duress. In a similar fashion, French Caribbean women playwrights innovatively remix performance conventions, cultural signifiers, and ways of knowing the past, present, and future. They stage creolization to extricate Caribbeans from the legacies of slavery and colonialism and to subvert long-standing systems of oppression that have persisted in contemporary, updated, and often veiled forms.

My analysis of seven plays by Ina Césaire, Maryse Condé, Gerty Dambury, and Simone Schwarz-Bart explores the aesthetics and cultural politics of staging creolization. As opposed to affirming Caribbean identity or history, these women play with historical ambiguity, set up ironic juxtapositions, mix multiple cultural influences and performance forms, upset established narratives, and rearrange accepted orders and epistemologies. By staging creolization, French Caribbean women playwrights invite audiences and readers to see Caribbeanness—and often the inheritance of slavery and colonialism—with fresh eyes. Creolization is also these women's response to cultural and literary movements in the Caribbean, largely dominated by men and male-centric perspectives. Refusing stasis, fixity, and anything that smacks of essentialism, the plays unhinge anticolonial and male-centric paradigms through this unpredictable aesthetics of creolization. They destabilize what it means to be a Caribbean person and, frequently, a Caribbean woman, by unsettling the very logic of the cultural hierarchies and established narratives they reject.

The plays additionally share a similar history of transatlantic, circum-Caribbean production and reception.[3] Césaire's first play, *Mémoires d'Isles*, was collaboratively devised and produced in 1983 in Bagneux, a suburb of Paris, and then restaged in English at Ubu in 1991. Two subsequent plays premiered at the Fort-de-France festival in Martinique and were restaged in the United States. *L'Enfant des passages, ou la geste de Ti-Jean* (The Child of Passages, or the Story of Ti-Jean) premiered in 1987 and was restaged (in the original French) at the University of Wisconsin, Madison, in 1994. *Rosanie Soleil* (Fire's Daughters) premiered in 1992 and was restaged in translation at Ubu in 1993. Condé's 1988 play, *Pension les Alizés* (The Tropical Breeze Hotel), premiered in Guadeloupe in 1988 and was restaged in translation at Ubu in 1995. Published one year later, her *An tan revolisyon: Elle court, elle court la liberté* (In the Time of Revolution) premiered before more than two thousand spectators in Guadeloupe in 1989 and was restaged in translation at the University of Georgia in 1997. Schwarz-Bart's *Ton beau capitaine* (Your Handsome Captain) premiered in 1987 in Guadeloupe; the production traveled with its original cast of actors to France, Martinique, Haiti, and Morocco, and the play was then restaged in translation three times (and once in French) by several different artists at Ubu from 1988 to 1990. Dambury's *Lettres indiennes* (Crosscurrents) premiered at the Avignon Festival in 1996 and was restaged in translation at Ubu one year later.

By reconstructing these plays' international production and reception histories, I reveal how dramatizing creolization engenders unpredictable and often unsettling performances. The productions and their audience reception materialized unresolved questions and tensions written into the plays and staged the contingency of Caribbeanness. I examine the stagings and audience reception of these plays, both the original productions and the U.S. premieres, not as the fleshing out or substantiation of the dramatic text but rather as another (often surprising) reinvention of it. Though the performances appear at times to contradict the playwright's intended meaning, I insist that these reinterpretations constitute a further, albeit often unsettling, reinvention of the creolizing impulses the playwrights set in motion. Insofar as these plays have been examined as dramatic literature, my analysis adds much to our knowledge of the plays and playwrights. It illustrates how their plays make meaning in performance and documents how this theatrical corpus has been received by international artists and spectators. I do not locate meaning in the play itself or the playwright's interpretation, nor do I privilege the performance. Rather I stress the interaction between text and performance, at various levels of creation, editing, production, and reception.

Staging creolization is akin to theatrical syncretism, which, according to Christopher Balme, "utilizes the performance forms of both European and indigenous cultures in a creative recombination of their respective elements, without slavish adherence to one tradition or the other."[4] In the first full-length scholarly study of French Caribbean theater, Stéphanie Bérard similarly insists upon this theater's hybrid "in-between" aesthetics, studying how French Caribbean theater artists appropriate a wealth of material, from European dramas to African-derived ritual, to "differentiate themselves from Western theatre and proclaim their Caribbeanness."[5] Alvina Ruprecht suggests that French Caribbean theater by women is already transcultural and translinguistic.[6] John Conteh-Morgan argues that francophone African and Caribbean playwrights deploy a "postcolonial performative," which combines a postcolonial approach with global postmodernism in order to instrumentalize (rather than simply validate) indigenous cultural practices while drawing freely from Euro-American, Greek, Arabic, and other theatrical conventions and performance practices.[7]

I expand upon these studies insofar as I contend that the syncretism of the plays is not a static, fixed creole aesthetics but rather a dynamic process of creolization in motion, informed by history, and based in the African-derived principle that performance is a space of creativity and transformation that connects past, present, and future. My analysis reaches beyond the hybrid aesthetics of the plays themselves, as I underscore how their performances embody, carry forth, and materialize the process of creolization.

Women Playwrights

With several pathbreaking plays, Césaire, Condé, Dambury, and Schwarz-Bart revolutionized the theater scene in Martinique and Guadeloupe and reached international artists and audiences. Their work represents a second wave of French Caribbean theater, which Conteh-Morgan has qualified as "post-nationalist," insofar as the playwrights of this generation self-reflexively looked beyond national and anticolonial agendas.[8] While the French Caribbean theatrical scene had previously been dominated by men and overshadowed by the titanic contributions of Aimé Césaire, the majority of playwrights in this second generation were women. The women playwrights featured here write across literary genres, and they are also cultural activists, academics, and public intellectuals.

Why did these influential women writers turn to theater? Césaire, trained as an ethnologist, was first attracted to theater as a means of making her ethnological research, focused primarily on French Caribbean women and storytelling, accessible to nonspecialists. She has authored at least twenty-five plays and adaptations, which stage "her people's voice," to quote Christiane Makward.[9] Condé, though better known for her novels, actually began writing theater first, in the early 1970s; she has written at least twelve plays and adaptations, which have been staged in the Caribbean, Africa, France, and the United States.[10] Theater has fascinated Condé since childhood; it serves for her as a means of telling uncomfortable truths and provoking her spectators.[11] Schwarz-Bart, also better known for her novels, has written only one play to date, which was inspired by an encounter with her Haitian neighbor, who had migrated to Guadeloupe in order to make a (meager) living and was perpetually separated from his wife at home in Haiti. Theater was the vehicle for Schwarz-Bart to transmit and imaginatively reinvent this man's plight. Guadeloupe-born writer, theater artist, translator, and cultural activist Dambury has written at least thirteen plays. A community-based artist, she is drawn to theater's social relevance and collective processes. Her dramatic corpus is provocative, probing, and often ethically motivated.[12] Though lesser known (and younger) than the three other women, Dambury writes prolifically across genres and recently won the prix Carbet de la Caraïbe (won earlier by Condé and Schwarz-Bart). She runs her own small publishing house, which has printed several of her plays.[13]

All four of my book's featured playwrights hail from Martinique or Guadeloupe, two former French slave colonies that are now French overseas departments located in the Caribbean. These islands both *are* and *are not* French, to paraphrase Stuart Hall. This dual identity represents for him an example of Caribbeanness as constituted through an ongoing and ever-changing interplay of difference within identity.[14] Today Martinicans and Guadeloupeans carry French (EU) passports. They are French, but they are also distinctively Caribbean. As a reflection of this unique neocolonial status, theater from Martinique and Guadeloupe oscillates between an investment in universal humanity and an articulation of (Caribbean) cultural particularity. In the words of Bridget Jones, theater is "a privileged arena, a site where the paradoxical strains of dependency and difference can be enacted."[15]

While the playwrights are Guadeloupean and Martinican, these unresolved tensions between human unity and cultural particularity, and dependency and difference, are often negotiated through an imaginary comparison with Haiti. Connected yet also separated by history, Haiti is, to quote Condé, "ever present in the hearts and minds of the writers from Martinique and Guadeloupe."[16] Also a former French slave colony, Haiti fought and won independence from France in 1804. As the first independent black nation, Haiti is a symbol of anticolonial triumph. At the same time, many of Haiti's contemporary realities—poverty, economically driven migration, the Duvalier dictatorships of the twentieth century, and the boat people, or refugees—illuminate certain practical advantages of Martinique's and Guadeloupe's dependence on France. Whereas male dramatists of the 1960s and 1970s dramatized the histories of the great Haitian male leaders Toussaint Louverture and King Christopher, French Caribbean women playwrights dramatize Haiti's past and present, showing, as Makward has argued, the triumph of the Haitian Revolution while also valorizing the daily lives of ordinary people and recognizing Haiti's ongoing struggle.[17] Their interest in broader historical legacies while honing in on everyday people's lives and struggles constitutes one of the critical ways French Caribbean women writers move beyond nationalist and anticolonial problematics.

In her influential 1993 essay, "Order, Disorder, Freedom, and the West Indian Writer," Condé distinguishes French Caribbean women's writing from men's by arguing that women introduce creative disorder. The dominant "order," that is, the rules for writing Caribbean literature, at the end of the twentieth century was the Créolité movement, which Condé has criticized in several essays for being prescriptive, restrictive, and shortsighted.[18] In 1998 she stated, "The Martinican school of Créolité is singular because it presumes to impose law and order." According to Condé, Créolité "reduc[es] the overall expression of creoleness to the use of the Creole language . . . [and] is terrorizing in its detailed catalogue of accepted literary themes."[19] At the risk of oversimplifying the complexity of Créolité thought—the two collaborative foundational texts (1989 and 1991) and the larger oeuvres of Patrick Chamoiseau and Raphaël Confiant—it is important to distinguish between the unstable process of creolization that I argue is dramatized and enacted by French Caribbean women's theater and the "order" that Créolité prescribed, at least in the late 1980s and early 1990s.[20]

Led by men, the Créolité movement insisted on the emancipatory value of Creole (plantation-derived and syncretic) language and culture, particularly the heroic figure of the storyteller, the *conteur*. Though they embraced postmodern cultures, the Créolists inadvertently reified a fixed idea of creoleness, effectively excluding women, East Indians, and other cultural and racial groups (besides black and *mulâtre* men) from their purview, as A. James Arnold has argued.[21] To this order,

French Caribbean women playwrights brought ambiguity and contradiction. As opposed to instilling a new order, one that would stem from an intimate or womanist perspective, these women embraced "discontinuous conjunction," to borrow Antonio Benítez-Rojo's characterization of the Caribbean,[22] in culture, history, and knowledge production. They counted Caribbeanness not as an identity but rather as an ever-changing, performance-based process.

In studies of French Caribbean theater, the corpus of women-authored plays of the 1980s and 1990s is often qualified as intimate and feminist. These plays deploy what Melissa McKay calls women-centered, "intimate" content and Makward calls a "feminine discourse."[23] Carole Edwards, in a book that analyzes plays by six French Caribbean women dramatists (the four women featured here plus the Martinican writers Suzanne Dracius and Michèle Césaire), argues that these women construct a "feminine consciousness," emphasizing bodily expression and performance.[24] As Makward points out, this corpus reevaluates the historical hero and favors women's lived experience.[25] It develops, as Judith Miller has argued, vibrant black feminist sensibilities that differ from French feminisms.[26]

The prism of creolization helps me to expand upon these studies by showing that gender is not a static signifier of identity or a fixed position from which to write for these playwrights; rather it is a fluid, ever-changing performance. The plays subvert binary distinctions between (among other dichotomies) the public and private realms and reinvent the meanings of gender inherited from slavery's sexual systems of subjection. These women-authored, apparently intimate plays did more than affirm the importance of women's writing and cultural production; they also subverted and transformed the status quo of the gendering of cultural production in the French Caribbean. In fact they should be characterized by their destabilization of femininity and womanhood, along with any fixed notion of Caribbeanness.

French Caribbean women playwrights "rewrite postcolonialism," as Carine Mardorossian has theorized the objective of contemporary Caribbean women's fiction.[27] Like the novels Mardorossian studies, the plays configure race and identity as fluid and relational and undo the binaries that oppose victimization to agency. Whereas postcolonial binary oppositions such as colonizer-colonized, black-white, French-Creole, and man-woman suggest that liberation from systems of oppression will begin with fixed (even if multiple) subject positions and categories of identity, these women playwrights write from places of ambiguity, imbrication, and entanglement. Yet, crucially, their insistence on cultural instability, remixing, and relationality should be understood not as free-floating but as grounded in the Caribbean historical past, in the lived experiences of the plantation, and in the syncretic performance practices of storytelling, song, and dance.

Diaspora Performances

The transatlantic performance history of these seven plays, though remarkable, is by no means unique. In addition to the seven plays explored in this book, two other French Caribbean women's plays were restaged by Ubu: Condé's *Le Morne de Massabielle*, which premiered in France in 1970 and was produced by Ubu in 1991,[28] and Michèle (Ina's sister) Césaire's *La Nef*, which premiered in Martinique in 1993 and was selected for a staged reading (rather than a full-scale production) at Ubu that same year. Another woman-authored play that made a similar journey is Dracius's *Lumina Sophie dite Surprise*, which was produced by Ubu's successor, Act French New York, in 2010. Other French Caribbean women's plays were not re-created in new stagings by U.S.-based artists but instead were reprised in the original mise-en-scène, traveling with their original Caribbean cast to the United States. The original production of Condé's *Comédie d'amour* (in French and Creole) traveled from Guadeloupe to Washington, DC and New York in 1993.[29] Similarly the 2007 Guadeloupe-based production of Condé's *Comme deux frères* circulated to several U.S. cities, including Chicago and New Orleans.[30]

Stéphanie Bérard calls this phenomenon "the migration of Caribbean theater to the North American stage." French Caribbean plays at Ubu, most written by women, were the beginnings of this larger trend. Whereas French Caribbean theater of the 1960s, 1970s, and 1980s was commonly staged in the Caribbean and France, the last decade of the twentieth-century marked a new path of circulation, in the United States and Canada, and thus a new global positioning for French Caribbean theater artists. "Artists from Martinique and Guadeloupe have ceased to seek recognition from France, which no longer acts as a hub, and are turning toward geographically closer horizons," Bérard writes.[31]

Though a new path of circulation, generally speaking, for *French-language* Caribbean playwrights at the end of the twentieth century, the pathway from the West Indies to the United States was well traveled by migrant anglophone Caribbean writers and actors. As Errol Hill and James Hatch have documented, the "Caribbean connection," that is, collaborations and exchanges among African American and anglophone Caribbean artists, has enriched theater production across the black Atlantic since the seventeenth century. Caribbean artists have been influential in the history of African American theater, and the United States in turn has offered vital resources and opportunities for Caribbean artists. In fact, as Hill and Hatch note, "the first known black theatre company in the United States was founded by a West Indian seaman in 1821."[32]

For francophone Caribbean artists, however, such exchanges are complicated by language barriers and the risks and challenges of cultural translation. The overwhelming influence of Frenchness—French culture, the French language, and the French theatrical tradition—looms over French Caribbean theatrical production. And many U.S.-based theatergoers saw Frenchness and blackness as somehow mutually exclusive, which made the act of translating and staging French Caribbean plays in the United States particularly challenging.

I interpret the processes of staging, performing, and receiving these plays in the United States as a second phase of creolization in theater by French Caribbean women, which I call "diaspora performances." These productions glanced back toward the Caribbean while locating the plays in the U.S. context and fostered links and commonalities among African American and French Caribbean artists and spectators. Aimé Césaire poetically deemed the states of the American South to be lands connected by blood to Martinique: "Land red, sanguineous, consanguineous land" (*terres rouges, terres sanguines, terres consanguines*).[33] Yet this shared inheritance must be understood as framed, to invoke Hall, simultaneously by two axes or vectors: similarity/continuity and difference/rupture.[34]

Whereas Caribbean histories tended to erase blackness and Africanness, in the United States it was racial hybridity that was largely forgotten. Generally speaking, U.S.-based artists and spectators in the 1980s and 1990s emphasized the ways these plays depicted blackness and black womanhood. For the French Caribbean women playwrights, in contrast, Caribbean identity, though encompassing several aspects of U.S.-based definitions of blackness, is quintessentially unstable. In privileging "authentic" blackness or Caribbeanness over unstable translation, the performances at Ubu contradicted the plays' portrayal of culture as fluid. Yet they nonetheless staged creolization, insofar as they reinvented the play's (cultural) meanings and resisted the status quo of white-dominated New York theater and the rigidity of American identity politics at the end of the twentieth century.

To return to the tribute quoted at the start of this introduction, while Ina Césaire compellingly speaks of the affective experience of rediscovering herself as a transnational black woman, she locates Caribbeanness and blackness in the diasporic experiences of dispersal, movement, acculturation, hybridization, relationality, and translation that scholars like Stuart Hall, Édouard Glissant, and Paul Gilroy associate with Caribbean and black Atlantic identity, experience, and aesthetics. In his essay "Cultural Identity and Diaspora," Hall defines the origin of Caribbeanness as translation itself: "How, then, to describe this play of 'difference' within identity? The common history—transportation, slavery, colonisation—has been profoundly formative. For all these societies, unifying us across our differences. But it does not constitute a common *origin*, since it was, metaphorically as well as literally, a translation."[35] By reinventing the plays' meanings, the diaspora performances of French Caribbean women's plays in New York returned to this shared origin of cultural translation.

Theorizing Creolization as Transformative Performance

Creolization generally refers to cultures in contact, conflict, and mutual transformation, specifically in the context of plantation slavery and its aftermath. Creolization is not an end product but rather a process or a practice—like theater and performance. Édouard Glissant distinguishes creoleness (the identity) from creolization (the process), which brings cultures, identities, knowledges, and aesthetics into relation with one another: "If we posit *métissage* as, generally speaking, the meeting and synthesis of two differences, creolization seems to be limitless *métissage*, its elements diffracted and its consequences unforeseeable."[36] While creolization is limitless, ever-changing, and unpredictable, it is nonetheless anchored in the particular historical situations, social structures, and inequalities of plantation slavery and colonialism. As the practice of intercultural, transformative encounters, creolization always involves power, conflict, and struggle. In Hall's words, creolization is "forced transculturation," necessarily entailing power disparities and domination.[37]

Whereas Glissant posits the origins of creolization in the abyss of knowledge and identity, what he calls the "womb abyss" of the slave ship,[38] I consider creolization to be a performance practice based in the principles of African-derived ritual and harnessed by enslaved people as a creative response to slavery's social structures and practices of subjection. As Saidiya Hartman argues in her seminal *Scenes of*

Subjection, slavery involved everyday assaults on the enslaved person's sense of self. She contends that we can find resistance to slavery not only in histories of insurrection but also in quotidian acts like slipping away for nocturnal visits to a loved one, feigning illness, or gathering together for secret meetings, dances, and storytelling. The traces of such performance-based acts of survival, meaning making, cultural reinvention, and everyday resistance can be found in what performance studies scholar Diana Taylor has influentially called the "repertoire" of so-called ephemeral, embodied practices, including (though not limited to) the syncretic performance practices of storytelling, dance, and theater.[39]

Creolization, in other words, is an embodied inheritance that present-day Caribbeans may strategically embrace by reinventing its meanings. On the plantation, according to Françoise Vergès, creolization was "an invention of everyday life, an aesthetics and a creative practice in a world dominated by brutality, domination, violence." She encourages the inheritors of this creative practice to embrace its malleability. Vergès characterizes intellectual and literary responses to slavery's histories and legacies as generally entailing either nostalgia for what was lost or idealization of plantation-derived creoleness. In contrast, she urges an ongoing practice of creolizing the past, of remaking its meanings for the sake of the present: "We must reappropriate the past of creolization yet we must reinterpret it, have a critical approach."[40]

By insisting upon the present-day Caribbean person's agency in reappropriating and reinventing the past, Vergès implicitly positions Caribbeans as performers of African-derived ritual, which also enables communication with the ancestors. In her canonical study of Yoruba ritual, Margaret Drewal underscores the transformative power of ritual and the agency of the performers. This core principle of African belief systems is distilled in the Yoruba concept of *asé*, the power of transformation: "the power to bring things into existence, to make things happen. This is the real 'work' of a ritual performer; indeed, it is in essence what the act of representation is all about."[41] In her multisited study of vodou, Yoruba, and candomblé ritual in the Americas, ethnographer Yvonne Daniel identifies a continuity from the African-derived rituals to the plantation and beyond, which is premised on this power of transformative performance. She writes, "The dancing body allowed temporary escape from the extraordinary hardship of enslavement and continued as a primary vehicle for spiritual communication and for both spiritual and artistic expression. In the Americas today, the dancing body still functions within ritual communities as a source of spiritual communication, aesthetic expression, and the site of extraordinary transformations."⁴²

Caribbean artists mobilize the performative power of *asé* by remixing, reassembling, and reinventing culture, historical memory, and identity. Derek Walcott has described Caribbean art as a creative act of reassembling fragments of historical memory:

> Break a vase, and the love that reassembles the fragments is stronger than that love which took its symmetry for granted when it was whole. The glue that fits the pieces is the sealing of its original shape. It is such a love that reassembles our African and Asiatic fragments, the cracked heirlooms whose restoration shows its white scars. This gathering of broken pieces is the care and pain of the Antilles, and if the pieces are disparate, ill-fitting, they contain more pain than their original sculpture, those icons and sacred vessels taken for granted in their ancestral places. Antillean art is this restoration of our shattered histories, our shards of vocabulary, our archipelago becoming a synonym for pieces broken off from the original continent.⁴³

Wendy Knepper views this creative act of reassembling fragments through Lévi-Strauss's concept of bricolage: "Creolization can be seen enacted through *bricolage* as the art of the disparate and fragmentary: the art of adopting and adapting multiple cultural fragments or artifacts as well as elements of imaginative, ideological, cultural, social, or religious practices, experiences, and beliefs."⁴⁴

Though the *bricoleur* artist's agency is key, she or he does not ultimately control the outcome of the creative act, since creolization necessarily involves surprises, inassimilable grit, contradictions, ambiguities, and coexisting oppositions. Fernando Ortiz famously used the image of the ajiaco soup to describe creolization, or what he called transculturation.⁴⁵ The ajiaco stew of vegetables, meats, and chili pepper synthesizes diverse flavors, combining its multiple ingredients into a thick broth. In addition to evoking the synthesis of cultures, the ajiaco metaphor recalls how creolization is an ongoing process: the stew remaining after a meal is not polished off or thrown away but saved and then renewed by the addition of new ingredients the following day. Though a powerful metaphor, the ajiaco fails to adequately acknowledge, as Margarite Fernández Olmos and Lizabeth Paravisini-Gebert point out, the "undissolved ingredients" of cultural synthesis. They cite Cuban art critic Gerardo Mosquera, who insists upon the "bones, gristle, and hard seeds that never fully dissolve, even after they have contributed their substance to the broth."⁴⁶ Hall uses the metaphor of translation to describe the importance of such leftovers: "Translation is an important way of thinking about creolization, because it always retains the trace of those elements which resist translation, which remain left-over, so to speak, in lack or excess, and which constantly then return to trouble any effort to achieve total cultural closure."⁴⁷

While creolization is an inherently unpredictable process, studying it gives rise to an ethics of global understanding, borrowing, and respect. With his notion of "opacity," Glissant derives an ethics from this fact of creolization's incomplete assimilability. He asserts that people, cultures, and epistemologies cannot be reduced to transparent meanings (as Western thought requires). The notion of opacity goes beyond acknowledgment or affirmation of difference, since "difference itself can still contrive to reduce things to the Transparent." In contrast, an ethics of opacity means "understanding that it is impossible to reduce anyone, no matter who, to a truth he would not have generated on his own."⁴⁸

Informed by these diverse theories, *Staging Creolization* views Caribbean theater as a means of both transmitting and reinventing culture by reassembling and reflecting upon multiple cultural influences, points of view, epistemologies, and traces of the past. I position French Caribbean women playwrights as *bricoleurs* who work, as in Walcott's description, from cultural, historical, and epistemological fragments. I observe how the international performances of their plays enacted this process of creolization in ways that inevitably surprised and sometimes unsettled the playwright herself. In other words, I locate the practice of creolization in both dramatic literature and performance, and (given that *asé* is present in all beings and all things) I blur the line between an artist's intentional act and the unconscious practice of cultural change.

I am indebted here to Joseph Roach's theorization of performance in the circum-Atlantic rim. In *Cities of the Dead*, Roach shows how collective memory is not so much preserved as remade through performance; performance transmits and reinvents collective memory through "surrogation," that is, an ongoing process of imperfect substitutions. Remembrance, Roach argues, always involves forgetting, and performance is the vehicle that drives this unstable process of cultural making and remaking: "The social processes of memory and forgetting, familiarly known as culture, may be carried out by a variety of performance events, from stage plays to sacred rites, from carnivals to the invisible rituals of everyday life. To perform in this sense means to bring forth, to make manifest, and to transmit. To perform also means, though often more secretly, to reinvent."[49]

By privileging the power of transformative performance over the playwright's conscious intentions, *Staging Creolization* revisits a formative question to the field of Caribbean theater studies: how to cultivate and theorize a Caribbean theatrical form that would be both political and popular. I view performance broadly, counting stage plays and ritual together as performance practices that carry out cultural reinvention. Glissant, in contrast, influentially distinguished, in a 1971 essay, between conscious theater and unconscious performance practices. In "Theater, Consciousness of the People," he privileges theater's role in providing the "conscious reflection" needed for Martinicans to develop a collective sense of self and historical awareness. "Theater is the act through which the collective consciousness sees itself and consequently moves forward," he writes. Glissant sees theater as akin to essays and reflective thought.[50] According to him, while participation in cultural activities, such as a *gwo-ka* (the traditional Guadeloupean percussion and dance practice) or storytelling evening, could be done more or less mindlessly, theater ideally involves reflective representation, integration, and regeneration of knowledge.

Glissant privileges theater over ritual and other communal performance practices, which he views as raw materials from which Caribbean artists should draw. The basis for his theater is "folklore," or "popular beliefs," terms he uses to refer to oral traditions, festivals, rituals, dance, and song. Glissant's folklore is the nonarchival, so-called ephemeral knowledge that Taylor would call the repertoire. Yet whereas Taylor privileges the repertoire as a source of knowledge in the Americas, Glissant describes French Caribbean folklore as paralyzed and deficient. He believed that, due to the trauma of the Middle Passage and the impingement of Frenchness following *départementalisation*, folklore in Martinique had become touristy and static, a problem he called "folklorization." Glissant concludes that theater needed to be a "willed act," which would "facilitate the transition from lived folklore to the representation of consciousness."[51]

The Trinidadian playwright, actor, and theater historian Errol Hill made a similar argument at the turn of the century in his inaugural Sir Philip Sherlock lecture and essay "Perspectives in Caribbean Theatre: Ritual, Festival, and Drama." He suggests that Caribbean theater artists never adequately "incorporated the meanings and methods, signs and symbols associated with the religions, rites, festivals, myths, storytelling and other forms of enactment belonging to their culture." "Had this development occurred," he continues, "the present quest to identify and establish an indigenous Caribbean theatre would probably be unnecessary." Much like Glissant, Hill makes a distinction between "formal" (which he also calls "conscious") theater and "informal" ("subconscious") folk performances, though he acknowledges the ways in which the two are blurred.[52]

Glissant's and Hill's essays both urge Caribbean theater artists to search for an authentic, popular, yet nonetheless reflective and critical Caribbean theatrical mode, which these authors view as absent or underdeveloped. Yet in their very efforts to describe this problem, Glissant and Hill effectively characterize what I see as the crux of Caribbean theater and performance. If we accept that Caribbean theater stages creolization, we see that it is based in the very contradictions, losses, and ambiguities these two men so compellingly describe.

As I read it, French Caribbean women's theater embraces creolization's inassimilability, contradictions, ambiguity, and misrecognitions. French Caribbean women playwrights stage creolization not only because their theater creatively remixes Western theatrical conventions and African-derived performance forms while incorporating further intercultural elements, but also because it acknowledges (both consciously and unconsciously) the ways such recombinations inevitably involve loss, coexisting oppositions, power hierarchies, and domination. It should be noted that Césaire, Condé, Dambury, and Schwarz-Bart would each implicitly disagree with some aspects of Glissant's essay on theater, either for the view of folklore as "deficient" (in Césaire and Schwarz-Bart's cases) or for the idealized vision of organic knowledge production (in Condé and Dambury's). Nonetheless their dramatic texts correspond with Glissant's manifesto insofar as they play with cultural influences as well as different forms of knowledge production in order to remember, reflect upon, and remake Caribbean history, identity, and aesthetics.

Reassembling Theater History

In order to analyze both the U.S. and original performances, I must reconstruct these performances. Much like the practice of creolization, my methodology reassembles fragments of memory. To reconstruct the performances, their collaborative rehearsal processes, and their audience receptions, I draw from personal and public archives comprising photographs, playbills, publicity, director and stage manager notes, costume and design sketches, lighting plots, correspondence, interviews, and, in select cases, videography. I have also conducted more than forty

17 *Introduction*

personal interviews with the playwrights, translators, actors, directors, designers, and audience members, which have enabled me to rescue important details that would otherwise have been lost.

As *bricoleur*, I combine, put into dialogue, test, and corroborate various perspectives and different forms of cultural memory, ranging from the archive-based traces to oral histories and performance-based knowledges.[53] In studying my archival sources, I have attended to their social and material contexts and uses. I distinguish "direct" sources that are involved in the production (e.g., a director's promptbook or costume sketches) from "indirect" sources that report on it (e.g., critical reviews or correspondence),[54] and I am mindful of the subjective positions from which narratives and archives are generated. In analyzing photographs, I consider whether each picture has been staged (a publicity photo) or taken during dress rehearsals.[55] I recognize that my interviews constitute, to cite Suk-Young Kim, a "moment of archival creation [in which] knowledge arises out of human bodies and interactions as embodied experience."[56] In conducting and interpreting interviews, I am mindful of verbal and bodily cues, the subjectivity of each narrative, the cultural positioning (as will be further discussed below) of the interviewer and interviewee, and the tricks of memory, particularly several decades after theatrical events. When appropriate, I make my own acts of bricolage apparent to my readers. I use phrases such as "he speculated," "she reported," "the director remembered," or "both actors believed" in order to convey the limited information I have while being transparent about the instability of my archive.

The challenge of *Staging Creolization* is the unevenness of my archive. U.S. theater productions are documented most completely, followed by the premieres that took place in France and then those in the Caribbean. Though numerous artists and scholars generously shared their time and personal archives, material traces of the original productions, particularly those staged in the Caribbean, are scarce. Until recently, theater criticism in Martinique and Guadeloupe was virtually nonexistent, and Caribbean performance archives from this period are very limited.[57] Because there is a wealth of materials held in Ubu Repertory Theater's archives at the Bibliothèque nationale de France, I was able to address the U.S. productions of these plays in separate chapters.

In contrast, my documentation of the premiere performances varies. In the Caribbean and other postcolonial contexts, cultural institutions often lack appropriate funding to organize collections, make them accessible, and protect them from natural catastrophes. That I was unable to reconstruct the premiere of Césaire's *Rosanie Soleil* is largely due to the fact that Haitian director Syto Cavé's personal archives, containing his notes and other physical traces of this production, were sadly lost in the earthquake in Haiti in 2010.[58]

My choice of plays was admittedly impacted by their accessibility and preservation. With the exception of Schwarz-Bart, each of these playwrights has written other noteworthy dramatic texts, many of which, though previously unpublished, are now accessible in print. To be sure, the fact that these seven plays were published facilitated their international circulation and restaging. As Bérard notes, the number of original plays staged each year in Guadeloupe and Martinique significantly exceeds the number of plays published, largely because it has been difficult for French Caribbean playwrights to find publishers.[59]

Creolizing Knowledge

Central to my study of both the plays and their production and reception histories is the question of cultural literacy, that is, how artists and audiences develop the knowledge, competency, and familiarity required to understand Caribbean theater. I am indebted here to VèVè Clark's concept of "diaspora literacy," which she develops by drawing from Condé's writing. Diaspora literacy is "the ability to read and comprehend the discourses of Africa, Afro-America, and the Caribbean from an informed indigenous perspective." This skill "demands a knowledge of historical, social, cultural and political development generated by lived and textual experience."[60] To interpret the plays from an informed perspective, attuned to the cultural and artistic practice of creolization, I draw from diverse critical tools ranging from Creole and African-derived belief systems, the Caribbean literary tradition, historiographies and ethnographies illuminating the lived experience and aftereffects of slavery and colonialism, and theories of theater and performance studies.

I emphasize the question of cultural literacy in my analysis of the production and reception histories. In Phillip B. Zarrilli's words, theater is "not a simple reflection of some essentialized, fixed attributes of a static monolithic culture but an arena for the constant process of renegotiating experiences and meanings that constitute culture."[61] I have attempted to document these processes of cultural renegotiation (what I call creolization) by giving voice to multiple perspectives and interpretations. I am interested in participants' and attendees' opinions, which I synthesize and put into dialogue with one another. This enables me to uncover conflicts, misrecognitions, and tensions in the collaborative act of staging and receiving these plays, as well as surprises and unassimilated complexities. Though always mindful of each interlocutor's opacity (to borrow Glissant's concept), I position key artistic and interpretive agents in terms of their culture, race, gender, and intellectual and affective investment. Like a performance ethnographer, I am also conscious of my own positioning as a white American woman, Armenian and Jewish, who has researched, taught, and made theater between the United States and the francophone world and who has taken deep inspiration from the words of French Caribbean women writers.

The book is organized to develop the cultural literacies and knowledges appropriate for my study of French Caribbean women's theater and, more broadly, useful for any investigation of Caribbean theater and performance. The first three chapters are organized around three transhistorical themes that underscore how creolization is caught up in the legacies of slavery and colonialism. Chapter 1 introduces dramaturgies of creolization as a response to French Caribbean women's contradictory experiences of slavery's sexual legacy and a dominant postcolonial culture that largely excludes women from public spaces of resistance. I argue that creolization is a means whereby French Caribbean women playwrights help Caribbean women to break away from the pernicious social scripts, inherited from the time of slavery, that limit their participation in the postcolonial, public sphere. The historical stereotypes of "the Chestnut" and "the Marilisse" abstract French Caribbean women's bodies, counting women either as passive, asexual sufferers and mothers or as willful seductresses. I argue that Césaire's *Rosanie Soleil* and Condé's *Pension les Alizés* subvert these sexualized stereotypes. Considering women's participation in a historical anticolonial revolt and the contemporary love endeavors of a Guadeloupean nude dancer in Paris, respectively, Césaire's and Condé's plays defy those stereotypes by means of creolization. Rather than replacing the myths and clichés of black womanhood with a more accurate historical truth, they play with ambiguity, ironic juxtapositions, and coexisting, contradictory modes of meaning making. The original performance of Condé's play further creolized her text by enacting unresolved questions regarding an aging woman's seductive powers.

Chapter 2 explores how three thematically diverse plays by Condé, Césaire, and Dambury reorder and remix the binary opposition between universal humanity and cultural difference. This chapter, with a focus on collaborative creation and cultural reception, argues that the playwrights, as opposed to representing a fixed Caribbean identity, present

Caribbeanness as an unfolding performative process of creolization. In plays treating revolution, Caribbean women's lived memories, and black-Indian relations, respectively, Condé, Césaire, and Dambury mobilize the conventions of intercultural and postcolonial theaters in order to refuse racial essentialisms, enact a constant interplay of unity and difference, and thereby reinvent the racialized legacies of slavery, colonialism, and East Indian indentured servitude. The original performances, in either the Caribbean or France, revealed the contingency of Caribbeanness and materialized the unresolved questions raised by the plays.

Chapter 3 argues that Césaire's *L'Enfant des passages* and Schwarz-Bart's *Ton beau capitaine* use theatrical syncretism to renew and question the life lessons inherited from the time of slavery. The creole concepts of *débouya* (making do with cunning) and *bigidi* (imbalance), which evoke religious and moral codes in order to adapt and bend them, are maintained and transmitted by the syncretic performance practices of storytelling and dance. The plays stage, question, and renew these performance practices. Césaire adapts a folktale about the trickster hero Ti-Jean. Schwarz-Bart tells the story of a Haitian sugarcane worker in Guadeloupe who dances to release and make sense of his feelings when his wife, at home in Haiti, confesses to adultery. Through theatrical syncretism, these two plays and their original performance histories raise unresolved questions about how to live with slavery's moral inheritance.

The final two chapters explore the English-language translation and performance of five of these plays at Ubu Repertory Theater of New York. Chapter 4 extends the analytical tool and theatrical practice of creolization developed in previous chapters to study diaspora performances of French Caribbean women's plays at Ubu. I investigate the staging of three plays by Césaire and Dambury at Ubu. By reconstructing the plays' rehearsal processes, performances, and audience receptions, I unveil the multiple, heterogeneous, and conflicting interpretations that undergird sentiments of cross-cultural unity and understanding felt by artists and audience members. In order to make French Caribbean women's plays accessible to American audiences, Ubu categorized the plays as "black" and "women's" writing; it balanced between evoking the cultural particularities of the Caribbean and reanchoring the play's themes in the United States. Race was a key signifier, but also an unstable and somewhat untranslatable one, since its meanings differed widely for the playwrights and artists involved. The performances fixed racial and cultural identities and thus denied the fluidity of the plays' creolizing aesthetics. But they nevertheless extended the process of creolization by reinventing the plays and their meanings, sometimes in ways that surprised or unsettled the playwrights themselves.

Chapter 5 more explicitly considers the themes of gender relations and heterosexual love in Ubu's diaspora performances of two plays by Condé and Schwarz-Bart. In Ubu's multiple performances of these plays, the actors playing the female leads were recast, and the question of how to stage the Caribbean heterosexual couple provoked anxious remodeling. How to stage the shared yet differently nuanced (in the United States and French Caribbean) inheritance of slavery's fundamental assault on black women's freedom to love for Ubu's international and interracial audiences? This proved an ambivalent and unstable task, premised on coexisting oppositions and conflicts in meaning making. The performances were pervaded by missed encounters, misrecognitions, and last-minute substitutions, and the textual translations were revised. The plays misfired insofar as Frenchness and blackness were seen by some collaborators and spectators as mutually exclusive. The question of how to best translate and stage these plays in the United States remains unanswered, which prompts ongoing acts of theatrical and interpretive recasting.

My performance analysis of Ubu's productions of French Caribbean women's plays raises a question that has preoccupied scholars of creolization across disciplines: To what extent can creolization be generalized beyond the Caribbean? Even though Ubu's team sought to expand the reach of Caribbeanness to a "universal" spectator, the material realities of theater complicated their efforts. Thus the production and reception histories test the influential proposition, advanced notably by Glissant, that the Caribbean is a microcosm for interculturalism and relational identity in our contemporary globalizing world.[62] Though this may be true, performing Caribbeanness outside of the Caribbean carries with it the risk of misrecognition, appropriation, and depoliticization. How should we stage and teach creolizing knowledges in the United States?

My coda expands upon my study of the aesthetics and cultural politics of staging creolization by exploring these ethical questions through an examination of two productions at U.S. universities in the 1990s: Césaire's *L'Enfant des passages*, performed in French at the University of Wisconsin, and Condé's *In the Time of Revolution* at the University of Georgia. In addition to completing the production history, the university productions enable me to foreground theater's pedagogical and ethical implications and possibilities. I observe how the two directors (who are also professors) cultivated critical, cultural literacy among their ensembles and audiences and fostered learning based on cultural encounters, points of tension, adaptation, reinvention, and reciprocal exchange. Informed by meticulous research, these performances privileged Caribbean histories, cultures, and knowledges, while reinventing the plays' meanings for the particular context of their universities. They combined traditional academic study with embodied and experiential knowledge and defamiliarized ready-made notions of race and gender. Like the plays, these productions enacted a conscientious performance of creolization as a dynamic, performative process, pervaded by coexisting oppositions, continuities and discontinuities in time and space, and ambiguities and inconsistencies in what and how we know. Performing creolization outside of the Caribbean, I conclude, is an ethical act when it engages participants and attendees in creolizing ways of knowing, rearranging our epistemological systems, challenging our ready-made paradigms, and fostering dialogue surrounding the uneven politics of our shared pasts, presents, and futures.

1 Unsettling the Gendered Stereotypes of Plantation Culture
Ina Césaire's *Rosanie Soleil* and
Maryse Condé's *Pension les Alizés*

In Maryse Condé's first novel, *Heremakhonon*, her protagonist, Veronica, a contemporary Guadeloupean woman, goes to a Caribbean festival in Paris with her lover, a white French man. The couple is spotted by a group of militant Caribbean men who all hiss at Veronica, "Marilisse! You're making yourself Marilisse!" Just after the men call out to Veronica, Condé cuts to a notice announcing the sale of a young enslaved black woman named Marilisse, whose master is leaving his plantation and thus no longer requires her sexual service: "Due to his forthcoming departure, Sieur Cazeau . . . has put up for sale a young negro girl of pleasant features named Marilisse. Good laundress. Can be taken on a trial basis."[1] In an interview, Condé explains that she took the figure from history: the Marilisse was "a Negro slave who lived with a White man and bore his children."[2] The insult "Marilisse" interpellates Veronica historically, holding her accountable for interracial sexual relations under slavery. Yet the announcement of the sale reveals that Marilisse was not a seductress who preferred white men so much as objectified property, sold by one white man to another. Condé shows how the sexualized system of subjection inherited from the time of slavery is ambiguously experienced at the site of Veronica's body. Though it is only within the symbolic universe of Condé's novel that the name "Marilisse" carries these complex historical meanings, the accusation underlying the insult—that enslaved women chose white men and betrayed black men—is a common, albeit often unspoken trope in the French Caribbean.[3]

"The Marilisse" is one of two historical stereotypes—images and clichés lingering from the time of slavery—that continue to impact how gender in the Caribbean is imagined and lived. For the second stereotype, I turn once again to Condé, who, in her 1993 book of literary criticism, *La parole des femmes*, cites two Creole proverbs to unveil a set of social restrictions insidiously imposed upon Caribbean women's roles. Whereas the image of the Marilisse figures Caribbean women as treacherous seductresses, these proverbs insist upon women's moral superiority and strength, particularly in opposition to weak and unfaithful men. The first, "Fem-n cé chataign, n'hom-n cé fouyapin" (Woman is a chestnut, man is a breadfruit), stresses the resilience of women compared to men. Condé explains that, although the chestnut and the breadfruit trees look alike, when their fruits ripen and fall to the ground, the hard chestnut remains intact but the breadfruit splatters into white puree.[4]

The proverb pays homage to Caribbean women's toughness, but it also instructs women to accept men's infidelity, mistreatment, and abuse. Suggesting that women have a natural ability to bear hardship, it implies that women should efface their own desires for the sake of their children and out of respect for black men's fragility. I call this second historical stereotype "the Chestnut," though the terms *potomitan* (center or stronghold of the family, like the central post in a vodou ritual) and *femme matador* (the strong black woman) are phrases more commonly used to refer to this ubiquitous image of the courageous French Caribbean woman, who is devoted to her children whom she raises in the absence of a reliable father.

The Marilisse and the Chestnut are examples of what sociologist Patricia Hill Collins has called the "controlling images" of black womanhood—clichés of black women's roles and sexuality that originated under slavery and continue to regulate black female bodies to reinforce the status quo.[5] Despite the successes of anticolonial movements, Caribbean and French societies continue to see Caribbean women as both passive, unaffected sufferers and deceptive, nefarious seductresses. While the stereotypes may seem to be opposing, both limit women's participation in the public sphere, prescribing that they wield power only through sex or in the domestic space of the home. Paradoxically even as the stereotypes deny women political agency, they position women's bodies as contested sites of political struggle.

Caribbean Canadian writer M. NourbeSe Philip poetically argues that the "inner space" between black women's legs "becomes, in fact, a public space. A thoroughfare."[6] This is because enslaved black women were valued on the plantation for their strength as physical laborers but also for their promise to service both white and black men sexually and to reproduce, providing new slaves. Thus the inner space between black women's legs becomes an outer, public space, which Philip calls the fulcrum of the plantation:

25   Gendered Stereotypes of Plantation Culture

S/Place. Where the inner space is defined into passivity by, and harnessed to, the needs and functions of the outer space—the place of oppression. Run it down even further into Caribbean English: s/place mutates into "dis place." "*Dis place*": the outer space—the plantation, the New World. "*Dis place*": the result of the linking of the inner space between the legs with the outer place leading to "dis placement." "*Dis place*"—the space between. The legs. For the Black woman "dis placed" to and in the New World, the inner space between the legs would also mutate into "*dis place*"—fulcrum of the New World plantation.[7]

In Philip's formulation, the plantation is the site of black women's sexual domination and exploitation and also of the political abstraction of women's bodies.

In this chapter I show how two French Caribbean women playwrights creolize gender, theater, and knowledge of the past in order to unsettle these two stereotypes and reinvent the sexualized legacy of abstracting women's bodies. I investigate how two plays stage creolization—in this case, how they deploy juxtaposition, dissonance, ambiguity, and multiple meanings—to trouble the historical stereotypes and transform the meanings of gender in the French Caribbean.[8] Ina Césaire's *Rosanie Soleil* (Fire's Daughters), first produced in Martinique in 1992, reinvents the Chestnut stereotype by portraying a family of revolutionary women in the domestic space of their home and yard. Condé's *Pension les Alizés* (The Tropical Breeze Hotel), which premiered in Guadeloupe in 1988, uses irony and exaggeration to unveil and unsettle the insidious ways in which the Marilisse stereotype resurfaces in Caribbean society and romantic relationships.

To creolize the inheritance of slavery's sexualized systems of subjection, Condé and Césaire deploy historical and moral ambiguity. Both plays destabilize established, male-centric narratives of the past. Yet rather than contesting the stereotypes or attempting to uncover the truth surrounding Caribbean women's historical experiences, they address the history of enslaved women's sexual exploitation obliquely. By dwelling in the unassimilated historical complexity of Caribbean womanhood, they dramatize a performative process of creolization that rearranges and muddles distinctions between past and present, memory and forgetting, victimhood and agency, bodies and speech, and the public and private spheres. Moreover the plays—and *Pension les Alizés* does this more overtly—unsettle the very logic of the moral hierarchy implicit in the Marilisse and Chestnut stereotypes by remixing the binary opposition between the long-suffering Chestnut and the treacherous Marilisse.

Transhistorical Abstractions of Women's Bodies

Rosanie Soleil and *Pension les Alizés* share a focus on women's bodies.[9] Both plays star Caribbean female characters whose bodies serve as creative sites for unveiling and reimagining the pernicious ways in which the historical stereotypes of the Marilisse and the Chestnut repeat and resurface across time. Harvey Young's concept of phenomenal blackness is useful for clarifying my meaning here. He argues that while there is no so-called authentic black experience, black people share the experience and awareness of a repeating scene of being seen. Inasmuch as popular ideas of blackness are commonly projected upon individuals' bodies, the embodied black experience entails living alongside *the black body*. "This second body, an abstracted and imagined figure, shadows or doubles the real one."[10] Young's theorization of the black body, like Frantz Fanon's notion of the "historical-racial schema" imposed upon his body, transcends gender and sexuality differences.[11] In contrast, Césaire and Condé consider how women live alongside *the black female body*, or *the female body of slavery's legacy*.

On the plantation, enslaved women were counted both as the passive property of their masters (and/or husbands) and as seductresses who allegedly acquired power through their willful submission to white men. At the time of slavery, these dual myths of the black female body were imposed upon enslaved women to justify rape and sexual exploitation as well as to deny slavery's fundamental violence. Rape, Saidiya Hartman theorizes, was displaced by the discourse of "seduction—the assertion of the slave woman's complicity and willful submission."[12]

Though Hartman's analysis of the scenes of everyday terror that, as she argues, both enacted subjugation and constituted black subjects, develops from the U.S. context, her insights regarding the discourse of seduction resonate powerfully in the French colonies of the Caribbean, where there were relatively few white women, a preponderance of miscegenation, and a good deal of anxiety from France surrounding "libertinage," that is, moral depravity. In the French colonies, as Doris Garraway has shown, sexual practices and fantasies were an important means whereby colonists secured domination and denied the brutality of slavery. Drawing on evidence that extends from missionary accounts to literature, laws, travel narratives, and treatises, Garraway argues that, though France criticized colonists for libertinage, white men were not ultimately held accountable for their coerced and unlawful interracial sexual relations. Rather the

27 Gendered Stereotypes of Plantation Culture

blame was displaced onto the black women with whom they had sex and their mixed-race children.[13]

The moral hierarchy and contradictory logic embedded in this colonial discourse of seduction has been reproduced in popular, male-centric narratives of the past and formulations of postcolonial resistance. It is commonplace in the French Caribbean to attribute troubled gender relations to the history of slavery. To give a characteristic example, in an interview with Carole Edwards, the Guadeloupean writer Gisèle Pineau stated, "Women used their bodies to get freedom so that their children could be free; and men, reduced to slave status, saw that. So there is a sort of conflict that has not been settled between men and women in the Antilles."[14] Pineau's choice of the verb *used* assumes that enslaved women had agency over their bodies under slavery and thus downplays the preponderance of sexual exploitation as well as the fact that rape and sexual assault were denied in order to justify slavery's violence. Her explanation echoes the colonial rhetoric of seduction, insofar as it blames enslaved women for interracial sex.

Popular postcolonial narratives more or less equate slavery's violence with the emasculation of Caribbean men. One might trace such a male-centric point of view to French abolitionist rhetoric, which condemned slavery for denying black men rightful ownership of their wives and children.[15] Into the twenty-first century, one still finds such a male-centric point of view pervading the media and daily conversations about gender.[16] The ubiquitous stereotype of the hypermasculine, sexually aggressive male, ethnographer David Murray observes, "is supported [in Martinique] by men and women across racial, class, and educational lines and acts as a central symbol in combatting the historical, racialized imagery of the weak and powerless colonized male subject."[17]

In the literary and cultural spheres, postcolonialism is often articulated from within this male-centric understanding of slavery and its aftereffects. In an influential essay, A. James Arnold argues that leading French Caribbean male intellectuals, from Frantz Fanon and Aimé Césaire to the Créolists, have made cultural production a masculine or masculinist activity by rehashing the symbolic geography of the plantation, with its emasculation of black men. Due to this transhistorical gender topology, Arnold argues, women are excluded from the postcolonial cultural sphere.[18]

Male-centric (and heterocentric) narratives that justify men's infidelity and domestic absence by evoking slavery are so pervasive that they are even repeated in academic scholarship. For example, in her study of gender in the French Caribbean novel, critic Bonnie Thomas argues that a "prominent legacy of slavery was the creation of a phenomenon of 'strong women' and 'weak men,' which, although certainly representing a simplified version of gendered relationships, finds resonance in much contemporary literature."[19] While insisting that novels by both women and men present gender as a fluid cultural category, Thomas nevertheless identifies a central gender opposition running through the works, which she, following Condé, explains using the same proverb I quoted at the start of this chapter: "man as breadfruit [weak and irresponsible] and woman as chestnut [strong, morally superior]."

Informed by her interviews with esteemed authors, including Patrick Chamoiseau, Maryse Condé, Gisèle Pineau, and Raphaël Confiant, Thomas attributes these stereotypes to black men's emasculation and the history of black men's inability to act as fathers under slavery. As the old story goes, Caribbean fathers are perpetually absent.[20] Thomas conceives of Caribbean men's promiscuity and domestic abuse of their romantic partners as a kind of "partial redress" for slavery, which women accept "out of a feeling of guilt for the slight advantages they experienced under slavery." Though she acknowledges the burden of sexual and reproductive labor, Thomas sidesteps enslaved women's experiences of rape and the daily threat of rape. She even goes so far as to claim that "some female slaves were able to transform their oppression into a means of autonomy by using their body as a bartering asset."[21]

Were enslaved women able to obtain freedom for themselves and their children through sexual liaisons? We know that in the French Caribbean at the end of the eighteenth century, women and children were freed three times more frequently than men, though the numbers were relatively small.[22] Yet even if some women did obtain freedom through relations with white men, more women remained enslaved. Furthermore, as the historian Arlette Gautier stresses throughout her book, enslaved women were classified as property and subject to rape and the threat of rape as a device of everyday terror. To claim that as a group they used their bodies for strategic advancement and personal gain is to distort the picture gravely.

The discourse of "colonial seduction," historian Myriam Cottias argues, occludes our understanding of enslaved women's everyday lives, relationships, pleasures, and pains.[23] Such histories of lived experiences cannot be easily recovered. Whereas there exist in the United States female slave narratives that address the ubiquity of sexual exploitation,[24] no accounts written in French by enslaved women (or men) remain. The female experience of slavery's sexual system of subjection in the French Caribbean remains obscure. This gap in historical knowledge is filled by the Marilisse and Chestnut stereotypes.

Performing gender in the French Caribbean is a way of creolizing slavery's memory. Joseph Roach might call this "surrogation," cultural remembering and forgetting driven by substitution, or "memory imperfectly deferred."[25] When a French Caribbean woman performs her gender through the social norm of the Chestnut stereotype, she transmits (and reinvents) slavery's memory. Even as her performance of the morally superior Chestnut anxiously tries to erase the Marilisse, it encodes the damning seductress, bodily. Through drama Césaire and Condé reinvent such everyday performances of gender and slavery's memory. Instead of replacing an insufficient historical narrative of slavery's sexual violence with a more accurate account, Césaire and Condé destabilize dominant hierarchies and clichés through that ongoing process of imperfect and often contradictory cultural reinvention—creolization—that continually furnishes collective memory and notions of gendered Caribbean identity.

Ina Césaire's *Rosanie Soleil*: Revolutionary Women Reinvent the Chestnut and Play with Ambiguity

Featuring four revolutionary women, Césaire's *Rosanie Soleil* remixes and revises the Chestnut stereotype against the backdrop of a Martinican historical revolt known as the Southern Insurrection. The play shows a family of four women—the Mother (also called Mama Sun); her twin daughters, Rosanie and Eïnasor (Roseanna and Annarose in the English translation); and the women's neighbor Voisine Fumée (Sister Smoke)—as they go about their daily chores. In Césaire's words, the major theme of the play is the "daily reality as lived by four women during a period of tremendous political upheaval."[26] Slyly masking their participation in the revolt, the women speak in code to each other to allude to the mob killing of the white overseer that began the revolt and to the burning of plantations taking place outside. Because they periodically leave and return, it is inferred that these women are participating in the insurrection between scenes.

The women's differing attitudes toward resistance are introduced and debated, but always surreptitiously. Through their veiled speech, Sister Smoke and Roseanna reveal themselves to be radical revolutionaries. Annarose, though involved, more modestly wishes to think through the implications of her participation in the revolt. The Mother, for her part, declines to disclose whether she participated in the revolt and evades any direct discussion of it. Because she wishes to protect her daughters, she dissuades the others from speaking of the insurrection as well. Another reason for the Mother's reticence is her wish to protect a fugitive black man, whom she is hiding from the authorities seeking to quell the revolt and arrest the insurrectionists. This man may be the insurrection's leader and her twin daughters' long-lost father.

The play is a glimpse into these four women's lives during the historical revolt, but its characters are also glancing backward—toward slavery. Alluding to the experiences of black Caribbean subjection and resistance repeating across time, the play imaginatively unites the time of slavery (1635–1848), the time of the great Martinican rebellion (1870), and the time of writing at the end of the twentieth century (1992). By encouraging spectators to embrace historical ambiguity, the play does not seek to uncover the historical truth but rather to conjure and creolize a complex, multivalent inheritance of injustice and resistance that has been passed down through generations. As Christiane Makward notes, the play is about lived history, transmitted by way of women's mouths.[27] Césaire's dramaturgical style, influenced by Caribbean performance practices, shows these women's lived experiences as suspended in time (hovering between past and present) and entangled in diverse, coexisting forms of knowledge production.

Legacies of Resistance

The Southern Insurrection took place in 1870, twenty-two years after slavery's final abolition in the French colonies. Over the course of approximately five days, Martinicans of color violently protested a trial that crystallized the problem of ongoing antiblack legal practices. The event spurring the revolt was the condemnation of Lubin, a young black agricultural worker, for the revenge beating of a white man. After the white man beat him, Lubin had gone to authorities to report the incident, but his complaint was dismissed. When Lubin beat the same white man in turn, however, he was prosecuted. Although a racially mixed jury had been selected by random drawing for Lubin's trial, the French-controlled judicial system replaced the jurors of color with four white jurors, including a notoriously severe overseer named Codé. In August 1870 this all-white jury sentenced Lubin to five years in prison and a heavy fine. One month later, when Martinique received word of the proclamation of the French Third Republic, the Southern Insurrection erupted. With the participation of numerous women, several of whom acted as leaders, insurrectionists killed Codé, the white overseer, and his black servant, and they set fire to at least twenty-five plantations.[28] In the style of a Creole folktale, Césaire's play addresses this history obliquely. Césaire does not explain the context, nor does she name the Southern Insurrection directly.

In two scenes that bookend the play, insurrectionists who fought in the revolt are named in onstage performances of different forms of knowledge production, different means whereby one can learn about the past. In the prologue, Césaire draws from archived court records in order to announce the names, ethnicity, age, vocation, and place of residence of various revolutionaries, concluding with the eponymous heroine Roseanna Sun (Rosanie Soleil). Her stage directions stipulate that a "monotone voice—which signifies the official legal system" will read this list of the accused. Before Roseanna, we hear the name Magdeleine Clem, who the voice tells us is "known as 'Smoke'" (thus the women's neighbor) and qualifies as "Wanted."[29] Clem, the historical figure, was an aggressive female revolutionary who was sentenced to death for having participated in the assassination of Codé and the pillaging of plantations but escaped from prison.[30] The closing scene draws from the repertoire of performance practices—drumming and vodou ritual—to announce the revolution and honor revolutionary ancestors from both Martinique and Haiti. Preparing the women to fight, the onstage ritual alludes to the rally of Bois Caiman in 1791, a vodou ceremony that instigated the Haitian Revolution. Those who participated in the revolt are named again, but this time they are honored with colored scarves characteristic of vodou ritual. The use of legal documents and Caribbean performance practices onstage self-reflexively parallels the ways spectators and readers too might engage with the past while acknowledging contradictions, continuities and discontinuities, and unknowns.

The use of Caribbean storytelling, in particular, enables Césaire to highlight slavery's legacy, as opposed to figuring slavery as a contained history that ended with abolition. While the prologue and final scene address the Southern Insurrection directly, throughout the play the women use "unsaid parables, understatement, proverbs, images, and allusions (elements which constitute traditional oral expression in the Antilles)."[31] Led by Sister Smoke, the women tell the story of the Southern Insurrection as though it were a timeless folktale.[32] Acting as a traditional Creole storyteller, Smoke deliberately confuses details surrounding the revolt to give a more general picture of slavery's legacy. In her telling, Codé confronts a black man named Lindoret on the road and whips him. Here Smoke confuses Lubin with Lindoret, who was an eighteenth-century Martinican slave who defied his master and whose legacy is commemorated in the Creole folk song "Aie Lindôr." When Annarose points out that Smoke is confusing her characters, Smoke proclaims, *"(with dignity)* I know what I mean and I mean what I say!"[33]

More important to Smoke than the fact that she is conflating men and time periods is the continuity that she identifies between the stories of oppression under white patriarchy and black resistance to injustice. Her tale emphasizes that injustice against black Caribbeans endures, even as laws and conditions change. From the enslavement of Africans to the unjust conviction of their descendants by a French-administered legal system after abolition in 1870, and then, by extension, to the more insidious cultural and economic problems characterizing the time of the play's writing in 1992 (for instance, the imbalanced allocation of resources), institutionalized antiblack discrimination continues. Like their enslaved ancestors before them, the women, led by Smoke, retell stories to make sense of their situation and to mask their secret subversion. Storytelling also protects them. As the women wait for the possible arrival of the authorities, who are searching for the leader and working to quell the revolt, Smoke tells a folktale to mask their awareness of and involvement in the revolt.[34]

Generalizing Revolutionary Women

Reflecting and remixing Caribbean women's historical experiences, the play blurs distinctions between public and private histories. Whereas the Marilisse and Chestnut stereotypes obscure the history of enslaved women's revolutionary activities by prescribing that women can wield power only through sex or in the private space of the family and home, Césaire's play insists on women's participation in acts of political resistance. Yet rather than offering a revisionist history, that is, a new, more just narrative of the past, Césaire embraces ambiguities and unknowns. In her author's note, Césaire clarifies that the play is not intended to be a "historical drama"; it is a more intimate, personal play, like a "chamber play" *(pièce à caractère intimiste)*.[35]

Though her title character, Roseanna, "really did exist," Césaire is uninterested in writing history.[36] To be sure, the play tells a somewhat forgotten story of Martinican resistance and privileges the role played by women. As critics have noted, it challenges the concept of the (male) hero and inscribes historical memory through vibrant black feminist sensibilities.[37] But rather than putting the historical events of the Southern

Insurrection onstage the play dramatizes the exchanges and experiences of four women in what seems to be an everyday context. Césaire shows a story unfolding in the private sphere that has a decisive impact on the public sphere.

Even as the play tells an intimate, familial story, it constructs generalizable archetypes of Caribbean culture and history. To generalize the figure of the Martinican woman, Césaire invents for Roseanna a twin sister, Annarose. Together the girls represent the differing attitudes and phenotypes of Caribbean women. They are false twins, and their mother endearingly refers to them as her "geminis" (*doublons*).[38] Césaire specifies that the daughters are "both the same and different. Their anagrammatic names introduce them even on the physical plane as inverted reflections of the same mirror." While Roseanna (called the Gabber) is fiery, cheerful, and outspoken, Annarose (the Gazer) is contemplative and introverted. Roseanna challenges her mother overtly, pressing her with questions about her life under slavery and about the twins' father. Annarose, by contrast, respects her mother's silence and protective attitude. Physically Roseanna is black and Annarose "chabine," a phenotypic category in the French Caribbean that refers to a woman who is light-skinned, probably with freckles, and perhaps blonde or blue-eyed.[39]

In Césaire's telling, the generalizable Caribbean woman is both a revolutionary and a Chestnut. As a family of women, with no men visibly onstage, the characters seem to be strong black women who rule over the domestic sphere in the absence of reliable men. Their bodily behaviors seem to reiterate this stereotypical expression of gender. For example, from the domestic setting of their home and yard, the women hang the laundry, shell peas, and pick through lentils.[40] But the Chestnut performance is subtly undermined by their coded speech, which reveals their participation in the revolt. In fact their performance of the Chestnut stereotype masks deeper truths about their lived experience and thus acts as a strategic façade.

Much like enslaved blacks obeyed white plantation owners by doing their daily chores while reiterating a secretive culture of resistance through everyday practices like Creole storytelling, the women in *Rosanie Soleil* perform the expectations that patriarchy imposes upon their bodies while secretly participating in the revolt. Performing the Chestnut thereby enables the women to remain safe from the authorities—and to protect a black man they are hiding.[41] As mentioned, this wounded maroon figure (a runaway rebel) may be the daughters' father and the Mother's long-lost love. He may also be the leader of the insurrection.

From the outside, the women's slyly subversive performance might seem apolitical, but Césaire teaches us that this view is misinformed. Like their secret participation in the revolt, the women's undermining of the Chestnut stereotype, which turns on storytelling and occluded speech, recalls enslaved blacks' veiled resistance to white planters.

The Marilisse: Forgotten but Not Gone

The myth of the Marilisse haunts the women's performance—and reinvention—of the Chestnut onstage. Throughout *Rosanie Soleil*, the Marilisse is subtly conjured, but she is addressed only obliquely, thus signaling that the figure of the treacherous seductress is encoded bodily, "forgotten but not gone."[42] In choosing to make Roseanna and Annarose laundresses, Césaire gestures toward Fanon's denunciation in *Black Skin, White Masks* of the author known as Mayotte Capécia, a literary figure he used to blame Martinican women for the social problem of internalized racism. Fanon argued that Capécia's (narrator's) choice to become a laundress mirrored her preference for white men. According to him, both her career (involving bleaching) and her sexual preferences marked the ways she "endeavor[ed] to whiten [the race] in her body and mind."[43] Insofar as Roseanna and Annarose are of starkly different complexions, their bodies onstage conjure Caribbean legacies of interracial sex, which the play treats ambiguously.

The Mother symbolically represents the inaccessibility of enslaved women's experience of love and sex. She evades questions about her daughters' father, about whom she gives selective information. When Roseanna probes whether her mother was happy, Mama Sun pretends to be angry as she retorts, "That's none of your business, little girl!"[44] Mama Sun's secretive attitude toward the past marks what historian Darlene Clark Hine might call a "culture of dissemblance," which enables the Mother to protect her daughters as well as "the sanctity of inner aspects of [her life]." As Hine argues, black women have historically performed dissemblance as an adaptive response to the experiences of rape and domestic violence. But this strategy also poses a historiographic problem, insofar as it may have contributed to the "absence of sophisticated historical discussion of the impact of rape (or threat of rape) and incidences of domestic violence on the shape of Black women's experiences."[45]

In an early monologue, the Mother suggests that the history of slavery as a sexual system of domination may haunt the bodily juxtaposition of her twin daughters. Due to the difference in the daughters' complexions, rumors have circulated about a potential liaison between the Mother and a young white priest. Alone onstage, the Mother recalls the voices of her gossipy neighbors, who accused her of lasciviousness. Yet the voices do not reproach her for choosing white men over black men, as in the image of the Marilisse. Rather they suspect that she may have enjoyed sex with men of both races: "Two daughters, Girl? One light and one dark? You're doubling your pleasure? Girl, tell me now, wasn't that young white priest in on the fun?"[46]

In response to these voices that she herself conjures, the Mother angrily insists that her daughters have "got the same papa!" She explains, "In the prime of my youth, I fell hard in love with only one man."[47] By forcefully linking fatherhood to the true quality of a mother's love, the Mother offers a new definition of the family under slavery that dismisses the legitimacy of relations by force, coercion, or what Hartman calls the "extremity of constraint."[48] Nevertheless, throughout her monologue, the Mother never refuses the possibility of a sexual liaison with the young white priest or states whether she willed the affair. Furthermore it is possible that this "priest" may be a guise for her slave master, as spectators and readers familiar with the history of slavery might know. When French slave masters were accused of miscegenation and libertinage by religious men, some would order the enslaved women to testify that the religious men in charge of the investigations had actually fathered their mixed-race children.[49]

While the Mother dissembles her experience of sex under slavery through speech, Roseanna and Annarose raise the question of their paternity through their onstage corporeality. Whether or not they have the same biological father, their different skin tones bear witness to a white ancestor somewhere in their family tree. Having inherited a bodily trace of slavery's sexual system of domination, Annarose, the lighter-skinned sister, quietly contemplates the meaning of her light complexion.[50] As the play opens, she has "just barely emerged from a chaste silence that protected her childhood." Her darker-skinned sister, by contrast, has always spoken her mind. Annarose's childhood silence may be understood as conditioned by the ideological scripts controlling the sexuality of women of color. She may feel ashamed or afraid to discover the events leading to her conception. That Césaire chooses the word *chaste* (*pudique*) to describe Anna's previous silence reinforces the dramaturgical link between sex and silence.[51]

Interpreting Césaire's first play, *Mémoires d'Isles* (Island Memories), which I examine in chapter 2, Valérie Bada underscores the importance of silence, which she understands as "the playwright's search for a credible voice" despite the unspeakable nature of slavery's trauma.[52] Césaire scripts onstage performances in which bodies make ambiguous and contradictory meanings from within these silences. In *Mémoires d'Isles*, a mimed "archetypal rape scene" shows an enslaved woman on a bed raising her hand toward a white man in an "act of love or aggression?"[53] This stage direction, posed as a question, underscores the ambiguity surrounding enslaved women's historical experiences. It seems to say: This enslaved woman was a real person, and she did have sex with a white man, but we cannot know what happened when she, next to him, raised her hand. Instead of recovering the historical truth, this archetypical rape scene in *Mémoires d'Isles*, much like the juxtapositional narration and embodiment of paternity in *Rosanie Soleil*, embraces historical ambiguity.

Unity in the Unknown

Annarose, the contemplative sister, experiences the unknown past affectively and bodily. Through her own body, she accesses her Mother's daily acts, when younger, of laboring in the cane fields. Now twenty-four, the twins were only two years old when slavery was abolished, but their mother worked as an enslaved sugarcane binder for years. Annarose describes feeling her mother's experience bodily:

> THE MOTHER: (*affably*) And your jobs, daughters? How goes it? I'll wager you aren't nostalgic for the sugar cane fields?
>
> ROSEANNA: You know very well, Mama dear, thanks to you—and to God, of course—we never had to cut or bind cane.
>
> THE MOTHER: (*dreamily*) Laundresses ... That's a fine trade ... white starched lace, perfumed with citronella, freshly ironed. That's what's on your trays.
>
> ANNAROSE: (*a little short-tempered*) You might remember, Mama, there's a little matter of preliminaries: At Lézard River, you have to drop on all fours to wash the dirty linen on those flat rocks.
>
> THE MOTHER: (*rubbing her back*) Believe me, my child, you might crouch down to scrub your laundry, but your back takes less of a strain! There's nothing like a plentiful cane.harvest to nearly cut you in half!
>
> ANNAROSE: You think there's a chance pain can be passed on from mother to daughter? My back aches too, Mama.[54]

While Annarose's light skin is an uncertain bodily mark of a distressing history of interracial sex, her experience of inhabiting (moving and working in) her body is a site of intergenerational transmission. Her experience of her body gives her knowledge (albeit uncertain) of her Mother's physical labor. She thus intuits that her mother was never a Marilisse, that is, an enslaved women living in relative luxury with a white man while enslaved black men worked in the cane fields.

The play favors restorative gender relations over historical precision. According to historian Odile Krakovitch, at the urging of white officials many female revolutionaries, including Rosanie Soleil, testified against their male Caribbean partners. These women claimed they were not necessarily devoted to the revolution but their men pressured them into participating. This was a choice, Krakovitch stresses, that women made to mitigate their much harsher sentencing by a sexist French judicial system that saw women's place as being in the home.[55] Césaire, in contrast, shows women risking their lives to save a fugitive man.

Just as a storyteller may leave out parts of the story or embellish parts in any given telling, Césaire glosses over this history of gender division in order to communicate the desired moral to her listeners. She deliberately forgets this alleged "betrayal" of black men by black women and instead emphasizes the women's caring for, sheltering, and loving a black maroon man. Similarly, whereas she might have reclaimed the history of women maroons, as André and Simone Schwarz-Bart and Maryse Condé have done in their novels, Césaire leaves intact the masculine ideal of the fugitive black man as hero.[56]

The play's final scene prepares the women to fight and honors those historical figures who participated in the revolt. The Mother sings the Haitian song "Eyou Marassa," a celebration of the *marasa*, the divine twins of the vodou belief system.[57] In addition to endowing Césaire's twins, Roseanna and Annarose, with symbolic power to generalize the Caribbean female experience, the song signals that the scene (and the play at large) should be understood through the rules of diaspora literacy that VèVè Clark calls "*marasa* consciousness."[58] The *marasa* signals both unity and division and traditionally encompasses male and female. As a hermeneutic strategy, the *marasa trois* introduces a third option: it moves interpretation beyond binary oppositions into a new realm of discourse and creativity, one in which the persistent traces of slavery's system of subjection are not undone but are acknowledged and accepted.

This final, ritualistic scene unites the girls with their father (represented onstage by the drum) and conceptually unifies histories of resistance in independent Haiti with the lesser-known revolutionary history of the French overseas department of Martinique. It heralds a future of resistance to ongoing French neocolonialism that will be marked by cooperation between women and men. As the scene begins, the women listen and interpret the message of the drum: "Reunion! [C'est le tambour des retrouvailles!]"[59] The drum's message signals both a meeting of insurrectionists, like the ceremony that took place at Bois Caiman and instigated the Haitian revolution, and a symbolic, ritualistic unification of Haiti and Martinique, men and women. Recognizing their father in the Haitian Assator drum, the daughters bow before the drum and chant, "It's the same, the same island and the same drum." In this final scene, spectators learn that all four women are in fact devoted revolutionaries as they ritualistically prepare for the rebellion. The final lines of the play, though still a bit secretive, confirm this fact: the women announce that they will all go to "meet them," meaning to join the insurrectionists.[60]

Staging the daily activities and veiled conversations of four women who are secretly involved in an insurrection, *Rosanie Soleil* shows a generalizable female experience of diverse women resisting slavery and its ongoing impact from behind the Chestnut façade. Through the onstage use of vodou ritual and Caribbean storytelling, Césaire symbolically unifies women's and men's experiences and Haiti's triumphant legacy of resistance with Martinique's lesser-known insurrection. By embracing historical ambiguity and contradiction, the play remixes and reinvents the gendered stereotypes of plantation culture and the predominant, male-centric narrative of postcolonialism. Rather than presenting a revisionist, female-centered history, Césaire calls upon spectators and readers to embrace historical ambiguities and epistemological contradictions.

This lesson in the necessity of accepting the unknown resurfaced for me as a theater historian when I studied the play's performance history. *Rosanie Soleil* premiered in 1992 at the Festival de Fort-de-France, Martinique, where it was directed by Syto Cavé, one of the founding members of the Kouidor Haitian theater troupe. Cavé's staging emphasized the influence of vodou, a theme that runs through much of his work as a theater artist.[61] The play starred Haitian actresses Laurence Durand in the role of Annarose, Joelle Jean-Julien as Sister Smoke, and Toto Bissainthe as the Mother. Raphaelle Serreau (the daughter of Danielle Vanbercheck and the French director Jean-Marie Serreau, who collaborated with Aimé Césaire) played Roseanna.[62] Unfortunately I was unable to reconstruct this premiere performance, largely due to the fragility of the archive. Cavé's personal archives containing his notes and other physical traces of the production were destroyed in the 2010 earthquake in Haiti.[63] This fragility of personal archives like Cavé's highlights the importance of the cultural performance practices Césaire evokes, the repertoire, namely storytelling and vodou ritual, as an embodied means of keeping and transmitting history.

Maryse Condé's *Pension les Alizés*: Defamiliarizing the Logic of the Marilisse with Irony

A failed love story set in Paris in 1986, Condé's *Pension les Alizés* destabilizes the logic of the Marilisse and Chestnut stereotypes by remixing the binary opposition of the passive victim and willful seductress and by muddling the moral hierarchy upon which the stereotypes are built. By way of irony and exaggeration, Condé defamiliarizes Caribbean society's unstated assumptions regarding gender and heterosexual relationships. The play invites spectators to see the lived experiences of a Guadeloupean nude dancer with fresh eyes, and thereby unveils a transhistorical legacy of the abstraction and exploitation of Caribbean women's bodies.

In contrast with the women of *Rosanie Soleil*, Condé's Guadeloupean protagonist Emma is both chronologically and geographically distanced from the site of the plantation, and she shows no interest in making meaning from this history. Yet slavery's sexual legacy nonetheless permeates her behaviors and attitudes and impacts her romantic relationships and prospects. Emma is a former nude dancer, now aged past her prime, whose onstage performances repeat, exaggerate, and remake the stereotype of the Marilisse. Emma lives alone in her Parisian apartment, where she idly daydreams of returning to her homeland; she has not set foot in the Caribbean since arriving in France more than forty years earlier. When she welcomes Ishmael, a Haitian political refugee and dubious revolutionary, into her apartment, she imagines the possibility of an equal romantic and sexual partnership. But this ideal relationship does not play out, and Emma ultimately decides to stay alone in Paris rather than return to the Caribbean with him.

Condé creolizes her meanings by inviting multiple contradictory readings of her characters and message. The play invites audiences and readers to see Emma doubled: as both a victim of society's exoticization and abstraction, and as a smart woman who has strategically embraced the stereotypes to her own ends. More broadly, Emma is simultaneously a sympathetic character with whom audiences will identify and an antihero whose life and sense of self-worth have been overtaken by the Marilisse stereotype. Stylistically Condé deploys the conventions of psychological realism and Brechtian alienation. In an interview with Alvina Ruprecht, Condé calls this technique her "ironic alienation combined with tenderness" (*distanciation ironique mêlée à la tendresse*).⁶⁴ As discussed in a final section on the original performance, *Pension les Alizés* posed interpretive challenges to its production team and spectators. The original performance further creolized the text by glossing over some meanings, emphasizing others, and enacting contradictions, syncretisms, and disconnects in meaning onstage.

Performing the Ambivalent Status Quo

Emma performs how the gendered stereotypes of plantation culture can abstract real Caribbean women from their bodies. Condé disrupts the stereotypes by selectively dissociating Emma the person from the stereotype projected on her, while nonetheless showing how the Marilisse has overtaken Emma's life and person. The *female body of slavery's legacy* shadows her real body, so much so that the "idea of the black [female] body and [her] actual, physical black body interrelate and . . . blur together."⁶⁵ The clichéd memory of the Marilisse is ambivalently encoded in Emma's body and behaviors. Single, childless, and independent, Emma has refused the social scripts of the Chestnut stereotype and (perhaps in consequence) fallen into the Marilisse stereotype, ironically returning to the damning seductress whom the Chestnut had so eagerly tried to forget.

Through her life choices, Emma embodies the Marilisse stereotype insofar as she has "used" her body to obtain some luxuries and advancement. Though she no longer dances, she is modestly wealthy, bringing home caviar, fancy cheeses, fine wines, and champagne for Ishmael to enjoy. When Ishmael asks where she gets her money, she responds, "There was a man who really loved me. . . . He gave me everything he owned." At the end of the play, when Ishmael is preparing to return to Haiti, Emma uses similar rhetoric to explain how she was able to obtain a counterfeit passport for him "through a man who once loved me very much. He was high up in the police department. And he kept his connections."⁶⁶ We can assume that these men knew Emma as a nude dancer, meaning that her body was her primary means of acquiring material luxuries and social advancement, both for herself and for Ishmael. Through such everyday choices, Emma represents the myth of the Marilisse, reendowing it with meaning through repeated behavior.

Emma rationalizes her career choice through ambiguous and contradictory repetition that seems to alternate between intransigence and doubt. Against her parents' belief that nude dancing brings dishonor to their family, she maintains that she is proud. In her opening monologue, she describes herself as a "dignified black woman" and goes on to repeat the word *dignified* four times. Yet she fears that her houseguest Ishmael considers her a whore, and she feels certain that her friends and family in Guadeloupe have dismissed her as a Marilisse. "Yes, my dear, she shows her ass off to the whites!" she imagines her neighbors gossiping.[67]

Emma's self-conscious performances show a female actor playing a role that she embraces, though it appears to be scripted by someone else. Onstage she bows to an invisible crowd and struts about. In the two metatheatrical scenes that bookend the play, she applies makeup in front of her mirror and exclaims, "When I'd stick on my false eyelashes, that's when the show would begin!"[68] Through this use of metatheatricality, the play fosters critical consciousness surrounding the insidious ways in which the Marilisse stereotype is repeated and reified in the performance of everyday life.

It is important to note that *Pension les Alizés* was inspired by two black women actors faced with the challenges of limited opportunities in France. The play was developed out of Condé's conversations with Lisette Malidor, a Martinican dancer and singer who performed in Paris, though, in the end, Condé decided not to write a play about Malidor since the actress did not confide enough in her. Condé wrote the play for another Martinican performer, her dear friend Sonia Emmanuel, who both directed the play and played the role of Emma in the original performance in 1988. Because there were very few interesting roles at that time for Emmanuel, a black woman in Paris, Condé wished to "write a play for her so she could display her talents."[69] This theme of the lives and struggles of black women actresses is central to the play's structure.

Ironic Juxtapositions and Exaggerations

Condé uses irony and exaggeration in order to defamiliarize Caribbean society's expectations regarding gender and heterosexual romantic relations. She scripts an apparent contradiction: between Emma's self-avowed pride in her career choice and her struggle to live with the myriad ways her daily life is permeated by the stereotype's influence. As such, Condé slyly unveils the unstated moral hierarchies undergirding the Marilisse stereotype. Her novels are commonly celebrated for what Leah Hewitt has aptly called their "questioning of dogmatic positions and ready-made values" by seesawing between different points of view.[70] Or, as Dawn Fulton puts it, Condé sets up intricate interpretive "traps" for her readers.[71] *Pension les Alizés* uses juxtaposition, irony, and comedic exaggeration to invite its spectators into similar traps. By making spectators confront the contradictions and ambiguities of Emma's life choices, the play facilitates its audience's questioning of the ideas and behaviors inherited from the time of slavery that people tend to take for granted.

Defying the binary opposition between woman as passive sufferer or willful seductress, Condé questions the extent to which Emma might have *chosen* her role as Marilisse. On the one hand, colonial (and postcolonial) societies project ideas of black female sexuality on Emma's body. Condé explains in an interview, "Even when they are very intelligent, the way that most black women can succeed is with their bodies, through their figures. For me, Emma was an exemplification of that dilemma."[72] On the other hand, Condé scripts Emma making the stereotype of the oversexed black woman "work for [her]," to quote Emma's own words regarding her body.[73]

Though Emma does not choose to be exoticized, she seems to willfully embrace the objectification of her body. When a white man sees her potential as a nude dancer, she feels that he has ushered in her destiny. Emma reports, "I think it was God, God himself, who sent Guido to me. 'My dear, with your looks, you could have Paris at your feet!' And Paris couldn't grovel fast enough. (*She laughs.*)"[74] Emma's conclusion that God sent Guido to her is comically exaggerated, but her thinking is not naïve. She has understood that, in Paris, she is "overdetermined from the outside," to use Fanon's phrase: her social role is scripted by her appearance as a black woman.[75] Yet while her comments are smart and insightful, they also reveal her overestimation of the power she wields as a nude dancer, which serves to defamiliarize the myth of the Marilisse's seductive powers over men.

Though Emma acquiesces to the role of the Marilisse, her lived experiences contradict its myths. If she has acquired her financial and sexual independence, these successes come at a high price, for they have distanced her from her native land and from Ishmael. Even though she tries to use her money to take care of and please him, he resents her fancy meals and favors because they make him feel belittled and emasculated. Whereas the stereotypical Marilisse would abandon the black man, choosing instead to live in relative luxury with the white man, Emma remains loyal to Ishmael despite his clearly dubious character. In fact it is not Emma but Ishmael who acts treacherously. When she is out shopping, he tries to steal her money and run.[76] She forgives him.

Even as she shows that Emma is independent and capable, Condé exaggerates the Marilisse's infiltration of Emma's sense of self. To be sure, Emma is a strong and smart woman, as Christiane Makward rightly insists.[77] She keeps informed about current events, particularly throughout the African diaspora, and she responds to the news intelligently. However, her body provides her job qualifications, her income, her extraprofessional earnings, and her sense of self-worth. She first came to Paris to study medicine, but she reneged on medical school and became a nude dancer instead. It is unclear whether she herself aspired to be a doctor or if it was the dream her father (a nurse) had for her. Over forty years later, Emma is still rationalizing her choice. First, she explains that it was difficult to survive financially as a student, especially because of food rationing during World War II. Later she insists that her body is all she has of value: "Papa was wrong about me. I didn't have it in me to become a doctor. First of all, I can't stand the sight of blood! Secondly, I'm not very smart. My brain isn't the best thing about me. I only had a body. And I made it work for me."[78] Matter-of-factly Emma repeats the colonial equation of black women with corporeality and sex—along with the dismissal of black women's intelligence. Here Emma's verbal repetition reinforces the stereotype of the licentious black woman—the European prototype of the Marilisse—while her lived experiences reveal the fallacies of this myth.

Transhistorical Abstractions

The play situates Emma within a larger history of other black women performers (whether performers by choice or by coercion) who were made to negotiate the sexualized stereotypes of plantation culture. The cabaret where Emma used to work is called the New Venus, recalling "the Hottentot Venus," the stage name of Saartjie Baartman, a South African woman whose body was put on display, in life and in death, to entertain the crowds.[79] And Emma informs the audience during her opening monologue that, in the prime of her dancing career, she was called the "new Josephine Baker." An African American performer who found instant stardom in Paris in the 1920s, Baker was nicknamed "the Black Venus." Though Baker was an influential artist and icon, her acts deployed colonial stereotypes of the oversexed and so-called primitive black female body. Through these subtle allusions, the play suggests that if Baker was the new Venus, Emma is now the new Baker. In other words, Condé evokes a lineage of black women on whose bodies the Marilisse stereotype was imposed and who may (or may not) have "made it work for [them]."[80]

Yet Emma is not in communion with Baartman or Baker. Baker was a prodigious, empowered figure, an icon and a decidedly modern woman.[81] As a black woman who chose nude dancing, Emma might identify with such empowering visions of Baker. Instead, however, she judges and distances herself from Baker, much like Caribbean society condemns the Marilisse. Emma seems to believe that Baker modeled undesirable self-exoticization: "The new Josephine Baker, that's what they used to call me! But I never really liked being called that! When I saw it in the papers, I was mad. Because I refused to wear a belt of bananas. I was a dignified black woman."[82] Emma learns about the link between herself and Baker by reading French newspapers, and she does not seem to know anything about Baker's life beyond her dancing. For example, she does not know of Baker's work with the French Resistance, her civil rights activism, or her large adopted family. Nor does Emma seem aware of the possible allusion to Baartman in the name of her club. Someone else, presumably a white European man, has named it.

While Emma *embodies* a continuity with the past, her knowledge of slavery is pervaded by an absence of physical traces and connection—by forgetting. Whereas *Rosanie Soleil* shows how (uncertain) memory is transmitted intergenerationally, Emma is alienated both from her family and from Guadeloupe's slave history. Whether she is correct or misguided in her incredulity, she dismisses the repertoire of family stories surrounding slavery. She jokes about a maroon ancestor whose last name, according to her father, became the family name: "Some story! A maroon, you bet!"[83]

This detachment from family and from history is emblematized by the physical and emotional distance that separates Emma from her mother's grave. Emma's mother died shortly after Emma arrived in Paris, in the early to mid-1940s, and she has never returned to see her grave. Likening her pain over the loss of her mother to a painful wisdom tooth extraction, Emma insists that one should not "brood over the past."[84] Yet throughout the play, she does brood over the loss. Thus her efforts to forget past pain affirm that the pain will linger, just as her ignorance of slavery and its sexual legacy allows her to mindlessly repeat the Marilisse stereotype that slavery produced.

Failed Heterosexual Love

Critics have argued that Emma's ultimate decision not to return to Haiti with her lover represents her triumph as a strong woman.[85] In my reading, it is also a creolization—in this case, a critical reassembling and defamiliarization—of gender and gender relations inherited from the time of slavery. Melissa McKay attributes Emma's unhappiness and isolation to her status as a marginalized and exoticized black woman living in France.[86] I wish to stress Emma's contradictory experience of *the female body of slavery's legacy* as opposed to the politics of her identity. Similarly, while one is tempted (by Condé's dramaturgical traps) to read the play from within the emotional division, the perceived conflict, between men and women discussed earlier, I insist that Condé (like Césaire) undermines this gendered division through her disorienting aesthetics of creolization.

Emma's romantic relationship with Ishmael is not simply positioned as an individual love story, for it is scripted by the stereotypes of slavery's sexual system of subjection, which are ambiguously projected onto both characters' bodies and internalized by them. Through Ishmael's visit, Emma imagines the possibility of a reciprocal relationship with a Caribbean man, yet her efforts to love and be loved misfire and fail. Wanting to assert his masculinity, Ishmael asks Emma to act "weak" for him, which she, having forged an independent life in Paris, resents. For her part, Emma wants Ishmael to be faithful to her alone, but he is primarily interested in returning to Haiti and to his mistress, whom he loves. Emma dreams of returning to the Caribbean and believes that the only way she can do so respectably is with a man at her arm.[87] Ishmael, a doctor, seems to present this possibility, and he invites Emma to return to Haiti with him, but he already has two women (his wife and mistress) waiting for him there.

At the end of the play, Emma chooses not to return with Ishmael to Haiti, but her "choice" is not so much a decision between two possibilities as an acknowledgment and acceptance of a scripted outcome. Coming to terms with the loss of her fantasy, she speaks of what might have been, the relationship they could have had in an alternate reality. Emma and Ishmael could have found love, returned to the Caribbean, and studied to be doctors together. They could have had a daughter, who would have led a life free from the stereotypes projected on Emma. "She wouldn't have been familiar with winter, freezing maid's rooms, racism, or fear. No one would have said to her, 'Take off your blouse, cross your legs. Higher. Turn around.'"[88] In Emma's fantasy, her daughter is completely free from the reality of Emma's (and other black women's) embodied experiences of the Marilisse and the Chestnut.

Condé's play ends in an unsettling performance that unveils the moral and cultural hierarchies implicit in the stereotypes of the Marilisse and Chestnut. In the final scene, Emma, sitting alone at her makeup table, receives a phone call informing her of Ishmael's probable execution. She transforms her face into a Pierrot (the stock clown figure of the Commedia dell'arte) and, echoing the opening scene, declares, "I'll stick on my false eyelashes and the show can begin!"[89] Critics have theorized this final moment as a testament to Emma's strength, even her triumph over Ishmael.[90] By contrast, I maintain that it offers a *gestus*, that is, a Brechtian moment, in which Emma's attitude and situation are revealed. The gestus encourages audiences to reflect critically on Emma's predicament. The whiteface represents her assimilation into French culture (analogous to whiteness in the French Caribbean context), which, in turn, entails her acceptance of the Marilisse stereotype that the French colonial and Caribbean postcolonial imaginaries project onto her body. Thus though Emma puts a white mask over her black skin to signal her assimilation, her body will continue to be marked and stereotyped every time she walks out her door.

By accepting her scripted role, she also performs her resignation to a loveless life in Paris. Sadly, yet comically, she embraces the divide between Caribbean men and women that is commonly understood to stem from slavery. Perhaps she accepts the blame that present-day French Caribbean women bear for the history of interracial sex. By inviting spectators to laugh (as they laugh at Pierrot), the clown makeup at the end of the play disrupts their complicity in Emma's bodily and moral abstraction. It may make spectators aware of earlier moments, when they laughed at Emma's exaggerated comments or her sexual behaviors and attitudes. In this moment of culturally conscious Brechtian alienation, her body is made strange, and audiences are awakened to everyday spectacles of race and gender.[91]

Emma's Body in Performance

The original performance of the play in 1988 represented a creolization of Condé's text insofar as it enacted continuities and breaks, converging and diverging from the script in new, unpredictable ways. The play was directed by Condé's close friend Sonia Emmanuel, who also played Emma, and was produced by her theater company, Libre Échange. Jacques Martial, a black French actor of Guadeloupean origin, played Ishmael. Though the play was rehearsed in Paris, it was performed in Guadeloupe and Martinique. In my reconstruction of this production, I have relied exclusively on interviews with Emmanuel and Martial. Both theater artists explained that they had wished to perform the play in Paris or Avignon (in addition to the Caribbean), but it was too difficult for them to rent a venue to perform the play in France.[92] Martial added that this was the case for most black and Caribbean productions at the time (and it continues to be a problem). Such logistical challenges were in some ways anticipated by the thematics of Condé's play. Though Condé's Guadeloupean protagonist Emma was able to perform in Paris, it was only as a nude dancer—thus from within the norms of the colonial imaginary of the black woman—that she could become a successful actress.

Emmanuel's staging of the final scene, in which Emma makes her face up into a Pierrot, modified this performative moment as scripted by Condé. Emmanuel did not use whiteface makeup since, as she explained to me, this stage direction did not work for her as an actress in this role. However, she did substitute white hair for the whiteface makeup, thus preserving a visual signifier of whiteness. Following Emmanuel's directorial vision, the white hair emphasized Emma's age and her emotional decline. Throughout the play, Emmanuel wore a wig to cover the white hair underneath, which spectators did not see until the final scene. At the play's close, Emmanuel revealed the white hair that Emma had previously tried to hide (as opposed to putting white makeup over her black skin). Emmanuel additionally used music to create a Brechtian alienation effect. She chose to play the last part of Schoenberg's *Gurrelieder*. She recalled that the piece's final notes resounded as Emma confronted herself, her age, and her situation. Emmanuel viewed this final moment as an end for Emma, perhaps even the end of her life in suicide.

Emmanuel did not stress slavery's sexual stereotypes in her artistic vision. By replacing whiteface with white hair, Emmanuel privileged Emma's dilemma as an aging woman who had previously relied on her body for money. I speculate that this interpretation, which downplayed the racialization of Emma's body, would have been better received in France than the provocative challenge issued to spectators by Condé's (scripted) whiteface gesture. Yet the company was nonetheless unable to perform the production in France, where they had created and rehearsed it.

While the performance glossed over the historical and racial dimensions of the Marilisse, it magnified the ambiguity surrounding Emma's sexual power already written into the text. In Condé's play, Emma's excitement at wielding power as a nude dancer (with Paris at her feet) is undermined by her aging body and Ishmael's tepid physical attraction to her. It is unclear whether Ishmael loves Emma—or even desires her sexually—or is using her for her money and shelter. Condé specifies in her stage directions that throughout the entire play a large portrait of Emma at thirty, or younger, will dominate an entire wall of her apartment.[93] Against an older Emma onstage, whom we can presume, based on Condé's chronology, to be roughly sixty years old, this portrait bears witness to her younger body as well as its aging.

Defamiliarizing the unstated yet ubiquitous myth of the Marilisse, this juxtaposition reinforces that Emma is caught up in a complex system of sexual subjection that she can nevertheless strategically harness to limited ends. It raises questions (without answering them) about the emancipatory potential of a woman's sexual power, particularly as she ages. Reflecting on the experience of acting in the play, Martial recalled having experienced a disconnect between his own viewing of Emmanuel onstage ("a beautiful woman," he remembered) and his character's sexual disinterest in Emma, due to her older age. Moreover Martial specified that this disconnect for him as an actor was not due to the actress's age, since Emmanuel "was and *is* a beautiful woman" (twenty-six years later).

Taken out of context, Martial's comment might sound inconsequential, perhaps like flattery or a lighthearted joke. But it is in fact an important testament to his experience—as an actor—of a poignant, unresolved tension in Condé's text. Does Emma wield sexual power in her relationship with Ishmael? If so, is it liberating? Can it be love? Defamiliarizing her audience's unstated assumptions about Caribbean heterosexual relationships, gender relations, black women's sexual roles, and sexual power and aging, Condé encourages critical questioning (without providing answers).

Of course because *Pension les Alizés* is a multivalent play, it would be difficult to conscientiously address every theme evoked in a single performance. Indeed Martial told me that he would like to play his role again now, as a more experienced actor, in order to do full justice to Condé's complexity, particularly the intense feeling of emptiness the play evokes. Based on the interviews, I have gathered that the play's premiere production reproduced Condé's irony without making its spectators overly uncomfortable. But there is evidence that some spectators were nonetheless offended by this provocative play. According to Condé, an open letter written by a Guadeloupean communist woman criticized her for her unflattering portrayal of the Guadeloupean city Pointe-à-Pitre.[94] To be sure, such a criticism misses the point of Condé's irony. But it also speaks to the challenges involved in staging Condé's unsettling of the Marilisse stereotype and her characteristic anti-essentialist refusal of positive, postcolonial propaganda and slogans. My evidence is too sparse to make any conclusions regarding the reception of the original production in the

Caribbean, but Emmanuel recalled that the play was enthusiastically welcomed in Guadeloupe, where the company was asked to prolong the run.

In my analysis of *Pension les Alizés*, I have emphasized how Emma's words and behaviors, along with the portrayal of the failed romantic relationship, critically expose and remix slavery's sexual legacy. While the myth of the Marilisse ascribes traitorous agency to French Caribbean women, Condé shows how Emma's body becomes a site upon which abstracted ideas of *the black female body* are confusingly projected and internalized. Using irony to defamiliarize the Marilisse, Condé questions the extent to which a woman who "uses" her body wields power over white and black men. Refusing to classify Emma as either a victim to her exoticization by society or a willful seductress who uses her body toward her own ends, Condé shows the complex and contradictory ways Emma lives alongside the gendered stereotypes of plantation culture, thereby creolizing the status quo. The play's final scene, in which Emma dons whiteface, drives home Condé's disruption of the stereotype.

While Emmanuel's staging softened Condé's irony, the original production nonetheless communicated Condé's critical questioning of Emma's sexual power and bodily experiences. Through the use of white hair and jarring music, the final scene reimagined Condé's whiteface gestus, thus repeating, with a critical difference, Condé's fragmented portrayal of Emma's lived experiences of love, sex, race, and cultural isolation. The performance creolized Condé's text: it repeated and reinvented the play's multivalent meanings.

Creolizing Gender

Césaire and Condé use theater to remix and reinvent the meanings of gender in the French Caribbean and to trouble the status quo of the Marilisse and Chestnut stereotypes. Though the playwrights deploy different dramaturgical styles and approaches, both create continuity with the slave past even as they expose knowledge gaps, contradictions, and ambiguities. Portraying female leads who live alongside, reinvent, or defamiliarize the gendered stereotypes of plantation culture, Césaire and Condé repair and unveil (respectively) society's unsaid assumptions about gender, sex, and heterosexual romantic relations. Though they position performance as a vehicle for social change, both plays question the extent to which emancipation from the past is even possible, and thereby acknowledge the inassimilable aspects of slavery's sexual legacy.

Whereas the gendered stereotypes of plantation culture limit women's participation in the public sphere, Césaire's and Condé's plays blur the apparent public-private opposition. They emphasize how gender, family, and love crucially intersect with the postcolonial, public sphere. In both plays, the female leads stand in for a larger collective of French Caribbean women. Césaire's twin sister protagonists, evocative of the *marasa*, or the divine twins, make meaning through creative oppositions. As in an allegorical folktale, they together embody a larger collective of Caribbean women. Condé's Emma, in a Brechtian manner, is a reflection of society's unexamined assumptions and social scripts. It is important to recognize Emma's "collective dimension," as Condé stated in an interview.[95] In both plays, apparently intimate stories of family and romance are connected to larger cultural trends and histories. What the female protagonists share with their Caribbean women spectators and readers is not a question of an essentialist nature, inner strength, or identity. Rather they share the experience of having slavery's sexual legacy projected on their bodies, of being seen and interpellated as Marilisse and/ or Chestnut when their lived experiences complicate and contradict the stereotypes.

The plays unhinge the gendered stereotypes of plantation culture through creolization as opposed to postcolonial resistance. Helen Gilbert and Joanne Tompkins argue in their far-reaching study of postcolonial drama, "The colonial subject's body contests its stereotyping and representation by others to insist on self-representation by its physical presence on the stage."[96] In this vein, Césaire and Condé reclaim Caribbean female bodies and roles from society's pernicious social scripts. However, the plays do not contest or resist the stereotypes so much as remix and subvert them, refusing their logic and defying the moral and cultural hierarchies upon which they are built. Rather than replacing the oppressive clichés with other, more empowering social scripts or with claims to historical truths, the plays reorder chronological time, mobilize diverse forms of knowledge production, and emphasize unassimilated tensions between past and present, bodies and speech, Haiti and the French overseas departments of Martinique and Guadeloupe, and in conflicting, popular narratives of the past. They destabilize the status quo by creatively enacting creolization as transformative, inassimilable performance.

2 Remixing Unity and Difference

Maryse Condé's *An tan revolisyon*,
Ina Césaire's *Mémoires d'Isles*, and
Gerty Dambury's *Lettres indiennes*

In the Caribbean, questions of humanity and subjecthood are tangled up in the legacies of slavery and colonialism. Slavery, Saidiya Hartman argues, made enslaved peoples subjects even as it subjugated them.[1] According to her, slavery was a dehumanizing system of subjection that also selectively ascribed humanity to black slaves in order to justify slavery's brutality and cultivate perfect submission. This history of racialized subjection did not end with slavery's abolition. For centuries, French Caribbeans of color have been selectively counted in and excluded from the categories of the human and the citizen. Revolutionary governments in 1794, 1848, and 1870 granted Caribbeans of color French citizenship, but these rights were revoked by subsequent regimes. The Code de l'indigénat in 1887 created an alternative and inferior legal status for natives of all French colonies.

Since the 1946 law of *départementalisation*, Martinique and Guadeloupe have been departments, or administrative divisions, of France. The islanders are French citizens; they benefit from French social and cultural policies, and artists can receive state-subsidized grants for their creative work. However, the contemporary problems of racism and the imbalanced allocation of resources (both by the French government and the economic market) continue. Martinicans and Guadeloupeans carry French (EU) passports, but there is a history of racialized and geographical exclusion that continues in economic and cultural policies. For hundreds of years, Caribbeans have experienced selective exclusion from bona fide French citizenship, evident in precarious access to rights, inferior official legal status, and unjust allocation of resources.

French Caribbean theories of identity combat the cultural dimensions of this ongoing political problem by striving to reclaim French Caribbean subjecthood from France's insidious control over notions of humanity and citizenship. For a long time France has attributed the allegedly universal concepts of justice, equality, and freedom to the French nation, the French Revolution, and the philosophical writings of white French men. I use the term *French republican universalism* to refer to a ubiquitous rhetoric which presumes that France's secular, humanist values transcend, race, gender, culture, ethnicity, and class while nonetheless, paradoxically, remaining "French."[2] Rather than disavowing French republican universalism altogether, many Caribbean authors have sought to reclaim it on their own terms. One salient aspect of the francophone tradition of Caribbean criticism, Nick Nesbitt argues, is that it "appears concerned not with individuals or with classes but with a series of abstract, universal concepts of relevance to all human beings and not to any specifically regional, racial, or gendered experiences."[3]

At the same time, however, French Caribbean writers have distrusted universalism and sought to affirm Caribbean particularity as a means of resistance. Leading theories of French Caribbean identity, from Aimé Césaire's Négritude to Édouard Glissant's Antillanité, and the Créolists' (Jean Bernabé, Patrick Chamoiseau and Raphaël Confiant's) Créolité, are each premised on the idea of difference, as Richard Burton has pointed out.[4] Theories of French Caribbean identity are built on an underlying tension between universalism and difference. Even as French Caribbean writers recuperate the human universal, they also reject the ways in which Caribbean culture and history have been dismissed as inferior. Caribbeans, to quote the Créolists, have been led to "beg for the universal in the most colorless and scentless way, i.e. refusing the very foundation of our being."[5]

In this chapter, with a focus on collaborative creation and cultural reception, I explore three plays by Maryse Condé, Ina Césaire, and Gerty Dambury that use performance not to propose another theory of identity but rather to creolize these unresolved tensions and interplay between universal humaneness and Caribbean particularity. Condé's *An tan revolisyon* (In the Time of Revolution) deploys postmodern historiography and storytelling traditions to revisit the lived histories of the events of 1789–1802 in Guadeloupe, Haiti, and France, and show that, from the point of view of the average Guadeloupean, the radical, universalist promises of the French and Haitian revolutions remain unrealized. Césaire's *Mémoires d'Isles* (Island Memories) performs Martinican collective memory by way of the reminiscences of two grandmothers and carves out a space in which Caribbean particularity and the human universal coexist. Dambury's *Lettres indiennes* (Crosscurrents), a story of a black Guadeloupean woman who befriends an East Indian man on an ambiguous island, dramatizes the overlapping experiences of the descendants of black slaves and Indian indentured servants and considers the historical experience of diaspora—dispersal from a homeland and integration into a new society—at the heart of Caribbean society.

Though these selected plays are quite different thematically, they each present Caribbeanness (whether the focus is on history, memory, culture, or identity) as a dynamic, unfolding historical process of creolization. Furthermore the plays were created in a dynamic process of theatrical creolization, that is, by combining multiple cultural viewpoints, knowledges, and theatrical traditions. Each of the three plays was inspired by the practices, aesthetics, and hallmark artists of the intercultural theatrical tradition. Both the plays and their staging and reception histories show that Caribbean identity and aesthetics, as Stuart Hall theorizes, are never complete but always in a process of becoming or (re)production, created simultaneously in points of similarity and difference.[6]

Intercultural and Postcolonial Theater

To negotiate between the opposing poles of sameness and difference, each of the three plays examined in this chapter mobilizes the conventions of intercultural and postcolonial theaters. On the one hand, as postcolonial artists, the playwrights affirm the specificity of Caribbean history and culture, and they resist French control over notions of the human and the citizen. On the other hand, they reclaim the universal human by aligning their Caribbean plays with intercultural theater and its efforts to uncover a shared human condition. I use the term *intercultural theater* to refer to the European tradition (commonly called anthropological theater) associated with artists like Peter Brook, Ariane Mnouchkine, and Eugenio Barba.[7] While postcolonial theater tends to affirm cultural difference in order to counter the cultural and political legacies of imperialism, intercultural theater is premised on notions of underlying human sameness.[8] According to postcolonial theater theorists Helen Gilbert and Joanne Tompkins, intercultural theater "aim[s] to enumerate similarities between all cultures without recognizing highly significant differences."[9]

Theater scholars have criticized intercultural theater by deeming it a politically ineffectual (and sometimes harmful) appropriation by Western artists of non-Western performance traditions. For their failure to acknowledge the politics of appropriation and difference, intercultural works of theater have incited such vehement critiques, particularly by

English-language scholars, that Ric Knowles deemed the debate surrounding intercultural theater the "interculture wars."[10] Probably the most controversial intercultural work is Brook's *Mahabharata*, an adaptation of the great Indian epic performed by an international cast. Indian critic Rustom Bharucha has claimed that Brook failed to incorporate the Indian cultural context and instead evoked a conceptually fuzzy and poorly informed "flavour of India." Additionally Bharucha criticizes Brook's intercultural method of research in India, citing in particular the reportedly disrespectful personal and financial interactions the company had with the Indian artists from whom they borrowed.[11] Brook, however, feels that he is not borrowing from or enacting Indian culture but rather attempting to uncover an underlying human connection—what he calls a "third culture" or "culture of links"—that will be unveiled only through endless discoveries of relationships and breakings of stereotypes.[12] In contrast with intercultural theater's investment in human sameness, postcolonial theater involves, to quote Gilbert and Tompkins, an "engagement with and contestation of colonialism's discourses, power structures, and social hierarchies."[13] As Christopher Balme points out, both postcolonial and intercultural theater are syncretic, insofar as they recombine Western and indigenous cultural and performance traditions, but postcolonial theater has the political objective of decolonization.[14]

By playing with the conventions of intercultural and postcolonial theater, the plays explored in this chapter remix the signifiers of universalism and difference. Condé, Césaire, and Dambury reclaim the intercultural theatrical tradition and thereby repossess the concept of the universal human. Their plays show how postcolonial objectives can coexist with intercultural theater's investment in universal humanity. According to Balme, intercultural theater usually involves a kind of theatrical exoticism, which "pays no heed to the original textuality of the elements it appropriates, whether they be costumes, masks, dances, or songs. They are arbitrarily recoded and semanticized in an entirely western aesthetic and ideological frame."[15] In contrast, the aesthetic and ideological frames developed by Condé, Césaire, and Dambury are neither strictly Western nor Caribbean, for—like Caribbean identity—they are in a constant process of reproduction. Staging creolization enables French Caribbean women dramatists to reorder and rearrange the opposing poles of human unity and difference and thereby reject the static or essentialist cultural and racial scripts imposed upon Caribbeans, while simultaneously affirming Caribbean culture, history, and lived experience.

In this chapter I am concerned with the remixing of Caribbean selfhood in the aftermath of slavery's racializing systems of subjection. The plays examined here explore race, culture, and subjecthood in a dynamic historical process of becoming. Rather than offering a theory of identity, they present a multiplicity of cultural and historical viewpoints, showing the fluidity of the Caribbean self in motion. Working from personal interviews as well as published reviews, publicity, and—in the case of Condé's *An tan revolisyon*—an abridged video,[16] I investigate the original performances, their creation, and cultural reception by audiences in Guadeloupe and France. To make meaning from Caribbean history and identity, as the plays and their original performance histories show, involves multiple, sometimes conflicting, transmutable viewpoints. My analysis of the production and reception histories of the plays illustrates how tensions in meaning making arose when artists and spectators negotiated their overlapping and contrasting ideas of what constituted Caribbeanness. These unpredictable performance and reception histories reinforce the tensions between universalism and difference and the contingency of Caribbeanness that the playwrights script.

Maryse Condé's *An tan revolisyon*: Revolution's Unfinished Inheritance

Condé's 1989 play *An tan revolisyon: Elle court, elle court la liberté* presents revolution—with its idealistic promises of equality for all citizens and liberation from colonialism and slavery—as an ambivalent and perpetually unfinished inheritance for the people of Guadeloupe. The play was first written while Condé was in residence at the University of California, Berkeley, where she conducted careful historical research in conversation with her historian colleagues.[17] It was then created in Guadeloupe, in close collaboration with director Sonia Emmanuel (who also directed *Pension les Alizés*); the two women lived together during the rehearsal process. The performance was an impressive outdoor spectacle in a large park. It involved approximately sixty actors, and more than two thousand spectators attended. From a dramaturgical standpoint, the play repeatedly shifts in its dramatic style and remixes sanctioned and unacknowledged histories. Condé quickly moves between different historical scenes and offsets moments of emotional tenderness with her characteristic ironic alienation.

Divided into three acts, *An tan revolisyon* shows the historical upheaval in France's Caribbean slave colonies and mainland France at three key moments in history: 1789, the French Revolution and the Declaration of the Rights of Man and of the Citizen; 1794, the abolition of slavery in the French colonies, with the defeat of the English in Guadeloupe and the advancement of the first successful slave rebellion, the Haitian Revolution, in Saint-Domingue; and 1802, when slavery was reinstated by Napoleon. The leader of the Haitian Revolution, Toussaint Louverture, was captured, but the revolutionaries in Saint-Domingue, now led by Jean-Jacques Dessalines, nevertheless declared Haiti the first independent black nation. Guadeloupe also fought for independence, but this island returned to the slave system until France's second abolition in 1848. According to Condé, staging this history "was to lead to dynamic reflection about the present."[18]

The play displays a postmodern, creolizing approach to history. It presents several deliberate anachronisms, which create jarring alienation effects but also suggest that different chronological times can coexist in one performative moment. Condé's deep distrust of political leaders and established ideology is evident in her deconstruction of her spectators' faith in historical heroes. *An tan revolisyon* mockingly cites the familiar history lessons that Guadeloupean children are made to recite in school. It deflates both colonial and anticolonial heroes, including Toussaint. Across scenes dramatizing complex historical alliances and ideological inconsistencies, Zéphyr, an enigmatic master of ceremonies and Caribbean storyteller (*conteur*), invites audiences to reflect upon their historical inheritance as well as the multiple meanings and uses of revolution (figure 1). "Revolution is like a woman: you do whatever you want with her. Soldiers of fortune sodomize her, poets read her poetry, the middle class makes her cough up the cash."[19] Zéphyr represents the author's own mediating voice, insofar as he connects past to present and sardonically deconstructs established narratives and clichés.

An tan revolisyon embraces multiple historical and cultural viewpoints and theatrical influences. Dramaturgically the style combines popular and intellectual theater, providing a dynamic outdoor spectacle from meticulous historical research. Rich in literary allusions, *An tan revolisyon* melds a wide range of tones, from comedic buffoonery to clever irony and Brechtian alienation. The play's farcical style can be attributed to Condé's collaboration with José Jernidier (who played the role of Toussaint) and the participation of his popular theater troupe TTC + Bakanal.[20] While Condé's text is written mostly in French, the performance contained several scenes in Creole, some scripted by Jernider and others improvised by members of the TTC + Bakanal ensemble.[21]

The play's larger message is likewise deliberately ambiguous and seemingly contradictory. *An tan revolisyon* was commissioned for the

57   *Remixing Unity and Difference*

Figure 1. Gilbert Laumord as Zéphyr in Maryse Condé's *An tan revolisyon*. Fort Fleur d'Epée, Guadeloupe, 1989. (Photograph by José Jernidier; private collection; courtesy of José Jernidier and Christiane Makward)

bicentennial of the French Revolution, ordered and financed by Félix Proto, who was president of Guadeloupe's Conseil Régional. Yet, as should already be clear, Condé's play did not commemorate the triumph of the French Revolution so much as show how the Revolution's idealistic promise of equality for all humans was a fallacy: the Declaration of the Rights of Man and of the Citizen, written in 1789, was not extended to black citizens in the colonies until 1794, and these rights were subsequently rescinded in 1802, when slavery was reestablished. Ironically Condé's play was performed in Fort Fleur d'Epée, the site of white Guadeloupean governor Victor Hughes's defeat of the English for revolutionary France. If the universalist project of *liberté, egalité, fraternité* was always ambivalent, and is still unrealized today, the play asks, why, then, should Guadeloupeans commemorate this bicentenary?

Condé's ambivalent attitude toward revolution plays out in a dynamic and multifaceted intertheater with Ariane Mnouchkine, and particularly the Théâtre du Soleil's production of *1789*. In fact Condé consulted a videotape of this production before writing *An tan revolysion*.[22]

The influence is clear, insofar as several of Condé's lines, along with the spatial arrangement involving podiums, are taken directly from that production. Noting the ways in which *1789* and (to a lesser extent) its sequel, *1793*, influenced *An tan revolisyon*, Deborah Gaensbauer qualifies Condé's play as "an ironic gloss [of Mnouchkine's, whose] intertextual weaving challenges the 'revolutionary' work of even such a liberal institution as [Mnouchkine's] Théâtre du Soleil."[23] To be sure, Condé's and Mnouchkine's plays share an interest in deconstructing the French Revolution's unfinished promises. As Judith Miller points out, *1789* "was conceived as a questioning of the founding myth of the French Republic."[24] Yet whereas Mnouchkine's *1789*, created in the context of disillusionment and exhaustion following the riots of May 1968, anticipates a future revolution to come, Condé's message is more ambiguous. The final scene of Condé's play begins, like Mnouchkine's, in a celebration—a *fête* characteristic of the Théâtre du Soleil's endings—but the tone quickly changes. As a crowd of Haitians and Guadeloupeans freeze their rallying cry and dances in anticipation of Guadeloupe's future independence, the play's storyteller Zéphyr walks through the crowd of frozen actors, asking the audience to judge whether those idealistic promises of independence and Haitian-Guadeloupean unity have been kept in the present time.[25]

An tan revolisyon foregrounds a pervasive disconnect between the universalist project of revolution and real people's lived experiences of historical change. Condé criticizes the French Revolution for failing to live up to its ideals, and she also questions the value of universalist ideals altogether. Her play unveils a series of uncomfortable truths by showing political leaders' corruption and everyday scenes in which average people become the victims of these leaders and of historical change. As opposed to telling a contained history, Condé shows revolution in its multiplicity, tracing the echoes and reverberations of the French and Haitian revolutions across geographical spaces and across chronological times. The play asks whether political revolution can bring about sustainable change, but Condé leaves that question unanswered. For this reason—and due to its many acts of provocation—the play's message was inassimilable for many spectators, though it was a popular success.

Critical, Fluid Histories

Inspired by postmodern historiography, Condé's play refuses History, that is, accounts of the past marked by key events, opposing forces, and Great Men. Instead the play blurs the lines between opposing sides, mocks well-known history lessons, and shows the buffoonery of the historical heroes Louis XVI, Napoleon, and Toussaint. Her characters include well-known historical figures, such as the three men just cited as well as less emblematic figures like Victor Hughes, the French-born governor of Guadeloupe, who beat the English and killed colonial royalists (those who refused the French Revolution) in the town square, and the *mulâtresse* Solitude, a legendary Guadeloupean female revolutionary, said to have been executed immediately after giving birth (figure 2). The play also features regular people, like Sergélius and Narcisse, who live the effects of historical change in their daily lives. She gives these fictional characters, unknown figures in history, the same status as the well-known historical heroes. In her treatment of these diverse historical agents, whether they have been acknowledged, celebrated, or forgotten by history, Condé declines to distinguish between heroes and "those anonymous figures whose names history does not remember."[26]

Condé refuses fixed victim-perpetrator roles and racial essentialisms. She shows how enslaved blacks and free people of color negotiated their own interests with and against different groups of white Europeans, the French revolutionaries, the French colonialists, the English, and the Spanish. In the French Caribbean colonies, the English sided with the colonizers, so Hughes's victory at Fort Fleur d'Epée was momentarily a victory not only for the French revolutionaries but also for the slaves who fought alongside them. (In Martinique, which was under the control of the English at this time, slavery was not abolished until 1848.) Though, as Condé's play shows, Hughes was indifferent toward the slaves, he did kill their oppressors, the French colonists. "Victor Hughes," Zéphyr recounts, "wastes no time in becoming the Robespierre of the tropics." He set up a guillotine in Sartine Square, where his executioner, a distinguished *mulâtre*, "cut heads like sugar cane. Clack, clack, clack."[27]

The play asks: To what extent does the signifier of race help spectators to make sense of this history? Pierrot, a former slave, cannot easily identify an enemy, and thus decides he is happy to kill whites from any country; he exclaims that the slaves "have come together like the fingers of a hand" against the whites. But even this solidarity among slaves is circumstantial and precarious, and Condé characteristically denies any kind of essentialist racial affinity. Zéphyr reminds us, quoting Toussaint, "Nèg ap trayi nèg dinpi nan Ginin," that is, "Blacks have betrayed Blacks even back in Guinea [which refers generally to Africa]."[28]

Early on in the first act, Condé examines the rigid three-tier racial caste system ubiquitous in the French Caribbean colonies: white Creoles

Figure 2. Anna Noverca as Solitude in Maryse Condé's *An tan revolisyon*. Fort Fleur d'Epée, Guadeloupe, 1989. (Photograph by José Jernidier; private collection; courtesy of José Jernidier and Christiane Makward)

at the top of the hierarchy, *mulâtres* or free people of color in the middle, and slaves at the bottom. The access to rights of *mulâtres* and free people of color was in constant flux, and their very existence defied French associations of race and servitude-citizenship status: the false dichotomy between white French citizens and black slaves. Members of this *mulâtre* class, the children of white plantation owners, were often protected by their fathers. They were commonly sent to France to be educated and often returned to inherit their fathers' wealth and plantations.[29] Nonetheless, in France many saw the *mulâtre* class as a shameful embarrassment, proof of the prevalence of interracial sex and white colonialists' *libertinage*. Through the play's dialogue, Condé addresses these common debates and the accusations surrounding the *mulâtre* class.[30] She also shows how, if the *mulâtre*'s status as citizen and human was debatable, the black slave was categorically excluded from the citizen and human categories.

Like Mnouchkine, Condé addresses the hypocrisy of the selective exclusion of blacks from the French Revolution's allegedly universalist rights of man and citizen. In a moment directly citing *1789*, an echo of the Declaration of the Rights of Man and of the Citizen is heard: "Men are born and remain free and equal in rights. Men are born and . . ." Hearing the reverberations of this idealistic promise, the slaves begin crying out in Creole, "Libèté! Libèté! Freedom! Freedom!" Monsieur de Jurement quickly responds, "Keep quiet! They're not talking about you. They're talking about men. Not about blacks!"[31]

In the second act, Hughes reads a declaration abolishing slavery and stipulating, "All people residing in the colonies, regardless of color, are French citizens entitled to all rights guaranteed under the constitution." Finally, enslaved blacks have been legally granted the status of citizen. The next line, however, reminds spectators that racism is as strong as ever and portends the subsequent retraction of these rights. An officer interjects, "Don't those animals understand anything? You are free! FREE!" Condé's play shows that, despite this legal decree, blacks continue to labor rigorously without pay. As Justin, a former slave, is dragged by a soldier back to Juremont's plantation, he matter-of-factly states, "I was sure that slavery would never end."[32] In the last act, set in 1802, slavery has been reinstated, and spectators are left to ponder whether it ever really ended.

Like *1789*, *An tan revolisyon* plays with deliberate anachronisms. While the play is set during the three specific moments of 1789, 1794, and 1802, it contains numerous anachronistic references, ranging from allusions to reading Victor Hugo (who was born in 1802) to more contemporary references like BMWs and the Duvalier regime in Haiti. Director Emmanuel explained to me that though she saw the play as set within the specific time period of 1789–1802, she also wished to capture this history's echoes across time periods and cultures.[33] Costume designer Micheline Damico crafted designs that were both postmodern and intercultural. For example, white colonizers, including Hughes and Napoleon, wore oversized white facemasks over period costumes and hats, marking them as white and slyly suggesting a connection between American football and colonialism. Plantation owners torturing a slave were dressed to evoke the Ku Klux Klan.

The performers accentuated this representation of multiple time periods. In one scene, Ignace removed his belt and threw it into the crowd like a rock star.[34] Following Zéphyr's performance of the guillotining of French royalists, in which he tossed heads up into the air, a janitor mopped up the heads and threw them into a trashcan. Contemporary music was mixed with period music. There were, in fact, two separate orchestras: the contemporary group Kafé and a classical orchestra that played the works of the Chevalier de St. Georges, an accomplished *mulâtre* violinist, composer, and fencer from the eighteenth century. Through these various staging choices, the production team enacted an experience of different chronological times coexisting, as in African-derived ritual. However, these anachronisms, like Mnouchkine's, were also used to disrupt audience expectations. They reinforced Condé's Brechtian estrangement effect and thereby invited spectators to reflect critically upon the aftereffects and meanings of these histories in the present.

Zéphyr, the Caribbean storyteller, facilitates the audience's understanding of these histories and legacies of revolution. With half of his face painted black, and the other white, his makeup recalled the *lwa* (a vodou divinity) Baron Samedi. Like Baron Samedi, Zéphyr dwells at the crossroads, bridging different time periods, points of view, and life and death. Instead of drawing a moral or lesson from history Zéphyr plays with the audience's expectations, teases them, and asks unanswered, controversial questions. He is a sardonic, enigmatic character, who Condé explains was "conceived to provoke."[35] The actor who played Zéphyr, Gilbert Laumord, recalled having worked during rehearsal to perform the character as neutrally as possible.[36] As Nick Nesbitt comments, "The *conteur* leads us through [historical events] less to interpret them than to undermine our faith in their epistemological cohesion."[37]

Condé's unsettling of historical and epistemological cohesion is particularly salient in Zéphyr's deconstruction of Toussaint. The play shows this hero of the Haitian Revolution acting despotically and making blacks in Haiti work like slaves. Zéphyr likens Toussaint to despotic rulers, but he quickly censors his own thoughts: "As for me, I found Toussaint Louverture a little frightening, in spite of all the respect to which he is entitled. You didn't? Didn't he remind you of anyone? No? Good! Too bad! Too bad for me; I'm kind of over sensitive when it comes to freedom! He reminded me of ... His manner was a little like ... No, nothing, no one. Let's talk about something else."[38] Zéphyr's performance of self-censorship serves to critique Toussaint's status as an untouchable hero. José Jernidier (who played the role of Toussaint) remembered having worked to cultivate a harsh image of the historical hero. He used sharp, forbidding gestures, and he sat on a chair that recalled the throne of the king.[39] Certain spectators found Condé's depiction of Toussaint irreverent and inappropriate. Condé recalls in an interview with Nesbitt that a group of Guadeloupean historians criticized her for having "portrayed Toussaint Louverture under the guise of a dictator."[40]

Revolution: Nestled in Its Mother's Womb

Condé uses the metaphor of the unborn child to address the theme of revolution. If Mnouchkine's *1789* anticipates a more radical revolution to come, Condé's play more pessimistically portrays revolution as the mother of a dead, unborn, or aborted child. Zéphyr repeatedly conjures the image of a child lost too soon. At the conclusion of the first act, he introduces the possibility of what the French Revolution *might have been*:

> That's it. Revolution is like a woman: you do whatever you want with her. Soldiers of fortune sodomize her, poets read her poetry, the middle class makes her cough up the cash. In the kingdom of France, revolution aborted the baby that had turned its womb into a mountain of justice. All that remains is a stinking pile of coagulated blood lying in the gutter. Yet it could have been beautiful, this child, born on July 14! I picture it dressed in white, blue and red, laughing in the new light of the sun! But the bourgeois didn't allow it to live.[41]

The pregnant *mulâtresse* Solitude's dreams for her unborn daughter, Aimée, parallel Zéphyr's hopes for the French Revolution. Before her execution, Solitude deploys language that recalls Emma's hopes in *Pension les Alizés* for her unborn daughter. Envisaging a life for Aimée in which "everything will be different," Solitude foresees a "beautiful tomorrow." But shortly after this moment of hope, Zéphyr coldly tells the audience of Solitude's execution. Reflexively anticipating the audience's expectations, he asks, "What do you want me to say? That I've invented a happy ending like in American movies? This time will be like all the others."[42]

In conceiving of the fruits of revolution as an unborn child, *An tan revolisyon* bridges the conventions of postcolonial and intercultural theaters. Condé does not foreclose the possibility of a universalist revolution to come, but she does show how the allegedly universalist ideals of the Revolution were never meant to benefit people in the Caribbean. Zéphyr reminds spectators of their particular inheritance as Guadeloupeans:

> For us in Guadeloupe not much has changed. Our men and women continue to have the taste of freedom in their mouths. Alas, they're still in chains and the blood of the dead continues to bleed in the silos of the earth until finally, in the evening dew, their spirits flutter in the air as fireflies. Be patient for my story isn't over. I still have a lot to tell you. A lot, a lot. After the days that taste bitter on your lips, the days without joy, the days that are rotten, be patient; other days will come! I can already feel the winds of change.[43]

Throughout the play, this glimmer of hope becomes progressively dimmer. While Zéphyr claims to have hope for the future at the end of Act I, he later becomes bitingly cynical. Contradicting his previous view of revolution as the mother of a beautiful baby who was never born, Zéphyr explains that revolution is "a witch. She feeds on fresh blood. She smears it all over her jowls. She licks it off her fingers. And then, in the colorless hours before dawn, she gives birth to monsters. The hopes of 1789 are so far, far away!"[44] Near the end of the play, he describes revolutionary histories as necessarily brutal and bloody, with no ultimate reward or recompense.

By way of this fundamental ambivalence, Condé bridges postcolonial and intercultural theaters. From a postcolonial perspective, *An tan revolisyon* sought to expose the largely unacknowledged plight of Guadeloupeans—and to unveil the hypocrisy of presuming that Guadeloupeans should celebrate the French Revolution, along with the defeat of the English in Guadeloupe. The program states that the first act of *An tan revolisyon*, "1789," "sets out to show that the French Revolution is above all a purely French metropolitan phenomenon."[45] Yet the play's treatment of the Revolution is less didactic than this program note might suggest. As an intercultural performance invested in universalist ideals, *An tan revolisyon* invites spectators to wish—and long—for a truly radical revolution. Through the image of the aborted child, Condé portrays the bitter loss of revolution as a dream for which one must grieve.

As the maternal images suggest, *An tan revolisyon*'s ambivalent treatment of revolution as an unborn child can be illuminated when considered through the African-derived metaphysical concept of the *abiku* or *ogbanje* child, named, respectively, in two identical Yoruba and Igbo myths.[46] The child repeatedly dies and returns, or looms close to death, threatening her or his parents with the harrowing prospect of dying before the parent. The result is a perpetually "jinxed" relationship between parent and child.[47] The concept can serve as a paradigm for understanding the reemerging effects of slavery's trauma in the African diaspora.[48] Generally, the *abiku* or *ogbanje* refers to an "unsettled condition of simultaneously existing in several spheres,"[49] for the child has been to the realm of death and returned to this world again. Condé's ambivalence toward revolution and her seemingly contradictory claims to the particular and the universal are characteristic of the *abiku* and *ogbanje*. Rather than anticipating recovery or radical change, the *abiku* and *ogbanje* evoke an unending cycle of rebirth and transformation.

In the Caribbean, the myth of the *abiku* or *ogbanje* took on more sardonic meanings under slavery. Common to Caribbean folklore is the image of the aborted child, or the *bolôm*. This folkloric reference subtly alludes to slavery by reminding us of abortion, which was one of enslaved women's tactics of resistance to rape, sexual exploitation, and interracial sex. Like Zéphyr's cynical views of revolution, the *bolôm* represents hope for the future intertwined with a profound past pain: a wish for an impossible future that might have been but will not be. Yet this pessimism is mitigated by each subsequent rebirth or pregnancy, which furnishes another opportunity to hope.

Haiti—and the dreams of its revolution—is figured as an unborn child. "What would old Toussaint think," Zéphyr asks, "if he came back to life and saw his country up for auction, handed over to the rage of the Tontons Macoutes [Duvalier's militia], his people bleeding from the eternal wounds of injustice and hunger?"[50] The play's final scene dramatizes unrealized hopes for a radical coalition between Guadeloupe and Haiti. In it, Guadeloupeans seeking refuge in Haiti are welcomed by Dessalines with open arms. Using call-and-response techniques to rally the crowd, Dessalines evokes an idealistic dream of solidarity among Haitians and Guadeloupeans:

DESSALINES: Don't cry! Aren't you at home here? Aren't Guadeloupe and Saint-Domingue one and the same?

THE CROWD: They're the same! They're the same!

DESSALINES: Don't we all come from Africa?

THE CROWD: Yes! Yes!

DESSALINES: Don't we all speak the same Creole?

THE CROWD: Yes! Yes!

DESSALINES: Don't we all dance to the same drum?

Beating of drums.

THE CROWD: Yes! Yes!

DESSALINES: Men and women of Guadeloupe, stop crying! Consider this your home!

This land is yours! We'll share with you, and even if there were thousands of you asking for refuge, we would welcome you in the same way!

Ovation. Drums. Applause.[51]

Dessalines's picture of Africanist unity is powerful, but, from their contemporary vantage point, spectators know it will not come true.

As Dessalines exclaims that he will always welcome Guadeloupeans, "even if there were thousands of you asking for refuge," the play slyly conjures the contemporary situation in which thousands of Haitian refugees in Guadeloupe are treated as second-class citizens. His hope for unity also glosses over real differences; for example, Guadeloupean and Haitian Creole are not the same. This final scene depicts a unification that *might have been*—had history played out differently. A man from Guadeloupe stands up and predicts that Guadeloupe will fight to its last breath to win freedom and independence at all costs. The crowd breaks into song and dances to the traditional *gwo-ka* drum. Then the actors freeze and the lights fade as Zéphyr enters a silent stage. Reminding the audience that this dream for freedom and independence was forged in 1802, the storyteller leaves them to "judge whether the promises that were made that year were kept; whether the dreams were realized or whether tomorrow still remains nestled in its mother's womb, waiting to be born."[52]

How did the play's spectators respond? Condé's deliberately ambivalent treatment of revolution appears to have been inassimilable to some spectators, though the play drew huge crowds. In an interview with Nesbitt, Condé calls the play a "very big popular success" but admits that she does not know "whether people appreciated the antiestablishment dimension that we tried to convey."[53] Though the play was performed on only two nights, it was sold out each night with more than two thousand spectators. Generally speaking, reviewers lauded the play, but critic Laure Rémy left "with profound bitterness."[54] Protesting Condé's disrespectful representation of Guadeloupean history, Rémy remarked that the play had "no humor but derision" and "that in the eyes of Maryse Condé we only have sham heroes."[55] As mentioned, a group of Guadeloupean historians similarly attacked Condé for portraying Toussaint as a dictator. The production was scheduled to air on television and radio, but it was boycotted.[56] The artistic team had high hopes that the production would travel to other Caribbean islands or to France and that it would play longer in Guadeloupe, but these dreams were never realized. Perhaps this ambivalent reception is due to the play's provocative nature and the way Condé rebelled against the project for which she was recruited: *An tan revolisyon* was commissioned for the bicentenary of the French Revolution, but it exposes how the French Revolution's idealistic promise of equality for all humans has yet to be fully realized in Guadeloupe.

Neither strictly postcolonial nor intercultural, Condé's play remixes notions of universalism and difference. While exposing the effects of the French and Haitian revolutions in Guadeloupe, *An tan revolisyon* poses unanswered questions regarding the concepts of revolution and history. Condé works in between postcolonial theater's emphasis on cultural difference and intercultural theater's assumption of universal human unity. Condé was clearly inspired by Mnouchkine's *1789* and her play makes similar points about the French and Haitian revolutions' unfinished projects. Yet Condé also questions the very value of revolutionary ideology. She criticizes universalist ideals and provides a careful consideration of history's complexities from a distinctly Guadeloupean point of view. As the Creole title suggests, *An tan revolisyon* decenters France, yet it does not focus on the Haitian Revolution either. Rather it portrays revolution in its multiplicity, showing its myriad, possible, performative iterations. Providing a sort of universalist critique of despotic power and corruption, Condé denounces violence, misogyny, and pride across colonial and postcolonial nations, with their diverse (yet similar) historical heroes. The play refuses essentialist notions of whiteness and blackness, even as it reminds us of the lived reality of the racialization of the category of the human. Condé's play, though clearly indebted to *1789*, goes beyond Mnouchkine's project by privileging tensions, disjunctures, and inconsistencies in history and political ideology. *An tan revolisyon* is simultaneously a postcolonial affirmation of Guadeloupean difference (against the expectation that Guadeloupeans should celebrate the French Revolution) and a universalist call for a more ethical, global future. The play's primary message is posed as a question: Will the unborn radical revolution, still nestled in its mother's womb, ever come?

Ina Césaire's *Mémoires d'Isles*: The Multiple Meanings of Caribbean Women's Reminiscences

If Condé remixes a complex historical inheritance and thus exposes the hypocrisy of French monopolization of the supposedly universalist categories of the citizen and the human, Césaire dramatizes ethnological research to enact a portrayal of collective Caribbean selfhood buttressed by an ongoing interplay of unity and difference. *Mémoires d'Isles* performs a Caribbean collective that is premised on juxtapositions. Rather than simply asserting Caribbean cultural particularity vis-à-vis French universalism, Césaire plays with the opposing poles of universal humanity and cultural difference, creatively cycling between the two. The play begins with a prologue, which draws from Caribbean Carnival traditions. The two actresses then move to a makeup table, where they transform themselves into grandmothers. The bulk of the dramatic action consists of these two elderly Caribbean women's reminiscences as they sit together on a veranda outside a wedding celebration.

Mémoires d'Isles was first performed in 1983 at the Théâtre du Campagnol in Bagneux, a suburb of Paris, for a culturally mixed (French and Caribbean) audience. Together Césaire, the director Jean-Claude Penchenat, and the two French Caribbean actresses, Mariann Mathéus (who played Hermance) and Myrrha Donzenac (Aure), collaboratively created the performance. Césaire later transcribed and published the script as a play, making some editorial changes that I discuss below. My reading of the play, which recognizes various levels of creation, editing, and performance, draws from several versions of the play script, critical reviews and publicity surrounding the original performance, and an interview with Mathéus. With a focus on the play's collaborative creation and reception histories, I aim to investigate how the play made meaning as a cultural performance. During the original performance, spectators were confronted with their varying familiarity with Caribbean realities and cultural memories. This served to challenge the way the human was invisibly equated with white, French men. Yet though the play exposes the fallacy of French republican universalism, *Mémoires d'Isles* does not reject the concept of universal humanity but rather anchors the universal within the diversity of lived experiences and memories.

Based in ethnographic interviews with multigenerational—especially elderly—Martinican and Guadeloupean women, *Mémoires d'Isles* documents nearly a century of Martinican history as lived and remembered by real women. The dialogue, which Césaire calls "monologues,"[57] consists of the two women's memories, which come to stand in for a larger, Caribbean collective memory. Speaking mostly in French, but accentuating their conversation with expressions in Creole, the two women share their memories: personal stories of childhood, family, marriage, and loss (figure 3). Intertwined with their personal hardships, triumphs, and lessons are references to larger events and periods in Martinican cultural memory, such as the Southern Insurrection of 1870 (the revolt depicted in *Rosanie Soleil*); the great hurricane of 1928; Dissidence, the resistance movement against the German occupation of France and its Caribbean overseas departments during World War II; and the assassination of a socialist mayor in 1935.[58] The women also recall embodied memories, likewise shared by a collective group of Caribbeans, such as the tradition of Creole dance balls, caterpillars cooked and eaten during the food rationings of World War II, and the memory of a mother's firm childhood hair-braiding (figure 4).[59] Through their stories, the two women

69 Remixing Unity and Difference

Figure 3. Myrrha Donzenac as Aure and Mariann Mathéus as Hermance in Ina Césaire's *Mémoires d'Isles*, Bagneux, France, 1983. (Photograph by Alain Fonteray; private collection; courtesy of Christiane Makward)

"remember the past and reinscribe the history of the island under the sign of women's quotidian reality," in the words of Christiane Makward and Judith Miller.[60]

Thematically *Mémoires d'Isles* resembles *Rosanie Soleil* insofar as both plays create a picture of unified Caribbean womanhood across difference through the juxtaposition of two counterpart characters. Aure is a light-skinned *mulâtresse* from the calm southern part of the islands. Well-educated and meticulous, she was a schoolteacher. Hermance, a dark-skinned, tall black woman, is from the wild northern part of Martinique, close to the volcano Mount Pelée. Working-class, uneducated, yet shrewdly intelligent, Hermance is charismatic and proud. As Césaire emphasizes, Aure's and Hermance's lives are "at once parallel and divergent." Their dialogue establishes that they are half-sisters: they share a father, who acknowledged Aure and her mother, but not Hermance and hers.[61]

Society's preference for lighter skin is evident in their father's favoring of Aure's lighter-skinned mother as well as the two women's opposing experiences of marriage and infidelity. Makward situates the play in the

Figure 4. Myrrha Donzenac and Mariann Mathéus improvise a hair-braiding scene from Hermance's childhood. Ina Césaire's *Mémoires d'Isles*, Bagneux, France, 1983. (Photograph by Alain Fonteray; private collection; courtesy of Christiane Makward)

context of Caribbean women's general acceptance of men's infidelity and abuse.⁶² Hermance accepted numerous instances of infidelity from her husband, including a six-month voyage to France with his pale-skinned mistress. Aure's husband, in contrast, was always faithful to her. In fact before he married Aure, he fathered another woman's child, but, as a service to Aure's family, he offered to pay her trip away from Martinique to Cayenne or Panama City.⁶³

My reading, attuned to the play's collaborative creation and intercultural reception, illuminates Césaire's unique ethnodramaturgical style and prompts a consideration of *Mémoires d'Isles* in light of the tensions between cultural difference and universal humanity. By drawing from the conventions of intercultural theater and ethnology, Césaire and the artistic team creatively reimagined Caribbean selfhood and collective memory. *Mémoires d'Isles* code-switches in its address to spectators of varying cultural literacies, who will interpret the play on different cultural terms. The play valorizes Caribbean women's historical experiences while nonetheless insisting upon a performance of universal humanity that is premised on a multiplicity of viewpoints. Building upon interpretations of the published play as dramatic literature,⁶⁴ I wish to privilege these dynamic tensions—between text and performance, universal, human unity and particular, Caribbean womanhood, and in memory's selective construction—that underlay both the script and its production and reception histories.

Performance, Editing, and the Politics of Remembrance

It is important to distinguish between the collaborative performance and Césaire's written play, published two years after the premiere. In contrast with the other plays analyzed in this book, *Mémoires d'Isles* was first a collaborative performance, which was then transformed into a published text that circulated throughout French Caribbean, French, and international literary circuits. Thus in this case, writing embodied performance is not only a question of creatively writing Caribbean performance practices (such as storytelling or dance) into a play but also of writing the original actresses' embodied movements and improvisation into the stage directions and dialogue. While the play lists Césaire as author, the script does not specify a playwright but rather stipulates that the texts were collected and adapted by Césaire and the two actresses.⁶⁵

The original performance involved numerous moments of improvisation, in which the actresses played different figures from the characters' memories. For example, in the hair-braiding scene, the two women reenact a moment from Hermance's childhood. Dance and song were also very important to the creative process. With the exception of several notable editorial changes that I will discuss, Césaire rendered the performance faithfully, and her published text more or less corresponds with the play script the actresses used.[66]

The embodied experience of performance was key to the play's creation and its conception of history. As the collaborators recognized, memories of the past are not only kept in printed documents and recorded testimonies; they are also stored in repeated behaviors and performance. In a personal interview, Mathéus described working meticulously on her voice, facial expressions, and stage movements in order to portray Hermance at many different ages, from the six-year-old to the woman of ninety, for which she used only small costume changes and no makeup.[67] Remembering the balls she attended as a young woman, Mathéus embodied Hermance's fierce spirit, coupled with the daily physical pains near the end of a long, laborious life, by dancing an immobile dance from her chair, with her aching leg up on a stool. Translating that performance into the stage directions of her play, Césaire wrote, "Motionless, HERMANCE, still humming her nostalgic tune. Only her foot keeps time with the music."[68]

The play's creation was guided by the production team's knowledge of Caribbean orality, music, and dance. Césaire's text renders Hermance's many tunes, ranging from traditional Caribbean songs to the production team's original creations. For instance, Mathéus, trained as a singer, recalled in our interview that she had created the song "Bouch nou oxydé" by putting a story collected during one of the ethnographic interviews she conducted to a popular beguine tune. The saying "Bouch nou oxydé," "Our mouth is rusty," recalls the collective, bodily memory of hunger in the Caribbean during the Dissidence movement, that is, resistance against Germany during its occupation of France and its overseas departments. Yet Césaire wrote her stage directions as if the song already existed and would be familiar to readers: "Laughing, she sings the song 'Bouch nou oxydé.'"[69] If Mathéus's recollection is correct, her performance would have expanded the repertoire of songs by which Caribbeans remember the time of Dissidence. Césaire's dramaturgy then would have fixed these performance aspects on the page. In any case, the published play now acts as a prompt for future performances, suggesting that other production teams also put the phrase to music.

In the publication phase, Césaire became the play's unique author and thus had ultimate control over the historical memories evoked. Though the published play more or less resembles the script the actresses performed, some notable editing choices served to universalize the play by making it accessible and comfortable for international audiences. In the published play, Césaire uses veiled language and evasion of specificity in order to paper over some of the harsher and more provocative elements of Caribbean history and culture.

The most significant change Césaire made in her text was to the prologue. In both versions, the two actresses conjure the tradition of Caribbean Carnival. In performance, they began the prologue by opening the door to Carnival, with Mathéus as a she-devil and Donzenac dressed as a man in drag, a common costume in Carnival. Soon after, the actresses became the two she-devils, Simeline and Déline. In Césaire's published text, however, the cross-dressing is omitted, as both women begin the scene as she-devils of Ash Wednesday. Mathéus remembered that, originally, Donzenac had proposed the prologue because she wished to bear witness to Caribbean history. But Césaire's text removes certain historical references. In Creole, the performance prologue glossed many important events and figures in Caribbean history, including the abolition and reinstatement of slavery, the Southern Insurrection of 1870, and the legacy of interracial sex between women of color and white men. The only history recounted in French was the story of Columbus's "discovery" of the New World. Césaire's published play deploys fewer historical references and less Creole: it uses riddles to refer more vaguely to the challenges of moving past the past in order to create a better future. Deleted entirely from Césaire's play is the she-devils' discussion of French Caribbean society's categorization of people (particularly women) by the degrees of blackness in their complexion and phenotypical traits. In the performance, Donzenac and Mathéus (as she-devils) evoked society's judgment of women's beauty according to complexion and referred to the very subtle differences between social categorizations of lighter-skinned women, such as the designations of "chabine Calazzaza" or "chabine dorée."[70]

When Césaire reissued the play, she took these universalizing editorial changes further. Since the original edition of *Mémoires d'Isles* was out of print, Makward included a version, entitled *Mémoires d'île*, in her 2011 anthology of Césaire's plays in French. In the text she gave Makward for this edition, Césaire deleted entirely what she called the "archetypal rape scene," an acknowledgment of the pervasive history of enslaved women's rape and sexual exploitation.[71] Mathéus recalled that the production team had created the scene together: Donzenac, dressed as a white, male plantation owner, "pays a visit" to Aure's grandmother, who is his slave. Already, in the first published edition, the scene appears to have become more ambiguous than the scene Mathéus described in our interview. This scene is included in the original 1985 French text of *Mémoires d'Isles* as a silent pantomime: "MALVINA is startled when the door opens. We can hear the creaking of a bed across which a body has thrown itself. MALVINA stands up slowly and leans over the bed. She raises her arm; is it a gesture of love or aggression?"[72] Césaire's stage direction posed as a question underscores the historical ambiguity surrounding enslaved women's experience and calls attention to enslaved women's agency. But this scene was deleted entirely from the 2011 text. Insofar as Césaire in 1985 designated this scene as "the only time the slavery era is recalled,"[73] she may have wished in 2011 to omit any direct reference to slavery.

These editorial modifications attest to the extent to which remembrance (commemoration and forgetting) of the past is both transmutable and political, that is, influenced by those in power. Césaire may have strategically anticipated her play's reception by a French readership, who might have been made uncomfortable by some of the harsher elements of slavery's history. Alternatively she may have wished to forget certain aspects of the past in order to free Caribbean spectators from painful memories. As Césaire explained to a journalist, the play evokes memories from the past in order to move forward:

> It is about accepting our past, it is not about being embarrassed, it is no longer about crying over it. We have acquired the right to no longer cry over our past, we must take responsibility for it and be able to move past it. To refer to our past is to show today our power to accept it despite the instability of our history. The simple fact that these women have survived, the courage, strength, as well as the desire to encourage their children to move forward is, for me, part of a life force that takes on liberating facets.[74]

Like the original performance, Césaire's published play showcases a multiplicity of viewpoints toward the past and its relevance in the present. More so than the original performance, the printed play imposes an order on the different memories evoked and universalizes the Caribbean women's experience by making it accessible to French readers. The play presents a restorative, forward-looking attitude. As the she-devils conclude Césaire's rewritten prologue, they triumphantly proclaim, "Tomorrow will be different!"[75]

Intercultural Creation

Mémoires d'Isles affirms Martinican women's memories and realities while also aligning itself with European traditions of intercultural theater, specifically the works of Peter Brook and Ariane Mnouchkine. Césaire met director Penchenat in Martinique, where he was working on a reality-based and collectively created theater piece and film, *The Bal*. Penchenat was a former member of Mnouchkine's Théâtre du Soleil. Césaire was excited by his interest in real people's stories, since she had been documenting Caribbean women's testimonies, and she discussed her idea for the play with him. She had recently seen Brook's *The Ik*, which whetted her interest in theater. She later explained, "I was inspired by the chance to take ethnology out of its ghetto of specialists and to give it back to those who are primarily implicated."[76]

Penchenat recruited the French Caribbean actress Myrrha Donzenac (who played Aure), with whom he had worked at the Théâtre du Soleil. Donzenac invited Mariann Mathéus (Hermance), a Creole singer who had no experience with theater at that time, to audition. As Mathéus recounted to me, at the audition she was asked to improvise with Donzenac, which set the precedent for the collaborative approach the team employed throughout the process. Their democratic process was similar to Mnouchkine's in several ways. For instance, as in the traditions of the Théâtre du Soleil, Penchenat told the actresses to come to rehearsal with their own costumes, and the costume designer Françoise Tournafond based her designs on their choice.[77]

Both the play's collaborative creation and its anchoring in ethnology valorized a multiplicity of viewpoints. *Mémoires d'Isles* renders the voices of countless elderly Martinican women whose stories Césaire had been collecting since 1980, as well as many women from Guadeloupe, where the actress Mathéus conducted ethnographic interviews with three mother-grandmother pairs.[78] The team also drew from other sources, including Luc Ponette's documentary *Berthilia*, which shows the life of a Guadeloupean woman,[79] and the Caribbean actresses' own families and memories. The two characters that emerged, Aure and Hermance, represent, respectively, Césaire's maternal and paternal grandmothers, who are discretely honored in the play's subtitle as Manman F. and Manman N. According to Mathéus, at that time Césaire had learned much about her maternal grandmother's life, but her paternal grandmother had been more or less silent. To substantiate her role as Hermance, Mathéus went to Martinique, where she interviewed Aimé Césaire's mother. As an ethnodramatist, Ina Césaire studied her interviews and worked on writing as older French Caribbean women speak. But Césaire explains that the dramaturgy was also significantly impacted by "the acting of the actresses, who are Caribbean themselves, and who helped me by bringing their experiences and memories to enrich the text (they found gestures naturally; the research was pushed into the realm of life) as well as the staging of Jean-Claude Penchenat, who is not very familiar—it's true—with the Caribbean, though he offered himself up to our service."[80]

In our personal interview, Mathéus likewise emphasized the play's collaborative creation. Because of his limited knowledge of the Caribbean, she recalled, Penchenat asked Donzenac to direct, but Donzenac insisted that the team would benefit from his directorial eye and vision. Thus Penchenat took the lead on the direction, as Césaire did on writing, but all four of the artists (author, director, and two actresses) contributed significantly both to the dramaturgy and to the mise-en-scène. Mathéus remembered that it was Penchenat who originally proposed the idea of crafting the two divergent yet parallel characters from the rich array of testimonies collected by Césaire and the two actresses. While Césaire and the actresses privileged their own memories and knowledge of the Caribbean, Penchenat had a different, more universalist point of entry into the play. He described it as dealing with "the mechanism of memory—something very dear to me!"[81] Césaire agreed; she called the testimonies of elderly Caribbean women she had collected "the memory of people and of cultures."[82]

Collaborators sought simultaneously to affirm Caribbean female cultural particularity and to create a theatrical experience of a unified community. Bridget Jones, who was present at the premiere production, described it as achieving a "sense of communion."[83] Indeed much as the play juxtaposes Aure's and Hermance's memories while foregrounding their mutual respect and sense of unity, it also combines ethnology and intercultural theater. By cycling between the opposing poles of universal humanity and cultural difference, the play ultimately inhabits a third option, akin to VèVè Clark's theorization of *marasa* consciousness.[84] Like the *marasa trois*, the performance both evokes and moves beyond binary oppositions lived by the two women—relating to skin color, education, language use—as well as the opposing poles of human sameness and cultural difference. In a 2001 interview, Césaire stated:

> We are no longer at the level of "Who are we?" . . . "What is our identity?" Identity *is*. Personally, I no longer ask myself the identity question, I feel

it very profoundly, without anxiety, without bitterness. . . . That can't be assimilated! When I read Dostoevsky, I'm not Russian, but I can enter into the skins of the characters in *The Brothers Karamazov*, and I'm passionate about it! I love Chekhov! So I believe that anyone can understand the soul of a Caribbean if he takes the time to penetrate it (and let it penetrate him) himself.[85]

Césaire views the Caribbean particular and universal human as coexisting within the Caribbean self. Likewise her ethnology-based play transcends these apparent tensions and can thus speak to spectators of varying cultural literacies.

Spectatorship by Cultural Literacy

Performed in an ethnically diverse suburb of Paris, Bagneux, the play drew an audience of varying cultural and linguistic literacies. Generally speaking, one might divide the spectators into two groups: French Caribbeans living in France (whom one could also refer to as French people of Caribbean origin) and white French people from France. Makward, who was present at the production, characterized the first, Caribbean audience as "fastidious . . . on questions of politics, linguistics, and skin-tone," while the French audience was "open-minded [given that they chose to go see the play] but modest, poorly informed of Caribbean realities, and possibly touchy on a patriotic soft spot."[86]

Spectators also likely had varying expectations regarding the artistic team's use of ethnology onstage. It is unlikely that in 1983 many audience members had seen plays written by French Caribbean playwrights and especially plays using the Creole language.[87] In contrast, it is likely that many of the French spectators were familiar with the performances of Brook or Mnouchkine, who was working on her Shakespeare cycle at the time, and thus used intercultural theater as a framework for interpreting *Mémoires d'Isles*. Whereas the work of Mnouchkine and Brook does not require cultural competency or literacy, Césaire's theater operates along the lines of Balme's theorization of the semiotics of postcolonial drama: it is divided into two discrete semiospheres in which semiosis takes place on different levels.[88] However, the French spectator, accustomed to intercultural or anthropological theater, was probably not expecting the "Caribbean" semiosphere. He or she was more likely anticipating song, dance, or performance of ritual used "purely for their surface appeal," to quote Balme's description of theatrical exoticism.[89] But since these French audience members were seated next to French

Caribbeans, who had the cultural competency needed to interpret both semiotic codes, *Mémoires d'Isles* challenged these expectations. It forced French spectators to recognize the "Caribbean" semiosphere and thus exposed the fallacy of French universalism and the problematic use of the universal spectator during anthropological or intercultural theater performances.

Mémoires d'Isles unveiled or "demasked," to use Gerard Aching's theorization of a carnivalesque political tactic,[90] these two audiences, which were otherwise invisible in a French society permeated by the ideology of universalism. The conventions of Caribbean Carnival enabled the collaborators to challenge the status quo in a veiled yet effective manner, much like Carnival functioned for enslaved peoples. The prologue, a parade of she-devils, sets the interpretive rules with which spectators will make meaning from the play. Marking the last day of Martinican Carnival, the actresses are dressed in black and white. In both the play and performance, they represent the she-devils of Ash Wednesday, companions of the Haitian *lwa* Baron Samedi, the *lwa* of death. Baron Samedi is portrayed at the crossroads into the next life and therefore signifies a transition into a new world in which the past life, like the painful Martinican history in Césaire's play, is accepted and moved beyond. The subversive potential of the play is rooted in this reference to Carnival,[91] which sets the rules by which spectators receive subsequent cultural references and code-switching to the Creole language. Corresponding to Lent in the metropole, Carnival was celebrated each year on plantations during the time of slavery. Those few days were the only time off given to slaves, who took advantage of this celebration to "symbolically invert the ethno-social pyramid."[92] Carnival is a time for celebration and dancing, a time for disguise, for pretending, a moment when hierarchies are inverted.

Carnival holds the subversive power to unmask uneven or hierarchical subject positions and to reveal the ideological underpinnings by which viewing subjects recognize the masked.[93] In the context of a mixed French and Caribbean audience in the suburbs of Paris, the reference to Carnival unmasks racism and cultural discrimination and reveals the ways these Caribbean realities have been denied by the ideology of French universalism. Contrary to practices in Western theater, Carnival puts no barrier between performer and audience. Thus the prologue asks the Caribbean spectator to participate as an agent in the reinscribing and re-creating of Martinican history. As the French audience member begins to recognize and validate Martinican difference, the Caribbean spectator, able to interpret the semiotics of a prologue communicated in the theatrical language of Caribbean Carnival, experiences a breaking of the fourth wall, an invitation to participate in the performance of *Mémoires d'Isles*, that is, the reinterpretation of history and the renegotiation of what might constitute universal, human unity.

From within this intercultural theatrical structure, the play's use of the French and Creole languages enacts further tensions between universalism and difference. Stéphanie Bérard has argued that *Mémoires d'Isles* offers a dynamic example of textual multilingualism that moves beyond the French-Creole dichotomy implied by notions of bilingualism and diglossia. As she points out, Aure's and Hermance's uses of French, Creole, and various hybrids of the two are a reflection of the two women's social status and relationship.[94] Yet even though the play shows language as necessarily power-laden, it also universalizes Caribbean realities and epistemologies by offering up Creole images and metaphors for shared human experiences. For example, Hermance describes life as a *morne* (a Creole term for a hill) and likens death to reaching the top of it.[95] As Bérard suggests, the Creole language's rich metaphor valorizes a larger Caribbean belief system, in which death is an integral part of life. This "universalist" dimension of the characters' speech invites all spectators and readers to identify with the two women's lived experiences.[96]

In production, the play's multilingualism also issued a challenge to its French spectators. Because the educated schoolteacher Aure speaks perfect French, the moments when she switches into Creole disrupt the spectator's expectations and thus unmask the limits of French universalism. Throughout the play, Hermance remodels and reconfigures French using Creole grammar, syntax, semantics, images, and structures, as Bérard has meticulously documented.[97] Whereas Hermance speaks in a familiar, Creolized language and often interjects Creole expressions into her speech, Aure generally deploys the elevated French of a schoolteacher.

Yet in a strategic moment Aure switches from French to Creole. The following excerpt matches up more or less with the various scripts. I quote the 1985 published text, followed by Miller and Makward's English translation (with Aure's last line, translated from Creole, shown in italics).

AURE: A ce moment-là je préparais l'Ecole Normale d'institutrices et j'assistais dans sa classe une certaine demoiselle Rosimond.... Une espèce de mulâtresse qui se coiffait avec deux gros macarons sur les oreilles. C'était cette dame qui toute la sainte journée, faisait chanter à ses élèves:

"La neige tombe sur Paris, la neige tombe sur Paris. . . ." Eti ou wè la nèj tombé pas isi- ya?

HERMANCE: (*Elle rit*): La neige!⁹⁸

AURE: At that time I was getting ready for the teacher training school exams, and I was helping somebody named Mlle Rosimond with her class. . . . A mulatto type who did her hair in two big macaroons over her ears. She was a woman who made her students sing every hour of the blessed day: "Snow's falling on Paris, snow's falling on Paris. . . ." *Ever seen any snow fall around here?*

HERMANCE: (*Laughing*): Snow!⁹⁹

Just as the infamous phrase *nos ancêtres, les Gaulois* (our ancestors, the Gauls) repeated by schoolchildren in African and Caribbean French colonies shows a failure to recognize local culture and realities (deeming every child a descendant of the blond, blue-eyed Gauls), singing "Snow's falling on Paris" in the Caribbean seems humorously out of context. Aure points out the ridiculous nature of the singing routine, choosing Creole to separate herself linguistically from those who would sing of and experience snow falling in Paris. Her choice of Creole unmasks the problematic nature of French universalism. It is interesting to note that Hermance repeats the word *snow* in French and not Creole, affirming the place of snow in a French mainland location and cultural context.

French spectators likely got the gist of the joke, perhaps anticipating it (being familiar with the complaint about *nos ancêtres, les Gaulois*), perhaps cued in by laughter, repetition, and likely facetious performance of the word *snow*. However, *Mémoires d'Isles* communicated a criticism of universalism to French spectators by forcing them to experience exclusion, thus unmasking the limitations involved in delimiting universal humanity (and particularly the lived history in the Caribbean of French republican universalism). Certain French spectators were indeed taken by this moment; two French reviewers for political newspapers note this moment in their reviews. A review in the leftist newspaper *Lutte Ouvrière* recounted that the actresses "denounce with humor colonial society, in which children learn to sing 'Snow's falling.'"¹⁰⁰ Likewise a critic for *Révolution* noted the exchange and interpreted it in conjunction with the reference to Columbus in the prologue, which was the only moment that used French in the somewhat inaccessible prologue: "At school they made us sing 'snow's falling on Paris,' remembers the former schoolmistress, not without smiling. Two lives drawn on the canvas of colonial depths, and it is obviously not for nothing that during the prologue, in costumes that oppose black and white, they make reference to Christopher Columbus and his ships."[101] Though this reviewer has missed the references to Carnival (the fact that the she-devils wear black and white because they are companions of Baron Samedi), he or she has understood the humor of the situation—and the criticism.

By playing with theatrical conventions and languages, the 1983 performance of *Mémoires d'Isles* made space for a subject to be both French and Caribbean, a third option—a *marasa trois*—that cycles between two otherwise mutually exclusive cultural identities (within the norms of French society at the time of the production). *Le Nouveau Journal* commented, "Martinique, Guadeloupe, whichever. French in any case."[102] Because French society generally did not recognize Caribbean cultural difference within Frenchness at the time of this production, making the French spectator aware of this cultural reality was both a subversive and a recuperative act. By nevertheless insisting on universal human unity and erasing certain elements of Caribbean history, the play refrains from confining the Caribbean spectator to the victim role (and the French spectator to that of the perpetrator). Caribbean spectators might begin to accept and move past their difficult and ambiguous memories, while French spectators can express empathy without feeling personally responsible for the histories of slavery and colonialism. A reviewer for a Parisian and (not coincidentally) Christian journal commented, "It is not about crying, pitying oneself, complaining, asking for pity. It is only about 'saying.'"[103]

In its multiple performative and textual iterations, and by way of its varying cultural receptions, *Memoires d'Isles* enacts tensions in Caribbean memory, identity, and selfhood. It figures Caribbean women's lived experience as accessible and relevant to all humans, thus universalizing ethnographic data through theater. At the same time, it issues a challenge to the French monopolization of the universal human. By making French spectators aware of their limited cultural literacy, the play invites them to experience exclusion and thus unmasks the fallacy of taking for granted that French culture represents universal values. By representing a multiplicity of historiographic and cultural standpoints, the play and its performance history propose an alternative, transmutable benchmark of the Caribbean self, in which the Caribbean particular and the universal human coexist.

Gerty Dambury's *Lettres indiennes*: Performing a Black and Indian Diaspora and the Contingency of Caribbeanness

While Césaire's and Condé's plays consider slavery's racializing legacies on a black-white continuum, Dambury's *Lettres indiennes* addresses ongoing systems of racialized violence at a point of intersection between blackness and Indianness. Set at the end of the twentieth century, against the backdrop of the closing of a sugarcane factory in an unnamed French overseas department, the play presents Caribbeanness as a fluid state that is continually negotiated via the process of diaspora, whereby subjects dispersed from their homelands create new, intercultural communities while maintaining a relationship with the homeland. Dambury shows black and Indian characters who together form a community on the island by negotiating, as in Hall's theorization of Caribbean identity, the opposing poles of unity and difference, continuity and change.[104]

Lettres indiennes turns on two interconnected stories of dispersal and cultural integration, the first involving a black Guadeloupean-born letter writer named Fructueuse, and the second, an Indian man named Paul. Newly arrived from Paris, Fructueuse befriends Paul and attempts to write about his life. She is drawn to Paul's community of mixed, black and Indian, friends and especially to the sugar factory where he works. When the factory closes, she accompanies Paul, now unemployed, as he returns to his family's house in a rural area of the island. There Paul's parents, disappointed in their son for never having married or fathered children, accuse him of failing to preserve their traditional Indian culture and values. As the play closes, Paul and Fructueuse look into each other's eyes as Fructueuse's notebook burns on top of Paul's deceased father's cremating body. Together they may now craft a new, intercultural home premised on tensions between unity and difference, mobility and fixity, and continuity and change.

To configure Caribbeanness as dynamic, multiple diasporas, Dambury remixes theatrical conventions, and, like Condé and Césaire, she strategically vacillates between depictions of cultural difference and universal human unity. She makes several strategic generalizations, and she plays with cultural ambiguity. She leaves the play's geographic setting deliberately ambiguous to emphasize cultural rootlessness and fluidity. While some allusions suggest that the play takes place in Guadeloupe, Dambury deploys several specific cultural references to the traditions of Réunion Island, such as *maloya* music.[105] Réunion, like Martinique and

Guadeloupe, is a former slave colony, now a French overseas department, and a site of creolization. However, Réunion's history is unique,[106] and it is geographically distant from the archipelago, located in the Indian Ocean, southeast of Madagascar. Dambury's conflation of Réunion and Guadeloupe is in many ways deliberate. As I will explain, Dambury's creative process imaginatively unites Réunion and Guadeloupe, much as the play enacts a unification of the black and Indian diasporas.

Working from photographs, critical reviews, publicity, and several personal interviews, I will discuss the original performance of *Lettres indiennes* at the Avignon Theatre Festival in 1996. This production and reception history creolized Dambury's text and materially enacted questions that were in many ways already written into the play. Whereas the play negotiates the opposing poles of continuity and difference in order to expose the overlapping histories of African slavery and East Indian indentured servitude and to propose a dynamic dramatization of Caribbean identity in reproduction, the performance reimagined those tensions in a way that obscured the Indian characters and culture. I insist that what appears to be a misrecognition of Dambury's dramatization of creolization—the forgetting of Indianness—was instead an unanticipated extension of it. As I will argue, varying cultural receptions of the play in performance illustrate the contingency of Caribbeanness and the disjointed role of Indianness as a signifier both of cultural particularity and of universalist diasporic existence in Dambury's text.

Fructueuse and Paul

Dambury's two main characters lead interconnected—oppositional yet parallel—stories, both involving migration and acculturation. Fructueuse, described in the list of characters as a letter writer, or *épistolière*,[107] arrives from Paris enthusiastic to "study" the people of the island. Notebook always in hand, she writes letters to a mysterious lover in Paris, who, she explains, is a "specialist," apparently a sociologist. Throughout the course of the play, however, she progressively abandons her letters, preferring human interaction over the hierarchized knowledge that her lover represents. Fructueuse's first object of study is Paul, an Indian man who works at a local factory, where Fructueuse observes him and then surreptitiously follows him home. While Fructueuse is introduced as a mobile, migrant character, Paul is anchored within his community: he is an important, stable support to his friends, notably a mixed-race couple, a black man and an Indian woman. Merchat, the man, is an alcoholic who beats his wife, Marie. Both seek refuge in

Paul's small apartment. Though clearly integrated into his community of friends, Paul too has left a community behind: his parents and his family home, to which he and Fructueuse go during the second part of the play. Paul left home because he wished to break from his parents' way of life and from Indian traditions; his mother sees him as his parents' "continuity."[108]

As the play progresses, Paul's and Fructueuse's stories further intertwine. Fructueuse becomes more invested in the ambiguous island and Paul's community of friends. Though she had previously insisted on her mobile status, she decides to stay. For his part, Paul confronts his parents and comes into his own as someone who will transmit Indian cultures (preserving some aspects and forgetting others). Though he has expressed disrespect for Indian ceremonies and traditions, when his father dies he proclaims that lighting the pile of wood for his father's cremation will be his responsibility. In the final scene of the play, Fructueuse, who had left Paul's parents' house for the city, returns for the cremation. She appears outside of the scene at first, but then slowly approaches. Having abandoned her distant lover and her letter writing, she places her notebook upon the body of Paul's father, and they burn together. Fructueuse and Paul "look into each other's eyes as a strange light envelops and isolates them from the world."[109]

Though Paul and Fructueuse's friendship appears to be platonic, the play's dialogue makes subtle allusions to the possibility of a romantic and sexual relationship between them. Fructueuse follows Paul because she is attracted by his masculine smell, a mix of cane juice, engine oil, and rum. She is intrigued by his fishing rods, and, in their first encounter, they speak of his job at the factory in simple, seemingly innocent language that plays slyly with sexual innuendo:

PAUL: Well, I'm a turbine specialist.

FRUCTUEUSE: That's nice.

PAUL: What do you know about it?

FRUCTUEUSE: Nothing . . . but it must be nice.

PAUL: That remains to be seen. . . .

FRUCTUEUSE: Don't you like it?

PAUL: It's very dirty work . . . and it's noisy.

FRUCTUEUSE: I'd like to see your turbines. Are they new?

PAUL: I think they're beautiful. They're . . . like new. The steel is smooth in places, all polished to the touch. The rust is creeping in, but I manage to keep them in shape.

FRUCTUEUSE: It makes me want to touch them.

PAUL: Tsk! Tsk! Certainly not!¹¹⁰

Paul and Fructueuse's unrealized romantic relationship is juxtaposed against Merchat and Marie's unhappy marriage. Merchat, formerly a soccer star, is an alcoholic. Though he regrets his behavior, he is irresponsible and abusive toward Marie, who regularly leaves him but always returns. Their children live with Marie's parents, who have disowned their son-in-law. In contrast with Marie, Fructueuse protects herself by attempting to remain objective, keeping a safe distance from love, from Paul, and from the community of islanders.

As Fructueuse becomes integrated into the ambiguous island, she abandons this commitment to objective distance. As her correspondence with her faraway lover becomes sparse, she embraces what she calls "reality." "How much longer will I be able to write to you?" she writes in her notebook. "Paul was right when he told me that to take notes you have to be on the outside looking in. I feel reality pulling me in and I am about to become one of the actors in this play."[111] This metatheatrical moment opposes theater to writing, and specifically to the social sciences, showing the former to be a site for active identity formation and community reproduction. Fructueuse is in fact no longer able to *write* about the sugar factory, Merchat's tragic absenteeism and abuse, Marie's beautiful expressions of sadness, or the black and Indian community into which she is becoming acculturated. But she is ready to experience these "realities" and to participate in the continuous (re)production of this community.

At the play's close, Fructueuse and Paul are poised to enact a new, ethical home by way of continual negotiations between continuity and difference. As Sandra L. Richards notes, a diasporic play can construct home as "an internalized idealization of community or solidarity that individuals are continually challenged to materially (re-)enact."[112] This theme of "home" in reproduction recurs throughout Dambury's play. Fructueuse proclaims that she feels "at home" (*comme chez moi*) or "almost at home" at Paul's house.[113] Paul too believes that, "in theory, it's only the heart that ought to say where home is." Though his father is disappointed by his son's lack of interest in Indian ceremonies and traditions, he understands that it is normal for a son to reject his father's way of life. Above all, the father reproaches Paul for his refusal to see the need for community: "When you refuse to belong to a community, you're on your own and you're wrong."[114] After Fructueuse decides to leave her lover and Paul's father dies, Paul and Fructueuse may become a romantic couple. (Though Paul rebelled against his parents' values, they both approve of Fructueuse.)[115]

As the body of Paul's father burns with Fructueuse's notebook, the two characters are freed from fixed ideas of their identities and origins. In the last lines of the play, Fructueuse says, "Today I am like one of them, since I can no longer trace exactly my bloodline. So perhaps I'm just as well here." She chooses to be part of the community and consequently takes on the burden of that community's past, but she nonetheless refuses to label her identity and origins. Her only hope is that they will accept her without finding her "too foreign" or asking her "those questions that frighten me: Who are you? What is your name? What is your bloodline?"[116] Without the trace of their bloodlines, the characters do not identify with a shared history of origins; instead they grapple with the dynamic process of the community's (re)production.

Staging a "General" Indian Diaspora

Diaspora is a central theme in Dambury's text; it was also key to her artistic process of creating the play. In conceiving of the play, Dambury brought together her own personal experiences with diasporic Indian populations in the Caribbean and on Réunion Island. In 1991 she was invited to Réunion to teach a writing workshop. Inspired by this experience, she dedicated *Lettres indiennes* to the students she taught during this trip: the sixth-grade students of Plateau-Goyaves Middle School.[117] Upon returning to Guadeloupe, she observed that Indian communities in Guadeloupe and Réunion had similar experiences. Indians in both islands were insulted for being Indian—called pejorative names such as "coolie" or "malbar." Furthermore both populations struggled with the question of whether they would assimilate into Caribbean, Creole culture or embrace their Indian culture's uniqueness.

Speaking to Stéphanie Bérard in 2003 of the play's conception, Dambury explains:

> In front of me were children who fought themselves every day, going back and forth between the shame of who they were, because the others made fun of them, and at the same time, the desire to affirm their culture. In the end, I tried to compare, to bring together what I had been able to take in while in Réunion with what was actually happening in Guadeloupe, something I was

directly confronted with because I was working at the time in Moule.... So I found myself working on something that had been growing in my unconscious while I was in Réunion and that, in my childhood, was quite present, because I went to ceremonies.[118]

Working in the Guadeloupean region of Moule, where there is a large Indian presence and quite a few Indian temples, Dambury returned to thoughts she had as a teacher in Réunion. Through the writing process, she brought her observations together. Creatively she forged a diasporic link between Indian communities in Réunion and Guadeloupe.

Dambury became especially interested in the exclusion of Indians and Indian cultural traditions from Caribbean culture. Speaking of her conversations with members of the Association of the Friends of India in Guadeloupe, she explained in an interview with Suzanne Houyoux, "They responded that they live in Guadeloupean society, that they are Guadeloupean, and that that society has evolved—it doesn't reject them like it used to. And that the more they had the sentiment of being rejected, the more they worked to assimilate, to marry outside of their community—with whites or blacks—to be better accepted."[119] While (white) Frenchness sets the norm for cultural superiority, (black) Creole identity is also somewhat exclusionary toward Indians.

From this vantage point, Dambury's play joins the contemporaneous Créolité movement, which, against the precedent of Négritude's valorization of Africa, attempted to expand the boundaries of Creole culture to include Caribbeans of Indian origin. Yet in spite of their well-known proclamation that they were "neither Europeans, nor Africans, nor Asians," the Créolists implicitly excluded both Caribbeans of Asian origin and women from their purview, privileging the standpoint of black and mulatto men, as A. James Arnold has convincingly argued.[120] In contrast, by dramatizing the overlapping black and Indian diasporas, Dambury shows Caribbean identity as a process of creolization. She includes Indians in Caribbean identity, not by re-delimiting its boundaries but by proposing generalizations about Caribbeanness that draw from the parallel or comparison between the African and the Indian experience in the former French slave colonies.

In addition to bringing visibility to Indian cultures in the Caribbean, *Lettres indiennes* explores the more generalizable experience of diaspora: forced migration, the loss of the homeland and of cultural traditions, as well as the difficulties and inequalities within the host culture. In order to dramatize an Indian diaspora, Dambury did research into many Indian cultures. She then incorporated certain findings into the play, reestablishing a lost diasporic link between cultural traditions in the Indian homeland and the contemporary practices of Indians in Guadeloupe and Réunion. One example is Marie's song, in which she narrates the stages of life of a woman from marriage to separation, revealing insight into her feelings toward her separation from her alcoholic husband.[121] This was based in Dambury's discovery in her research that women in North India sing their everyday stories.[122] Thus Dambury's play forged a link between Indians in Guadeloupe and a cultural practice that did not survive the journey to the Caribbean.

Dambury's efforts to restore a link to the lost Indian culture could be understood as a parallel to black Caribbeans' efforts to restore the ruptured relationship to Africa, pioneered by Aimé Césaire's Négritude movement. "I wanted to know if [Indians in Guadeloupe] would have the same desire to return to India that we have in terms of Africa," she explained to Houyoux.[123] Dambury joined the Association of the Friends of India on a "return" trip from Guadeloupe to India because she wished to observe how they would interact with Indian culture on the continent. "So actually, it's a kind of ongoing process of questioning about what leaves India, what arrives in our country, what lasts, what gets lost, what is at odds with the rest of society, what tries to be validated, but doesn't know how," she explained.[124]

Dambury attempted to generalize her portrayal of the Indian diaspora. On the one hand, she worked to distill the concept and practice of diaspora from the specificity of black and Indian cultures, thus crafting a performance that could be applicable to all migrants. On the other hand, she also delimited a translocal Indian culture in order to portray it on stage. "But I wasn't talking about Indians in Guadeloupe, or in Réunion," she explained to Bérard, "because I became interested in Indian culture in general."[125] This process of bringing together insights from Indian communities in multiple locations resembles what Peter Brook calls the "culture of links," insofar as she sought to uncover a generalizable essence of Indianness. This idea of "Indian culture in general" may be somewhat imprecise, but it reflects the contemporary realities of Indians in Guadeloupe. Though they are not fully integrated into Creole culture, they are also distanced from Indian culture. While the majority of Indians who came to Guadeloupe were of Tamil origin and of the Sudra caste, the caste system has not survived, and the Tamil language is hardly spoken.[126] Whereas most of the Indians who came to Guadeloupe were Hindus, their religion in the Caribbean is a syncretic form, influenced by Catholicism as well as Africanist practices. For instance, in Guadeloupe there are Indian priests who act as healers.[127] Though the majority of Indian workers came from Tamil-speaking French enclaves in southern India, Dambury was not incorrect to also research northern India, because some of the Indians arriving in Guadeloupe came from the North through a port in Calcutta.[128]

Dambury's attempts to access "Indian culture in general" and her interest in diaspora as a transcultural experience could be understood as a subset of her investment in a universalism of theater and of human experience. As she explained to Bérard, through writing she tries to access a "sort of empty space inside of us" that allows for connection among humans.[129] She also stated that she would like to see one of her plays performed in Russian, to see that it is possible for a Russian living in his own country to have "felt the same feelings as an everyday Guadeloupean."[130] Dambury's interest in the universalism of her theater reflects her alignment with intercultural theater.

Furthermore her process of creating the play was strikingly similar to the creation of the Théâtre du Soleil's *Indiade*, for which Hélène Cixous did library research into Indian customs while Ariane Mnouchkine and the troupe of actors traveled to India.[131] The placelessness of setting also recalls numerous productions by both Mnouchkine and Brook. Makward suggests that Dambury's characters are both Guadeloupean and "from here and elsewhere, 'universal' in their awkwardness with living and their need to communicate and to love."[132] Yet Dambury's universalism is rooted in creolization—diasporic experiences in the context of the aftermath of colonialism, slavery, and indentured servitude. Much like Césaire's, Dambury's attention to the universal human serves an ethical, political purpose.

Echoes of Slavery's Violence

Dambury dramatizes contemporary echoes of the overlapping histories of African slavery and East Indian indentured servitude. Symbolically Paul and Fructueuse's obscure relationship, of which Fructueuse is unable to *write*, might represent what Lisa Lowe has called the "intimacies of four continents," a range of global connections, contact, and unspoken intimacies, largely dissimulated by the colonial archive, "out of which emerged not only modern humanism but a modern racialized division of labor."[133] Bérard has argued that Dambury's plays operate in both the past and the present through an aesthetic of ruptures and openings, which enables voices from the past to resurface.[134] In *Lettres indiennes*, the violence of slavery (with East Indian indentured servitude counted as an extension of that violence) resurfaces in multiple ways. The play suggests that one might understand derogatory terms for Indians prevalent in the Caribbean, such as "coolie" and "malbar," as an echo of antiblack racism and a symptom of a larger, racializing, colonial discourse. The history of Indians who migrated to the Caribbean as indentured servants parallels the history of African slavery in striking ways, so much so that East Indian servitude was called "a new system of slavery" due to its brutality and miserable conditions.[135]

The Indian experience of racialized violence and exclusion is distinct even as it parallels the black Caribbean struggle. The majority of Indian workers brought to the French Caribbean through an agreement between France and England were poor and illiterate. With limited knowledge of French and geography, they likely did not understand the contracts they signed.[136] Into the twentieth century in Martinique and Guadeloupe, Indians, generally speaking, continued to be poorer than other Caribbeans and tended to be undereducated because they lived in rural areas and experienced prejudice. As late as the 1960s in Guadeloupe, illiteracy rates among Indian families were still extremely high.[137] At the end of the twentieth century, in the aftermath of *départementalisation*, all French Caribbeans experienced the problems described at the start of this chapter relating to selective, racialized exclusion from the French citizen and the "human." Caribbeans of Indian origin, however, additionally faced incomplete assimilation into and exclusion from Creole culture, particularly in Guadeloupe. In contrast with Indians in Martinique at the end of the twentieth century, who were generally acculturated into Creole culture, in Guadeloupe Indians remained relatively segregated and were more invested in reaffirming Indian cultural identity.[138]

Through her efforts to draw attention to the particular and often overlooked plight of Indians in the Caribbean, Dambury also sought to dramatize the underlying violence of slavery's racializing legacy. A sugar factory frames the dramatic action of *Lettres indiennes*. Further extending the idea that Indian indentured servitude replaced African slavery, the factory reminds spectators of an ongoing system of economic exploitation in slavery's aftermath: laborers of color in the Caribbean still provide sugar for the mostly white peoples of the Global North. Yet Paul, a mechanic, does not cut cane; he repairs the machines that have fundamentally altered the labor involved in the production of sugar.

For Fructueuse, who may be somewhat naïve, the factory is associated with the promise of mobility and change. At the play's opening, she has just arrived on the island and quickly happened upon the factory. In a letter to her lover, she poetically writes:

> I discovered this factory one evening by chance. I had lost my way. I took a path that I thought led somewhere and came upon this magnificent sight: hundreds of soaring chimneys making tracks between the sky and us; rusty objects everywhere, and because rust is the voice of time, I had the feeling I was drifting in another time, another world. . . . Then there was a noise. A thousand machine engines roaring at full throttle in the silence of the night, mingling with the irregular spluttering of the engines of the trucks parked in front of the scales, threatening to choke at the slightest moment of inattention by the drivers. Can you imagine me in the night watching the sky turn black as ink, the smoke spiral up, wrapped in the smell of sugar cane, the noise of the machines and the spasmodic acceleration of the trucks' engine after each splutter. . . . And the lights, little dots of light that were frozen in time. Magical![139]

Fructueuse insists that she likes the factory (and sugarcane), and she wants to use it as a research site.[140] After having spent a long time in Paris, she may long for a characteristically Caribbean experience, or she may be romanticizing industrialization.

However, Paul believes the factory is unfit for a woman to visit. The factory enables him to live independently from his parents, who grow sugarcane on their family farm, and to send money home to them as recompense for his absence. But as his mother points out, Paul "sweated for white men," just like his parents did.[141] An ambivalent signifier, the factory enables Paul to meet his basic needs and provides his financial independence from his parents. But as his modest house attests, he does not make a substantial profit, and his job is not secure. As a temporary solution to long-standing global economic disparity, Paul's job at the factory may mask slavery's enduring legacy. As Dambury's play makes clear, the factory conceals deeper socioeconomic and racial tensions on the island.

When the factory closes, violence and competition resurface. In the play's most aggressive scene, the "Player" (a black man playing checkers with Paul's friend Merchat) verbally assaults Paul. The characters have just heard the official announcement that the factory will be closing, and Paul and the Player are both put out of work. Yet rather than empathizing or expressing solidarity with Paul, the Player seems to displace his anger onto him.

> Player: Say Coolie, you're getting cheeky. Perhaps it's the peanuts you earned at the factory that made you think you're a man. . . . (*He gets up threatening.*)

But you're nothing, little Coolie, Malbar, Ratapunda. If we hadn't refused to be slaves, you'd still be rotting like a loser in India! When you arrived on our tiny island, you were nothing, nothing but a bunch of vagabonds, picked up by the white men on the side of the road. Nothing else, do you understand? So when I see a whippersnapper like yourself put on a bold face because we've lost our jobs, I only feel like doing one thing: grabbing you by the little skin there is on your body and chucking you over the ocean to see if you've got any family left over there.[142]

Using racist language to insult Paul, the Player conjures the histories of Indian indentured servitude and African slavery. His mention of "the peanuts you earned at the factory" might recall the fact that Indian indentured workers were commonly paid one half to one third the wages of free people of color.[143] His comment that blacks refused to be slaves associates blackness with resistance, thus figuring his black ancestors as both "greater" victims and stronger resisters in comparison with Indians, who are viewed as having taken their place as slaves. Wishing to violently expel Paul through a fantasy of "chucking" him back to India, the Player lays claim to Creole identity and slavery's legacy.

The Player is indifferent to the violence he inflicts on Paul and blind to the possibility that he now perpetuates racism—not antiblack racism but racism against Indians. He excludes Paul from those who have inherited memories of violence, even as he inflicts an echo of that underlying violence on him. The hostility dramatized here represents the larger trend of racism against Indians, recognizable in the epithets—coolie, malbar, ratapunda—the Player repeats. When Fructueuse tries to defend Paul, the Player responds, "You'd fight with me? You haven't got a chance. You're only a woman. Worse than an Indian. (*He bursts out laughing.*)"[144] In this scene, sexism parallels racism, underscoring the play's treatment of domestic violence against women, most conspicuously apparent in Marie's story.

The play portrays this originary, racializing violence as internalized by Caribbean society and subsequently resurfacing in unpredictable ways. Paul's attitude toward traditional Indian culture is conflicted. He rejects his parents' values because he wishes to escape colonial racism and exclusion, but he has also internalized this rhetoric. His father and mother put pressure on him to preserve Indian traditions and to respect their values. His father also charges him with the burden of collective representation, that is, the duty to act in a way that will reflect well on Indians as a group. Paul recalls his father's voice from his childhood: "We Indians, we've got enough problems! Don't make our case worse!"[145]

In the play's final scenes, Paul, previously docile, refuses the burden of his parents' expectations: "I'd have burnt everything, everything do you hear? The temples too! I'd have trampled on the sacrifices, the fruit, the flowers, the coconut that's too white and the rice. I recall the first ceremony I attended. I was meant to swallow the mashed banana, the coconut and the rice. Well, I spat it out while you weren't looking. I spat it out, do you hear? Spat! And I have never stopped spitting it out from that day on." Likening himself to slavery's resisters, who burned down plantations, Paul positions his parents as his oppressors, standing in the way of his assimilation into Creole culture. Confronting his father, Paul complains that his parents insisted that he preserve Indian culture while simultaneously teaching him to hate his own Indianness. The first word that came out of his father's mouth when Paul learned to speak was "Silence!" Rather than love for Indian traditions, his father taught him fear: "Fear of him, fear of the white man, fear of the creoles, fear of the gods. . . . Fear of the evening lurking with spells, fear of the master, fear of oneself."[146]

Through her portrayal of multiple, parallel racialized violences inflected upon and perpetuated by Caribbean society, Dambury figures colonialism and slavery in reverberations that echo across cultural groups and time periods. *Lettres indiennes* recognizes multiple, overlapping histories of violence simultaneously. Though the community shares that reverberating violence, their selfhood and collective existence is not defined by violence. Rather, much like Glissant's choice to open his *Poetics of Relation* with a scene from the hull of a slave ship, the "abyss,"[147] Dambury shows how new, ethical relationships grow from a shared history of cultural loss and violence. She situates Paul and Fructueuse's relationship and their black and Indian community within slavery's racializing legacy. In line with Hall's theorization of Caribbean identity as diaspora, Dambury's portrayal of intersecting black and Indian diasporas counts Caribbeanness not in fixed origins or identities but as an ongoing process of creolization. Performance, as opposed to sociology and letter writing, enables Fructueuse to take part actively in the community and its reproduction.

Performing Caribbeanness?

Lettres indiennes was created by Alain Timar's Théâtre des Halles for the 1996 Festival in Avignon. The play was staged in a collaborative spirit, and Timar recognized the importance of cultural competencies the actors brought to the rehearsal process. It starred many well-known French Caribbean actors: Raymonde Palcy and Gilbert Laumord (who also played Zéphyr in *An tan revolisyon*) in the roles of Fructueuse and Paul; Mariann Mathéus (who also played Hermance in *Mémoires d'Isles*) and Philippe Calodat playing Marie and Merchat; Serge Abatucci as Paul's father, and Firmine Richard his mother. All these Caribbean actors are black, and none is identifiably of Indian descent, which means that there was no visible, racial signifier onstage to distinguish between the black and Indian characters in Dambury's script. Working collaboratively with the actors and encouraging them to propose staging choices, Timar provided a basic structure while encouraging the actors to utilize their knowledge of Caribbean performance practices, such as *gwo-ka*, song, and storytelling. The scenic design, a warehouse-like space that was painted by Timar, who is also a visual artist, was abstract and minimalist. It enabled spectators to focus their attention on the actors' stage movements (figure 5). The artists collaboratively created a performance that enacted tensions in the meanings of Caribbeanness and diaspora.

Timar's staging emphasized stage movement and the theme of travel. In an author's note in the program, Dambury wrote, "The characters, therefore, travel, move about and evolve in a closed circuit which is really the major theme of the play."[148] The mutability of the stage space, with its delocalized, abstract aesthetic, as well as Timar's emphasis on movement and migration reinforced this theme. One reviewer from the newspaper *Midi Libre* remarked, "This could take place anywhere."[149] Laumord (Paul), who has worked multiple times with Timar since this project, commented that Timar has a sharp, geometric sense of space and of the actor's positioning.[150] Under his direction, the actors used the entire space, leaving large distances between them. The entire ensemble was always onstage; characters not involved in the scene sat or stood at the sides of the theater space. Suddenly and rapidly, actors would move across the entire space. Mathéus (Marie) explained to me that in her interpretation, Marie sings and dances to expel her experience of society's violence. Mathéus recalled that Marie's internal experience of domestic violence propelled her forcefully in ways that were even

95   *Remixing Unity and Difference*

Figure 5. The cast of Gerty Dambury's *Lettres indiennes*: Philippe Calodat as Merchat, Gilbert Laumord as Paul, Firmine Richard as the Mother, Serge Abatucci as the Father, and Mariann Mathéus as Marie (not pictured, Raymonde Palcy as Fructueuse). Avignon, France, 1996. (Photograph by Alain Timar; Collection of the Théâtre des Halles; courtesy of Alain Timar and Aurélie Clément)

surprising to Mathéus herself.[151] One review noted a powerful "drive that translates the interior movement of the characters."[152]

The underlying violence that Dambury exposes, and the ways the characters have internalized that violence, was evident in confrontations between them and was rendered abstract in stage movements and nervous tics. For instance, Laumord remembered a moment in which he silently twisted his shirt, communicating what he called an interior suffering.[153] Though this underlying violence was tangible to actors and spectators, it appears that it was not manifest in racism against Indians, which Dambury's play exposes. No reviews commented on this message. Mathéus recalled the experiences of violence against women and Guadeloupean society's internalized violence, but not racism directed against Indians.

While Dambury's play features Indian diasporic cultures, the performance drew largely from African-derived song, dance, and storytelling. Working collaboratively, the actors brought to the table their knowledge of and experience with Caribbean performance practices. As in Condé's *An tan revolisyon*, Laumord brought his knowledge of Creole storytelling traditions and his passion as a cultural activist for teaching and reinvigorating this tradition. Actor Philippe Calodat brought his expertise as a *gwo-ka* dancer, and Mathéus, as she did for *Mémoires d'Isles*, as a Creole singer. The theater's publicity associated the performance of *Lettres indiennes* with a performance by the Haitian storyteller-singer Mimi Barthelemy, who was also invited by the Théâtre des Halles. Though Dambury appreciated many aspects of the original production, particularly the actors' work with stage movement, she was troubled to see her writing staged under the sign of African-derived storytelling. She told Bérard in 2003:

> I don't want to be imprisoned in the oral world. I'm sick of the fact that every time a Caribbean or African artist writes something, they're sent back to orality, because you're an oral civilization, and blah-blah-blah. I'm not interested in that. So I don't write folktales. That's why it was so irritating when the fable in *Lettres indiennes* was turned into "yé krik ... yé krak" by the director Alain Timar. I detest "yé krik ... yé krak," and I say that really vehemently because I have had enough of this and I know they always take us back to the orality question.[154]

"Yé krik... yé krak" (the Creole spelling of *Yé Cric! Yé Crac!*) is a conventional call-and-response exchange between the Caribbean storyteller and the public. To Dambury's surprise, it was used to stage Paul's ritualistic chant, told despondently while he beats the drum, following the factory's closing.[155] The poem, which Dambury had researched, recounts the South Indian legend of the god Madurai.

Where did the storytelling stereotype come from? While it would be logical to attribute the choice to the director Timar, the use of storytelling was actually more likely proposed by the Caribbean actors themselves. Though neither could recall the details, both Mathéus and Laumord believed that one of the Guadeloupean actors (rather than Timar) first suggested staging the Madurai poem using the *cric-crac* call-and-response technique of Caribbean storytelling. Mathéus speculated that because the poem is long, they were probably searching for a way to bring it to life on stage. To Dambury, storytelling is an unnecessary stereotype (since there is no reference to Creole storytelling in her play), but for the actors, it enabled them to draw from their own cultural interests and expertise in order to collaboratively craft a mise-en-scène deemed Caribbean.

Though a Caribbean actor likely suggested the popular depiction of Caribbean orality, Timar, who is a white man of Jewish Hungarian,

Spanish, and Algerian origins, must have approved of the choice, since he kept it. Furthermore it corresponded with Timar's own interest in Creole culture, especially Patrick Chamoiseau's writing and the well-known Créolité movement. Timar staged adaptations of several of Chamoiseau's works. Indeed his theater scheduled a roundtable about Créolité to take place alongside the production of Dambury's play in Avignon. Along with Chamoiseau, Raphaël Confiant, Daniel Maximin, Ernest Pépin, and Franketienne joined Dambury for a discussion titled "Rebel Sons and Daughters of Aimé Césaire." The program introduces the stages of French Caribbean identity and emphasizes the Créolists' *Eloge de la Créolité* and the Creole language.[156]

While Dambury's play portrays overlapping black and Indian diasporas, the original production emphasized the black, Caribbean, and universalist aspects, thereby glossing over her interest in Indian cultures. As mentioned, in Timar's production all roles, including the Indian characters of Paul, Marie, and Paul's parents, were played by well-known black, French Caribbean actors. To be sure, the casting choice was likely made for practical reasons, since there were very few French Caribbean actors of Indian origin at that time. Yet this casting choice erased the visual indicator of Indian-black difference, subsuming Indians into black, Creole culture, despite Dambury's efforts to avoid that very trend.

Spectators must have experienced a disconnect between what they heard and what they saw: while the actors described Indian characters in their lines, they all appeared as black Guadeloupeans onstage. The title remained *Lettres indiennes* (literally, Indian Letters). One reviewer rationalized this confusion: "'Indian' Letters? Yes, Christopher Columbus' India, meaning the Caribbean."[157] When I asked Mathéus, who played the Indian woman Marie, about the Indian elements, she responded that, in the minds of the actors, there really were no Indians in the play.[158] What may have bothered Dambury more than the *cric-crac* stereotype was the erasure of Indians and Indianness. The play dramatizes Caribbeanness as a process in dynamic reproduction and thereby invites multiple meanings and transformations. Downplaying the Indian elements was an interpretation that did not sit well with Dambury, insofar as it reestablished the dominant social expectations against which she wrote. But her play does not take a fixed political stance so much as dramatize a creolizing impulse, the afterlife of which will necessarily be unpredictable and messy. Though the casting might appear to be a mis-staging of Dambury's text, it was a materialization of her aesthetics of creolization.

As in the other case studies, performance reveals the contingency of Caribbeanness. Even though the production contradicted Dambury's objective of breaking the silence surrounding Indian heritage in the Caribbean, it extended her dramatization of the tensions between particularity and universalism that make up diasporic, Caribbean realities. This point of interpretive tension materializes the unpredictable legacy of racialized subjection Dambury exposes. Several reviewers at the production questioned the meanings of Caribbeanness as well as the boundaries separating it from other cultures. One reviewer described the characters as searching for roots other than slavery.[159] Another identified Caribbeanness in the experience of happiness, even in the face of extreme poverty and misery.[160] The actors likewise questioned what it meant to be Caribbean. While Laumord described Paul's mother as a "poto-mitan," an equivalent to the stereotype of Caribbean womanhood that I have called the Chestnut, Firmine Richard deployed universalist language to explain that a mother is a mother, regardless of race or culture.[161] Across these varied interpretations, to perform Caribbeanness in *Lettres indiennes* meant to perform the fragmented Caribbean self, remaking oneself through creolization. In Dambury's play, dislocation and displacement gives rise to an intercultural ethics of conflict, dialogue, and community.

In their thematically diverse plays, Condé, Césaire, and Dambury dramatize Caribbean identity and historical memory in dynamic reproduction. While Condé critically questions the inheritances of the French and Haitian revolutions, Césaire enacts cultural memories that foreground Caribbean women's lived experiences and their various assimilations into, exclusions from, and rejections of the customs and values set by French cultural standards. In her focus on diasporic Indian populations and cultures, Dambury explores the experiences of dispersal, acculturation, discrimination, and community building at the heart of Caribbean societies. Each of the plays emphasizes the importance of a community, and the playwrights created these plays by drawing from various communities: working collaboratively with directors and actors, conducting ethnographic interviews, and immersing themselves in other cultures. Nourished by the process and spirit of collaborative creation, the plays feature a multiplicity of historical and cultural viewpoints. This facilitates questioning of the meanings of Caribbeanness, the inheritances of colonialism, slavery, and revolution, and the ways colonial power imbalances affect people's lives.

As opposed to articulating a theory of identity, the plays *enact* processes of dynamic identity formation and thus *stage* Caribbeanness as creolization, much as it has been theorized by Hall and Glissant. The plays each favor what Glissant calls "relational identity" over "root identity" and eschew the "hidden violence of filiation."[162] They privilege Hall's second understanding of identity as a "becoming" and thus join him in his belief that the notion of identity as "one true self" does not reflect "the common history" of Caribbean peoples, which was, "literally, a translation."[163] Indeed the plays stage ongoing processes of interrogating history, reproducing culture, and remaking community. Such translational configurations attempt to disrupt slavery's racializing, dehumanizing legacy: the precarious colonial history of making certain subjects of color "French" and then rescinding that decision or incompletely realizing the promise of *liberté, égalité, fraternité*.

Playing with the conventions of intercultural and postcolonial theater, the plays dramatize unresolved tensions between unity and difference, mobility and fixity, past and present, and continuity and change. The staging and cultural reception of the plays inevitably remixed those tensions in new, unpredictable ways, thus revealing once more the multivalent meanings of historical inheritance, the selective fungibility of power hierarchies, and the contingency of Caribbeanness.

3 Syncretizing Performance and Moral Codes

Ina Césaire's *L'Enfant des passages*
and Simone Schwarz-Bart's *Ton beau capitaine*

Two Creole proverbs teach life lessons inherited from Caribbean plantations: *Débouya pa péché* (Making do with cunning is not a sin) and *Bigidi pa tonbé* (Be off balance, but do not fall). Both evoke religious codes in order to bend and adapt them. The first revisits the Christian concept of sin, while the second modifies the quest for balance at the core of African religions. *Débouya* (making do with cunning) implies tricking the powerful, exploiting gaps in the dominant system, and doing whatever is necessary to get ahead. The French term *débrouillardise* (also known as *système D*) refers to clever, creative problem solving. In Creole, the concept additionally designates resourceful opportunism and engagement in illegal, unorthodox, or immoral activities.[1] *Débouya* is commonly associated with the trickster folktale heroes Brer Rabbit and Ti-Jean. While *débouya* is evocative of Creole folktales, the Creole word *bigidi* (permanent imbalance) is associated with Caribbean dance. *Bigidi* is central to the syncopated steps of a Guadeloupean *léwoz*, a popular rhythm of the *gwo-ka* dance and percussion tradition. The *léwoz* dancer, in communication with the drummer, repeatedly loses his or her balance but never touches the floor.[2] In common usage, the Guadeloupean proverb *Bigidi pa tonbé* teaches emotional strength: when times are tough, let yourself be off balance, but do not fall.[3] Insofar as many African-derived rituals seek balance, *bigidi* also symbolizes the need to remake religion and moral codes in the aftermath of the rupture with the African homeland, the brutality of the slave system, and the prohibition of African religious practices. Under the conditions of slavery, the balance and harmony for which African religions strive was not always a realistic or useful goal.

The concepts of *débouya* and *bigidi* both conjure embodied knowledge kept in Creole performance practices. When summarized in words,

101   Syncretizing Performance and Moral Codes

these lessons appear somewhat contradictory and perhaps outdated. Performance bears witness to past acts of syncretism: the ways in which, in Noel Erskine's words, the enslaved "merged African and Christian worldviews in the elaboration and explication of their faith."[4] Performance also offers the possibility of creatively reinventing the past, repurposing it for the sake of the present. Forged under the duress of the plantation, Caribbean syncretic religion embraces dualities, ambiguities, and dissimulations. It always carries with it a promise for transformative change. "More than simply a strategy for survival, this active, conscious, syncretic process demonstrates an appreciation for the intrinsic value of creativity, growth, and change as well as for the spiritual potential of other belief systems."[5] *Débouya* and *bigidi* remind us that the plantation's oppressive logic made the bending of moral codes necessary for survival, but they also celebrate the magnificent power of syncretic religion and Creole performance practices (storytelling, dance, and song) as tools for survival, empowerment, solace, liberation, redress, and transformative change. Still said in Martinique and Guadeloupe today, the proverbs expose a temporal continuity and discontinuity between past and present. Calling attention to the simultaneous continuities and fissures with the past, they raise unresolved questions: In what ways does the slave past continue to inflect and influence contemporary life? To what extent are the moral codes and life lessons inherited from the plantation still viable?

In this chapter, I investigate two plays that represent, renew, and question moral codes inherited from the plantation by playing with the life lessons summarized in the two proverbs. Written in 1987, Ina Césaire's *L'Enfant des passages, ou La geste de Ti-Jean* (The Child of Passages, or the Story of Ti-Jean) and Simone Schwarz-Bart's *Ton beau capitaine* (Your Handsome Captain) ask unresolved questions relating to slavery's inheritance and syncretize moral codes by updating the Creole performance practices of storytelling and dance. I have chosen to explore these two plays together since both feature apparent transgressions of Christian moral codes and dwell in the syncretisms, contradictions, ambiguities, and unresolved tensions of plantation-derived performance. Césaire's play, an adaptation of a classic Caribbean folktale, questions and renews the contemporary value of *débouya*. In the play, the folktale hero Ti-Jean, born into poverty, wins a mythical kingdom and a beautiful princess by being selfish, proud, and destructive. He reminds his spectators and readers of strategies for psychic liberation and survival that originated under the intense oppression of the plantation; Césaire's play mediates this inheritance for contemporary audiences. Set in the 1980s, Schwarz-Bart's play dramatizes a Haitian migrant worker in Guadeloupe who must make sense of his wife's infidelity from a distance. Listening to his wife's confession in a tape-recorded letter, Wilnor rejects his wife, Marie-Ange, but he comes to a deeper understanding of their situation through dance and embodied experimentations in *bigidi*. After analyzing the two plays with a focus on their adaptation of Creole performance practices, I draw from interviews and published reviews to investigate the original performances and their cultural reception. Given their moral provocations, it should not be surprising that both plays elicited fervent and conflicting responses from artists and spectators. The plays script unresolved tensions that disrupt an implied spectator's moralizing gaze; artists mobilized diverse theatrical conventions and cultural forms of knowledge production in order to perform these provocatively multivalent, syncretic plays.

Syncretic Performance as Moral Repossession

L'Enfant des passages and *Ton beau capitaine* reclaim the legacy of apparently contradictory moral codes inherited from the plantation through intercultural renewals of traditional, Creole performance forms. Césaire and Schwarz-Bart use storytelling and dance to convey embodied, historical knowledge of *débouya* and *bigidi*. But they do not aim to preserve these cultural traditions in their past iterations; rather the playwrights adapt the performance practices through deliberate acts of what Christopher Balme would call "theatrical syncretism," that is, the melding of multiple, culturally tangled—Creole, African, and European—theatrical conventions and semiotic codes within a dramatic text.[6]

The traditional Creole performance practices are already "reassembled behavior[s]," to borrow Leo Cabranes-Grant's term: Creole dance and storytelling are performative not only because they are repeated, recognizable acts but also because of the "relational relays" of which they are composed and which they reproduce.[7] They have "tangled roots," meaning that one cannot trace the geographical origin of Caribbean folktales or dances—even the names seem to derive from both Europe and Africa.[8] And their futures will be further entangled. Elements of Césaire's folktale, including her hero Ti-Jean, can be found in European, African, and American tales. Similarly, in the movements involved, the instruments used, and even their names, the dances Schwarz-Bart calls for in her stage directions resemble both European and African dances. By incorporating other intercultural elements, for example, the use of

Noh theater, ballet, or Brechtian theater, Césaire and Schwarz-Bart *reassemble* a Creole vision of life lessons, moral codes, and religion that was already tangled and intercultural, thus renewing its contemporary relevance.

The syncretic moral codes of *débouya* and *bigidi* appear contradictory in meaning. Creole belief systems are pervaded by split figures and double meanings that align empowering identities and allies with sources of oppression. In Creole folktales, the character of the Bon Dieu (Good God) has two distinct forms: he can be the Catholic God, all-powerful and awesome, or he can be the white plantation owner, a sinister character who exercised almost complete control over enslaved people's lives.[9] Similarly, in Haitian vodou, the supreme God, the Bon Dieu or Bondyé, can also be called the Gran Mat (Grand Master). While Bondyé is the supreme God, as in Christian monotheism, vodou practitioners believe that they are able to communicate with him only via the *lwa*, vodou divinities associated with African deities and Catholic saints. Still today vodou practitioners sometimes call their *lwa* devils (*diables*), in addition to angels, spirits, saints, invisibles, and mysteries.[10] Similarly, in the Creole quadrille dance, which I examine in my analysis of *Ton beau capitaine*, the caller (*commandeur*) is a relic of the African drummer, yet the term also means "slave driver."

By way of a focus on performance as a dynamic becoming, the playwrights inhabit these dualities. This enables them to refrain from moral judgment and to reject Creole myths of origins, claims to authenticity, and static visions of the past. In contrast with the contemporaneous Créolité movement, particularly Chamoiseau and Confiant's valorization of the Creole language and the male storyteller,[11] Césaire's and Schwarz-Bart's dramas count Creoleness not as an identity but as a historical process of creolization, akin to Joseph Roach's theorization of performance in the circum-Atlantic rim. There is no authentic Creoleness insofar as Caribbean identity, like storytelling and dance, is caught up in the ongoing, relational process of reproducing itself.

This focus on performance's syncretisms enables Césaire and Schwarz-Bart to implicitly position the influence of Christianity as, simultaneously, a force of both oppression and liberation. At the time of slavery, the French Crown imposed Catholicism on enslaved Africans. Today, however, the French Caribbean is significantly more Christian (Catholic and Adventist) than mainland France, which takes pride in its secularism. In fact Christianity is often viewed as a mark of Caribbeanness. As anthropologist David Beriss notes, the Christian religion is a means whereby present-day Martinicans and Guadeloupeans living in France distinguish their cultural identity from mainstream French values and organize activist Caribbean groups.[12] Yet though Christianity is empowering for many Caribbeans, when it is defined exclusively by French standards, its influence can cause present-day Caribbeans to disavow the legacy of *débouya*, label this Creole inheritance a sin, or judge it by a "standard of absolute morality."[13] Even Chamoiseau measures Creole morality against French, Christian moral standards inasmuch as he rationalizes *débouya* as a result of the plantation's "impossible moral universe," as Estelle Tarica rightly points out.[14] Césaire and Schwarz-Bart, in contrast, use theater to restage (and resyncretize) syncretic moral codes. They use drama to reframe and question slavery's inheritance and to renew the processes of intercultural exchange that drive the liberating, syncretic religion born from slavery: the plantation church, to borrow the title of Erskine's book.

Created on the plantation, under the slave master's watch, Caribbean storytelling and dance both dissimulate and transmit subversive messages, moral instruction, Africanist retentions and liberating, empowering meanings. These performance practices bear witness to a complex history of colonial society's contradictory uses of Christianity to subjugate the enslaved.[15] They also hold the traces of enslaved people's repossessions of Christianity on their own, liberating terms. Harnessing the transformative power of Yoruba and Fon ritual, slaves practicing vodou "took possession of Catholicism and thereby repossessed themselves as active spiritual subjects."[16] Though one does not find vodou practiced in Martinique and Guadeloupe, performance nonetheless enabled creative syncretism in these two islands.[17] Creole dances offered enslaved people a liminal, syncretic space in which to repossess their spiritual selves, while remaining faithful to Christianity on their own terms.

To take an illustrative example, in 1724 the priest Jean-Baptiste Labat observed a dance in Martinique that he found to be overly sexual, and thus opposed to Christianity. The enslaved Africans, by contrast, practiced the dance together with Christianity, even in a shared physical space. Labat wrote:

> [The dancers] strike their thighs, [the thighs of] some beating against the others, that is, the men's against the women's. To see this, it seems that they beat their bellies together, while it is however only their thighs that support their blows. They back away immediately, pirouetting, to recommence the same movement with completely lascivious gestures, as often as the drum

gives them the signal, which it does several times in succession. From time to time they interlace their arms and make two or three turns while always striking their thighs together, and they kiss one another. We see enough by this abridged description how this dance is opposed to decency. . . . They dance it in their churches and in their processions, and the nuns hardly stop dancing it even on Christmas eve upon a raised theater in the choir, behind a railing, which is open, so the populace have their part of these good souls giving witness to the Savior's birth.[18]

Labat's discomfort at the enslaved dancers' thigh contact may belie a deeper anxiety over the their repossession of their moral agency, which extended into their faith as Christians. Through dance one observes the amalgamation not only of African and European elements but also of the secular and the sacred.[19] As I will argue, by reframing the performance practices of storytelling and dance on the intercultural stage, Césaire and Schwarz-Bart encourage reflection on this embodied knowledge that storytelling and dance keep. The playwrights creolize slavery's moral inheritance, adapting it for contemporary life, by dramatizing continuities and discontinuities between the slave past and the present, representing the contradictions of Christian moral codes (as lived by Caribbeans), and renewing the syncretism of Caribbean religion and performance.

Césaire's *L'Enfant des passages*: Mediating Ti-Jean's Legacy

L'Enfant des passages, ou La geste de Ti-Jean is an adaptation of a series of folktales revolving around the character Ti-Jean, a young boy born into poverty (implicitly slavery), who finds fortune and success through selfish means and trickster strategies. Ti-Jean is the human double of Compère Lapin (Brer Rabbit); both characters incarnate trickster strategies, craftiness, and deception.[20] A classic Caribbean hero, Ti-Jean can be found in the works of several Caribbean writers and intellectuals, including a play by the Saint Lucian Nobel laureate Derek Walcott and two unpublished plays by French Caribbean theater artists Luc Saint-Éloy and Élie Pennot.[21] While Ti-Jean is a familiar archetype for virtually all Caribbean artists, Césaire has additionally studied the trickster boy at length in her work as an ethnologist. She recorded some sixty Ti-Jean tales, of which she transcribed three recurring stories in *Contes de mort et de vie aux Antilles*.[22]

Césaire's play is based specifically on the "Enfant terrible" tale, which is a sort of coming-of-age story, whereby Ti-Jean, born into misery, climbs the social ladder to become royalty. Orphaned at the play's opening, he and his older brother, Yinyin, own nothing but a small hut, left to them by their mother. When a rat enters, Ti-Jean quickly burns the hut to the ground, thereby signaling his characteristic insolence and, as Césaire explains, his outright refusal of poverty and misery, which society had already accorded to him.[23] By contrast with his passive brother, who wants little more than a few drinks of rum, Ti-Jean violently disrespects authority, etiquette, and social harmony.

As the boys journey through a series of fantastical lands, they encounter several common characters from Caribbean folklore, anthropomorphized animals whom Ti-Jean unscrupulously insults and murders. He kills the babies of a Tiger family who generously welcome the boys into their home. He insults the Eagle, king of the sky, who graciously picked up the boys, in desperate flight from the mother Tiger. He even kills and eats the Tortoise, an old healer who brought the boys back to life after Eagle dropped them from the sky. At the end of the tale, Ti-Jean saves the kingdom from eternal darkness by killing a seven-headed monster. As recompense, the king gives Ti-Jean the hand of his daughter in marriage, and Ti-Jean becomes heir to the throne. Since the play is based in this well-known tale, I will not analyze the plot but instead focus on the ways Césaire mediates the folktale through drama.

By adapting the folktale for the stage, Césaire reinvents Ti-Jean's cultural meanings, while nonetheless embracing the ambiguities and contradictions of his legacy. She transposes many parts of the folktale directly to the stage. However, she also incorporates elements from other stories, such as the Dame Kéléman witch (a sorceress who eats children and an archetype of Caribbean folklore), as well as her own creative additions. Thus Césaire the playwright becomes an invisible, behind-the-scenes storyteller. Without showing herself onstage, she mediates Ti-Jean's reception by audiences. She updates *débouya* for the present day, while questioning Ti-Jean's contemporary relevance. If Ti-Jean provided a liberating response to the complete submission demanded of the enslaved on the plantation, then what is his social role after abolition and *départementalisation*, when certain traces of slavery nonetheless persist? Refusing to view the folktale as static, Césaire follows Glissant's manifesto, discussed in the introduction, insofar as she cultivates critical reflection surrounding the folk hero.[24] Drawing from both Brechtian theatrical conventions and the performance practice of Creole storytelling, Césaire encourages her spectators and readers to question Ti-Jean's place in the popular consciousness.

Directed by Annick Justin-Joseph, the play premiered at the 1987 Festival de Fort-de-France. Césaire was the scenic designer, and the Martinican actress Sylviane Enéléda (not Christiane Enéléda, as others have mistakenly written) played Ti-Jean. In this premiere performance, tensions between different modes of knowledge production resurfaced. Furthermore Césaire's ambiguous interpretation of Ti-Jean provoked conflicting claims to ownership of Caribbean identity. In a review published in *Antilla*, Chamoiseau criticized Césaire, claiming that she had misunderstood the trickster folk hero, particularly his moral compass.[25]

Dramatizing Débouya

Like the folktale, Césaire's play communicates a lesson in *débouya*, and it refuses Catholicism's preference for the "good" slave. Seemingly anodyne and comical elements—the fantastical folklore world, the ubiquitous jokes, and the moments of vulgarity and uncouthness (for example, Tortoise saves the boys' lives by farting on them)—belie a subversive message. As Césaire notes in her ethnological writings, the lesson of the Ti-Jean tale is that all means of subverting and resisting exploitation (ingratitude, fraud, and even crime) are valid; this is the "ideology of *débrouillardise* [making do with cunning]."[26] While her ethnological writings explore and rationalize this ideology, her play scripts embodied performances, thus showing *débouya* to be a lived experience that will reproduce, renew, and transform itself across time. As Césaire explains in an interview with Stéphanie Bérard, she wanted to show the Ti-Jean story as if it were reality.[27]

To Césaire's mind, the "Enfant terrible" tale offers "a formidable summary of Martinique's history."[28] In contrast with *Rosanie Soleil* and *Mémoires d'Isles*, *L'Enfant des passages* does not recount historical events or lived memories. Rather the "history" to which Césaire is referring is the inheritance of syncretic moral codes, specifically *débouya*. The play highlights several moments in which Ti-Jean refuses dominant moral and social codes. At the play's start, he repeats several times to his brother, Yinyin, their mother's dying words: "The oldest obeys the youngest; the youngest does not obey the oldest."[29] A reversal of the traditional sibling hierarchy, this repetition shows Ti-Jean's disrespect for tradition, positioning him as the authoritative child. These early scenes show Ti-Jean to be braver, more decisive, and more reckless than his whimpering brother.

Ti-Jean's rejection of Christian moral codes becomes clear when the boys encounter a family of Tigers. In Creole folktales, Tigre is traditionally a dupe and thus represents a foil for the trickster characters. Tigre is the gullible and hard-working peasant (or slave), whom Rabbit (the animal version of Ti-Jean) repeatedly tricks.[30] Both Rabbit and Tigre are born into poverty, but the trickster conquers his condition, while the Tiger remains enslaved or exploited. In the play, Césaire emphasizes this connection between Christianity and the Tiger family. When Ti-Jean's brother asks for rum, Mme Tigre responds furiously, "No rum here, little boy! This is a Christian household!"[31] Rum, of course, is commonly drunk at vodou ceremonies and other Creole gatherings. Not only does Ti-Jean disrespect the Christian "good," by which the Tigers abide, but he goes so far as to carelessly murder their Tiger baby while the couple is out working in the fields. Soon after, the boys must flee from a furious mother Tiger. Eagle, the king of the sky, picks them up, but then drops them when Ti-Jean complains of the smell under Eagle's wings.[32]

Tortoise saves the boys, but Ti-Jean eats him. Traditionally Tortoise is an old healer and practitioner of Quimbois, an African-derived form of magic practiced in Martinique and Guadeloupe. In Césaire's play, Tortoise is an Africanist healer but also a Christ figure, and his murder is framed as Ti-Jean's initiation into the adult world and into a syncretic Christianity that he himself possesses. Even though Tortoise has just saved his life, Ti-Jean is hungry and plans to eat him. Shocked by his brother's insolence, Yinyin insists, "I will not devour my savior!"[33] But Ti-Jean, without a care, eats his fill. Disrespectfully he nourishes himself in an outright attack on what Nietzsche would call slave morality (which measures "good" against "evil"), but he also, ironically, performs his Christianity by eating the savior, as in the sacrament of communion. This moment marks the beginning of Ti-Jean's transition into adulthood. Much like the proverb *Débouya pa péché* encourages Caribbeans to make their own rules as Christians, Ti-Jean continues to subvert conventional, social expectations. He is not afraid to call the king an imbecile, and, when offered the beautiful princess, he responds that he is not ready to get married just yet.[34] The king forces him to marry Bebelle, but he does fulfill Ti-Jean's wish for half of the kingdom, to which Ti-Jean is, any case, sole heir.

By staging Ti-Jean's hallmark rejections of conventional morality and social codes, Césaire fosters reflection surrounding the legacy of *débouya*. Spectators are invited to see the archetypal characters of Caribbean folklore with fresh eyes and from a critical distance: to (dis)identify with and judge them rather than thoughtlessly recognizing the old familiar tropes.

109 *Syncretizing Performance and Moral Codes*

In other words, suppressing the mediating figure of the storyteller creates a Brechtian estrangement effect, since audiences are otherwise accustomed to hearing the Ti-Jean tale from the storyteller's mouth. In this case, theatrical mimesis encourages the estrangement effect, which contrasts with common expectations insofar as mediating devices—for example, projections, holding up signs, and addressing the audience directly—are generally understood to serve Brechtian purposes. An embodiment of the dualities that permeate plantation-derived moral valuation, Césaire's Ti-Jean is an ambiguous hero, with a history that some Martinicans might prefer to forget. To extend the analogy with Brecht, one might interpret Césaire's trickster folktale hero as a sort of Mother Courage figure, inasmuch as he is neither moral nor immoral, neither victim nor perpetrator, but rather a reflection of society's subterranean consciousness.

Mediating the Folktale

As an ethnodramatist, Césaire assumes a role similar to the storyteller, mediating the tale's preservation, transmission, and reinvention. In her play, there is no storyteller onstage, and there is likewise no planned or scripted interaction between the performers and the audience, such as the typical call-and-response phrases (i.e., *Cric! Crac!*).[35] However, there are detailed stage directions, which provide readers and theater artists with instructions for making meaning from the play. A detailed list of characters enables Césaire to prescribe an interpretation of the story's symbolism. As she explains, oppression coming from the exterior (presumably France) is represented by the Seven-Headed Beast, whom Ti-Jean kills. The king, for his part, is a *béké* (white Creole) or *mulâtre* member of the planter class.[36] Her women characters, particularly the beautiful but vapid Princesse Bebelle and Mme Tigre, an overbearing mother, offer exaggerations of the generally stereotypical and distasteful portrayal of women in folktales, portrayals that Césaire addresses in her feminist criticism.[37]

Much like the explicit nature of the character list, the play includes lengthy stage directions, which Bérard rightly views as the echo of the lost storyteller's voice.[38] For example, the key scene in which Ti-Jean ungratefully kills the baby Tiger (whose parents generously welcomed the boys into their home) is performed entirely in mime, as scripted by Césaire's meticulous stage directions. She also calls for a number of Creole songs and dances, such as the Dame Kéléman's *lérôz* (*léwoz*) and Ti-Jean's theme song, which bring to life the various worlds infused with Creole culture.[39]

As Césaire herself explains, theater enables her to "retransmit" the fruits of her ethnological research in order to give it back to the Caribbean people.[40] As an ethnologist, she has transcribed Creole folktales and interpreted them in scholarly articles and research presentations. But these works remain confined, Césaire has stated, to a "ghetto of specialists,"[41] contributing mostly to the social sciences in France, where Césaire is part of the prestigious national research organization, the CNRS. As a playwright, however, she works to creatively present her ethnological research to Caribbean audiences and a wider international community. This involves translating the play from one medium to another. As Bérard emphasizes, Césaire fixes the otherwise mutable oral tradition of storytelling on the page, and thus privileges dramatic writing, even as she inhabits an in-between space—between orality and writing, and French and Creole.[42]

But a play is not unlike a folktale, inasmuch as it scripts multiple performances. One night's performance is never the same as the previous iteration. Furthermore the published dramatic text, presented in a bilingual French-Creole edition, allows for stagings in both languages (or mixtures of the two). Thus Césaire's task is to mediate from one performance genre (storytelling) to another (theater). In Césaire's view, Creole storytelling is already a form of theater since the storyteller performs—dances, sings, falls, laughs, and even plays characters.[43] Nonetheless there is a challenge involved in translating the story's tone, since folktales communicate political messages in a dissimulated, veiled, and sarcastic manner, which was suitable to the conditions of enslavement. By contrast with theatrical mimesis, folktales offer what Césaire calls a "distorting mirror, not in the sense that folktales do not tell the truth, but because they reflect a sarcastic image of the truth."[44]

To mediate the sarcastic tone of the folktale, Césaire develops a syncretic presentational style that is at once reminiscent of Brechtian epic theater and Caribbean storytelling. The play's organization, in which Ti-Jean travels (sometimes with his brother and sometimes alone) through various worlds, emphasizes the boys' repetitive acts of walking, stipulated by the stage directions. This device takes them through the fantastical folklore world, and it is also a syncretic semiotic sign. The image of a child walking evokes the *abiku* (in Yoruba) or *ogbanje* (Igbo) child who traverses worlds.[45] It also emblematizes the perpetually displaced state of the descendants of enslaved Africans, who were made to cross worlds during the Middle Passage. Simultaneously this same sign conjures Brechtian epic theater, particularly Ervin Piscator's original German production of *Schweik*, in which the soldier Schweik wanders on a conveyor belt as the world around him is transformed.

The title reinforces this theatrical syncretism. On the one hand, the notion of the "child of passages" alludes to the traumatic, primal passage: the Middle Passage, which gave birth to Ti-Jean and to the Caribbean people. Yet Césaire's intercultural subtitle, *La Geste de Ti-Jean*, which Judith Miller rightly translates as *The Epic of Ti-Jean*, situates the tale within epic theater (and alludes to the Brechtian acting technique of the gestus) as well as the classic traditions of Greek and French Medieval poetry.[46] The play's presentational style and structure mirror the techniques of the storyteller, insofar as the play deploys powerful, multilayered, and sometimes mystifying allegory. This multidimensionality, Miller aptly notes, "establishes a time which is no time (because many times) and a space which is no space (because many spaces)."[47] Like a folktale—and like a Brechtian play—the action is episodic, which Bridget Jones, who attended the original production in Martinique, describes as one of the play's major shortcomings.[48]

The play's organization enables Césaire to communicate an academic reading of the tale, which she has advanced in her scholarly writings, by way of dramatic action. She structures the play's action spatially, distinguishing, as one would four acts, the four worlds that Ti-Jean travels: the real world, the imaginary world, the intermediary world, and the restored (*régénéré*) world. This spatial organization reflects Césaire's psychoanalytic reading of the folktale, in which Ti-Jean releases his destructive instincts in the permissive fantastical folklore world, so that he may enter a regenerated, alternative universe.[49] According to her, killing Tortoise is a sort of psychoanalytical release, which frees Ti-Jean from the oppression he had inherited (by default) in the real world and marks his initiation into adulthood.

Césaire's addition of the intermediary world fills in the transition between the second and third worlds. A short interlude that Césaire invents—the country where people live upside down—dramatizes philosophical questioning of Creole cultural and moral inheritance. In this upside-down world, Ti-Jean encounters L'Homme Inversé (the Inverted Man), who washes up with mud, sleeps standing up outside, and is not ashamed to admit that he is lazy and feeds off others.[50] The Inverted Man believes that everyone in the world behaves like him, but Ti-Jean explains that this is not the case: "There are countries where people live differently!"[51] A classic image of Carnival, the Inverted Man symbolizes the heterogeneity of cultures, as Césaire herself stipulates in the list of characters.⁵² He helps Ti-Jean to see that his own worldview is not the only valid one, serving, in Miller's words, to "foreground the relativity of all truth systems . . . and generally presents Ti-Jean with the possibility of reimagining his entire epistemological field."⁵³

In a play that questions the contemporary relevance of *débouya*, the Inverted Man introduces the possibility of understanding morality as dynamic and malleable—like storytelling and other forms of performance. As the Inverted Man suggests, morality and social codes can be viewed as intercultural, in perpetual translation, and created through encounters between people from different cultures who hold different values. As in Glissant's concept of relational identity, the Inverted Man's heterogeneity has a specific source, the Middle Passage, which becomes clear in his song comparing life to a boat. The Inverted Man sings a song that is in fact one of Césaire's original compositions, created with her cousin.⁵⁴ The song's nautical imagery seems to evoke the Middle Passage, and the refrain repeats, "Head down, feet up."⁵⁵ One might imagine that African captives en route to the New World, uprooted from their homeland, families, and communities, might have felt that all points of reference in life had been turned "upside down." The refrain "Head down, feet up" might also allude to the inhumane horizontal stacking of African captives on the decks of the slave ships.⁵⁶

Although the play is decidedly intercultural in its theatrical syncretism, it privileges Africa as the substrate and source of foundational wisdom. Africanist wisdom is incarnated by the character of Zamba, one of Césaire's creative additions. As Césaire explains in the list of characters, Zamba represents the African ancestors and wisdom: "memory, tradition, and forgotten history."⁵⁷ In her play, Zamba becomes a guide for Ti-Jean; he instructs him to go to the country of eternal darkness, and predicts that he will win the battle.⁵⁸ That Zamba speaks in French in both (Creole and French) versions of the play suggests that the Caribbean people's reconnection with African-derived knowledge will be mediated by the French language and French systems of thought. Zamba's preference for French parallels Césaire's own encounter, as a researcher, with the Ti-Jean tale.

Though Césaire had heard Ti-Jean tales in her childhood, she did not remember the "Enfant terrible" tale until she rediscovered it in France, via African cultures. In Paris she studied African languages and cultures, writing her dissertation on the nomadic Fula (Peul) peoples, and joined a CNRS research group focused on African oral traditions. She subsequently turned her attention from Africa to the Caribbean and was among a small group of Caribbeanists who formed the CNRS group focused on Caribbean cultures.[59] As Césaire studied African folktales, she was struck by their similarities with Caribbean tales. When she examined the Bambara story titled "Enfant terrible," it immediately brought back faraway memories from her childhood. She compared the two stories and was fascinated to note the ways in which the African tale's symbolism had been altered by the Middle Passage and the conditions of plantation slavery.[60] For example, while the boys are spoiled sons of the king in the Bambara tale, they are born into poverty (and probably enslavement) in the Caribbean version. Furthermore, in contrast with the African tale's reproachful attitude toward the trickster boy, the Creole tale values Ti-Jean's disrespect for authority, elders, and tradition. Bambara is not necessarily the story's source culture, since Ti-Jean, like many other folktale themes, appears in stories from across the entire world.[61] But Césaire's primary interest in Ti-Jean was sparked by his passage from Africa to the Caribbean.

Césaire's insistence on the importance of African foundations might prompt spectators and readers to reconsider the Creole origins of *débouya*. While *débouya* may have developed out of the conditions of plantation slavery, we might also understand Creole trickster strategies as derived from the teachings of Esu, the Yoruba trickster and boundary-crossing god who "seemingly delights in engendering chaos."[62] To judge *débouya* by absolute (French, Christian) moral standards is to misrepresent this Creole attitude, much as missionaries and scholars have misaligned Esu with Satan. Esu, an autochthonous and ambidextrous god, is neither good nor evil.[63] Similarly vodou ritual, though it offers ethical guidance, does not distinguish plainly between good and evil.

Both Esu and his Fon counterpart, Legba, find power in ambiguity. They "reveal the sacredness of ambiguity itself and enlarge the total pattern of meaning that is society, shaping it more closely to the design of the cosmos itself."[64] Certainly Césaire's Ti-Jean is not a god, but he transmits Esu's ambiguous stance toward good and evil. Like Esu, he inhabits the crossroads. This privileged (dual) view enables him to guide his spectators and listeners, showing them the need to syncretize moral and religious codes in the Caribbean. Viewed through the lens of these Africanist metaphysical influences, *débouya* is not a shameful product of the plantation's impossible moral universe. Rather it is a creative adaptation (suited to the plantation) of an Africanist understanding of the world's sacred mysteries.

Mediating the tale's reception, *L'Enfant des passages* situates the Ti-Jean story across chronological time by drawing from the synchronic world of folklore, while proposing allegories that renew Ti-Jean's lessons in 1987. For example, the thief who tries to take credit for killing the Seven-Headed Beast is a "Négropolitain"; that is, he is aligned with a group of Caribbeans who immigrated to France and have now returned. The military fish Poisson Armée becomes one of Duvalier's Tontons Macoutes.[65]

With other creative additions, Césaire questions the very concept of time. L'Homme Immortel (the Immortal Man) symbolizes the infinite repetition of time, which he tracks by his own heartbeats. But his insistence on quantifying time has precluded his *experience* of life as time passes. He regretfully admits that he and his heart have become so regular that he has forgotten to measure human experience and emotions.[66] Subtly the Immortal Man raises a question: To what extent is the experience of Ti-Jean still relevant in 1987? Furthermore should the answer to that question be guided by chronological measures of time or by experience and emotion? While Césaire's ethnological studies anchor the Ti-Jean tale clearly within the time of slavery, her play updates its teachings.

Compared to myths of origin, folktales are synchronic, as Césaire the ethnologist has noted.[67] However, as Césaire the playwright shows, we can understand *débouya* and the morality inherited from plantations as diachronic. By way of critical reflection, this inheritance can be harnessed as an empowering, albeit ambiguous, tool in the present. At the end of the play, Ti-Jean gives a speech at his own wedding and implores his guests (and the audience) to remember him: "Today I am celebrated and admired but you must have recognized me: my name is Ti-Jean Lorizon. I am an easily forgotten black man and, as you must also know, nothing is forgotten faster than misery. So, it is to you, all of you, that I toast, to all of us, may we not forget. Let's drink!"[68] By pronouncing his surname, Lorizon, Ti-Jean reminds audience members and readers of another Ti-Jean tale that refers more directly to slavery. The "Ti-Jean Horizon" tale recounts how Ti-Jean tricks the white plantation owner who is his godfather (and biological father, though the white man denies it) into asking for his own death: Ti-Jean speaks so glamorously of the horizon that the *béké* begs his godson to take him there and drop him into the sea.[69]

To remember Ti-Jean is to remember a practice of *débouya* that has endured and transformed across time. This is not a static inheritance but rather a dynamic, syncretic legacy that is just as malleable as a folktale. Césaire suggests that making meaning from Ti-Jean's legacy requires confronting, questioning, and renewing histories of oppression and misery as well as cunning and conquering by means of creative syncretism and the bending of conventional codes.

Staging Theatrical Syncretism

Through her theatrical syncretism, which mirrors the dualities and synchronicities of Caribbean history and contemporary life, Césaire scripts multiple possible performances and cultural interpretations. If *L'Enfant des passages* presents coexisting, sometimes contradictory views of Ti-Jean and his legacy, the premiere performance of the play enacted conflicts and misrecognitions that paralleled Césaire's ambiguous dramatizations of the inheritance of *débouya*. As a critical and multivalent text, the play was a challenge to stage. Theater scholar Bridget Jones, who was present at the original performance, described the play as a profound and ambitious yet somewhat didactic project that demanded critical thinking and patience from its spectators. Comparing Césaire's play to more popular adaptations of folktales for children's theatre, Jones concludes, "Ina Césaire's more ambitious project is to use the intense dramatization already present in storytelling: familiar protagonists, strongly structured plots, concise dialogue enhanced by mime, music and sound effects, in the service of more complex and challenging ideas."[70]

Director Annick Justin-Joseph staged Césaire's text with an emphasis on the actors' physicality. As the artistic director of Martinique's first professional theater, the Théâtre de la Soif Nouvelle, Justin-Joseph headed the Centre Dramatique Régional, tasked with developing Martinican theater and professionalizing local artists. In our interview, Justin-Joseph recalled having worked with Césaire, who was the scenic designer for this play, and who had previously given a workshop to the troupe's actors as part of their training, on the mise-en-scène. Justin-Joseph explained that she sought to evoke the fantastical quality of Creole folktales through an acting style nourished by traditional Caribbean performance practices; specifically she and the actors experimented with voice, song, dance, rhythms, and movement.[71] Speaking of her directorial vision, she cited the proverb *Débouya pa péché* as a trace of the lived history from which Ti-Jean was born: a violent world in which the enslaved, oppressed by an extreme system of domination, has only trickster strategies and insolence as tools to improve his or her situation. She described her theatrical aesthetic as one that allowed little space for pity but, on the contrary, by way of physical expression, ironized the effects and aftermath of a dehumanizing social order.[72] According to

Justin-Joseph, Sylviane Enéléda, who created the role of Ti-Jean, had a knack for conveying the character's instinctive, rebellious provocations. Based on these recollections, it appears that both the actress and the director were sensitive to Césaire's bold vision of Ti-Jean's ambiguous moral stance and aware of the folktale hero's legacy of liberating, cunning, and ruthless resistance.

When embodied directly onstage, without the mediating presence of the storyteller, Ti-Jean sparked impassioned responses. Given that Césaire dramatized Ti-Jean's dualities and contradictions, it is not surprising that spectators reacted to the character in starkly divergent ways. In the local press, Serge Médeuf, a Martinican cultural activist, praised the play for its Caribbean authenticity and described Ti-Jean as dwelling "in the heart of our people."[73] Médeuf spoke of a sentiment of recognition that Martinican spectators experienced upon viewing Césaire's candid dramatization, embodied onstage by Enéléda, of the trickster boy: "We come to terms with ourselves through an acknowledgement of our hero."[74]

In contrast, Chamoiseau criticized what he viewed as Césaire's misapprehension of the folktale hero. Though he congratulated Enéléda and the artistic team for their performance, he responded to the text with dismissive hyperbole. Addressing Césaire directly, he explicitly called the hero "your" (*votre*) Ti-Jean, so as to disidentify with the collective legacy she wished to unveil.[75] He ridiculed Césaire's psychoanalytic reading, which she had included in the program, and stressed that the play was dramaturgically nonsensical and empty, each scene serving no purpose other than to "underscore and underscore again Ti-Jean's incomprehensible, insolent cruelty."[76] Chamoiseau concludes by refuting the authenticity of Césaire's interpretation: "The message of the true Ti-Jean is one of amorality, not immorality."[77]

With this published review, Chamoiseau acted as a gatekeeper of so-called authentic Creoleness. He asserted his authority as a leading Créolist and as a man to delineate what he calls the "true" Ti-Jean. But this understanding of Ti-Jean and the folktale as definable and static actually contradicts the nature of storytelling as a transformative performance practice. Chamoiseau claimed that in the Creole folktale, Ti-Jean only kills, steals, and shows his malice in opportune situations from which he will benefit.[78] To be sure, Chamoiseau is familiar with the Ti-Jean stories, especially the "Ti-Jean Horizon" tale, which he has creatively adapted.[79] Yet with this comment, he discounts the "Enfant terrible" tale, upon which Césaire based her play. Césaire did not invent this tale, as Chamoiseau's comments might suggest, but rather transcribed it after it was told to her by a storyteller in Martinique.[80]

Ironically Chamoiseau's absolute claims reveal his own limited knowledge of Ti-Jean stories as well as his selective disavowal of the fluid nature of storytelling, a tradition to which he views himself as a privileged heir.[81] He even dismisses Césaire's sources, who were traditional storytellers, as "decadent [and] alienated."[82] Did he really believe that the "true" folktale was definable and fixed, and was he unaware of its multiple iterations? Whereas Césaire's play reminds us of the mutability of Ti-Jean, Chamoiseau's provocative comments lay claim to an authentic, essentialist Caribbeanness.

It is possible that Chamoiseau's emphasis on authentic Caribbeanness was facilitated by the premiere performance. Justin-Joseph's staging downplayed African-derived epistemologies and sought to valorize Martinican identity. Actors were dressed not as anthropomorphized animals but as traditional Martinicans. For example, Tortoise, played by José Dalmat, was portrayed as a traditional, elderly *quimboiseur*, that is, a practitioner of Martinican magic and healing practices. Justin-Joseph recalled that Dalmat portrayed the character as old and doddering but absolutely captivating, and insisted that spectators identified with him. It seems that, whereas Césaire had scripted a dual identity—as both the traditional *quimboiseur* and a Christ figure—under the guise of the animal Tortoise, the production team did not embody these multiple layers of meaning onstage. Thus the performance of Ti-Jean's eating of his wise savior might have glossed over certain nuances in my interpretation of Césaire's text. Chamoiseau identified this moment as particularly unsettling.[83]

Other liberties that Justin-Joseph took reiterated Césaire's portrayal of the dualities and ambiguities of syncretic culture. Seven dancers mimed the heads of the Seven-Headed Beast, and the Immortal Man was portrayed as a black man, stuck in a white man's discourse.[84] Justin-Joseph's choice of Enéléda, a woman, in the role of Ti-Jean introduced a disconnect between the audience's expectations (knowing that Ti-Jean is a boy) and his embodiment onstage. I expect this choice would have reinforced Césaire's interest in fostering critical consciousness surrounding the trickster hero and his enduring legacy.

By adapting the folktale to the dramatic form, Césaire's *L'Enfant des passages* asks its spectators and readers to confront, question, and renew Ti-Jean's attitude and acts of *débouya*, which enable him to climb the social ladder by bending moral codes. Through theatrical syncretism,

Césaire emphasizes the tale's changing meanings, as well as the multiple, apparently contradictory cultural epistemologies that inform it. The premiere performance extended and transformed the meanings scripted by Césaire's play. In performance, new dualities and disconnects appeared, while some of the text's complexities were glossed over. Like a storyteller, these theater artists transmitted Ti-Jean's legacy while reinventing it along the way.

Schwarz-Bart's *Ton beau capitaine*: Embodied Lessons in Imbalance

In her first and only play, *Ton beau capitaine*, the renowned Guadeloupean novelist Schwarz-Bart shows a husband reacting to news of his wife's infidelity through dance. In this lyrical play, Wilnor, a Haitian agriculture worker in 1985 in Guadeloupe, listens to an audiotape sent to him by his wife, Marie-Ange, who is at home in Haiti. The couple, likely illiterate, communicates by such recorded letters (as many migrant Haitians at that time did). In the recording, Marie-Ange begins her story quite indirectly and then becomes very frank, revealing that she has had sex on several occasions with the man Wilnor had trusted to deliver his money and gifts to her. She is now pregnant by this other man, and her own efforts to lose the baby have failed. Appealing to an otherworldly interpretation of reality, she explains her actions, describing how this other man was "in reality" her husband.[85] Though she anticipates that Wilnor will want to end the marriage, she implores him to understand her point of view and to embrace *bigidi* (imbalance), more specifically the unresolved tensions at the heart of the play and the couple's situation.

Marie-Ange's voice guides Wilnor to embrace *bigidi*, which he repossesses for himself by way of dance. "This is earth, Wilnor, and on earth everything is whirlwind and smoke. There are none of the straight, wide lanes of heaven. So I beg you, stop shaking your head and figure it out," she tells him.[86] In *Ton beau capitaine*, syncretic performance practices guide Wilnor as he copes with Marie-Ange's transgression of Catholic marital codes. By experiencing physical and emotional *bigidi*, Wilnor is able to confront his reality and forgive his wife. Marie-Ange (according to the stage directions) is not visible on stage, but her voice communicates her emotions and experiences in a palatable way. Wilnor is alone in his modest hut as he makes sense, before the spectators' eyes, of the fact that the world as he has known it and his vision of himself as a man and husband are crumbling. The play might be qualified as a solo performance for Wilnor, but Marie-Ange is an equally significant character.

Ton beau capitaine underscores unresolved tensions between Marie-Ange's presence and absence and between the ritualized communication between the couple and the reality of their physical separation (emblematic of the socioeconomic marginalization of Haitians). If we have faith in the realness of Marie-Ange's ethereal presence, we might also believe her statement that the other man was "in reality" Wilnor. But the play leaves these questions unanswered. During the premiere performance in 1987 in Guadeloupe, the director Syto Cavé (who also directed *Rosanie Soleil*) chose to have the actress playing Marie-Ange present on stage. This choice privileged the otherworldly, ritualized communication between the husband and wife over the physical distance separating them.

Like *L'Enfant des passages*, Schwarz-Bart's play uses theatrical syncretism to question and revive the life lessons and practiced behaviors inherited from the plantation. By creatively reassembling historical time and performance conventions, Schwarz-Bart renews the inheritance of *bigidi* through deliberate acts of interculturalism. By building upon the work of other critics who have foregrounded her use of song and dance, and extending insightful readings by Alvina Ruprecht and Stéphanie Bérard of the play as structured by vodou ritual, I investigate the ways in which Schwarz-Bart counts dance as a source of historical knowledge and a relay for transformative, social change.[87] As I will argue, by scripting continuities and discontinuities between the slave past and the time of writing, 1987, the play questions and renews the legacy of *bigidi* for readers and spectators.

Symbolically the couple stands in for all of Haiti and for all African diasporic populations, disenfranchised by slavery's aftereffects and wielding the powers of syncretic religion and performance. The play's use of interculturalism—its incorporation of Noh theater and ballet—blurs the binary opposition between the individual (associated with Western drama) and the collective of African-derived rituals. As Schwarz-Bart explains in her author's note, the dances "have a dramatic function; they express the different moments of an individual drama rather than a collective state of mind."[88] But Wilnor and Marie-Ange's individual drama calls to mind the collective inheritance of slavery's sexual systems of subjection. As a black woman who has transgressed sexual and social norms, Marie-Ange's body is implicitly subject to the moralizing gaze of (white) patriarchy. Since her body is absent from the stage, it is not Marie-Ange but Wilnor who must confront and cope with slavery's aftereffects.

Scripting Wilnor's Syncretic Dances

Dance punctuates and conveys Wilnor's reaction to his wife's infidelity. As Wilnor listens, Marie-Ange's voice recounts the initial coercion (according to her, the affair began because the man threatened to withhold Wilnor's money if she did not give in to his sexual desires) and then a long list of days on which she willfully welcomed this man into her bed. At first Wilnor is emasculated. He rejects his wife and reaffirms his threatened masculinity through insults and lies. He calls her a "tramp," and he fabricates stories of his own sexual exploits. Feeling duped for having remained faithful, he calls himself "the biggest jackass under the stars." Soon after, however, he *dances* his way to a new understanding of the situation. The *léwoz*, Creole quadrille, and an unnamed closing dance, which Bérard associates with the *nago* or *congo* of vodou, prepare and enable him to forgive his wife and to embrace his role as father of the child.[89]

At the end of the play, Wilnor records a sympathetic letter to Marie-Ange, in which he instructs her to take good care of herself and the child. "Remember," he tells her, "I want that child as beautiful as an angel." As Wilnor signs off from his letter, he no longer knows how to name himself in relation to his wife, who had called him the handsome captain of her ship earlier in the play. Now doubting his command—and his normative masculine identity—he repeats the appellation several times, as if trying to find the correct enunciation. At the play's close, he poses this name—his image in his wife's eyes?—as a repeated question: "Your handsome captain?"[90]

Dance is scripted into the text as a tangled, syncretic theatrical sign that transforms Wilnor's experiences of reality. As Schwarz-Bart stipulates in her author's note, dance and song constitute an "additional language that the main character has at his disposal."[91] This notion of the additional (*supplémentaire* in the original French) language clarifies that dance, like the African-derived talking drum, has communicative powers.[92] *Ton beau capitaine* is divided into four tableaux, the last three of which end in a dance. At the end of the second tableau, as Wilnor dances, he expresses his inability to deal with Marie-Ange's infidelity and his feelings of being overwhelmed. "Enough, god, enough!" he pleads: "Enough angles!"[93] Here he dances a *léwoz* dance, the most common rhythm of the Guadeloupean *gwo-ka*. Associated with African-derived dances, the *léwoz* involves small hops side-to-side, experimentation with imbalance, and communication between drummer and dancer. As in the proverb *Bigidi pa tonbé*, the *léwoz* dancer is *bigidi*, but he never falls.

In other words, Wilnor tests and loses his balance, but he never touches the ground.

Through subsequent dances, Wilnor comes to embrace physical and emotional *bigidi*. When the third tableau comes to a close, Marie-Ange has confessed to multiple sexual encounters with the man. Furious, Wilnor dances a Creole quadrille with three invisible partners. An Africanist adaptation of European contredanse, the quadrille resembles a square dance and is led by a caller or a *commandeur*, which was also the term for the slave driver. In this dance, Wilnor becomes his own caller, as Ruprecht has also noted,[94] calling out insults to Marie-Ange and the lies he told of his own sexual exploits. Yet these expressions of his frustration lead him to question his perception of reality. "Life, O.K., life; but where is life, where is it?"[95] As Bérard argues, this dance reveals Wilnor's profound solitude and his social status as a migrant worker, inasmuch as he is forced, like his enslaved ancestors, to obey the caller.[96] But the dance also appears to transform and even liberate him. "What a beautiful quadrille!" he exclaims at the start of tableau 4. "A bit more and I would have flown away."[97] In the embodied experience of dance, he remembers to embrace precarious imbalance, which empowers him to face his destitute reality. To feel the earth, he scrapes the ground with his foot and then expresses sympathy for Marie-Ange. He records a response, in which he divulges his feelings and fears honestly. As the play closes, he dances again to the *ti-bois* percussion sticks. His last dance is desperate, violent, and brief.

The play's structure can be broadly understood as a quadrille dance, for which Marie-Ange represents the *commandeur*. In other words, metatheatrically the play is one long Creole quadrille, in which Marie-Ange calls Wilnor's emotional journey. Her voice, whether real or imagined by Wilnor, guides him. Though the caller doubles as the slave driver, in the African diasporic context the *commandeur* might also constitute a transposition of the African talking drum, whose full communicative possibilities did not survive the slave trade.[98] Both Marie-Ange and then Wilnor assume the role of the *commandeur*, but Wilnor is always guided by his wife's voice.

Marie-Ange is well positioned to call Wilnor's life choices, insofar as she is an inspiring singer and storyteller. In fact Wilnor used to say that the first time Marie-Ange sang a song for him was the moment that "convinced [him] to tie the knot—a winged woman who sings like a dragonfly despite the tons of sorrows dragging on her skirts." Her repeated song, which is heard from the tape recorder and later emanates audibly from Wilnor's mind, the last time distorted by a synthesizer, affirms the value of Creole, embodied knowledge. "Moin n'aime danser, moins n'aime chanter" (I like to dance, I like to sing), she sings in Creole.[99]

Through dance Wilnor achieves ritualized communication with his wife that, though one might question how real their communion is, exceeds the possibilities offered by the tape player. Ruprecht contends that Wilnor experiences something similar to a vodou possession, which is also a sexual possession, triggered by his wife's voice.[100] This ritualized performance of the couple's communication and love is premised on the embodied Creole concept of *bigidi*. Choreographer and dance scholar Léna Blou has theorized *bigidi* by studying the symbiotic relationship between the dancer and drummer of the *léwoz*. According to her, this vital communication between dancer and drummer, also called *makè*, involves mutual improvisation, syncopation, surprise, frenzy, and silence. Léna Blou's dancer comes close to falling, but his or her (though traditionally the *léwoz* is danced by men) body never touches the floor.[101] This moment of communication between dancer and drummer might be compared to *rasé* in Haitian vodou, when a *lwa* mounts a devotee like a horse. Both *rasé* and the communication between dancer and *makè* are characterized by precarious balance and imbalance.

Wilnor's ritualized communication with his wife is cast as a religious experience. He attributes his coming to terms with Marie-Ange's actions by way of dance to the grace of the gods. He records this response:

> Marie-Ange . . . (*Pause.*) When I read your cassette, for an instant, one brief instant, I almost doubted you. (*Pause.*) For one instant. (*Pause.*) Fortunately, I've always been appreciated by those in heaven. That's my good fortune, that I'm appreciated by those who live on high. And here I was believing without believing, doubting and not doubting, when all of a sudden I heard your voice right here at my house, your voice coming and going just like in bygone days, and suddenly I saw the light: it came to me! It may have been a kind gesture, an act of mercy from St. Anthony of Padua. Or perhaps it was a god from Guinea, Legba, oh yes, or Damballah Ouedo, or perhaps Erzulie Freda Dahomey, the good, dear one. I don't know who it was, I don't know, but I've always been appreciated by those up there. And suddenly I saw the light, bright and clear.[102]

Though the audience cannot hear or see Marie-Ange's response to Wilnor's spiritual transformation, it is clear that he becomes closer to her emotionally through ritual. Both theatrical and religious syncretism enable Wilnor to join in solidarity with his wife, even as the couple remains separated by physical distance and socioeconomic immobility. Wilnor's Creole dances are akin to vodou, insofar as it is *the movement itself* that brings about the restorative balance that the ritual seeks.[103] That balance is necessarily *bigidi*, and it must be continually reinvented.

To dynamically revive Caribbean dance, Schwarz-Bart draws from several cultural performance forms, including the conventions of ballet. "Traditional Haitian dances are choreographed in a way that they become balletic," Schwarz-Bart writes in her note.[104] In other words, ballet, though it will not likely appear on stage in a recognizable form, will be used to remodel traditional Haitian dances. Some might argue that ballet, a style commonly thought of as classical dance, serves to elevate or uplift so-called primitive Caribbean dances by way of the European form. However, the use of ballet here does not Westernize Caribbean dance so much as renew its creative acts of syncretism.

The incorporation of the ritualistic tradition of Japanese Noh theater deepens *Ton beau capitaine*'s theatrical syncretism. In fact it was Noh that inspired Schwarz-Bart to translate what she sees as the dynamic relationship between gestures and words, central to Caribbean lived experience, for the stage.[105] She discovered Noh by way of the French director Jean-Louis Barrault's work on the twentieth-century Noh-inspired writer Yukio Mishima.[106] Schwarz-Bart's short note stipulates that the play should create through music and dance an "imaginary space, like the one in the Noh theatre, for example."[107] Ruprecht points to several aesthetic similarities between Schwarz-Bart play's and the Noh tradition, such as the two characters and the fact that percussion (in this case, rhythms from the *ti-bois* percussion sticks) accompanies and guides Wilnor's movements.[108] As Kathleen Gyssels writes, "Just as in the Nō tradition, the text of the play and the movements of the actors make manifest unspoken and imperceptible realities."[109]

With such deliberate acts of interculturalism, Schwarz-Bart crafts a Caribbean play—a written text—that relies on Caribbean dance in order to make meaning in both text and performance. In other words, though it may seem counterintuitive, Schwarz-Bart's published play privileges embodied knowledge, which it scripts through its meticulous stage directions. As Schwarz-Bart explained in an interview with *France-Antilles* at the time of the play's premiere, for this particular story she needed to turn to theater because "in our culture, body language and gestures often replace the textual; how we move and hold our bodies is just as important as what we say. The two work together."[110]

The new, imaginary world of the play is created through the playwright's intentional cultural reassembling. By remixing performance traditions, literary genres, and cultures, *Ton beau capitaine* forges a syncretic form of theater that is suited to Wilnor and Marie-Ange's story. Rather than evoking a return to authentic Creole or African-derived dance, Schwarz-Bart updates these syncretic dances by incorporating new cultural influences. This act of creative reassembling is also reflected in her use of syncretic language. The play is written in lyrical French, but its rhythms and turns of phrase are reminiscent of the Creole language. It is not surprising that Max Kenol, the Haitian actor who originated the role of Wilnor, has translated the play into Creole (*Kapten Wilnor!*).[111]

Slavery's Echoes and Reverberations

The inspiration for *Ton beau capitaine* knocked on Schwarz-Bart's door one afternoon at her home in Goyave, Guadeloupe. She has recounted on at least two occasions that her Haitian neighbor, an agricultural worker, asked to borrow her cassette player since his was broken. He needed to listen to a letter from his wife and respond to her right away, before a friend—an intermediary who carried the tapes between them—returned to Haiti the next day.[112] Touched by the injustice of her neighbor's situation, Schwarz-Bart immediately scratched a few pages upon his departure as a way of easing her bitter feelings.[113] The play born from those pages acknowledges the reality lived by the neighbor and so many Haitian migrant workers, who are impoverished, stateless, and separated by distance (brought about by socioeconomic marginalization) from the ones they love.

In Guadeloupe, Wilnor relives, with a difference, the experiences of his enslaved ancestors. He is an agricultural worker who must leave his home in order to make money from rigorous, manual labor under austere living conditions. As an individual character, he is representative of a larger collective; his is a common scenario for Haitian men.[114] As Wilnor explains to Marie-Ange, in Guadeloupe he is "their black man, the black man's top black man," or the "nègre des nègres" in the original French.[115] Schwarz-Bart's play recognizes the systemic racism and disenfranchisement Wilnor suffers. At the same time, like the Ti-Jean folktale and play, *Ton beau capitaine* refuses pity. Instead it shows Wilnor's and Marie-Ange's dignity and emphasizes the resilience of Wilnor's love for his wife. The play is a tribute to the magnificent power of Haitian song, dance, and religion. These embodied inheritances, like the legacy of Ti-Jean, are tangled up in slavery's systems of oppression and aftereffects.

Ton beau capitaine situates the power of Wilnor's syncretic dances within a picture of slavery's echoes and reverberations. With lyrical language that moves seamlessly between the slave past and the present situation, the couple laments their physical separation. Wilnor repeats that separation is an ocean: "Ah yes, separation is a big ocean, which muddles everything; it shakes things up like a cupful of dice. You start seeing with your ears, hearing with your eyes and feeling with your hands things that are very far away, while the things nearby that surround you, you notice no more than a puff of smoke."[116] His description of separation as a grand, disorienting, distorting ocean parallels the Inverted Man's maritime song ("Head up, feet down") from *L'Enfant des passages*. This metaphor, along with the nautical imagery Marie-Ange utilizes to describe sensually her love for Wilnor, evokes the Middle Passage, as Judith Miller has also noted.[117]

Wilnor has experienced a rupture that is both analogous to and critically different from the trauma experienced by African captives, uprooted from their homes in Africa and forced to journey across the ocean to their enslavement in the Caribbean. As Sandra Adell remarks, Wilnor's exile was "imposed on him by an economic order that makes it all but impossible to eke out a living in his own land."[118] Since the play is set in 1985, the Duvalier reign of terror may have affected his decision as well. Though Wilnor finds work in Guadeloupe, Guadeloupeans scorn him, treating him as "their black man," despite the fact that Haitians and Guadeloupeans share the aftereffects of slavery's systems of oppression. As Marie-Ange asks, "Is there no country on earth where we Haitians can work and send a little money home from time to time without being reduced to formless gusts of air?" Her news that Wilnor's friend has drowned along with some thirty other Haitians on a raft destined for the United States reiterates the parallel between past and present.[119]

While slavery's aftereffects confine Wilnor to a destitute daily reality, he simultaneously internalizes colonial scripts of masculinity. He left Marie-Ange to make money, and it is his money that he thinks of almost immediately after learning of her infidelity. This money was meant to provide for a comfortable life and happy retirement with his wife, but it also serves, psychologically, to affirm Wilnor's masculinity. Marie-Ange remembers how his ambitions grew: "You went away to earn a wayfarer's daily bread. But you—whose soul was always full of marvels—you wanted daily bread, the whole loaf, and more. You spoke of striking it rich; you dreamed of buying land by the river and a cow." In earlier tapes, Wilnor has claimed to be "as fat as a prize pig and living in a large house with pillars, a big front door, and so many electric light bulbs that [he was] floating among the stars." This description, which Marie-Ange plays back to Wilnor, suspecting it to be untrue, starkly contrasts with the one-room shack, furnished with only a mattress on the ground and a soap box, stipulated in Schwarz-Bart's description of the set.[120] In the first part of the play, Wilnor strives to assert his manhood, which he measures by the standards of white patriarchy. His fantasy of the house with pillars recalls a plantation, as Miller has also noted.[121] And the pig, a common character in Caribbean folktales, is representative of the white plantation owner. In contrast, Marie-Ange urges him to creatively reinvent his role as man and husband. She implores him (perhaps belatedly) to return to Haiti: "I beg you on my knees, come back. Come back my dear Wilnor, even if it's without the land, without the cow."[122]

Whereas *Rosanie Soleil* and *Pension les Alizés* put women's stories and bodies center-stage, Schwarz-Bart's play foregrounds Caribbean men's lived experiences and their performative agency in bringing about transformative social change. Like Césaire and Condé, Schwarz-Bart undoes the logic undergirding the binary opposition of the Caribbean woman as either a passive victim or a willful seductress and instead explores the ambiguous ways in which slavery's aftereffects inflect the couple's lived experiences and social roles. Yet in contrast with the female leads considered in chapter 1, Marie-Ange's body is absent from the stage. "By metonymically displacing Marie-Ange to the cassette," Miller argues, "Schwarz-Bart has uncannily side-stepped the difficult issue of the 'male gaze,' and the possibility that the public has learned to see as a gendered male, always positioning the staged female character as its object of desire."[123] In so doing Schwarz-Bart additionally frees Marie-Ange from the *moralizing* gazes of her audience. Marie-Ange subverts both the image of the "good" black Christian woman and the misogynist label "tramp" (which Wilnor himself uses before his transformative dance). Refusing both assaults on her moral autonomy, Marie-Ange occupies a new role that bends dominant moral codes. Yet it is not Marie-Ange but Wilnor whose body appears onstage and who must creatively reinvent the couple's love story.

Even as Marie-Ange's story provocatively defies social scripts for Caribbean women, her adultery parallels the experience of her enslaved female ancestors. Black women often had multiple sexual partners due to sexual exploitation and rape, while black men were denied sex by an institution that figured the white plantation owner as the (incestuous) father to a "family" including his slaves. Marie-Ange does report having been coerced by Wilnor's supposed friend.

"Listening to [Marie-Ange]," John Conteh-Morgan writes, "gives one the impression that words are inadequate to express her complex and complicated emotions in which intense erotic desire, guilt, *and* innocence . . . are combined."[124] When Marie-Ange tells of the man's second visit, she betrays her attraction to him, a "handsome young man wearing a jacket. . . . But who cares how he was dressed?"[125] However, her desire does not make her a willful adulterer, for, as she explains, this man became a proxy for her absent husband. Couching her story in the third person, she explains:

> Suddenly, she is moved, so deeply moved on seeing the young man, she has the impression that he's bringing her some of her husband's world, some of his scent. She looks at the eyes which had seen the absent one. (*She gives a small sob.*) She touches the hands which just the day before, just yesterday, had touched the absent one. My God! (*She gives a small cry.*) . . . Finally, she's completely confused (*She sighs.*) and ends up in bed with the young man. (*She sobs.*) But, in reality, it's her husband. (*Pause.*) Seemingly with the young man, but in reality lying by her husband. Do you understand, Wilnor? *Do you understand?*[126]

Marie-Ange will admit shortly afterward that this "grand, pious lady, with a soul as pure as spring water, truly someone exceptionally moral" at the heart of her story was in fact her, and she will go on to insist that this other man was in reality her husband.[127]

To what reality is she referring? Could Wilnor and his friend have been the same person through a ritualistic possession? To what extent is the couple's reality in the 1980s distinct from their enslaved ancestors' lived experiences? Schwarz-Bart's textual tricks raise many questions, and, as Jones says, "there are no easy re/solutions."[128] Slavery's echoes and reverberations blur the spectator's points of historical and moral reference. The play replaces those expectations with unresolved tensions and continuities and discontinuities, which enable new, syncretic meanings.

Wilnor's (dancing) realizations lead him to abandon his money. "Marie-Ange's adultery," according to Miller, "gives Wilnor the chance to dig out from under the weight of the myth of money and possessions."[129] Though he has been sending most of his savings to Marie-Ange, he has been keeping a small amount for himself. As he confesses to her that he too feels lonely, he takes out this money and gradually burns each of the bills, naming the dreams he abandons with each one: a veranda, a couple of goats, a cow, enameled dishes, a white dress with matching shoes, and a "radio/cassette recorder that we would own so we wouldn't have to rent one and we could listen to all the cassettes of all of these years—all the years on cassette."[130]

After he has abandoned his ambitions and relinquished his previous ideas of masculinity, Wilnor hears Marie-Ange's voice again, first distorted, as if run through a synthesizer, and then closer and closer to him. Now he records his gratitude to the gods and his understanding of separation's distorting effects. He forgives Marie-Ange and even accepts the other man's child, whom she had tried desperately to abort, as his own.[131] The play ends on a precarious yet vital note—an expression of *bigidi*. Wilnor and Marie-Ange have reconstructed their family, and the child (perhaps an allusion to the *bolôm* of Caribbean folklore) will live. Though Wilnor is not the biological father, they are a family—*bigidi*. But given that Wilnor has now burned all his money, how will he finance a return trip to Haiti? Will he be reunited with his beloved wife in the physical space and time of this world?

Performing Unresolved Tensions

Ton beau capitaine premiered in 1987 at the Centre des Arts in Pointe-à-Pitre, Guadeloupe. Directed by Syto Cavé, the production starred Haitian actor Max Kenol in the role of Wilnor and the Guadeloupean Mariann Mathéus as Marie-Ange. The Guadeloupean theater artist and cultural activist Michèle Montantin, who recalls having encouraged Schwarz-Bart to complete the script, produced the play.[132]

Ton beau capitaine poses challenges to artists insofar as it scripts unresolved tensions between the ritualized communication that Wilnor achieves through dance and the reality of the distance separating husband from wife. In other words, there is a disconnect between Wilnor's rather bleak, material reality and the otherworldly space of love and divine communication that he inhabits throughout the play, guided by his wife's voice. Ruprecht calls this central dynamic a "tension between the visible and the invisible."[133] In an interview with *Le Quotidien* when the premiere performance was showing in France, Schwarz-Bart explained, "Without dreams, life would be impossible on the islands. The real is constantly compensated by dreams."[134] *Ton beau capitaine* teaches, much like the Creole proverbs, that apparently contradictory experiences coexist. Wilnor, as in vodou ritual, inhabits multiple realms simultaneously: dream and reality, visible and invisible, ritualized communication and separation. The play's ending, while joyous and triumphant, is also profoundly ambivalent and bittersweet. During the premiere performance, onstage conflicts and misrecognitions materialized these unresolved tensions.

Given Cavé's interest in incorporating vodou ritual into theatrical production,[135] it is not surprising that the premiere performance privileged Wilnor and Marie-Ange's otherworldly, ritualized communication. This was largely due to Cavé's somewhat controversial decision to physicalize the voice of Marie-Ange by placing the real actress's body visibly onstage. As he explained in an unpublished interview with Ruprecht, Cavé chose to show Marie-Ange onstage as she records her letter to Wilnor because it enabled the artistic team to work between the two physical spaces (Guadeloupe and Haiti) and to reinforce the couple's relationship.[136]

Staging choices established a performance space that operated between different spatial, temporal, and epistemological realms. The set design emphasized Schwarz-Bart's nautical imagery, with a boat hull and mast represented onstage; Mathéus, who performed much of the play from within a large hexagonal fishing net, initially entered through a tear in the netting.[137] While Mathéus spoke some of Marie-Ange's lines aloud, others came from the cassette recorder. This choice both acknowledged and blurred the temporal distinction between the time of her recording and the time of Wilnor's listening. It also showed Marie-Ange in her dual, self-contradictory relationship to Wilnor, simultaneously mediated by the cassette recorder and live, that is, speaking to him from a shared physical and temporal realm.

Mathéus recalled working to communicate this apparent contradiction. By way of her voice, song, and stage movement, she sought to show both the distance separating herself from Wilnor and their proximity. Though she did move about, she did not interact with Kenol or address him directly; instead she spoke to what she described as the image she had of him in her mind.[138] Nonetheless she used her voice in order to guide Kenol and bring him closer to her. This performance technique, which she developed in collaboration with Cavé, required a great deal of concentration.

In line with his emphasis on ritualized communication, Cavé foregrounded Caribbean performance practices. As a director, he valued input from the actors and sought to create his mise-en-scène from the gestures and diction they proposed.[139] Mathéus drew from her rich knowledge of Creole songs, vocal traditions, dances, and performance cultures. She recalled infusing her performance with song, entering, for example, singing a song about the Haitian village Jacmel. Likewise contributing his experience with Haitian performance cultures, Kenol performed the dances called for in the script. According to Mathéus, he more or less followed the stage directions. She remembered his experimentations with imbalance (*bigidi*) during the *léwoz* as well as the images of vodou he conjured through his acting style. For example, she recalled that, in a striking moment, he drank and then spit out rum in a picturesque fountain that caught the glimmer of the stage lights.

Cavé's choice to put Marie-Ange onstage has sparked lively disagreements. Ruprecht contends that it radically transformed Marie-Ange's signification.[140] The author, Cavé, and Montantin had many discussions about whether Mathéus should appear onstage.[141] In our interview, Mathéus maintained that, though Schwarz-Bart disagreed with Cavé's preference at first, the author changed her mind upon viewing the actors' performance.[142] Montantin cites a text written by Schwarz-Bart in which she emphasizes the interplay between the visible and the invisible as well as the real and the imaginary. "One possible way of staging the play is to adorn the female voice with a body," she ambiguously concludes.[143] Gyssels claims that the play "has never been staged exactly as [Schwarz-Bart] would have wished: there have always been significant discrepancies between her vision and the interpretations of the various theatre companies."[144] It seems that Schwarz-Bart, who privileges the epistemological disconnects scripted by her text, sees multiple interpretive possibilities. But perhaps a single mise-en-scène cannot render the multivalent complexities of her syncretic play. Noël Jovignot's 2004 production (with Ruddy Sylaire and the voice of Yna Boulangé), like Françoise Kourilsky's staging at Ubu, used only a voice.[145] Cavé, for his part, has affirmed that, if given the opportunity to restage the play, he would choose again to put the actress onstage.[146]

After opening in Guadeloupe, the premiere production traveled to the International Francophone Cultural Festival in Limoges, the Chaillot National Theatre in Paris, Morocco, Martinique, and Haiti. Reviews consistently displayed an appreciation for the gravity and injustice of Wilnor's situation and an admiration for the vibrancy of Haitian culture and love. Overall the critics, many of whom expressed enthusiasm that the renowned novelist had turned to theater, lauded the play.[147] A reviewer for *Le Figaro* called it "a love story stronger than absence," while another for *Libération* exclaimed, "Simone Schwarz-Bart knew how to give a dimension of complete dignity to Haitians, too often scorned in Guadeloupe."[148]

Mathéus recalled that the warmest reception the artistic team received was in Haiti. She told me that at that time there were regular blackouts, with only two hours of electricity each day and no water. Cavé tried to arrange to do the play during those two hours of electricity, but a blackout nonetheless occurred during the performance. It cut off the recording of Marie-Ange's voice, which was playing from the cassette recorder, since Cavé had decided that some lines would be spoken onstage by Mathéus and others would be recorded. Mathéus recounted that, without losing a beat, she began speaking the recorded lines, which she had never expressly memorized, realizing that she knew all of them by heart. In the absence of stage lighting, she and Kenol performed with only Wilnor's small gas burner lighting them. Mathéus told me that, at the play's close, several spectators told the artistic team that their most striking performance actually took place that evening of the blackout. Insofar as the actress replaced the cassette recorder, it would seem that, during that blackout performance, Marie-Ange's presence decidedly overpowered the distance separating her from Wilnor. If spectators preferred that performance, perhaps this was because it decidedly favored Marie-Ange's presence, thus offering a more unqualified tribute to the resilience of Haitian dance and song, and the couple's love.

In text and in performance, *Ton beau capitaine* shows syncretic dance and religion not as a memory from the past to be preserved but as a vital, changeable, embodied experience that will continually be updated to suit the present day. Marie-Ange's unborn baby, whom Wilnor evokes just before signing his letter at the play's close, represents a future that is ripe with possibilities yet also (perhaps troublingly) unknown. The ending of *L'Enfant des passages*, Ti-Jean's wedding, likewise suggests a baby to come, even as Ti-Jean reminds spectators to remember him—particularly those aspects of his personality and story they might wish to forget.

As opposed to recovering a memory of the past, these plays (like those discussed in previous chapters) privilege creolization as a historical, performative process. Performance enables the playwrights to engage simultaneously with the past and present, while gesturing toward an uncertain future. With meticulous stage directions, Césaire and Schwarz-Bart update and adapt the Creole performance practices of storytelling and dance for the stage, thereby mediating, questioning, transmitting, and reinventing the meanings of *débouya* and *bigidi*. Through theatrical syncretism, they renew their enslaved ancestors' legacy of bending moral codes and embodying empowering, creative syncretic religion.

The multivalent plays examined in the first half of my book reject fixed identities and histories while exposing continuities and discontinuities between the slave past and the present, between text and performance, and between various cultural forms of knowledge production. The plays stage creolization insofar as they show—in both thematic content and aesthetic form—performance's transformative power to reproduce and remake Caribbean culture, identity, and subjectivity. When performed onstage, new synchronicities, tensions, and conflicts emerge in artists' interpretations and audience responses. Such onstage surprises might appear to oppose the authors' intentions. But inasmuch as creolization is a reinvention often involving contradictions, unforeseen outcomes, and inassimilable grit, I have theorized such unexpected and unsettling choices as material realizations and extensions of the creolizing impulses the playwrights script.

The history of unforeseen staging choices in the performance of plays by French Caribbean women authors does not end here but rather travels to the United States. When performed in this circum-Caribbean context, what new meanings did these plays accrue? What new syncretisms might those performances have created? What tensions, contradictions, and ambiguities might have resurfaced? And how might an analysis of these performances prompt us to consider yet again how theater enacts a performative process of creolization that develops from, builds upon, questions, and transforms the legacies of slavery and colonialism? I will take up these questions in the second half of my book.

4 Diaspora Performances at Ubu Repertory Theater in New York

Following their premiere performances in Martinique, Guadeloupe, or France, all seven plays examined in previous chapters promptly traveled to the United States. Five of these were translated into English and staged by the foremost Franco-American theater, Ubu Repertory Theater. Plays by French Caribbean women were quite popular at Ubu.[1] The theater was an important site for the promulgation of black francophone theater as well as French-language works by women. In the United States, fixed ideas of blackness and womanhood impinged upon the reception of the plays, and artists sought to offer an authentic portrayal of the Caribbean. Cultural signifiers (of Caribbeanness or Indianness) were portrayed as static, and the plays' presentation of Caribbeanness as fluid and ever-changing was thus downplayed. However, French Caribbean women's plays were remade and reinvented in ways that challenged the cultural and theatrical status quo in New York. These performances—by way of their heterogeneous reception by artists and audiences—further creolized the plays.

In this chapter I focus on Ubu's restaging of three French Caribbean women's plays in English translation: Dianne Kirksey-Floyd's production of Césaire's *Island Memories* (*Mémoires d'Isles*) in 1991; Ntozake Shange's 1993 staging of Césaire's *Fire's Daughters* (*Rosanie Soleil*); and in 1997, Ubu founder and artistic director Françoise Kourilsky's production of Dambury's *Crosscurrents* (*Lettres indiennes*). How were these women-authored, francophone, Caribbean plays translated, publicized, performed, and received by Ubu in New York? In this and the subsequent chapter, I draw from various sources to provide nuanced and educated responses to that central question. In Ubu's archives, I have consulted documented traces of the performances, photographs, playbills, director and stage manager notes, costume and design sketches, lighting plots, and correspondence. I have also conducted personal interviews with the playwrights, directors, actors, designers, attendees, and translators. These sources have enabled me to reconstruct the performances and to draw several informed speculations regarding the plays' cultural reception by artists and audiences in New York.

By way of this performance analysis, I theorize a second phase of creolization in theater by French Caribbean women, which I call "diaspora performances." Building upon theorizations of theater as a "cultural translation,"[2] I interpret these performances as cultural translations of the source (French Caribbean women's) play in a target (U.S.) culture, specifically the context of Ubu. Yet I also acknowledge the ways in which Ubu sought to muddle the binary of source and target culture, and I am attuned to elements that transcend the distinction—for example, the shared transatlantic history of slavery as well as the performance practices (such as African-derived song, dance, and storytelling) that have circulated and developed throughout the circum-Caribbean.

While the United States and the Caribbean share a history of slavery, performances at Ubu point to the ways slavery and its legacy are differently configured in different cultural contexts. Generally speaking, in the United States at the end of the twentieth century, the concept of race took center stage in representations of slavery's legacy. Gender, another highly charged signifier, was interpreted not as intertwined with slavery's legacy but as a separate consideration. Intersectional enactments of Caribbean culture (Dambury's portrayal of the overlapping black and Indian diasporas) were difficult to translate at Ubu.

Ubu's Cultural and Pedagogical Context

Ubu Repertory Theater was founded in 1982 by Françoise Kourilsky, a French woman of mixed French Catholic and Hungarian-Russian Jewish origins and a professor of American theater. Between Ubu's founding in 1982 and its closing in 2001, it translated and staged 251 plays by French-language playwrights in New York. Ubu was as much a cultural hub as a theater company. It organized roundtables, panels, and cultural events and reached out to local communities, teachers, and students. Ubu was also a translation center: it commissioned translations, which were completed in consultation with the playwrights. Having developed a reputation for its translations, Ubu regularly received contemporary French-language plays from writers and their agents.[3] Before proposing full-scale performances, Ubu often organized staged readings of the translations. Though most performances were in English, a few plays were staged in the original French.

Ubu was originally conceived as a means of promoting French-language theater in the United States, but it quickly became a meeting place for international and interracial artists. Kourilsky made a point of inviting every French-language playwright featured by Ubu to New York (and financing their trip), so that they could attend rehearsals, meet the New York artists involved in restaging their plays, and of course watch the performances. Ubu's New York–based artists were encouraged to bring their personal experiences of their own culture, race, gender, and sexuality to the staging. While the textual translation was intended to remain meticulously faithful to the original French, Ubu's artists were asked to transcend—through the performance—the play's original language in order to enact transnational solidarities. While Ubu's publicity labeled the plays "francophone," meaning part of a larger French-language cultural empire, their performances by Ubu artists served to simultaneously recode them under cultural signs familiar to New Yorkers.

Ubu packaged, publicized, and performed its plays under multiple cultural signs. To make French-language plays relevant to U.S. audiences, Ubu categorized them following U.S. identity politics, calling the plays "black theater," "theater from the West Indies," "international women's plays," and "gay plays," among other labels. Yet even as Ubu marked the plays according to the culture, gender, sexuality, and race of the playwright, it also privileged theater's ability to reach universal audiences. Kourilsky stated in an interview at the time, "I look for plays that are rooted in their culture and therefore have universal meaning."[4]

Ubu's investment in universal humanity was evident not only in its rhetoric and publicity but also in its intercultural theater aesthetic. The core team of designers met at Ellen Stewart's LaMama ETC, and the costume and set designers, Carol Ann Pelletier and Watoku Ueno, directed an intercultural company called Yara Arts Group. Ubu's theatrical aesthetic of interculturalism emphasized placelessness and mobility. In concert with this investment in intercultural exchange, Ubu sought to perform international blackness. Working to foster links and commonalities across the African diaspora, the theater commissioned African American directors and actors for Caribbean plays, contacted black and African studies departments at local universities, and sent invitations to public schools in New York's majority-black neighborhoods.

Ubu's performances, roundtables, and publications were associated with knowledge production and cultural activism. The theater had a particularly close relationship with universities; in addition to French and theater departments, it collaborated with black and African studies as well as women's studies departments. It is perhaps for this reason that audiences and artists interpreted Ubu's plays within the framework of the international black diaspora or international feminist solidarities. Alongside this emphasis on transnational performances of race and gender, cultural particularities of the Caribbean island from which the play hailed were also performed.

Diaspora Performances

Diaspora generally refers to the experience of dispersal from the homeland and integration (coupled with the experience of discrimination) into a host culture, while maintaining a relationship (real or imagined) with the homeland. But the term has also been used to describe the transnational links and commonalities among diasporic populations in different parts of the world. Ubu's performances of French Caribbean women's plays in New York can be theorized as diaspora performances on several different levels. First, the performances simultaneously glance back toward the Caribbean homeland and relocate the plays in the U.S. context, the host culture. Second, they foster solidarities and affiliations among different diasporic populations, notably francophone Caribbeans and African Americans. Third, they enact unresolved, ongoing tensions between mobility and fixity, sameness and difference. Diaspora identities, as Stuart Hall theorizes, are "those which are constantly producing and reproducing themselves anew, through transformation and difference."[5] Diaspora performances are likewise constantly translating, transforming, reproducing, and reinventing the meanings of the play. The performances at Ubu led artists and spectators to delimit ideas of fixed and so-called authentic Caribbeanness, blackness, and womanhood, as well as to rediscover the instability of creolization as a transformative, performative process.

In line with Paul Gilroy's concept of the black Atlantic, the term *diaspora* is commonly used to refer to links, commonalities, and a sense of belonging among African-descended peoples across the world. Deploying the chronotope of the slave ship, Gilroy argues that routes (as opposed to roots) unite the inheritors of the transatlantic slave trade's triangulated crossings and shared suffering.[6] Extending Gilroy's claims, Brent Hayes Edwards emphasizes that sentiments of African diasporic unity do not preexist black international intellectual and artistic collaborations. Rather Edwards theorizes diaspora as a practice akin to translation. Black international unity is always formulated in a specific historical moment and always articulated across difference. Edwards conceives of diaspora as a conceptual prop or prosthetic that enables African-descended peoples to form a seemingly cohesive unity across gaps and uneven ground. Hence diaspora necessarily involves misapprehension, misunderstanding, and mistranslation.[7]

To speak specifically of diaspora theater one must also consider the particular convergences and divergences of text and performance. In his introduction to *Totem Voices*, an anthology of black diaspora plays (including translations), Paul Carter Harrison argues that African-derived performances transcend questions of linguistic translation. To illustrate this point he recounts a personal anecdote: During a trip to Brazil, he was invited to hear a black Bahian poet read his poetry. Harrison found that he understood the poet's performance in Portuguese—a language Harrison does not speak or read—much better than in the poet's halting efforts to translate his words into English. In the Portuguese poetry performance, Harrison heard the poet's "word/song," that is, the performative and musical force of the black diasporic artist's word, which, according to him, transcends language through the affective technique of ritual.[8] Given these variable and flexible conceptions of diaspora performance, as Sandra Richards points out, the question of what is at stake in invoking diaspora inevitably arises: "What commonalities of experience are diaspora people recognizing in each other? What experiences of difference are they ignoring in order to produce unity, and for what purposes is this unity being mobilized?"[9]

Diaspora performances necessarily involve conflicts and tensions. I attempt to excavate such conflicts and use them as an opportunity to analyze this theater as a global cultural practice. Rustom Bharucha has advanced a similar approach,[10] and it is indebted to Arjun Appadurai's hallmark theorization of the contemporary globalized world as constituted in tensions between cultural homogenization and heterogenization. According to Appadurai, scholars can effectively explore the cultural dimensions of globalization with a focus on the "disjunctures and difference" that inevitably occur in the interactions between global flows.[11] Accordingly I will emphasize moments of conflict and misrecognition in these plays' stagings at Ubu, which reveal illuminating interpretive tensions in Ubu's system of theatrical meaning making as well as in the dramatic texts themselves.

Ubu's diaspora performances involved both textual and extratextual acts of translation that served to negotiate the opposing poles of sameness and difference, mobility and fixity, old and new. They were differently negotiated in various semiotic realms: set, costume, sound, and lighting design; blocking (that is, the actors' movements and their spatial relationships to one another), the individual actor's body language and gestures, and choreographed dances; and the spoken text and the actors' performance of it. Because Ubu was a repertory theater, that is, a company devoted to the promulgation of French-language plays in the United States, it prioritized what Kourilsky and her team perceived as fidelity to the cultural particularities of the text. At the same time, however, Ubu used performance to enact black diasporic unity and other global cultural affiliations. In each of the case studies that follow, misrecognitions and conflicts point to the contingency of cultural and social signifiers, namely Caribbeanness, race, and gender, and the ways in which slavery's legacy is differently configured in different national contexts. Such tensions in meaning making are inherent in diaspora performances, and they also reinvent the unpredictable process of creolization the playwrights foreground in their plays.

Césaire's *Island Memories*: Behind the Black Sister Connection

The 1991 production of Césaire's *Island Memories* illustrates that Ubu's diaspora performances of French Caribbean plays were necessarily multivalent, coded and received under multiple cultural signs, and always undergirded by tensions and coexisting oppositions. As discussed in the introduction, after attending a rehearsal of her play in English translation in New York, Césaire reported having experienced a black diasporic sister connection.[12] My interviews and consultation of archived accounts have revealed that several participants and spectators experienced similar sentiments of unity and communion during the New York production. A deeper look into that production and its cultural reception, however, reveals that such sentiments of unity were necessarily propped up across tensions, misrecognitions, and conflicting claims to cultural authenticity.

Sentiments of Unity

Island Memories is based in ethnographic interviews with elderly Martinican and Guadeloupean women and constitutes a tribute to Césaire's own grandmothers, two real women whom Césaire knew well. Nonetheless Ubu's reinvention of *Island Memories* felt authentic and deeply meaningful to Césaire. Carmen De Lavallade, the dancer and choreographer, played Aure, and Ernestine Jackson played Hermance (figure 6).

Figure 6. Ernestine Jackson as Hermance and Carmen de Lavallade as Aure in Ina Césaire's *Island Memories*. New York, 1991. (Photograph by Chester Higgins Jr., © Chester Higgins Jr./chesterhiggins.com; Ubu Repertory Theater Collections; courtesy of the Bibliothèque nationale de France)

With these women, as well as the African American director Dianne Kirksey-Floyd and choreographer Marie Brooks, Césaire experienced a "black sister" connection. It is worth quoting Césaire's tribute once more:

> A great emotional moment: my arrival in the simple room of a dance school where they are having the last rehearsal of my play, *Mémoires d'Isle*, which has become *Island Memories* for the occasion. . . . In this room where they are rehearsing my text in another language, I am welcomed with great warmth, a little like a sister they always knew. They are not discovering me, they are recovering me. These truly are my black American sisters, whom I am finally meeting. . . . The last rehearsal begins and it is immediately the magic of true theater: the two magnificent actresses are instantly transformed into old women, at once strong and broken (my own grandmothers, gone now). Despite my precarious English, I recognize each phrase, each expression, each gestural tic reminiscent of the dear old ladies to whom this text is dedicated, and tears come to my eyes.[13]

Césaire describes feeling, through theater, a powerful sense of unity and communion but also a return, a sense of original belonging. Her testimony introduces an apparent contradiction between translation and shared origins. But this tension is in fact definitive of both Caribbean and diaspora identities and experience. As Hall explains, the "common history—transportation, slavery, colonisation—has been profoundly formative. For all these societies, unifying us across our differences. But it does not constitute a common *origin*, since it was, metaphorically as well as literally, a translation."[14] In other words, reinvention, translation, and transformation return Caribbean people to their formative histories. At Ubu, Césaire may have felt reminded of the performative process of creolization that drives her play.

Césaire was not the only spectator to feel emotional communion during Kirksey-Floyd's production of *Island Memories*. Archived stage manager notes describe the audience as "wonderfully responsive,"[15] a sentiment emphatically echoed by Ronnie Scharfman, now a retired professor of francophone literature at SUNY Purchase, who attended the production in New York. Scharfman told me the performance of *Island Memories* was one of Ubu's most spectacular and compelling productions, and she believed that audience members were quite touched. "[Aure and Hermance] could have been two African American women in the South," she said; "the whole audience related."[16] Scharfman's remark is revealing of Ubu's universalist goals. That she evokes two African American women from the South recontextualizes Césaire's ethnographic play within U.S. histories.

As Césaire continues her tribute, she sends out a "thought for the translators, Judith Miller and Christiane Makward, who found a way of uncovering, even beyond language, the depths of authentic Martinican culture, always oscillating between laughter and tears."[17] Makward and Miller are French professors and experienced translators, but in Césaire's view, it is not their linguistic mastery alone that gives them access to Martinican authenticity, since she stipulates that the translation goes "beyond language." This rhetoric recalls Harrison's conclusion that the black diasporic artist's word transcends language through the affective technique of ritual. But Makward and Miller's successes in capturing authentic Martinican culture cannot be attributed to their cultural inheritance or racial identities and experiences, since they are both white women. Indeed according to Césaire, the translators' whiteness, the black diasporic performance, and the authentic re-creation of Caribbean culture all coexist.

These memories of affective unity raise the question of who has the authority to delineate and judge an "authentic" performance of Caribbeanness. Césaire states that Caribbean authenticity is located in the words of her play. It is Césaire herself, as playwright, who embraces the role of cultural expert. This role was offered to her by Ubu: when she arrived in New York in 1991, she quickly became an authority, visiting Rutgers and SUNY Purchase and participating in a roundtable at the West Indies Festival. It follows that she herself judges whether the translators and theater artists succeeded in authentic re-creations of her play. While this understanding of Césaire's authorial (and authoritative) voice was very much in line with Ubu's processes, it appears inconsistent with the collaborative creation of Césaire's ethnodramaturgical play.

Caribbean Memories, Universal Performances

Island Memories was staged as part of Ubu's first West Indies Festival in 1991, alongside *A Tempest* by Aimé Césaire and *The Hills of Massabielle* by Maryse Condé.[18] In an artistic director's note in the program, Kourilsky boasted that these three plays showcase the diversity of contemporary West Indian drama. She grouped them together because all three "belong to what I would call a lyrical theater in touch with the very problems of our times. They are deeply rooted in the reality of the West Indies, and, precisely because they express the individual and social history of a specific group, they have a universal appeal."[19]

Aimé Césaire's dramatization of black diasporic unity in an adaptation of Shakespeare's *Tempest* melds cultural references from the Caribbean, Africa, and black America. The play is better known than Ina Césaire's *Island Memories*. Yet a reviewer for *Theater Week* preferred the daughter's play to the father's. The reviewer is critical of Ubu's production of *A Tempest* (directed by Robbie McCauley) for its lack of drive, or what she calls its "centripetal force," but she describes the New York run of the daughter's distinctively Caribbean play as "all too brief."[20] The popularity of *Island Memories* at Ubu suggests that, as Kourilsky's rhetoric stipulates, the cultural particular might yield a so-called universal performance. To be sure, Ubu's production of *Island Memories* illustrates how Caribbean particularity, when performed in a transnational context, can give rise to new, transnational performances of race and gender that transcend Martinican locality. But these diaspora performances were necessarily undergirded by tensions and misrecognitions. Drawing from multiple subjective accounts, photographs, and notes and sketches generated during the artistic process of staging the play, such as the stage manager's promptbook,[21] I will chart Césaire's text's mediation by Ubu.

Though Ubu preferred to craft its own translations, Makward and Miller had already translated the play by the time Ubu elected to produce it. Specialists in French-language theater and the French Caribbean, Miller and Makward had slotted Césaire's play to appear in their critical anthology of plays by French-language women playwrights.[22] Their translation was meticulously informed and annotated, partly thanks to discussions with the original actresses and the playwright. Nonetheless the translators confronted challenges in making their knowledge of the play and its cultural context resonate in the United States.

While Césaire's text is written in French and Creole, Makward and Miller decided to translate both languages into Standard English rather than use a language with an analogous relationship to Standard English, for example, anglophone Creole, such as Jamaican pidgin or Patois, or a black American dialect, in place of the Martinican Creole. In their published text, lines originally written in Creole are italicized to indicate the original language. However, audience members, unlike readers, had no clear means of distinguishing between lines in Creole and in French. The subversive potential of the Creole language was thus lost in translation, though Césaire's meanings were nonetheless enacted through different onstage signifiers. This linguistic subtlety likewise modifies the presentation of the two women. Aure, the highly educated schoolteacher, is associated with the French language in the original play; in the English translation, her linguistic affiliation is boiled down to the more general question of intellectual and cultural capital.

As in the original production, the play made meaning primarily by way of the juxtaposition between the two main characters. In her directorial concept, Kirksey-Floyd emphasized the relationship between the two women and the way their different lives and experiences come together throughout the course of the play.[23] The director explained to me that as part of her extensive research on the script, she studied Martinique's complex relationship to France, but the actresses on stage could not perform these cultural complexities—that is, the island's unique departmental status. It was the two half-sisters' relationship, Kirksey-Floyd emphasized, that enabled the audience to embrace the play on an emotional level.[24]

In Ubu's production, differences relating to class and complexion upstaged Aure's and Hermance's differing access to Frenchness. The actresses' different skin tones facilitated audiences' understanding of the two women's different social statuses and reinforced the play's consideration of internalized racism in the Caribbean. A reviewer for *Black Ivory* stated that the play "juxtaposes the similar, yet divergent lives of two sisters in a world where skin tones determine public response."[25] As this account suggests, even without the distinction between the French and Creole languages, Aure's social class as a *mulâtresse* and society's preference for lighter skin likely resonated with spectators in New York. The class difference between the women also appears to have been communicated to audiences. A critic with *Theater Week* emphasized the two women's different socioeconomic classes, calling them "two grand old ladies of Martinique, one rich and one not-so rich."[26]

Claims to Authenticity

On- and offstage cultural signifiers served to imbue Césaire's play with a performance of Caribbean authenticity. An early press release echoes the tricks of the tourism industry by proclaiming that the "sights and sounds of the French West Indies will come to Manhattan."[27] Taking a more educational approach, the festival's program billed *Island Memories* as "an oral history of Martinique."[28] For their part, the production team worked to perform authentic Martinican cultural traditions in New York. By relying on her research and the expertise of her designers, Kirksey-Floyd sought to steep the production in the culture of Martinique.[29] Notes housed in Ubu's archives document these efforts.[30] Acting as both music consultant and choreographer, Marie Brooks incorporated and taught traditional Martinican dances, such as the Creole Waltz, the Haute Taille, and the Mazurka Piquée. The team likewise searched for original Creole songs called for in the script. Sound designer Michael Sargeant played recordings of these songs (rather than compose new intercultural "world" music, as musicians did for many of Ubu's productions, including the two analyzed below). Additional sound cues that played throughout the performance, such as crickets and waves, served to create an atmosphere of the Caribbean and perhaps to figure the Caribbean as a tourist destination to be visited by way of the performance. This might even have served to increase business for the main financial supporters of Ubu's West Indies Festival, the Martinique Tourist Office and the Regional Agency for Tourism Development (in addition to the regular support provided by the Cultural Services of the French Embassy).[31]

Césaire herself cinched Ubu's performance of Martinican authenticity. When she arrived in New York, she taught the actresses several of the Creole songs called for in her script and instructed them in tunes to be hummed throughout the performance, including the "Bouch nou oxydé" song. As discussed in chapter 2, the actress and musician Mariann Mathéus recalled having composed this song based on her ethnographic interviews. This history of the song's composition is not evident in the published play, which refers to the song as if it preexisted the play's creation. At Ubu the "Bouch nou oxydé" song became part of Césaire's repertoire of cultural practices that could be taught to the African American actresses and labeled as authentic Martinican culture. Like all Ubu playwrights, Césaire acted as a cultural ambassador. Ubu's archived notes and correspondence confirm that she visited U.S. universities and gave interviews with the *Amsterdam News* and the magazine *Black Ivory*. It seems that, in New York, Césaire was viewed as the authority delineating authentic Martinican culture as well as the single author to a play that had originally been a collaborative, collective creation.

Césaire's text—which was written after the performance was created—held ultimate authority at Ubu. Kirksey-Floyd studied the play and remained carefully faithful to the text.[32] Based on various photographs and documents consulted in Ubu's archives and my personal interviews, I gather that the tone of *Island Memories* at Ubu was light and joyful and thus corresponded with Césaire's desire to move past difficult memories. The past was "surpassed," to quote an addition Césaire made when she rewrote the prologue.[33] Humming, dancing in their seats, the two women elegantly incarnated Césaire's grandmothers. For instance, as the stage manager notes document, Jackson twirled her cane above her head. Carol Ann Pelletier's costumes contributed to this tone. As she-devils of Ash Wednesday, the women look joyful, not a bit dangerous or menacing (figure 7).

In another point of contrast with the original production, traditional gender roles were respected. In the original production, Donzenac was dressed in drag, in line with Caribbean Carnival traditions, for the first part of the prologue. At Ubu both women wore their she-devil costumes, which accentuated their femininity, throughout the entire prologue. As in the original production, the women were dressed in black and white, showing that they are companions of Baron Samedi. Yet they nonetheless looked opulent and carefree, wearing one white shoe and one black. Their costumes also featured question marks made of glitter, in order to call attention to the fact that they speak in riddles.

Besides Césaire, several prominent African American artists assumed the role of cultural expert for Ubu's West Indies Festival. Ubu's

Figure 7. Ernestine Jackson and Carmen de Lavallade as the she-devils of Ash Wednesday in Ina Césaire's *Island Memories*. New York, 1991. (Photograph by Chester Higgins Jr., © Chester Higgins Jr./chesterhiggins.com; Ubu Repertory Theater Collections; courtesy of the Bibliothèque nationale de France)

roundtable at the festival was devoted to teaching Americans about the Caribbean. Césaire sat alongside Ntozake Shange, Amiri Baraka, and Laurence Holder; though they did not attend, Toni Morrison and Derek Walcott had also been invited to participate.[34] At that time Ubu was not viewed as a "black theater" by all or even most African Americans in the New York *theater* scene, but it had established a reputation as a theater doing (political) work relevant to the black diaspora. Through this roundtable, Ubu performed its identity as a black diaspora theater and invited Caribbean and African American artists to perform their shared cultural expertise.

Simultaneously coded as Caribbean, black, and universal, the production of *Island Memories* at Ubu was permeated by diverse claims to Caribbean authenticity. While the play was based in numerous Caribbean women's real-life testimonies, at Ubu—even more so than in the original production—theater artists took on the roles of cultural mediators and experts. Whereas the original production code switched in its address to Caribbean spectators, familiar with the reality portrayed, and French spectators, whose implicit cultural hegemony was challenged by the performance, at Ubu the play was made equally accessible to audience members of all cultures, races, and nationalities. As a consequence, the play's subversive political message, rooted in the references to Caribbean Carnival, was mitigated. However, Césaire was empowered to "recover" her blackness and the process of translation and reinvention at the heart of Caribbeanness. It also appears that U.S. spectators related to their history of slavery in ways that seemed both familiar and new to them.

Ubu's diaspora performance positioned the text as simultaneously distant from and familiar to the target culture. The production team balanced between communicating the cultural and historical particularities of Césaire's ethnology-based play and finding analogies relevant in the New York context. While Ubu's artists sought to make *Island Memories* accessible to American audiences, they also preserved certain elements of the original context, employing what Gershon Shaked has called a "productive misunderstanding" that asks audience members to respect difference, reminding them that the culture portrayed onstage is not entirely accessible to their own limited view.[35] By staging the play under multiple cultural signs—Caribbean, black, and universalist—Ubu counted slavery's legacy as the inheritance of its entire interracial audience rather than as a separate African American history. At the same time, however, the production preserved the Caribbean setting, and thus distanced Aure's and Hermance's memories from the United

States. While this distancing enabled a performance of Caribbeanness in New York, it may also have mitigated the play's subversive potential of unmasking and challenging French (white, male) monopolization of the category of the universal human. Such transformations and misrecognitions crucially coexist with the affective performance of unity described by Césaire and others.

Césaire's *Fire's Daughters*: Conflicted Receptions of Race and Gender

Two years later, in 1993, Césaire's *Fire's Daughters* was directed at Ubu by Ntozake Shange. Ubu presented the play under multiple cultural signs. Even more so than Césaire's ethnographic drama, her glimpse into the everyday lives of four black women at the time of the Southern Insurrection was recoded and interpreted in New York as a "black" play. And, probably because of Shange's reputation as a black feminist theater artist, many saw *Fire's Daughters* as a black feminist piece. In selecting Shange to direct, Ubu framed and encouraged a black feminist reinvention of Césaire's play, which was also facilitated by Ubu's intercultural aesthetic and undergirded by conflicts and misrecognitions. On several occasions, Ubu associated French Caribbean women's plays with Shange's theatrical black feminism, particularly her renowned choreopoem and Broadway success (it was a Tony nominee) *For colored girls who have considered suicide / when the rainbow is enuf.* In addition to collaborating with Shange herself, Ubu appointed two actresses from the play's original cast, Seret Scott and Saundra McClain, to direct other productions of French Caribbean women's plays.[36]

The Text

For the translation of *Fire's Daughters*, Ubu commissioned Judith Miller (cotranslator of *Island Memories*), who crafted a textual translation that was meticulous yet accessible to readers unfamiliar with Caribbean culture. As she had done with Makward, Miller provided detailed historical and cultural notes and found English-language equivalents for an array of distinctively Martinican proverbs, foods, and customs. To take a specific example:

> ROSA: Les contes d'aujourd'hui ressemblent à ceux d'avant. Si j'ai bonne souvenance, ça commence toujours par la faim. . . . (*Geste significatif.*)
>
> EÏNA: Et ça se continue par la fin. . . . (*Geste significatif.*)[37]
>
> ROSEANNA: Today's tales are just like yesterday's. If I remember right, they

always begin by "lending an ear." (*Gesture.*)

ANNAROSE: And they always go on till the "ending is near." (*Gesture.*)[38]

Where Césaire's veiled use of French communicated the Creole tradition of storytelling, Miller found an analogy in English. To give a bit of context and a brief review, Sister Smoke draws from the tradition of Creole storytelling in order to conflate several stories of antiblack oppression and resistance across time. In the quotation above, to reinforce Smoke's account and to register their own commitment to subversive resistance, the sisters allude to the Creole tradition of storytelling. The original text turns on the word play between *faim* (hunger) and *fin* (end), which are homophones in French. Acting as storytellers, the sisters perform their cultural literacy and knowledge of Caribbean folktales, which almost always begin with the theme of hunger. Miller's analogy in English is a catchy rhyme that enables the sisters to perform their knowledge of storytelling without alienating readers and spectators unfamiliar with the specific Caribbean cultural literacies necessary to grasp the original. Similar to the case of *Island Memories*, the subversive potential of the Creole language and culture is somewhat mitigated in translation, but the themes of resistance and storytelling are clearly communicated to U.S. readers and spectators.

Despite these challenges, Miller's translation reproduces (with a difference) many of the play's core qualities and meanings. Capturing Roseanna's fierceness, Annarose's quiet contemplation, their mother's overly protective love, and their neighbor Sister Smoke's storyteller-like subversive riddles, Miller compellingly rendered the emotional ties and interpersonal relations among Césaire's family of revolutionary black women. Miller also took care to reproduce the culturally expansive qualities of the play, such as the parallels that Césaire establishes between Martinique and Haiti. In her translation of the title, Miller alluded to the transatlantic history of enslaved people's resistance to their masters. Whereas *Rosanie Soleil*'s eponymous heroine (Roseanna Sun in translation) is a historical figure that very few people outside Martinique would recognize, Miller's title, *Fire's Daughters*, recalls the flames of slave resistance (the burning of plantations, which took place not only under slavery but also after abolition—notably throughout the course of the Southern Insurrection). Moreover the title emphasizes the theme of matrilineal filiation and the female-centric family unit at the heart of the play. Thus the translated title anchors Roseanna's story within a larger community of women of color who resisted slavery, colonialism, and the forms of structural antiblack discrimination that endured after abolition, like the legal practices that spurred the Southern Insurrection. The title also follows the playwright's own author's note, in which she stipulates that the play is not a historical drama and insists upon the juxtaposition between the twins, Roseanna and her anagrammatic sister Annarose (a character Césaire invented).[39]

Once again the diaspora performance was achieved through various onstage signifiers, which exceeded the communicative possibilities of the text alone. A reviewer of Ubu's anthology, Harold A. Waters, described *Fire's Daughters* as dramatizing a history specific to Martinican culture that, he predicted, would not be of interest or accessible to U.S readers and audiences: "Although it is interesting to learn of 1870, I would not say this is an exportable play."[40] Based on my research in Ubu's archives and personal interviews, however, it seems the production presented the play as quite exportable: resonating across the black diaspora and reaching Ubu's heterogeneous audiences. Onstage, dance and performance were used to recast the local Martinican history of the Southern Insurrection as a global, black diasporic, feminist narrative.

Both Francophone and Black Diasporic

At Ubu *Fire's Daughters* was simultaneously framed as part of the Francophonie (that is, the global community of French-speaking people and countries) as well as a black diasporic play. It was scheduled as the first production in the Ubu International 1993 Festival. Kourilsky specified in her note as artistic director that this festival was "not organized around a specific country, theme or region."[41] *Fire's Daughters* was slotted alongside Belgian playwright Paul Emond's *Talk about Love!* and the Quebecois Michel Marc Bouchard's *The Orphan Muses*. In the press, Kourilsky and her team emphasized that this multicultural program was a testament to the diversity of French cultures and to the broad compass of the French language.[42] Nonetheless the plays were grouped into categories in Ubu's publicity, and *Fire's Daughters* was among the African diaspora plays that Ubu labeled in the festival's program "New Plays from the West Indies and Africa."[43] The two other plays, which were given staged readings rather than full-scale productions, were Michèle Césaire's (Ina's sister) *The Ship* and Koffi Kwahulé's (Ivory Coast) *That Old Black Magic*.

Shange was invited to direct *Fire's Daughters*. Kourilsky explained that she made this choice because Shange was an important and intelligent theater artist and was interested in Martinique.[44] Ubu might have also selected Shange in order to frame Césaire's play as an international black feminist piece and to draw African American spectators; Shange certainly had cachet. Casting choices made by Shange and casting agent Adrienne Stern embodied diasporic connections among French Caribbean and African American women. African American actresses Harriet D. Foy, Darlene Bel Grayson, Alene Dawson, and Cee-Cee Harshaw played the family of four Martinican women (figure 8). Saundra McClain, who had acted in *For colored girls*, was the assistant director. The production appeared in a listing of Beth Turner's *Black Masks* and the "Community Affairs Calendar" of the *Amsterdam News*, both of which would have drawn African American spectators.[45] Shange, as a previous participant on various panels and workshops at Ubu, including the roundtable at the 1991 West Indies Festival, had already been involved in the company's efforts to cultivate black diasporic links between African Americans and black francophone playwrights.

Perhaps because she was familiar with Ubu, or perhaps because she was already preoccupied with finding a black diasporic mode of expression across languages,[46] Shange embraced her role as cultural mediator. Knowledgeable about the French Caribbean, she situated the play within a Martinican intellectual tradition even as she stressed generalizable African diaspora themes. "In much the same way the island of Hispañola, Haiti, spawns painters and heroes," she wrote in her director's note, "poets and thinkers bloom in Martinique."[47] Before reading Miller's translation, Shange studied Césaire's original play in French and Creole. In place of some of Miller's anglicizations, she chose to retain certain Creole phrases. For instance, where Miller had replaced the *soukougnon*, a Martinican transformative werewolf-like figure, with *hobgoblin*, Shange chose to keep the Creole image.[48]

Shange's directorial vision put a distinctively Martinican culture on stage, while at the same time seeking transcultural aesthetic experiences with which African Americans, white Americans, and other interracial and international audiences could identify. In Shange's understanding of Césaire's play, it was the history of shared violence and domination that made it relevant across black diasporic populations. As she said to a journalist at the time, "There is a very precarious nature to these lives, and the violence of their lives ricochets all over Africa and the Caribbean." Additionally articulating her directorial concept under a black feminist sign, she stressed the unification of domestic and political spaces, calling the play "a presentation symbolically of the elements of struggle of people whose battlefield is their own house."[49] Following

Figure 8. The cast of Ina Césaire's *Fire's Daughters*: Alene Dawson as Annarose, Cee-Cee Harshaw as Roseanna, Darlene Bel Grayson as Mama Sun, and Harriett D. Foy as Sister Smoke. New York, 1993. (Photograph by Dominique Nabokov; Ubu Repertory Theater Collections; courtesy of the Bibliothèque nationale de France)

Césaire's stage directions, the actresses performed characteristically gendered chores, such as hanging the laundry, as they slyly alluded to the Insurrection (See figure 9).

The Intercultural Elements

Shange communicated her concept to Ubu's regular designers, who integrated her black diasporic vision with their intercultural artistic process. Ubu's longtime set and costume designers had met Kourilsky through collaborations at LaMama ETC, and, as mentioned earlier, they ran their own intercultural company, Yara Arts Group. In personal interviews, they each recounted their memories of their artistic processes. Set designer Watoku Ueno commonly integrated his skills as a painter into his set design and crafted work that was influenced by the aesthetics of his native Japan and characteristic of the intercultural genre associated with such artists as Peter Brook, Ariane Mnouchkine, and LaMama founder Ellen Stewart. In line with Shange's concept, Ueno crafted a set that blurred the boundary between public and private spaces. He

Figure 9. Mama Sun and Sister Smoke speak in code while Annarose hangs the laundry in Ina Césaire's *Fire's Daughters*: Darlene Bel Grayson, Harriett D. Foy, and Alene Dawson. New York, 1993. (Photograph by Dominique Nabokov; Ubu Repertory Theater Collections; courtesy of the Bibliothèque nationale de France)

placed domestic symbols within an outdoor space that included trees, grass, and a blue sky. His artfully constructed tree represented an outdoor space but simultaneously served as part of the house.[50] For a backdrop, he painted hills, which recall the dwelling of the runaway black man, whom the women protect, and the legend of maroon resistance to slavery (figure 10). However, Ueno's hills did not seem to be in the Caribbean; in fact they looked like they could be the Himalayas.

Having previously researched traditional Martinican dress for *Island Memories*, longtime costume designer Carol Ann Pelletier did cultural research into the traditions of vodou for this production. On Shange's recommendation, Pelletier read Zora Neale Hurston's memoir *Tell My Horse: Voodoo and Life in Haiti and Jamaica*. She also discovered the writing of experimental American filmmaker Maya Deren, who collaborated with Katherine Dunham and documented Haitian vodou rituals in ethnographic film.[51] Also a member of Ubu's regular crew, set designer Greg MacPherson thought about the "warm" atmosphere of New Orleans in making his color choices.[52]

Figure 10. Watoko Ueno's set of Ina Césaire's *Fire's Daughters*. New York, 1993. (Photograph by Watoko Ueno; private collection; courtesy of Watoko Ueno)

Although she was happy with the production at large, delighted with the actresses' work, and grateful to Kourilsky for selecting her play for a full-scale English-language production, Césaire told Stéphanie Bérard that she was disappointed with the intercultural aesthetic. In a published interview, she called the aesthetic "folkloric"; she associated Ueno's hills with a touristic, cartoonish map of Martinique and found Pelletier's choice of traditional Caribbean dresses better fit for old, chic ladies than for her revolutionary women.[53] Perhaps Ueno's symbolic expression of the history of maroons was too delocalized for Césaire's artistic sensibilities. Pelletier's period costumes, in contrast, might have struck Césaire as too specific—in contradiction, perhaps, with her trans-chronological dramaturgical approach, or misaligned with the women's social class.

Césaire's comments to Bérard suggest that she may have worried that Martinican culture had been simplified or even exoticized. *Folklore* as Césaire uses it here does not refer to the African-derived and Creole popular performance practices that she, as an ethnologist, researches and documents. Rather, as Édouard Glissant defines it in his essay on theater, folklore is a static trace of a culture from the past. In order to create a people's political theater, according to Glissant, folklore must be transcended and moved past.[54] To avoid folkloric portrayals of culture on display, Ubu sought to re-create each play within the New York context. In this case, the aesthetic re-creation may have struck Césaire as already fixed or relying on signifiers that she perceived as simplistic, exploitative, or incorrect. This folklorization of culture, which makes Caribbeanness static and unchanging, undermines the fluidity of Césaire's creolizing aesthetics.

Ubu's intercultural process was also evident in the music. Whereas the production of *Island Memories* sought to reproduce traditional Martinican music, *Fire's Daughters* involved new compositions that combined delocalized music with specific Caribbean elements. The artists worked with a Brazilian musician and composer, Mauro Refosco, whose music Kourilsky characterized as "world music," explaining that he integrated Brazilian and Caribbean musical traditions into his new intercultural compositions.[55] Notes housed in Ubu's archives reveal the production team's efforts to reproduce traditional songs. A note from Césaire provides the lyrics and tunes for several songs (it refers to an enclosed cassette tape), such as the folksong celebrating the legendary slave Lindôr and a song for Vaval (king of Carnival).[56] She recommends that the team seek out Haitian individuals familiar with the song "Eyou Marassa" (originally provided in the premiere performance by the Haitian actress Toto Bissainthe). The song, as discussed in chapter 1, celebrates the divine twins, a concept of diaspora literacy that is embodied in this play by Roseanna and Annarose. The music, like the set design, was described as suspended between the cultural particular and the universal. According to a review by Ubu collaborator Rosette C. Lamont, which stressed the play's resonance across cultures, the music "was like the voice of an oppressed people."[57]

Performing Unity

The women actors' re-creation of Africanist dance appears to have achieved a representation of African diaspora unity, akin to the diasporic dances of artists like Katherine Dunham and Zora Neale Hurston.[58] The actresses created the final scene collaboratively with assistant director Saundra McClain, who recalled in our interview that she largely took over working with the actresses once Shange had finished table work. McClain explained that they created these dances through improvisation, guided by the musician, and by mobilizing their own training in African dance (especially Harriet D. Foy's). In using their own knowledge of African diasporic movement to create a new dance together, the artists drew from a repertoire of bodily knowledge to reinvent a black diasporic performance. Whereas Marie Brooks brought her specialized knowledge of Martinican dance to *Island Memories*, for *Fire's Daughters* black actresses were given cultural authority to create African diaspora dance. Relying on the resonance of Shange's choreopoem, Lamont described the production as a "lyrical stage poem inhabited by magnificent black women." Her review also pitted the four women characters against a global, transhistorical construction of the white master: "Both this adventure [the Haitian Revolution] and the aborted insurrection symbolize to this day the pride of slaves rising against their white masters."[59] Lamont's comment echoes Sister Smoke's onstage retelling of the insurrection, insofar as it conflates post-slavery white hegemony and racism with the violence of the white planter class against slaves.

Along with African diaspora unity, Ubu's production of *Fire's Daughters* communicated a sentiment of shared humanity across races and genders. Throughout the play, the actresses portrayed their characters as what Shange called "ritualistically absorbed,"[60] and thus prepared audiences for the final vodou ritual, which many described as the culminating point of the performance. Makward remarked that the scene was "superbly" staged by Shange, and D. J. R. Bruckner, a reviewer for the *New York Times*, deemed this scene "a spectacular march—a dance, really—that makes the eyes prickle and the ears ring after the lights have gone out."[61] Critics also described how this moment prompted an engagement with Césaire's play on a level that transcended the textual and the linguistic translation from French to English. Lamont celebrated Shange's ability to forge a visceral expression beyond language, as if her staging touched some sort of a primal human instinct: "Her interpretation went beyond words, reaching for the guts and blood of a people."[62]

It is likely that some spectators additionally interpreted the production as evocative of world feminism under the sign of "international women," which was a common category used in Ubu's publicity and anthologies. In an earlier article publicizing Ubu's fall season, "Ubu International 1993," Lamont, a white Jewish woman, called attention to the play's valorization of the personal or private domain—a convention of feminist theater—and Césaire's focus on real women and their daily lives: "The four female characters on the stage create an atmosphere of intimacy and feminine complicity."[63] Ubu's use of the category "international women" as well as its reputation as a largely women-run enterprise might have encouraged women of all racial identifications to engage empathetically with the feminist messages of the play.

While Shange is associated with black feminism, the play's Caribbean feminism might be qualified as interracial, though necessarily intertwined with slavery's legacy. *Fire's Daughters* creates a women-centered world, while explicitly including Martinican women of different skin tones under the sign of Caribbean women. Ubu's enactment of international feminism was not at odds with Césaire's own political views. She has stated elsewhere that she views feminism as a "universal" struggle, shared by all women.[64] Staged under multiple cultural signs, Ubu's production of *Fire's Daughters* enacted affective sentiments of unity that, like diaspora, were propped up over conflicts and tensions. Césaire's play resonated on multiple levels, ranging from Martinican specificity to the black feminist register, international feminism, and the generalized experience of oppression and resistance.

Conflicted Viewings and the Multiple Meanings of Race

Evidence of diaspora performance's underlying tensions and misrecognitions surfaced poignantly during a postperformance discussion. An African American woman spectator asked translator Judith Miller, "Why did *you* translate this play?"[65] While some might discount the spectator's question as indicative of little more than one individual's displaced irritation or faux pas, confrontations like this one occurred several times at Ubu. I wish to dwell momentarily on this confrontation not to uncover the spectator's motivations but rather to consider the larger cultural dynamics with which the question begs me to reckon.

In this moment of cross-viewing, to cite dance scholar Susan Manning's concept, the spectator and translator "[caught] a glimpse of subjectivities from social locations that differ[ed] from their own." According to Manning, spectatorship is inflected (though certainly not determined) by a spectator's multiple, overlapping social identities.[66] At the theater, spectators are aware of the presence of other spectators from social locations that differ from their own, and they may watch each other watching. Thus this moment of conflict seems to have stemmed from a moment of cross-viewing, in which the African American spectator watched the white translator engaging with Césaire's play; Miller, for her part, caught a glimpse (made tangible in the question posed to her) of how that spectator saw her engagement.

To be sure, the question was a challenge to Miller's authority (not for her particular background, I presume, but as a generic white woman) as translator of Césaire's play. The spectator may have meant to assert her ownership over Césaire's play or to clearly label it as "black" and not "intercultural," or not belonging to the category that Ubu labeled "international women." Blackness would thus be understood as something a person must *be* rather than something a person can study. (Miller had studied Césaire's writings, French Caribbean history, vodou, and Creole storytelling.) In other words, this woman may have excluded Miller, due to her complexion, from those who can understand and faithfully render black cultural and literary production. Yet such a claim to authentic blackness fixes meaning and is therefore antithetical to the play's portrayal of Caribbean identity and memory as created by way of a dynamic process of creolization.

Though it fixed black identity, the spectator's question additionally served to unveil one aspect of slavery's legacy that New York's theater scene had largely forgotten: the larger historical pattern of racialized knowledge production in which white women were (and still are) commonly given authority to speak for all women. Such a structure was certainly relevant at Ubu, since Kourilsky, a white woman, held the ultimate authority in all of the company's decisions.

Because Ubu was involved with universities and through its roundtables and other extratheatrical events performed its investment in the dissemination of knowledge surrounding the Caribbean and the African diaspora, it might be helpful to consider the makeup of the U.S. academy at that time. In the fall of 1992, one year before the production at Ubu of *Fire's Daughters*, non-Hispanic black women composed only 2.4 percent of all full-time and part-time instructional faculty and staff in institutions of higher education, while non-Hispanic white women made up 28.4 percent.[67] Set against these statistics, one can imagine how Ubu's publicizing and packaging of plays according to U.S. identity politics could lead to sentiments of frustration over the theater's failure to address the larger pattern of intellectual authority being unequally distributed with respect to race.

Ubu's universalist approach to black francophone drama, though suited to these French Caribbean women's rejection of racial and cultural essentialisms, was, generally speaking, at odds with the racial climate of New York theater in the 1980s and 1990s, which was dominated by white artists and relatively segregated. Despite the successes of such black theaters as the New Federal Theatre and the Negro Ensemble Company, African American actors and directors were still afforded relatively little work compared to their white counterparts. Yet Ubu was among the New York theaters making work for African Americans and other nonwhite theater artists. To take two examples from the productions examined here, Kourilsky ushered in the directing career of African American theater artist Saundra McClain, who was previously known for her acting, and brought visibility to the Indian actor Aasif Mandvi.[68] When I asked Kourilsky whether she expressly chose black translators and directors for black plays, she responded that perhaps sometimes she did but that matching by race and gender was certainly not her priority. "I consider the work of the professional. The most important [factor] for me is the quality of the work," she insisted.[69]

While Ubu's performance of *Fire's Daughters* enacted a sentiment of unity for many artists and spectators, this moment of conflict exposes an underlying misrecognition—specifically, differing conceptions of race and racism. Whereas white domination of hierarchized art and appropriation of black culture were likely to be recognized as racist in the United States, unjustly relegating artists to their race as a means of defining their work was the more common definition of racism recognized in France and the French Caribbean.[70] The choice of a white woman to translate Césaire's play could have been viewed as perpetuating the inequality of knowledge production manifest in the statistics cited earlier. Yet the choice of a black woman translator, by virtue of her race, over Miller, a specialist in the field, could have been viewed as perpetuating a definition of racism prevalent in France: the commodification of an individual human or work of art as a token representative of a particular culture.

Ubu's diaspora performance of *Fire's Daughters* was pervaded by interpretive tensions, conflicting claims to cultural authority, and misrecognitions. When examined critically, such tensions defamiliarize our ready-made assumptions. They unveil different configurations of the signifiers of Caribbeanness, race, and gender and different understandings of the ways in which slavery and its legacy influence racial, gender, and cultural discrimination and belonging. Such coexisting oppositions were negotiated in the theatrical process. As Ubu collaborators repeatedly stressed, their English translations were supposed to remain meticulously faithful to the original French (and in this case Creole), thus illustrating the scope and importance of the Francophonie, while their productions were expected to "transcend" language under an intercultural or African diasporic sign in order to engage U.S. audiences and attest to the plays' universal appeal. Césaire's scripting of Caribbean women's embodied experience was textually rendered in Standard English and through Anglicized equivalents of Martinican culture. The diaspora performance deployed African diaspora dance and ritual, as well as the Creole language, which was spoken and sung onstage considerably more frequently than it appeared in the published translation. It was through such an unstable cultural coding of text and performance that Ubu's *Fire's Daughters* performed transnational black womanhood while, at the same time, figuring black women's experience as already intercultural and interracial.

Dambury's *Crosscurrents*: Fixing a Creolizing Diaspora

While Césaire's dramatizations of Martinican ethnology and history educated audiences about the Caribbean and evoked black diasporic unity, Dambury's more abstract dramatization of the processes of creolization and diaspora (and particularly her portrayal of overlapping black and Indian relations) was received neither as Caribbean nor black at Ubu. Rather Dambury's migrant, anti-essentialist play was interpreted as an exploration of cross-culturalism and an Indian (as opposed to African) diasporic performance. Nonetheless Ubu's reinvention of Dambury's play challenged the status quo of white-dominated New York theater, particularly the underrepresentation of South Asians.

Dambury's antiracist message was largely transformed. Generally speaking, Indians were not read as Caribbean in the United States, though certain spectators familiar with East Indian servitude did grasp the play's complex treatment of slavery's legacy. As in the other productions, dance and music were used to transcend place and to evoke the ambiguous island space on which Dambury's play is set. Providing a stylized interpretation of this surreal and self-reflexive play, Kourilsky's 1997 production made the play accessible and engaging to U.S. audiences. Yet the production coded the play's treatment of cultures in a way that Dambury found to be static. By fixing cultural identities, it denied the fluidity of her creolizing aesthetics, while reinventing the play's meanings in ways that surprised Dambury herself.

Insofar as *Lettres indiennes* is a reflection on diaspora, exile, and cross-cultural relations, it resonated well with Ubu's mission and artistic process. Kourilsky first encountered Dambury's play at the Avignon theater festival in 1996. She found Alain Timar's production fantastic, both in terms of his visual aesthetics and the actors' work with stage movement, but when she later read the text, she found the staging to be a departure from what she perceived as the play's meanings.[71] Just one year later, in 1997, Kourilsky directed a production at Ubu in a translation by Richard Philcox (Maryse Condé's husband), whom Dambury had suggested.

Kourilsky based her directorial concept on the encounter of African and Indian cultures on Réunion Island, while also stressing the play's relevance across cultures. A critic with *France-Amérique* said the success of her staging lay in its respect for the play's social fabric, while nonetheless moving beyond the confines of "narrow realism."[72] As in the Césaire productions, Ubu's intercultural aesthetic, alongside the team's use of music, dance, and stage movement, facilitated the coexistence of cultural particularism with performances of shared humanness. Once again, between these two poles of cultural-historical specificity and human universalism, a performance of diaspora emerged. For this production, however, it was not a black diaspora but an Indian diaspora. Though Ubu worked to teach spectators about Réunion, New York audiences were generally unfamiliar with the ways black and Indian diasporas overlap in the Caribbean. It is therefore not surprising that Indianness was performed and received as a somewhat static cultural signifier.

Dambury's dramatization of black-Indian relations in Guadeloupe (and Réunion) was difficult to transpose to the New York context. The major challenge in this restaging was that South Asians in the United States were not indentured servants and thus do not share with African Americans the historical experiences of slavery. Furthermore, generally speaking, Indians in the United States are more socially advantaged than African Americans, which contrasts with the situation in Guadeloupe, where Indians have tended to be the more disadvantaged group, poorer, less educated, and experience more discrimination than black Caribbeans.[73] It was likely for these reasons that Dambury's scene dramatizing black racism against Indians most overtly, in which the drunken checkers player insults Paul (scene 12), was cut from the Ubu production. A more general antiracist message was nonetheless made clear. As one reviewer wrote, "How familiar to our own racism, multi-cultural collisions; dysfunctional families, and sang froid of the underclasses!"[74]

While Dambury's play cultivates diaspora consciousness across African-descended and Indian-descended peoples, this specific intersectional diaspora consciousness did not resonate at Ubu. Insofar as the play decenters blackness, spectators did not interpret it as a black diasporic performance, and few related the issues addressed with the economic ramifications of slavery and its ongoing neocolonial legacy. Archived spectator responses suggest that audiences tended to interpret the play from two opposing poles: either they were happy to learn about another culture, or they were grateful for Ubu's meaningful interrogation of more general questions relating to differences and similarities across cultures, intergenerational conflict, and social class.[75]

Cross-Cultures

Ubu's production emphasized the theater's hallmark cross-cultural exchange, which was associated with Kourilsky herself. As Rosette C. Lamont, regular critic and friend of Ubu, wrote at that time, cross-culturalism came "naturally to [Kourilsky as] a transplanted Parisienne with Russian roots."[76] Collaborators conducted cultural research into multiple contexts. Kourilsky was, above all, enthusiastic to learn about Réunion Island, where the play seems to be set. She became intrigued by the diversity of cultures existing on Réunion.[77] La Tonya Borsay, an African American actress who played Fructueuse, on the other hand, went to the library to research Guadeloupe, home of her character and the playwright (as well as the culture from which Dambury drew most material to craft her portrayal of Indians and black-Indian relations).[78] Costume designer Carol Ann Pelletier researched traditional Indian dress. Kavi Ladnier (then Ramachandran), who played Marie, drew from her personal spiritual experience with Indian devotional songs and her knowledge of traditional Indian dance in order to create movement pieces and her song. Ladnier also incorporated into her artistic process what she described as her personal, situated knowledge as an Indian woman.[79]

This research into multiple cultures sought to arrive at one unified point of crossing, representative of the characters' migrant community, and the translated title reinforced this theme. Rather than using a literal translation of *Lettres indiennes*, "Indian Letters," for the title, Philcox renamed Dambury's play *Crosscurrents*, which conjures images of diverse cultures and cross-cultural conflicts. Dambury recalled that she herself proposed this concept for the title, while Philcox found the particular word.[80] The new title may suggest that a more general idea of a crossroads of cultures replaced Dambury's specific agenda of bringing visibility to Indians, though the term additionally evokes the currents of the ocean, on which both enslaved Africans and indentured Indian laborers were brought to the Caribbean.

As in the productions of Césaire's plays, throughout the intercultural artistic process of staging *Crosscurrents*, collaborators enacted multiple cultural particularisms even as they performed affective sentiments of unity. As she explained to me, Ladnier viewed the play as being about "islanders," stressing the particular diverse community enacted by the

Figure 11. Kavitha Ladnier (née Ramachandran) performing Marie's dance in Gerty Dambury's *Crosscurrents*. New York, 1997. (Photograph by Jonathan Slaff; Ubu Repertory Theater Collections; courtesy of the Bibliothèque nationale de France)

production. She saw her work as guided not so much by the Indian traditions from which she drew as by what she called "the humanity" of the piece and the community in which it was anchored (both on and off stage). Ladnier said her dance was not just an expression of Marie's character but "representative of the play, the people" (figure 11). Borsay echoed a similar sentiment explaining that the production created a "new place" and took audiences there.[81] She attributed this to Kourilsky's directing style, which she described as both "European" and "international," as opposed to the realism of the Actors Studio and the dominant acting techniques of the U.S. tradition.

As in other Ubu productions, music and dance were key in crafting the intercultural sentiment of affective unity. Led by Kourilsky and musician-composer Genji Ito, who, Kourilsky recalled, was present at all rehearsals and an integral part of the collaborative creative process, Ubu's team experimented with the affective transcendence of location and language.[82] The team's emphasis on music as part of the rehearsal process allowed them to craft an aesthetic and embodied experience that the actors described to me as transcending the usual confines of existence. Borsay spoke of a "fourth dimension" that was reached through her work with Ito and Kourilsky, for it "engaged all of [her] senses." These moments occurred for the actresses during songs and dances. Rather than evoking how characters would actually act in the real time and space of the present or a given historical period, Kourilsky was "always in a dream-like or memory place."

The set was also representative of Ubu's intercultural aesthetic, as evidenced in an image from the final scene, the cremation of Paul's father (figure 12). Watoku Ueno crafted huge industrial wheels, meant to symbolize the factory, while incorporating fabrics that suggested Indian influence and multiple levels of platforms to reflect the conflation and confusion of place. Design and staging choices evoked placelessness and offered an intercultural collage. Through this aesthetic, the production cultivated an international affinity, reflective of Ubu's international team.

The production facilitated universalist readings of Dambury's text. While the play seeks to transcend place, creating an imaginary island that is an amalgam of Guadeloupe and Réunion, it also explores black-Indian relations across islands and cultivates a political consciousness of intersecting diasporas in the aftermath of slavery and colonialism. The New York production, in contrast, did not foreground black-Indian intersectionality so much as the intercultural, affective unity. The

Figure 12. The cremation of Paul's father in Gerty Dambury's *Crosscurrents*: Bryan Hicks as Merchat, Aasif Mandvi as Paul, La Tonya Borsay as Fructueuse, Kavitha Ladnier (Ramachandran) as Marie, and Bina Sharif as the Mother. New York, 1997. (Photograph by Watoko Ueno; private collection; courtesy of Watoko Ueno)

reviewer Bruckner likely meant to refer to the intergenerational familial conflict when he wrote, "It happens on La Reunion, an island in the Indian Ocean, but of course it is next door; everyone everywhere who is over 30 will recognize this situation and its familiarity arouses much pleasant laughter."[83] Another critic summarized, "We are left with existential human questions of exile, and the nature of what is 'home.'"[84]

Departing from such universalist readings, other reviewers insisted on the places and cultures of Réunion and India. Though the *News India-Times* described the play as looking at "race and the diaspora," it situated these themes in a "remote island in the Indian Ocean."[85] In this case, the two coexisting, opposing poles of universalism and cultural specificity were reordered in a way that may have obscured the specific points of intersection that Dambury foregrounds. This apparent misstaging, however, also extended the performative process of creolization by remixing the cultural signifiers and cultivating a new global consciousness that resisted the cultural politics of the New York theater scene at that time.

Figure 13. Fructueuse at Paul's childhood home in Gerty Dambury's *Crosscurrents*: La Tonya Borsay, Aasif Mandvi, and Bina Sharif. New York, 1997. (Photograph by Jonathan Slaff; Ubu Repertory Theater Collections; courtesy of the Bibliothèque nationale de France)

Performing Indianness

Whereas the original production of *Lettres indiennes* in Avignon, which starred black Caribbean actors in all of the roles, downplayed the Indian elements of Dambury's play, Kourilsky's staging of *Crosscurrents* foregrounded them. Ubu's production featured Indian actors, traditional Indian dress for costumes, the Hindi and Tamil languages, and traditional Indian music and dance. This Indianness was most conspicuous when Fructueuse traveled to Paul's childhood home (figure 13). To attract Indian spectators, Ubu publicized the production in Indian newspapers in New York, and casting agent Stephanie Klapper worked to find Indian actors at a time when the New York theater scene was not yet very diverse and outreach to cultural groups was much more difficult than it is today.[86] She cast two Indian actors who have gone on to successful careers in theater and television: Kavi Ladnier and Aasif Mandvi, now well known for his work as a correspondent with Jon Stewart's *The*

Daily Show and his book *No Land's Man*.⁸⁷ Because Klapper could not find enough professional actors of Indian descent willing to work within Ubu's budget and methods, she cast Jay Palit, who was not a professional actor, to play the Father. Though Kourilsky said it was difficult to work with actors who had not had professional training,⁸⁸ it is clear that, in this case, she prioritized cultural visibility and Indian descent over the actor's experience and training.

During the collaborative rehearsal process, Ubu's team valued personal, situated knowledge the actors brought as Indian men and women. For example, Bina Sharif (the actress playing Paul's mother) taught costume designer Pelletier how to tie a sari.⁸⁹ Kourilsky asked Ladnier, who played Marie, to make use of cultural gestures and knowledge she had learned from her family and her Indian community. As Ladnier described the process of creating Marie's songs and dances, the specific movement came out of her own knowledge of traditional Indian dance, but she relied on her "instincts" as a performer to create the performance pieces.⁹⁰ She additionally incorporated an Indian devotional song that she knew from her own spiritual journey and drew from her understanding of what it meant to be an Indian woman. Just out of college, at the young age of twenty-three, Ladnier said she interpreted the character in a genuine but perhaps naïve way.

Similar to Césaire's critique of the folkloric representation of Martinique in *Fire's Daughters*, Dambury worried that Ubu's representation of Indianness seemed static and tokenistic. She explained to me that she never imagined that Marie, Paul, and his family would be costumed in traditional Indian dress, with the women wearing bindi on their foreheads. This surprised her, since Indians in the Caribbean dress in the same Western clothing as black Caribbeans. Though Dambury described Kourilsky's production as a "fair" and "honest" enactment of her text, she was disappointed in its reliance on fixed representations of culture.⁹¹ "Something appeared to me when I saw the production at Ubu," Dambury told me. "I saw that my text could make someone think that I'm trying to give an image of a community. Something like folklore emerged." In this case, it was not Caribbean culture that was commodified, as Césaire feared when she saw Ueno's set for *Fire's Daughters*, but rather Indian culture, which was figured as distinct from the Caribbean. "I love Indian culture and would like to see more," one audience member wrote.⁹²

From Text to Performance

Both Kourilsky and Mathéus remembered having difficulty finding ways to bring Dambury's text to life onstage. The play has a poetic quality and includes sequences of poetry. Bruckner noted this in his review, mentioning that the play "has the emotional grip and stimulation of a metaphysical meditation in four voices, in spite of Francoise Kourilsky's energetic direction of a spirited cast."[93] Whether through Creole storytelling or traditional Indian dress, both productions struck Dambury as stereotypical representations of culture. Yet it was challenging for the artists to enact Dambury's self-reflexive treatment of cultures materially onstage without relying on static signifiers. Dambury herself explained that, throughout the process of researching and writing *Lettres indiennes*, she became interested in "Indian culture in general."[94] And her play unites Réunion and Guadeloupe. Kourilsky's production performed this focus on cultural sameness or generality, partially taking its cue from Dambury's text. A glossary included with the published play was reproduced in Ubu's program; it lists terms from multiple sites across the diaspora, showing how multiple particularisms of Indian cultures and belief systems inform Dambury's portrayal of the Indian diaspora.

Although African American reviewers and spectators attended the play, they did not label it "black," as they did for many of Ubu's productions of plays by black francophone playwrights. A review in the *Amsterdam News* stressed social class rather than blackness: "Crosscurrents is billed as [a] 'story of migration and memory in paradise lost.' What are lost are jobs when the sugar cane factor where everyone works shuts down."[95] Dambury's dramatization of slavery's echoes through an overlapping black and Indian diaspora became more imprecise in the United States. Nonetheless this imprecision encouraged spectators and collaborators to reflect on different aspects of racial and cultural politics. For instance, Ladnier recalled that the production made her think about black-brown relations, about racism by South Asians against African Americans, and how U.S. society clearly values lighter skin. Though perhaps somewhat taken out of the context of the aftermath of slavery and East Indian servitude, the echo of the sugar factory nonetheless resonated on socioeconomic and cultural levels. Furthermore it appears that the production fostered attentive cross-cultural dialogue. One reviewer commented that it "reveal[ed] that there are more similarities than differences between races and cultures, if only we would keep the dialogue open."[96]

Ubu's diaspora performances of Césaire's and Dambury's plays offer materializations or enactments of diaspora performance, negotiated through textual translation and extratextual performances, including intercultural designs, music, and dance. At stake in Ubu's English-language performances of French Caribbean women's plays were different meanings of Caribbeanness, gender, and race—and the question of who had the cultural authority to identify whether the performance was "authentic." Ubu's diaspora performances were crafted by interracial artists, who worked in collaboration and conflict, deploying realism and antirealist aesthetics, local and transcultural references, and music and dance to make French Caribbean women's plays accessible to U.S. audiences. While these productions sparked dialogue, educated their audiences, and fostered community, they were permeated by misrecognitions, disagreements, and conflicting claims to cultural authority and ownership over Caribbeanness and blackness.

One salient factor at work in Ubu's diaspora performances was an ongoing negotiation between late twentieth-century U.S. identity politics and the plays' dramatizations of culture and race as inherently unstable. Generally speaking, whereas many U.S. collaborators saw race in terms of a black-white binary, the women playwrights—like other French Caribbean artists, particularly those writing in the aftermath of the Négritude movement—viewed race along a continuum. Furthermore French and francophone Caribbean artists held to a discourse of cultural universalism that was in many ways incompatible with U.S.-based identity politics of the 1980s and 1990s. Whereas Ubu's productions tended to treat race, culture, and gender as fixed signifiers, the plays emphasize their entanglement with the lived histories and aftereffects of slavery. Some of Ubu's artistic choices might appear to contradict the playwrights' intentions. But by putting these different views of race and culture into dialogue with one another, Ubu's productions challenged the cultural status quo of New York's theater scene.

5 Recasting the Francophone Caribbean Couple at Ubu Repertory Theater

Between 1988 and 1990 Ubu Repertory Theater produced Simone Schwarz-Bart's *Ton beau capitaine* four times. Three different actors played Wilnor and four actresses played Marie-Ange. The number of actor switches during this short time period suggest Ubu's ambivalence over casting choices. But Kourilsky's difficult decision—in the middle of the 1989 production's run—to replace the talented African American actress playing the voice of Marie-Ange, Catherine Slade, speaks to the challenges of re-creating in the United States the role of this enigmatic Haitian woman, who is unflinchingly strong, infinitely loving and sincere toward her husband, but nonetheless unapologetic about her affair. In Ubu's archives, the 1989 show's program, in which Slade's name and bio are pasted over with her successors' in the playbill, beckoned me to investigate why this francophone Caribbean couple proved so difficult to adapt to the New York stage. Though there were no such eleventh-hour substitutions for Maryse Condé's *Pension les Alizés*, which only received one full-scale production at Ubu (1995), Kourilsky questioned the appropriateness of the actress who played Emma, Jane White. When an excerpt from Condé's play was produced as part of "Bravo Ubu," a tribute organized for the theater's closing in 2001, Emma was recast. Why so many recastings of the francophone Caribbean couple?

In this chapter I deploy the theoretical concept of "recasting" in order to expand upon my analysis of Ubu's diaspora performances of French Caribbean women's plays. Like the productions analyzed in the previous chapter, Schwarz-Bart's and Condé's plays made meaning on multiple, sometimes conflicting registers when they circulated to the United States. I suggest that enacting the francophone Caribbean heterosexual couple onstage, in English, at Ubu proved an ambivalent and inherently unstable task. Conflicts, tensions, and misrecognitions prompted the continuous recasting of the couple. To be sure, theater always involves recasting, remodeling, and reimagining. No two productions of a play are alike, and, even within one production's run, every performance is different. Yet in the cases of these two particular plays—each centering on the Caribbean heterosexual couple—collaborators were never satisfied with a single casting; each production prompted a desire to recast and restage the play. These plays were anxiously reshaped and remodeled throughout Ubu's engagement with the dramatic text, as collaborators confronted what they saw as perhaps irresolvable challenges in their translation into English and adaptation to the U.S. context.

Recasting, as Christiana McMahon theorizes, is the process whereby artists at international theater festivals transform (trans)national affiliations and reassign cultural groups to new roles in hierarchies of power relating to race, gender, and colonial histories. She points out that the term has two meanings: replacing an actor or reassigning a role, and shedding new light on master narratives to change the way dominant ideas or ideologies are received.[1] At Ubu the two connotations clearly worked in concert: actors were recast in order to present the play and the culture from which it hailed in a different light. When Kourilsky reallocated roles, she sought to rectify what she perceived to be the actor's misrepresentations of the character or the play's meanings. Even the role of translator was reallocated. In both cases, the original translators, Jessica Harris and Barbara Lewis, were asked to work together with Ubu's literary manager, Catherine Temerson, whose job was to correct the translations according to Ubu's standards. In both publications, the two women are credited as cotranslators. Ubu's multiple recastings point not only to possibilities for social change, like the recastings of race, gender, history, and the nation McMahon foregrounds, but also to the instability of cultural signifiers onstage and their discontinuous reception by artists and spectators.

At stake in these performances was the representation of the postplantation heterosexual couple. Both plays consider slavery's aftereffects on love, sex, and romantic intimacy insofar as the Caribbean couple's efforts to find or sustain love are portrayed against the backdrop of harsh socioeconomic conditions and self-imposed exile. While Condé shows Emma and Ishmael's failed romantic relationship, Schwarz-Bart dramatizes Marie-Ange's confession to Wilnor of her infidelity. Showing spectators a glimpse into an emotionally charged moment, in which the romantic relationship could either deepen or end, the plays explore love's instability and its possibilities, situating the theme of love against

Caribbean realities and the possibility of the romantic partner's substitution. Absent or failed love is conceived as a facet, albeit an unpredictable and contingent one, of slavery's legacy.

Diasporic Love and Trouble

Schwarz-Bart's and Condé's portrayals of failed or absent heterosexual love in the Caribbean converge with black feminist sociologist Patricia Hill Collins's influential writings on the "love and trouble tradition" in the African American context. According to Collins, while heterosexual black men and women love each other deeply, tensions and troubles run through their relationships. Suggesting that problems with love stem from slavery, Collins considers slavery's fundamental assault on enslaved people's freedom to love. Though originating in slavery, the condition of "love and trouble" is not simply a consequence of the past, for it is perpetuated by society's intersecting ideologies of oppression and structures of power. As Collins explains, intersecting systems of oppression influence individual interpersonal relations, yet institutionalized oppressions must nevertheless be analytically distinguished from individuals' sentiments and actions.[2] Similarly, while the love portrayed in Schwarz-Bart's and Condé's plays is inflected by slavery's legacy, the playwrights nonetheless insist upon their individual characters' freedom to love as they choose.

Like Collins, Schwarz-Bart and Condé illuminate the politics of postplantation love while acknowledging the importance of each individual's choices and emotions. For both Caribbean women, writing about love, sex, and romantic relationships is an inherently political act. When Schwarz-Bart was asked in an interview with the Antipodes radio station whether her play *Ton beau capitaine* was political, she responded that the very fact that Wilnor and Marie-Ange are separated is already a political critique.[3] And Condé argued in her influential essay "Order, Disorder, Freedom and the West Indian Writer" that Caribbean women writers "imply that before thinking of a political revolution, French Caribbean society needs a psychological one."[4] In Condé's plays, the "creaking of bed-springs tends to replace the rattling of machetes," to borrow Bridget Jones's words.[5] Or, as Christiane Makward puts it, "A man who gives love a chance is already a useful revolutionary."[6] In *La Parole des femmes*, Condé identifies a politics of love in Schwarz-Bart's best-known novel, *Pluie et vent sur Télumée Miracle*, insisting that it is "the social structure of a dominated country, the exploitation of blacks, that does not allow people to be happy and destroys couples."[7]

During Ubu's performances of Schwarz-Bart's and Condé's plays, a black diasporic reading of heterosexual love in slavery's aftermath emerged that, as in my theorization of diaspora performance, was premised on conflicts and tensions in meaning making. The staging of love repeatedly challenged Ubu's artists' and audiences' expectations. In Ubu's productions, Condé's and Schwarz-Bart's dramatizations of the complexities of love and trouble were simultaneously coded as Caribbean, universal, and black diasporic. The French language, and a general performance of Frenchness, was perceived by some as a marker of authenticity and by others as an impediment to the performance of Caribbeanness or black diasporic unity. Collaborators disagreed over the meanings of love and victimhood, as well as the onstage coding of bodies in relation to race and gender. Multiple acts of recasting marked the performance of black diasporic love as well as the translation of the texts. My analysis of these performances—hinging on multiple acts of recasting—underscores the instability of the plays' meanings regarding love, race, culture, and gender.

Schwarz-Bart's *Your Handsome Captain*: Re-creating Haiti, Recasting Love

In a personal interview, Kourilsky recalled that she first discovered *Ton beau capitaine* at the International Francophone Festival in Limoges.[8] Sensing that something was missing from Syto Cavé's production, she read the play and was immediately touched and intrigued by the theatrical device of Marie-Ange's voice—how Marie-Ange's emotional and spiritual presence preoccupies Wilnor even though she is never physically present on stage. Cavé chose to put Marie-Ange (played by Mariann Mathéus) onstage, thus privileging the couple's ritualized, otherworldly communication over the reality of the physical distance separating them. However, Kourilsky felt that this staging choice did not achieve the delicate balance of emotional presence and physical absence that she read in Schwarz-Bart's text. Committed to realizing the play's unique theatrical expression, Kourilsky thus began a two-year relationship with *Ton beau capitaine* that culminated in her final staging of the play, in French, with two Haitian actors in 1990. Kourilsky was, as she put it, "very attached" to the play.

Ubu staged *Your Handsome Captain* four times, with various actors and two directors. For their first production, in 1988, Ubu invited Seret Scott to direct; she is a pioneering African American actor who originated one of the roles in Shange's *For colored girls*. But Kourilsky felt that Scott's staging was not quite right, perhaps because Scott also chose to put Marie-Ange on stage at one point. In 1989 Kourilsky decided to stage the play herself. In 1990 she reprised it in English, and then directed a similar production in French. As these multiple restagings suggest, Kourilsky was dissatisfied not only with Cavé's and Scott's productions but also with her own. Her impression that the play was somehow misrepresented onstage was informed by her discussions with Schwarz-Bart, who attended several rehearsals and productions during two separate visits to Ubu.

In Kourilsky's view, the problem with these various productions was not that they were unfaithful to the original but rather that the act of adaptation was inadequate. According to her, translating and staging a francophone play in the United States and in English involves "recreating" the text in a new light, refashioning it. This occurs on several levels, beginning with the textual translation, and includes staging choices—music, dance, an actor's performance style—as well as publicity. After multiple efforts to refashion the play, Kourilsky believed that she succeeded only in French, during her last production, in 1990. I viewed this production's documentation on video in Ubu's archives at the Bibliothèque nationale de France.[9] Though Schwarz-Bart did not attend this final production, Kourilsky speculated that she would have finally approved of her play at Ubu. Rather than analyzing this or other specific productions, I will interpret Ubu's work with Schwarz-Bart's play across its various stagings in order to explore the multiple acts of recasting that occurred.

Translating a Syncretic Text

Even before the Ubu performances, the history of the textual translations of Schwarz-Bart's play was already pervaded by efforts to recast and recode the author's language. The poetic language of *Ton beau capitaine* is syncretic and proved difficult to translate into English. The play is written in the French language, but with the spirit of the Creole language. Schwarz-Bart's lyrical and poetic French turns on repetitions and word play and conjures the Creole language's rhythms, images, proverbs, and styles. In fact both Schwarz-Bart and Condé use the French language in innovative ways that qualify as Caribbeanesque. Whereas Condé's anti-essentialist approach emphasizes the translational quality of writing and the influence of multiple, recombining cultures, Schwarz-Bart reinvents the cadences of the Creole language. Writing specifically of Schwarz-Bart's style, Condé notes that "the absent corpus of the

Creole language cries out to us."[10] Schwarz-Bart herself has described her writing as syncretic, composed of several coexisting levels: "the Creole level, the French level, the Creole-French level, and then the product, the new term, the new language."[11] At which level, then, should a translator begin?

In an article in *Translation Review*, Rosannne Kanhai-Brunton proposes an answer based in what she describes as the reality of the Caribbean and the translational Caribbean subject. A translator and scholar from the anglophone Caribbean working and living in the United States, Kanhai-Brunton had already begun translating Schwarz-Bart's text before learning that Ubu held the rights. Her translation remains unpublished, representing a missed encounter between Schwarz-Bart's play and the English language. As Kanhai-Brunton theorizes, Schwarz-Bart's text is "already distorted, already translated," since Caribbean people are themselves in "a state of translation, one that is removed from its own sources."[12] She believes the translational quality of the original justifies taking liberties with the translation, and she suggests translation choices that would more firmly anchor the play in the English-language Caribbean (which is itself, like the francophone Caribbean, already translational) context.

Ubu's translation, in contrast, was quite literal and preserved the play's cultural coding as French, sometimes at the expense of its Creole qualities. For instance, consider the language Marie-Ange deploys to preface the story of her infidelity:

> Wilnor, au sujet de l'histoire qui m'était restée dans la gorge, hier, tu vois ce que je veux dire? Finalement je me rends compte qu'il n'y avait pas lieu d'en faire tant de cas. Tant de vent pour une si petite barque, tant de mousse pour si peu de chocolat.[13]
>
> Wilnor, about the story that stuck in my throat yesterday, you remember? I realize, finally, that there was no point in making such a fuss about it. So much wind for so small a ship, so much mousse for so little chocolate.[14]

Schwarz-Bart's rich use of imagery recalls the Creole language, specifically the art of the *conteur* (Creole storyteller). The image of the story "stuck in [Marie-Ange's] throat" evokes the storyteller in both the original and the translation. But the reference to the French dessert of mousse au chocolat makes meaning differently in the two languages. In the original, it represents part of a local cultural syncretism that includes French influences; in the English-language context, it resonates as cuisine for the elite. Kanhai-Brunton finds the allusion to mousse au chocolat too far estranged from the social realities of poverty in the Caribbean: she suggests using *froth* as a more appropriate anglophone Caribbean term.[15] While the term *froth* recodes the play culturally, it also makes it more readily legible as Caribbean in English. Though Kanhai-Brunton appears to have taken more liberties overall, Ubu's translators did not always select the most literal option. Marie-Ange's question "Tu vois ce que je veux dire?" is translated as "You remember?" rather than a more literal equivalent: "You see what I'm trying to say?" Thus Marie-Ange's communication of the insufficiencies of language—which relates, of course, to the need for dance as a supplemental language—is downplayed or perhaps lost in this moment of linguistic translation.

As this example suggests, such subtle acts of recoding Schwarz-Bart's language have important ideological implications. To take another example, Wilnor's false confession of his infidelity brings to mind the religious syncretism of Christianity coexisting with *quimbois* (practices of African-derived magic, healing, and sorcery): "Et puis je suis tombé dans la fosse, je suis tombé dans le sortilège, tout comme toi."[16] Harris and Temerson translate literally: "And then I fell into the pit; I fell under the spell just like you."[17] In contrast, Kanhai-Brunton proposes replacing Wilnor's untrue confession that he "fell into the pit," meaning that he too was adulterous, with the anglophone Caribbean expression "fall into the bamboo." According to her, while the pit evokes a Christian hell, bamboo "suggests confusion and bewilderment, but with a measure of temporariness, and thus leaves open the opportunity to resume one's intended commitment, as happens at the end of the play."[18] In de-emphasizing Christianity and adding a specifically anglophone Caribbean reference, Kanhai-Brunton foregrounds the play's Creole worldview and privileges its subversion of slavery's moralizing legacy.

At Ubu, Kourilsky ultimately oversaw the translation and cultural coding of the play's language. For her, Schwarz-Bart's syncretic use of language was first and foremost a display of the French language's diverse possibilities. To be sure, Kourilsky, like Cavé, was sensitive to Schwarz-Bart's unique writing style, which she called the "Creole music" to the French text. But as founder and artistic director of a theater devoted to celebrating the diversity of the French-language dramatic repertoire, she prioritized the French language as keeper of the play's poetics and core meanings. She found that African American professor Jessica Harris's translation did not effectively reproduce what she perceived as the play's "music," and thus asked Ubu's Temerson to correct it.[19]

Here Ubu's choice of translators, as in the previous chapter, implicitly coded the play and its performances. Individual translators bring unique expertise and cultural competencies. Furthermore, at Ubu, translators (like the actors involved in the production and other collaborators) were read by Ubu's team and by audiences as culturally positioned. Educated internationally, Harris is a professor and a specialist in African diaspora and Creole cuisine. Temerson, a white woman who was brought up in a bilingual household, had studied at a French *lycée* and then in the American university system.[20] Though she had studied Russian literature in college, she was familiar with francophone plays, since she held a steady position at Ubu. While Harris was familiar with the cultures of the African diaspora, Temerson's primary qualification was her bilingualism. (But Temerson told me that Harris's French was quite good.) Temerson recalled that the two women, who knew each other from the culinary world, worked collaboratively. In Ubu's published translation, both women are credited as cotranslators. Nonetheless it appears that Kourilsky believed Temerson's mastery of French enabled her to reproduce Schwarz-Bart's rhythms and language. Kourilsky assured Schwarz-Bart in a letter that Temerson was "perfectly bilingual" and a professional translator.[21] This attests to the way Ubu privileged the French language rather than a multilingual Caribbean in its textual translation.

Outside critics, like Kanhai-Brunton, found Ubu's translation insufficiently Caribbean. When the pioneering African American theater Rites and Reason at Brown University produced Schwarz-Bart's play, they modified Ubu's translation. *Ton beau capitaine* was the first play produced in translation at Rites and Reason. The text was adapted by VèVè Clark, Micheline Rice-Maximin, Tanya Little, and Leah Gilliam, who worked to find appropriate analogies in the context of the anglophone Caribbean. For example, Ubu's title, *Your Handsome Captain*, was changed to *Your Fine Captain*; the director explained in a program note, "In our working dialogues about the play, we recognized 'FINE' to be a compelling and culturally grounded translation of 'BEAU' that has the poetic resonance and ambiguity close to the meanings and memories that are invoked by the original French text."[22]

Implicitly Kourilsky may have agreed with the critics who found Ubu's translation too far removed from the Caribbean, insofar as she believed that her final production, performed in French by two Haitian actors at the Alliance française in New York, was Ubu's best performance of the play. In fact both Kourilsky and Temerson believed that Ubu best captured the spirit, poetics, and aesthetics of Schwarz-Bart's play in this last production. This final act of recasting marked the play as decidedly Haitian (rather than French or Anglo-Caribbean) and reanchored the play's authenticity in the francophone world. Ubu's choice to perform in French may have been sparked by reviews in *Haiti Progress* and the *Guardian*, which described the play as "not seen under the best linguistic conditions" since it was originally written in French but shows people who speak Creole, and was subsequently translated (again) into English.[23] In other words, as these reviews aptly note, Harris and Temerson were charged with translating Schwarz-Bart's French language, which was itself already a translation of a scenario that would have unfolded in Creole. Kourilsky remembered that, when Temerson saw the production in French, she confessed that she could not express the profound beauty of Schwarz-Bart's language in translation.[24]

Re-creating Haiti in New York

Through publicity and performance, Ubu sought to situate the play within the pan-Caribbean world as well as, more specifically, within Haitian cultural and performance practices. That Ubu scheduled Schwarz-Bart to do an interview with the *Calabasse Creole* radio program and with *Carib News* attests to these pan-Caribbean links.[25] Yet the production was framed, above all, as Haitian. This emphasis on Haiti was guided by Schwarz-Bart herself, who consulted with Kourilsky on the staging. As Kourilsky recalled, in preparing to direct the play, she wished to travel to the Caribbean, but Schwarz-Bart advised her to travel to Haiti rather than to Guadeloupe. In Haiti, Kourilsky immersed herself in musical and performative cultures, which inflected her directorial vision. She recorded music and attended vodou ceremonies.[26]

Haitian music and vodou culture inspired Kourilsky's work with the actor playing Wilnor. As the different stagings progressed, she deepened her focus on Haitian performance practices and worked particularly closely with the Haitian actor Patrick Rameau, who was the final actor to play Wilnor at Ubu in the English- and French-language productions in 1990. Kourilsky's focus on performance took its cue from Schwarz-Bart's play, which scripts extratextual communication, particularly through dance. As Kourilsky explained in an interview with Alvina Ruprecht, she wished to invent a new ritual from the dramaturgical language presented to her: "Our aim was not to copy a ritual but to invent one."[27] To do so, as she did in other Ubu productions, Kourilsky worked closely with a musician, first the well-known African American jazz artist Henry Threadgill and then Frederick D. Berryhill. By the final staging, the musician had become so integral to the performance that he was onstage with the actor at all times.[28] Viewing the video recording of the final production, I noticed that, though they did not look at each other, the actor and the musician were clearly engaged in a dialogue, as in traditional Caribbean and African-derived dance.[29]

While Ubu's early performances had recast the play in the African American context, the final production coded the play as Haitian. Before Rameau and the Haitian actress Michelle Marcelin, African American actors Stanley Earl Harrison and Reg E. Cathey played Wilnor (figure 14). African American actresses Sheila Gibbs, Catherine Slade, and Sharon McGruder played Marie-Ange. Kourilsky told me she was pleased with many of these performances, particularly McGruder's and Cathey's, but she remembered that no actors could match the work of Rameau and Marcelin performing in French. In an effort to frame the show as African American in 1989, Kourilsky had gone so far as to invite Denzel Washington to play the part of Wilnor.[30] The black diasporic reading was more strongly present in earlier productions, particularly in the show directed by Scott. Reviewers for these productions interpreted the play as black by virtue of the collaborators' racial identities. A review for the 1988 production coded the play as black, pointing out that the author was black, as was the translator Jessica Harris, and calling it a "black love story."[31] A 1989 article stressed that, like the playwright, Harris was black.[32] In the final production, this previous focus on blackness had been overshadowed by the themes of migration, poverty, and the Francophonie. The black diaspora seems to have been upstaged by the French language, perhaps due to the final performance location: the Alliance française, a francophone cultural hub.

Much like other plays at Ubu, *Ton beau capitaine* was framed as simultaneously Caribbean and universal. Correspondence regarding a proposed tour of *Your Handsome Captain* to U.S. universities succinctly states, "Through rooted in the social and political realities of the Caribbean, [*Your Handsome Captain*] encompasses the wider themes of exile, separation, love and jealousy."[33] Schwarz-Bart's treatment of intimate relationships as political was very much in line with Ubu's interests. Kourilsky, who often selected plays that were political, antiracist, antisexist, or antihomophobic, was particularly interested in the intersection between what she referred to (in various Ubu flyers, publications, press releases, and correspondence) as the poetic and the political. Many spectators responded to the play's treatment of these so-called universal themes, particularly at the universities.

179 *Recasting the Francophone Caribbean Couple*

Figure 14. Reg E. Cathey as Wilnor in Simone Schwarz-Bart's *Your Handsome Captain*. New York, 1989. (Photograph by Georgina Bedrosian; Ubu Repertory Theater Collections; courtesy of Marianna Fisk and the Bibliothèque nationale de France)

In 1990 Ubu toured Kourilsky's production with Rameau and McGruder to the University at Albany. Students who attended the performance wrote response papers, many of which explained how they related personally to the love story. One student commented that, though the culture represented onstage was very different from his own, the emotions were universal. Another student related to the way separation endangers love; when she left home for college, she intended to stay together with her high school boyfriend, but their relationship did not last.[34] At Ubu, exile was conceived to be a "universal idea," in Kourilsky's words, cited in the Albany student newspaper.[35] Ubu's universalization of exile resonated with its efforts to cultivate black diasporic links, since African-descended people across the Americas share the memory and inheritance of the Middle Passage. Both Schwarz-Bart's and Condé's plays position contemporary exiles as repetitions (and reinventions) of that primal journey. Exile was also a recurring theme in Kourilsky's own life, as her grandfather had emigrated to France as a Russian Jew, and she was now self-exiled in New York, where she worked with an international team of artists. As she speculated in 1999, her passion for

Caribbean plays may have been related to her personal experiences of exile.[36]

Recasting the Voice

Ubu's multiple recastings of the role of Marie-Ange appear to reflect the challenges involved in enacting onstage the dualities and interpretive tensions of the character of Marie-Ange. Wilnor's wife defies simple distinctions between faithful and unfaithful, victim and culpable, regretful and unremorseful. Notes housed in Ubu's archives explain Kourilsky's reasons for replacing Catherine Slade, an African American actress and professor. Though Slade is a vocal coach, she could not perform the voice in a way that satisfied Kourilsky or Schwarz-Bart. In a series of notes to Slade, Kourilsky attempted to guide her in her performance of the voice. As the notes stress, Marie-Ange is a simple, strong woman, a fighter, and not a victim, who does not cry often or easily. One of the letters urges Slade to return to a cheerful tone, a lightness, and a love for life she had shown in previous performances: Marie-Ange should not show self-pity and must speak in a way that is simple and direct.[37] These notes reveal that Schwarz-Bart herself was particularly adamant that when Marie-Ange makes her confession of infidelity, she should not cry. In a final letter, Kourilsky regretfully announces that she will have to replace Slade in the middle of the show's run. Insofar as Slade is an accomplished actress who specializes in voice, it is surprising that she could not succeed in incorporating Kourilsky's repetitive notes in a way the director found suitable.

There may be larger, cultural stakes involved in Slade's (perceived) misrecognition of Marie-Ange's character. To briefly review, Schwarz-Bart's play dramatizes the legacy of bending and adapting moral codes and liberates Marie-Ange from the moralizing gazes inherited from the time of slavery. Provocatively Marie-Ange transgresses Christian marital codes and is unapologetic for her infidelity. It seems that these moral provocations proved difficult for some Ubu spectators to accept. In a review for the *Amsterdam News*, Barbara Lewis (cotranslator of Condé's *The Tropical Breeze Hotel*), expressed her inability to make sense of the power dynamics portrayed between the black woman and the black man. Presumably writing for the *Amsterdam News*'s African American readership, she describes Wilnor's plight within a larger African diaspora context, explaining that his "dilemma is faced by many Black men today whatever their country of origin or native language."[38] Yet Lewis goes on to explain that Wilnor is not a typical black man, for he is the victim of Marie-Ange's adultery (rather than the inverse). She recounts that she could not accept the woman as "transgressor and the man as injured party."

Through discussions with the actors, director, and playwright, however, Lewis came to understand the play in a new light, which led her to transmit an inclusive black feminist message to her readership:

> It is the prerogative of the writer not simply to reflect but to expand reality in order to expose a higher truth.
>
> It is the Black man who must act, who must bridge the gulf of division. In action, a man empowers himself, shakes off the shackles of psychological containment, claims his manhood, and earns the respect of his woman.
>
> The issue is harmony, and it must be achieved no matter what the cost in superficial pride. Whatever our sins against each other, the Black man and woman must understand and forgive each other. Ultimately, we have no security except in each other. Money alone will not shield us; money alone will not suffice. We are our salvation.[39]

Likely cued by Schwarz-Bart's message of spiritual communion, Lewis calls upon black heterosexual men and women to unite against the plantation-derived status quo of "love and trouble." She captures Schwarz-Bart's wish to task the black man—as opposed to the woman—with cultivating redress. In his review, African American playwright and translator Townsend Brewster calls Wilnor a "man whose true strength rises above his machismo."[40]

As a prism through which to view Schwarz-Bart's play, recasting was relevant not only at Ubu but in other performances of the play as well. What Kourilsky perceived to be the major directorial challenge and crux of the play—Marie-Ange's simultaneous presence and absence—has inspired a wealth of vehement debate by both critics and artists. In a scholarly argument very much in line with Kourilsky's thoughts on the staging, Judith Miller argues that Marie-Ange's presence dominates, even as Schwarz-Bart forecloses the possibility that she will become the object of desire for the male gaze.[41] But her analysis raises the same question that preoccupied Kourilsky: How should this complex dynamic be realized onstage? While Alvina Ruprecht and Kathleen Gyssels insist that, to accord with the author's intentions, the actress should not appear onstage, Michèle Montantin, who produced the premiere, argues that Schwarz-Bart ultimately preferred for the woman playing Marie-Ange to be present onstage, as in Cavé's production.[42]

If the man is alone onstage, it is clear that he is responsible for redressing the challenges of post-plantation heterosexual love. Indeed

Schwarz-Bart's play reverses social expectations not only because it is the woman who is adulterous but also because it is the man who must cope and find a way to forgive her. The man, in other words, takes on the responsibility of mending the couple's love in the woman's absence. But Schwarz-Bart's play ends with a question, as Wilnor wonders how to name himself in relation to his wife: "Your handsome captain?" The tensions Schwarz-Bart dramatizes, between the power of the couple's love and the reality of their separation, between presence and absence, are left unresolved—and thus perpetually open to further acts of recasting.

Schwarz-Bart herself—and her own romantic relationship—was interpolated into the performance of black diasporic "love and trouble" during a postperformance discussion. In our personal interview, Professor Ronnie Scharfman recalled that an African American man stood up and asked Schwarz-Bart why she had married a white man.[43] As a questioning (and presumably a judgment) of her interracial marriage, the spectator interrogated the extent to which Schwarz-Bart herself can love free from slavery's legacy. Perhaps the spectator disagreed with the radical message of black men's responsibility, or maybe he viewed Schwarz-Bart as living in contradiction with the reunification her play urges—as having abandoned black men. As in the incident involving Miller, this spectator was responding not only to the play but also to Ubu's offstage performance that contextualized it.

During that discussion, Schwarz-Bart's and her husband's bodies were read as culturally and ideologically coded. Schwarz-Bart's husband was present in the audience, and she publicly addressed their collaborations during the discussion. André Schwarz-Bart, best known for his prize-winning novel *The Last of the Just*, had lost his entire immediate family in the Shoah when he was just a child and lived most of his adult life in Guadeloupe with his wife. The husband and wife together considered the overlapping histories of blacks and Jews.[44] As Scharfman recalled, Simone Schwarz-Bart's answer to the spectator was that love knows no color. It might seem that Schwarz-Bart was simply repeating Ubu's rhetoric of love as a universal signifier, but she was also asserting her freedom from the moralizing gazes inherited from the plantation and her freedom to love as she chooses.

Throughout Ubu's multiple recastings of *Ton beau capitaine*, Kourilsky tried to do justice to what she identified as Schwarz-Bart's central theatrical device: the voice of Marie-Ange, a powerful presence who is never physically visible onstage. To embody this apparent contradiction, Kourilsky insisted that audiences should hear Marie-Ange's live voice from the wings. The actress should never be visible onstage, but her voice should never be prerecorded either. The challenge that preoccupied Kourilsky was how to show Wilnor's intimate connection with Marie-Ange while keeping her physically absent. By the final production, Kourilsky had succeeded in establishing that intimacy in several ways: Wilnor's performance of his love for his wife, including his cuddling with the cassette player, and his playful mouthing of her familiar greetings; Wilnor's onstage relationship with the musician; and Wilnor's vodou-inspired dance, which takes him beyond his hut in Guadeloupe.[45] But even if this final production satisfied Kourilsky, the urge for recasting remained in the unresolved tensions of post-plantation love that Schwarz-Bart scripts. In each act of the play's recasting, the script's epistemological tensions and unanswered questions reemerged.

The Tropical Breeze Hotel: Recasting Caribbean Irony as French Reality

Maryse Condé's *Pension les Alizés* shares with Schwarz-Bart's play an emphasis on the trials and tribulations of a francophone Caribbean heterosexual couple. While Schwarz-Bart's treatment of "love and trouble" hinges on an apparent contradiction between physical absence and ritualistic presence, Condé deploys irony in order to explore and nuance the theme of black diasporic heterosexual love. In comparison with Schwarz-Bart's ambiguous ending, Condé's play concludes on a bleaker note: Ishmael's execution and Emma's (seemingly inevitable) romantic isolation.

Condé's ironic and exaggerated portrayal of "love and trouble" was difficult to translate for U.S. spectators, particularly in Ubu's interracial setting, where black collaborators may have felt the burden of collective representation, that is, the responsibility to enact racial uplift through a positive representation of black communities. Whereas Ubu often relied on categories of identity ("black," "women," "gay") to make francophone plays accessible to U.S. audiences, Condé provocatively defies all racial, cultural, and gendered essentialisms. She has stated that she agrees with Hall's anti-essentialist theorization of Caribbean identity as diaspora identity: that which constantly produces and reproduces itself anew.[46] Her play portrays both Caribbeanness and black diasporic "love and trouble" as unfinished, in a process of becoming, and always in translation. How to translate a representation that is already in translation? At Ubu, apparent tensions between the French language and the performance of blackness posed particular challenges.

In 1995, five years after the final production of *Ton beau capitaine*, Ubu staged Condé's *The Tropical Breeze Hotel*. Though Kourilsky chose to invite a guest director to stage the play, the production was nevertheless dear to her, as she explained to me, since she knew Condé and appreciated the complexity of this particular play.[47] Four years earlier, in 1991, as part of the West Indies Festival, Ubu had produced Condé's *The Hills of Massabielle* (translated by her husband, Richard Philcox), a satire about tourism in the Caribbean, under the direction of Cynthia Belgrave. Even earlier in 1986, Condé had sat on Ubu's "Theater and Social Change" panel as part of the Festival of New Plays from French-Speaking Africa and the Caribbean, which included two Martinican plays by Aimé Césaire and Julius Amédé Laou. Condé was an ideal collaborator for Ubu, since she is both a scholar and a creative writer and had been teaching at various U.S. universities since 1978. Furthermore she had lived in Guadeloupe and continental France and in Africa (Ivory Coast, Guinea, Ghana, and Senegal). However, Condé, who has stated many times that once her texts are translated, she no longer thinks of them as her own,[48] never became actively involved in Ubu's artistic process. She preferred to work in solitude as a writer, and then to allow the production team to do their own work in turn, as she told me. She nonetheless remembered Ubu fondly, since the interest Kourilsky took in her theater encouraged her to write more plays.[49]

Condé's irony proved difficult to translate for U.S. audiences, and the subtleties of Emma and Ishmael's relationship posed challenges to Ubu's team. The play was not staged under the sign of Caribbean culture or the black diaspora. Rather the setting in France was foregrounded in Ubu's production, and the play was staged using psychological realism, according to director Shauneille Perry's vision. Though the role of Emma was not recast during the production's run, Kourilsky viewed the actress, Jane White, as fungible. Kourilsky had chosen to do the play with a specific actress in mind, Saundra McClain, but McClain was not available. The process of staging and receiving the play at Ubu was pervaded by misrecognitions and missed encounters between Condé and the production team. Condé's opaque writing style likely contributed to this dynamic. The question of how to best translate this play remains unanswered.

Translating Condé into English

Pension les Alizés was first translated independently and titled *Hotel les Alizés* by Barbara Lewis, an African American theater critic, scholar, and translator, who became interested in Condé's theater after reviewing Ubu's 1991 production of *The Hills of Massabielle* for the *Amsterdam News*.⁵⁰ As in the case of Harris's translation of *Ton beau capitaine*, Kourilsky, who was a purist when it came to the French language and preferred to commission her own translations, asked her literary manager, Temerson, to read through Lewis's text. Lewis was not brought up bilingually, like Temerson, but she did attend a French Canadian school. While Temerson had a wealth of experience in Ubu's translation center, Lewis was completing a master's degree in translation and had just finished a translation of Chamoiseau's story "Red Hot Peppers."⁵¹ As Temerson explained to me, her job was to go through the two texts word by word in order to ensure fidelity and prevent any mistranslations—what the French call (the dreaded) *contresens*.⁵² She recalled spending long hours on the text and making substantial changes—for which Kourilsky, who was meticulous about paying and crediting Ubu's translators, chose to acknowledge Temerson as cotranslator.⁵³

Temerson did not remember any specific changes she made. Neither could Lewis recall any details surrounding the changes Temerson made, but she remembered taking a pragmatic approach.⁵⁴ Knowing that Temerson was Ubu's gatekeeper, Lewis was happy to "take a backseat" to ensure that the translation would be staged. Temerson recalled that Kourilsky was quite satisfied with her corrections (of which Condé, following Ubu's process, also approved). However, in retrospect, Temerson wondered if she may have corrected translation choices that seemed like semantic mistakes but were actually liberties Lewis had deliberately taken in order to make Condé's text better resonate in English and for (black) U.S. spectators. When I asked Lewis about this possibility, she responded that, as a translator, she does have a "poetic tendency," but this discussion remained speculative, and Lewis's original translation has been lost.

As in previous discussions of Ubu's selection of translators, Kourilsky's recasting of the translator had both cultural and ideological implications. Once again Temerson, a white woman, was given authority by Kourilsky (another white woman) to judge and correct the work of a black woman, Lewis. Temerson's bilingualism and knowledge of French were favored over black diaspora literacies. In our interview, Temerson conscientiously reflected that, because her job was to correct linguistic errors, she might have seemed like the "French police."⁵⁵ It is important to keep in mind that, if Kourilsky was zealously committed to upholding the sanctity of the French language, this was a reflection of larger

French anxieties at the end of the twentieth century about globalization and the infiltration of English and *anglicismes* into the French language. Two-thirds of Ubu's funding came from the French Ministry of Culture. In fact when Kourilsky first created Ubu, the Ministry wanted her to perform the plays in French, but she insisted that they would do translations. Though Ubu sought to decenter metropolitan France, the French language was always the string holding together their various readings, productions, publications, and acts of community outreach.

It appears that Lewis had originally approached the text mindful of the theme of "love and trouble" in the larger black diaspora. She had engaged Condé in a discussion of the reoccurring elements of black women's lived experience in an interview conducted while she was translating the play. Emma exemplified a black women's dilemma, Condé told Lewis: "Even when they are very intelligent, the way that most black women can succeed is with their bodies, through their figures." Lewis also asked Condé to speculate about the similarities and differences in the "crisis with our men" in the French Caribbean and black America, to which Condé replied, "All over the black world, men are spoiled. They are like very small babies. You have to do everything for them. But we don't have a crisis in the West Indies. We believe that they have to amend their ways, to change, to become more responsible, but they are still very nice. The feeling is more ambivalent. We would like them to change. So the crisis is not as dramatic as it is in black America, it seems to me."[56] That Lewis and Condé took the time to discuss similarities and differences in post-plantation heterosexual love relationships in the Caribbean and in the United States might suggest that Lewis's translation likewise explored black diaspora "love and trouble." Might this translation have resonated differently in the United States? We cannot know, since Lewis's original translation remains a missed encounter between Condé and her U.S. readers and spectators.

Condé's writing style offers many challenges to the translator. *Pension les Alizés* is replete with the characteristic contradictions, surprises, traps, and conceptual seesaws that critics have identified in her writing at large.[57] Her dramas are fundamentally provocative; they pose many challenges to readers and spectators—and the production teams who stage her plays. Condé defies the same social scripts and cognitive schemas readers and spectators are likely to deploy in order to interpret her texts. Her writing encourages readers, interpreters, and spectators to reexamine their assumptions, particularly relating to the meaning of Caribbeanness and what constitutes Caribbean writing. From a postcolonial standpoint, Condé does not write in a language of resistance, insofar as she does not privilege the Creole language, which was historically dominated by French. Once an oral language, Creole's writing has been standardized by Creole activists, Hector Poullet in Guadeloupe and, in Martinique, Jean Bernabé.[58] Previously prohibited in schools, it is now taught at the University of the Antilles and French Guiana, and even in secondary schools since the 2001 French law on regional languages. For the writers known as the Créolists, Patrick Chamoiseau and Raphaël Confiant, Creole is a fundamental tool for literary resistance. By contrast, Condé writes in a language that is much closer to the French intellectual and classical literary tradition than to the Creolized French that has become Chamoiseau's trademark.[59] Condé has been criticized by the Créolists for writing in French (rather than Creole) and for making her writing too easily accessible to a French public. Her provocative answer is that she writes "neither in French nor in Creole. But in Maryse Condé."[60]

What does it mean to write in Maryse Condé, and how might this unique language be translated? Condé expertly deploys not only French and Creole (and other languages) but also global landscapes, musicalities, layers of intertextual references that range from the canonical to the obscure, and, above all, irony. The result is a writing style that, to quote Philcox, is "very esoteric . . . [and] makes its readers work."[61] Writing about his experience translating Condé, Philcox stresses the need to find a new register and tone with which her complex text can resonate. One must be "unfaithful to the French-speaking context and faithful to the music and register of a canon in the English language."[62] In order to find this register, Philcox considers contextual and extratextual information to which only he, as Condé's husband, is privy: texts that she was reading at the time, the places and sites they visited together, and the music she was listening to.[63] He goes so far as to "relive the experience that inspired the original work."[64]

Gayatri Spivak has theorized the politics of translation as a question of intimacy: the ethical, feminist translator must be intimately familiar with the text's original language and attuned to the "ways in which rhetoric or figuration disrupt logic."[65] Stated more simply, the translator must be intimate with not only words but also the silences between the words: the language of the original text and writer's artful ways of undoing, restructuring, and playing with that language. One wonders whether such intimacy with Condé's writing is possible for any translator other than her husband. Even despite his zealous efforts, Condé remains uninterested in his translations—which Philcox regrets.[66] Yet the act of translation itself may already be intimately tied to Condé's writing. The challenges her texts pose to translators are rooted in their construction as already translational, translinguistic, and transcultural. Insofar as Condé's rhetoric and writing style reflects nomadic Caribbeanness, as Rachelle Okawa has argued, the process of translating her texts mirrors the dislocations that her works enact. According to Okawa, both Condé's texts and the act of translation thus construct Caribbean identity as a problem based on a series of past dislocations—that is, the Middle Passage, slavery, and exile.[67]

Speaking specifically of Ubu's production of *The Tropical Breeze Hotel*, Condé has commented that the play's ironic content did not translate well into English.[68] Ubu's translation clarifies some of Emma's opaque speech, thus downplaying her clever irony and making the character fairly serious. Consider, for example, Emma's language early on in the play as she remembers her first days in Paris:

> Les jours étaient noirs comme les tableaux d'une salle de classe, des tickets de rationnement pour tout. La viande, on ne savait pas ce que c'était ! Qui avait la tête à étudier ?[69]

> Those were dark days, as dark as the blackboard in a classroom. Everyone was on rations. Meat was an unattainable luxury! Who could study?[70]

The translation is quite literal inasmuch as it reproduces Emma's images and references. However, it privileges clarity of meaning over the humor, hyperbole, and uniqueness of her speech. Emma's clever, dramatic personality becomes less discernible. For instance, her provocatively exaggerated description of the paucity of meat—"La viande, on ne savait pas ce que c'était!"—might have been translated as "Meat? People didn't even know what it was!" But I suspect that Ubu's translators worried that this reproduction of Emma's speaking style might have confused spectators and readers unfamiliar with the French rationing during World War II. People culturally distanced from the text might have tended to take Emma's exaggerated comments too literally. Instead the phrase is replaced with the much more straightforward exclamation that meat was an unattainable luxury. Throughout the text, in glossing over Emma's complexity, the translation does not quite adequately capture how she fluctuates between light, clever humor and bittersweet clarity.

Several staging choices in the Ubu production appear to have miscommunicated the driving themes of the black woman's alienation in white patriarchal society and the way slavery's sexualized legacy undermines romantic relations between black Caribbean men and women.

Much like Condé presents challenges to her translators, she also catches the artists who produce her plays in interpretive traps. I agree with Okawa that translation (though it does not interest—and perhaps somewhat vexes—Condé) is in many ways a further realization of the translational quality of Condé's writing. Likewise, interpretive choices that Ubu collaborators—and Condé herself—perceived as misrecognitions or misperformances of her play represent unsettling embodiments of her staging of creolization.

Enacting Irony with Psychological Realism

The pioneering African American director Shauneille Perry was selected to direct the play. Perry had not been involved with Ubu before signing on to do the production as a freelance director, and her approach to the play was quite different from Ubu's habitual intercultural aesthetic and process. She described her method to me as distinguishing between a character's "inside" human elements and *how* they express those shared insides, which is cultural conditioning coming from the "outside": "A violent person is a violent person, but *how* they are violent is determined by their cultural surroundings."[71] Thus Perry emphasized meticulous cultural research into the specific location and customs that Condé evoked, while generalizing the nature and psychological state of the characters. This method, a culturally conscious form of psychological realism, has the advantage of forestalling the possibility of a folkloric (static) representation of Caribbean culture, of which Césaire and Dambury complained. However, it was very much at odds with Ubu's common process of deploying an intercultural aesthetic to invite U.S. audiences to identify with the francophone play. As Kourilsky described the production, "it was all realistic, different from Ubu's usual work."[72]

Following Perry's directorial concept, the designers employed psychological realism as the major means of communication. Watoku Ueno, Ubu's longtime set designer, used a more straightforward and realistic approach for *The Tropical Breeze Hotel* than he did with other Caribbean productions (figure 15). His set presents a small studio apartment. The spectator can easily imagine that Emma lives in this space insofar as it displays furniture and objects that she uses in her daily life: a couch, a table, her makeup table, her clothing, and worn-out rugs. Following Condé's stage directions, Ueno painted a portrait of the lead actress, Jane White, which he hung on the wall. He portrayed a younger White in the painting, which stands in for Emma's feelings: her nostalgia for her glamorous days as a nude dancer. Old photographs reinforced this theme of nostalgia. The

Figure 15. Watoko Ueno's set of Maryse Condé's *The Tropical Breeze Hotel*. New York, 1995. (Photograph by Watoko Ueno; private collection; courtesy of Watoko Ueno)

Japanese influence that was recognizable in other sets is not visible in his work for *The Tropical Breeze Hotel*, which displays an array of knickknacks rather than the large, symbolic pieces that are his trademark. Greg Macpherson explained that his expressionist lighting, which used mostly reds, sought to evoke Emma's inner state, her psychology or feelings. Pelletier recalled that her costumes were based in contemporary French dress and emphasized the generalized concept of a faded diva.[73]

The actors also portrayed Condé's characters using a realistic style. The well-established Broadway actress Jane White, a lighter-skinned black woman who often played colorblind roles, was cast as Emma. The Haitian-born actor and regular Ubu collaborator Patrick Rameau (who also played Wilnor in *Your Handsome Captain*), known for his starring roles in two films by Haitian director Raoul Peck, played Ishmael.[74] Based on my personal interviews as well as my consultation of production photographs and critical reviews, I have gathered that the two actors succeeded in playing the moments of friction and misunderstanding between the two characters (figure 16). However, it appears that they did not communicate the moments of tenderness that also run through the play. Many interviewees described the unsatisfying on- and

191 *Recasting the Francophone Caribbean Couple*

Figure 16. A moment of tension between Patrick Rameau as Ishmael and Jane White as Emma in Maryse Condé's *The Tropical Breeze Hotel*. New York, 1995. (Photograph by Jonathan Slaff; Ubu Repertory Theater Collections; courtesy of the Bibliothèque nationale de France)

offstage relationship between White and Rameau, explaining that they did not get along or like each other and that the stage chemistry simply was not there.[75] Condé concurred; through she reported to me that she was happy with the staging on the whole, she felt that the actors did not bring Emma and Ishmael's romantic relationship to life.[76] Translator Barbara Lewis, in contrast, recalled being fascinated by the stage chemistry—what she described as "an electricity" between White and Rameau.[77]

In an interview with Ruprecht, Condé additionally observes that the director, Perry, was not sensitive to the text's "transitions between moments of irony and tenderness."[78] These transitions in tone, which produce the Brechtian alienation effect discussed in chapter 1, are certainly present in the English-language text, but they are more apparent in the French. They would be very difficult to reproduce on stage using psychological realism, since they occur very quickly and abruptly.

I imagine that an actor working with Stanislavskian character motivations would have much difficulty structuring his or her portrayal of these roles. In fact such an approach seems somewhat incongruous with Condé's larger philosophy toward her characters.

Condé emphasizes not the unity of the character's motivations or the actor's performance of a single, cohesive driving interpretation of the role (central to psychological realism as it is commonly practiced in the United States) but rather the actor's plasticity—which enables the communication of fragmented, contradictory emotions. Condé explains that she writes plays with certain actors in mind, who share the quality of being emotionally ambiguous and malleable. Her favorite actors are skillfully able to act comedy and tragedy at once and to play a character as simultaneously happy and sad.[79] I believe that this plasticity of the actor, as Condé calls it, could facilitate communication of the play's creolizing, political meanings on stage. Mastery of such a craft might enable the actors playing Emma and Ishmael to perform the ways slavery's sexual legacy inflects and obstructs their romantic behaviors and attitudes without prescriptively portraying the characters as helpless victims to white patriarchy or to history.

One key rapid change in tone occurs in the play's final moment. Ishmael has returned to Haiti, and Emma receives a phone call informing her of his likely execution (figure 17). In a moment that echoes the play's opening, she sits alone at her makeup table and proclaims, "I'll stick on my false eyelashes and the show can begin!" However, as Condé's stage directions specify, this moment is crucially different from the opening, insofar as Emma makes her face up into a clown, a Pierrot: as Condé specifies: "Slowly at first, then faster and faster, transforming her face into a clown's face [Pierrot]." In Emma's donning of the whiteface clown makeup, Condé's unmasking of slavery's sexual legacy is crystallized. Covering her black skin with a white mask, Emma affirms in this final scene her complete assimilation into French culture, her acceptance of the stereotype of the Marilisse and of the impossibility of any form of sustainable love with a Caribbean man. That this moment seems to come out of nowhere strengthens its disruption of spectators' complicity in the myth of the Marilisse.

This subversive moment proved difficult to render in performance. In the original production, Sonia Emmanuel replaced the whiteface makeup with white hair. The whiteface was even further removed from Perry's realistic vision of the play and from White's portrayal of Emma as a psychologically motivated universal diva. As far as I can gather, in the Ubu production, Emma used bright red lipstick in place of the clown

Figure 17. Jane White as Emma alone at her makeup table in Maryse Condé's *The Tropical Breeze Hotel*. New York, 1995. (Photograph by Jonathan Slaff; Ubu Repertory Theater Collections; courtesy of the Bibliothèque nationale de France)

makeup. Pelletier speculated why this stage direction was likely ignored: "The way Jane portrayed the character, that kind of frenetic behavior would have seemed incongruous."[80] Incongruity in the actor's portrayal of a role is a flaw according to the rules of psychological realism, but I wonder whether it might have facilitated a performance of Condé's more political, creolizing meanings. Rosette C. Lamont's review in *Theater Week* interpreted this final moment as Emma's triumph rather than a performance of how slavery's sexual legacy traps her in assimilation and leads her to play the clown. Lamont calls Emma's final proclamation "a brave line worthy of Giraudoux's *Madwoman of Chaillot*."[81] Of course, the reference to Giraudoux here serves to label the play as French, which some spectators found to be incompatible with its coding as Caribbean or black.

French, not Black or Caribbean

As in the productions already analyzed, in order to attract spectators, Ubu coded Condé's play under multiple cultural signs. In 1994 Ubu staged a reading of the play as part of the Festival of New Plays by Women, and the published text likewise appeared in their international anthology of plays by women. In contrast, the full-scale production was part of the Spring French West Indies Festival, paired with Laou's *Another Story*. Echoing Condé's dramaturgical positioning of Emma (a former nude dancer) within an intergenerational community of black women whom society equated with their bodies, virtually every press release and flyer likened Emma to Josephine Baker.[82] At the same time, the play was framed as a universal love story. The opening on February 14, 1995, Valentine's Day, was followed by a fundraising party. "Bring your sweetheart or meet one," suggested an invitation for the benefit.[83] Though a clever fundraising tactic, the party's theme was incongruous with the pessimistic vision of love presented by the play. Furthermore, inasmuch as the failure of Emma's romantic relationship with her Haitian house guest Ishmael is a symptom of slavery's sexual legacy, a party universalizing the theme of love may have mitigated the play's sociopolitical impact. Such incongruities represented another unsettling materialization of the play's aesthetics of creolization, even though they undermined the political message.

Despite its placement in the French West Indies Festival, *The Tropical Breeze Hotel* was interpreted by many collaborators and spectators as French rather than Caribbean. Though Perry was familiar with the Caribbean, and had even worked in professional theater there, the French language and setting took precedence over Caribbean cultural signs in her mediation of Condé's play. Perry understood her role as cultural mediator as involving primarily a negotiation between the French and U.S. worldviews rather than the creation of a black diaspora performance. She explained to me that a director has the difficult role of the "middle person" who makes all the pieces come together and that this task may be more difficult in an international setting because of linguistic differences. A director must be privy to the meanings of the text, she explained, and an English-speaking director is more likely to understand those meanings with an English text than one written in French or German. She was quite happy that Rameau, a former student of hers at Queens College, was involved in the production because of his fluency (as a Haitian) in the French language. She saw his language expertise as an advantage but did not stress her own mastery of black diaspora theater forms as a relevant qualification.

Given Ubu's history of enlisting visible and talented African American artists, it was likely because of Perry's reputation and expertise in black diaspora theater that Kourilsky chose her to direct the piece. Yet Ubu's interest in cross-culturalism was flexible and inexplicit, and it appears that no one communicated this interest in black diaspora performance to Perry. Perry associated Ubu not with black theater in particular but with the French language. She told me that, before signing on to this show, all she knew about Ubu was that they did francophone work. She did not see it as a diasporic theater or recognize it particularly for its ties with the African American community. Attentive to detail and following her commitment to realism, Perry sought to reproduce the location of the play: Paris. Stage manager notes document her reminders to cast and crewmembers of the setting and her request that they "establish a sense of Paris (French in nature)."[84] Paris, which for Emma is a place of assimilation into French culture, occupies a different space in the imaginaries of Guadeloupean and U.S. spectators. Paris was in many ways a place of freedom from U.S. racism for Josephine Baker. For Emma, in contrast, it represents loneliness—the price of independence.

Meticulously conscientious, Perry's production privileged the text's setting and the characters' scripted words over the generalizable narrative of embodied black female experience. "Whatever Ms. Condé wrote," Perry summarized, "that's what I tried to do."[85] In chapter 4, I observed how, in Shange's production of *Fire's Daughters*, African dance enabled the actresses to perform a transnational construction of black womanhood, which corresponded with Césaire's emphasis on Caribbean storytelling, songs, and other performance practices. Condé's text, in contrast, shows the black female body not as a transmitter of knowledge so much as a site upon which sexual stereotypes are confusingly projected across chronological time.

This may be why Perry did not stress the body as a viable transmitter of knowledge or a repository for performance material. When I asked her how she staged the Haitian merengue that is written into Condé's text, she replied that she did not remember exactly, and then concluded that she must have engaged "someone who knew the particular dance." A short but happy moment for the couple, the merengue looks awkward in a production photo (figure 18). In Condé's script, it represents a brief moment of unity between Emma and Ishmael and across Guadeloupe and Haiti, coexisting—and juxtaposed—with the text's portrayal of critical differences. In Ubu's production, the dance did not communicate black diaspora unity but rather served as a reminder of the crucial differences that Condé also scripts. Though Emma, from Guadeloupe, has lived in Paris for more than forty years, she owns Haitian music and

Figure 18. Emma and Ishmael dancing the merengue in Maryse Condé's *The Tropical Breeze Hotel*: Jane White and Patrick Rameau. New York, 1995. (Photograph by Jonathan Slaff; Ubu Repertory Theater Collections; courtesy of the Bibliothèque nationale de France)

knows how to dance the merengue like her Haitian house guest. Poking fun at her elite French tastes, Ishmael teases, "Maybe you like opera, but you are a real black woman. . . . One who knows how to dance."[86] In coding the dance as culturally situated movement, Perry and the production team missed the opportunity to perform the merengue's potential as a signifier of black diaspora unity.

Ubu expressly sought out additional Caribbean and black audience members for most Caribbean productions, but for *The Tropical Breeze Hotel*, efforts seem more actively targeted to French American spectators. Chris Kapp, who did the marketing, remembered putting the production on the list of the Theatre Development Fund, which gave spectators discounted tickets with purchased deals and catered to public school teachers and others in education. She also publicized on a francophone Caribbean radio station and reached out to French-language newspapers and to the French consulate. She even sought out a French American audience by targeting the affluent suburb of Mamaroneck.[87] Though the production was listed in *Black Masks*, which was well circulated within the African American theater community, and though Ubu invited *Black Arts NY* to review the show, to my knowledge no reviews of *The Tropical Breeze Hotel* in African American publications appeared.[88] I take the lack of such a review to suggest that, generally speaking, African American reviewers did not see the production as relevant to the canon of black theater, and neither did they interpret the play as related to slavery's legacy. Picking up on Condé's bittersweet tone but attributing the failure of Emma and Ishmael's romance to the universal human experience, Bruckner of the *New York Times* wrote, "There is a sad message in 'The Tropical Breeze Hotel,' by Maryse Condé: in matters of the heart, age confers wisdom, but wisdom brings pain and gives no consolation."[89]

Perry's production of *The Tropical Breeze Hotel* emphasized the French language and setting. It appears that the majority of spectators did not interpret the play as a black diaspora performance of "love and trouble" but rather as a foreign text (staged out of context in New York) that offered insight into the universal human condition. *The Tropical Breeze Hotel* reimagines and refutes the categories of black, French, Caribbean, and women, even as it performs them. The play dramatizes the experience of a black Guadeloupean woman living in exile in France, who stands in symbolically for the French Caribbean people at large, many of whom live alongside and within French culture, especially following the 1946 law for *départementalisation*. Condé's concept of Caribbeanness in fact resembles Kourilsky's intercultural interest in exile, which led her to direct French Caribbean plays.[90] If *The Tropical Breeze Hotel* scripts embodied alienation and the dislocation and fragmentation of Caribbean selfhood and love, Ubu's 1995 production—as another act of translation—performed that dislocation (albeit in ways that collaborators did not anticipate) on the global stage.

Recasting Emma: Diva or Black Woman?

Although the role of Emma was not recast, there was much debate over who should play her. Kourilsky had originally chosen to do Condé's play with the understanding that Emma would be played by Saundra McClain, who had done a staged reading in 1994 of the part for Ubu's Festival of New Plays by Women.[91] However, when it came time to begin work on the full-scale production in 1995, McClain was not available. Perry cast White, with whom she had worked before and whom she believed to be a "great actress."[92] Kourilsky did not agree with the casting choice, but she left the direction to Perry. At the occasion of the "Bravo Ubu" performance in 2001, Kourilsky recast Emma, giving the role again to McClain.

Beyond the artists' personal preferences, at stake in the recasting was the communication of the heterosexual couple in the black diaspora. White was a light-skinned black actress, known for doing "classic roles," often Shakespeare.[93] A darker-skinned black actress, McClain would have been more readily intelligible as a "black woman" for spectators who did not know of White's family background. Beyond the visual cue of McClain's complexion, her interpretation of Emma's motivations and psychology might have also encouraged spectators to see her as part of the black diaspora. Based on my discussions with Ubu collaborators and attendees and my consultation of reviews and photographs, I gather that White embodied Emma—or perhaps that her lighter-skinned body was *read* as embodying Emma—as a "diva." Inasmuch as a diva character is obsessed with her own desires and success, White's interpretation of Emma may not have conveyed a woman of color hampered by slavery's sexual legacy.

McClain, on the other hand, appears to have interpreted Emma's character through a generalized, embodied experience of a black woman living within white patriarchy—and one that would have resonated more readily in the United States. Describing her experience of the character, she remembered, "[Emma] had a difficult time dealing with her dark complexion and a feeling of inferiority based on color. She dealt with self-esteem problems. She was beautiful but she felt she was not."[94] McClain's interpretation might have more easily cued U.S. audiences to see how Emma is ensnared by slavery's sexual stereotypes, exoticized each time she steps out the door.

Though it may have discouraged black diasporic readings of "love and trouble" for U.S. spectators, White's interpretation of Emma as a diva makes sense. In fact it corresponds with Condé's own comments to Pfaff: "[Emma] reflects the rise and fall of a person. She is the old prostitute, the aging whore. These are themes found frequently in the theater."[95] Whereas other Ubu collaborators downplayed Condé's irony, White seems to have been attuned to Condé's scripting of Emma's exaggerated (sexualized) behaviors and self-delusions—the crux of the play's ironic tone. However, particularly since the play was staged using psychological realism and was coded as French, and due to the way U.S. spectators likely read White's body, Emma's diva-like qualities seem to have occluded the creolization of gender relations. In other words, at Ubu, many viewed Condé's ironic treatment of Emma's self-delusions and her consideration of slavery's sexual legacy as mutually exclusive. How could the production team have communicated these two facets of Emma to Ubu's audiences? One might imagine a creolized version of Emma in whom White's and McClain's seemingly opposing interpretations would coexist.

For Condé, it is precisely by way of her irony that she exposes and defamiliarizes the Marilisse. Lifting the veil from the Marilisse, Condé encourages her audiences to *think* about Emma's predicament and her entrapment in romantic isolation. Condé's challenge to U.S. identity politics may have proved difficult for U.S. spectators to receive, particularly since her provocative exaggerations of Emma's sexual behaviors and delusions must have overturned the rules of interracial decorum in 1995. She has long refused racial essentialisms and the burden of collective representation.[96] Furthermore she has provocatively criticized dominant views toward race in the United States for "turning a blind eye to biological hybridity" and holding to an "obsolete cultural principal" that "a person with a drop of black blood is in fact black."[97]

Regrettably there seems to have been a missed encounter between White and Condé. Though both influential women refused racial essentialisms, their innovative approaches to writing and performing race did not converge in the context of this production. White was the daughter of Walter White, an important activist and longtime executive secretary of the NAACP, who identified as African American but passed as white and was thus able to infiltrate and write about lynching mobs and race riots.[98] Jane White inherited not only her father's light-skinned complexion but also his desire to use the privileges it afforded him in order to better the world in which he lived.[99] As a performer, Jane White worked against the industry's (and her audiences') expectations about race. "I've just always been too 'white' to be 'black' and too 'black' to be 'white,' which, you know, gets to you after a while, particularly when the roles keep passing you by," she said in a 1968 interview.[100] Her ambivalent relationship to race resonated with Emma's own assimilation into French (white) culture. The final whiteface moment that Condé scripts (had Ubu's production team decided to follow the stage directions) might have opened interesting interpretive possibilities for White, whose complexion was already light. But such a provocative performance of Emma was never realized on Ubu's stage; its potential thereby represents a missed encounter between Condé and White.

At Ubu, Schwarz-Bart's and Condé's plays were recast, restaged, and reinterpreted several times, as collaborators sought to resolve challenges in translation and to adapt each playwright's unique writing style for U.S. audiences. Ubu's process of intercultural meaning making enabled artists to collaboratively reconfigure these plays, even as Kourilsky, the production's director, and sometimes the playwright herself held to interpretations they perceived to be accurate or appropriate. In the end, those artistic agents who held power or laid claim to knowledge of so-called authentic Caribbean culture ultimately controlled Ubu's decisions. I sought to investigate Ubu's multiple acts of recasting the two plays and to illuminate the conflicts, misrecognitions, and missed encounters materialized by Ubu's rehearsal process and performances. Variously coded by language, geography, and cultural performance practices, the plays facilitated unsteady and contradictory readings, especially of the theme of love, which was simultaneously figured as universal, Caribbean, and black diasporic. The unresolved tensions of "love and trouble" that Schwarz-Bart and Condé dramatized were reinvented on Ubu's stage, provoking unpredictable responses and multiple, often conflicting meanings.

The ambivalence over the casting choices of Slade as Marie-Ange and White as Emma illuminates the ways in which these female characters embody conflicting and contradictory impulses. Marie-Ange is both present and absent, both innocent and guilty of adultery, and "a woman who sings like a dragonfly despite the tons of sorrows dragging on her skirts."[101] Emma has made her own choices in life, though they were scripted by slavery's sexualized legacy. Emma fluctuates between light, clever humor and bittersweet clarity. She is a diva, self-important, obstinate, and somewhat delusional, yet she also gives selflessly to Ishmael and makes sense of the world with ample insight and generosity. By juxtaposing White's and McClain's divergent interpretations of Emma, I have illuminated the character's apparent contradictions. Ubu's ambivalence over Emma raises the question of whether any single performer could embody Condé's protagonist. If the same is true for Marie-Ange, perhaps that is why Kourilsky insisted that the woman playing her should never be present onstage. Whereas Kourilsky and Ubu's production teams and collaborators generally remembered the productions explored in chapter 4 as successes (though the playwrights themselves had some misgivings), Kourilsky was ambivalent about Ubu's productions in English of Schwarz-Bart's and Condé's plays. But whether perceived as successes or failures, each of these productions provides a lens through which to explore creolization at work in theater by French Caribbean women.

Conclusion

Taking its cue from a group of deeply insightful, inspiring, and conscientious Caribbean women playwrights, *Staging Creolization* has foregrounded creolization as a performative process of cultural remembrance and reinvention that subverts established narratives, puts diverse points of view into dialogue, and challenges the status quo. Plays by Césaire, Condé, Schwarz-Bart, and Dambury juxtapose bodies with speech, lived experience with ideology, African-derived performance practices with European theatrical conventions, and different conceptions of the past's influence on the present and future. They reinvent the sexual stereotypes of plantation culture, remix unity and difference, and syncretize performance and moral codes. These dramaturgies of creolization encourage critical reflection and social change by embracing ambiguity, contradiction, and inassimilable complexity.

As their transatlantic production history suggests, the plays engaged interracial artists and spectators in the parallel French and U.S. contexts as both nations were grappling with slavery's legacy. Citing the importance of Ubu Repertory Theater to French Caribbean theater history, Alvina Ruprecht suggests that scholars must ask whether Ubu, in its efforts to adapt to its U.S. audiences, significantly transformed the original texts.[102] In chapters 4 and 5 I answered Ruprecht's question in the affirmative and meticulously documented these transformations. Yet precisely by way of transformation, the Ubu productions extended the creolizing projects of the plays. While some aspects of Ubu's productions appear to counteract the playwrights' original intentions, the conflicts and tensions that occurred in performance were in many ways scripted—in other words, prefigured, though not necessarily dictated or prescribed—by the multivalent plays. The unsettling surprises that occurred at Ubu remind us that creolization necessarily involves inassimilable grit, leftovers, and unresolved tensions.

I have aimed to privilege the cultural literacies, epistemologies, and theatrical processes creolization produces. Following Shu-mei Shih and Françoise Lionnet, I have regarded cultural, historical, and theatrical "encounters as situations that produce the possibility of a theory or a method that can itself be conceptualized as creolization."[103] Specifically, as a theater scholar my creolizing method involves shifting between the study of dramatic literature and performance analysis in order to illuminate the multifaceted, complex, and dynamic meanings scripted and enacted by these plays. As Sandra Richards has noted, given that the African American folk aesthetic privileges juxtapositions, syncopation, and creative syncretism, we as critics of theater and performance must "scrutinize those meanings we produce based upon the multiple discourses in which we and the script are embedded, but we also need to imagine and to write into critical discourse how these interpretations imply contradictory positions that are likely to result from the materiality of theatre, that is, from the semiotics of movement, tones, silences, costumes and spatial arrangements on stage as well as from the reactions of spectators in the auditorium."[104] I have worked to craft a methodology attuned to such creolized and creolizing meanings written into the plays, mindful of contradictory positions, juxtapositions, fragments, ambiguities, multiple discourses, positionality, and continuities and discontinuities in time and space.

In my performance analysis, each play's "absent potential," to borrow Richards's term, was further investigated by using theater—the play's production and reception histories—as a laboratory. In France and the Caribbean, I observed conflicts and disagreements over gender relations, the "authentic" characteristics of Caribbean identity and history, and the interplay of African-derived and European forms of knowledge. Performances in the United States were permeated by similar misrecognitions, claims to cultural authority, and conflicts—particularly surrounding race, racism, and racialized knowledge production—provoked by collaborative acts of making meanings from these plays in Ubu's interracial and international theatrical context. The Ubu productions tended to make race and culture static, which irritated several of the playwrights, but they nonetheless challenged the cultural status quo of the white-dominated New York theater scene. I have taken such moments of misrecognition and conflict to be materializations of the performative process of creolization. Creolization connects past, present, and future as well as spatial and geographical configurations through what Antonio Benítez-Rojo calls "discontinuous conjunction."[105] Ubu's creolization of these plays defamiliarizes our assumptions and reminds us of the contingency of Caribbeanness, race, and gender as well as the ways in which these social signifiers are differently inflected in various cultural contexts.

My exploration of this second phase of creolization at Ubu raises a question: To what extent can creolization be generalized beyond the Caribbean? This question has preoccupied theorists of creolization across disciplines.[106] While creolization is an apt critical, comparativist tool, overgeneralizing the term also risks stripping it of its sociocultural and political meanings. "Unmoored uses of the concept of creolization," Lionnet and Shih warn, "can take it in the direction of merely playful bricolage or transculturalism. Without an anchor in history, creolization can become too pliable."[107] While I have chosen to view staging choices

203 *Recasting the Francophone Caribbean Couple*

that unsettled and surprised the playwrights themselves as an extension of their aesthetics of creolization, I also note that some of these choices (for example, replacing Emma's whiteface makeup with red lipstick) represented a depoliticization of the play's meanings. To be sure, writing for the theater and moving beyond postcolonialism both entail, to some extent, relinquishing control over the political meanings produced by a play. But these particular moments of conflict also raise ethical questions. How to evaluate and enact a politics—and ethics—of performing creolization, particularly in the United States? I take up this question in the book's coda.

Coda

Creolizing Knowledge in
U.S. University Performances

Françoise Vergès views creolization as, at its core, an ethics of encounters, transformations, and borrowings: "Creolization . . . must be distinguished from cultural contact and multiculturalism because, at heart, it is a practice and ethics of borrowing and accepting to be transformed, affected by the other. In the current era of globalization, processes of creolization appear in the zones of conflict and contact. They are the harbingers of an ongoing ethics of sharing the world."[1] How do we grasp such an ethics of global encounters and mutual transformation? And how do we anchor these ethics of such a seemingly boundless project in the embodied inheritances of slavery and colonialism? How do we, in other words, avoid depoliticizing, overgeneralizing, and disembedding creolization from its Caribbean historical and cultural contexts? How do we preserve—and reinvent—its critical, political, and ethical potential? More specifically, how do we do so, ethically, from U.S. universities? How can we teach creolization in our classrooms?

If creolization is, as I have theorized it in this book, a performance-based practice of cultural and epistemological transformation via mixing and conflict, then performance must be key to answering these questions. Embodied knowledge is necessary to any effort to grasp the ethics of creolization, to learn from the legacies of slavery and colonialism, and to look ahead toward our shared future. My coda considers how U.S.-based students, teachers, artists, and audiences might collaboratively create and re-create creolizing knowledges through a series of ethical, performative encounters facilitated by collaborative theater making. Analyses of the productions of Césaire's *L'Enfant des passages*, staged in French at the University of Wisconsin in 1994, and Condé's *An tan revolisyon*, performed in English translation (*In the Time of Revolution*) at the University of Georgia in 1997, complete the theater history and enable a self-reflexive addendum to my study by offering a privileged view into theater's pedagogical and ethical possibilities when U.S.-based students and teachers (re)produce knowledge by performing and adapting Caribbean plays.

The university productions crafted diaspora performances that resonated in the United States while privileging Caribbean theater, culture, and knowledge. Much like the approach I have adopted in *Staging Creolization*, these performances aimed, to cite Maryse Condé, to "expand the notion of the Caribbean" to encompass the United States.[2] To be sure, creolization is part of our inheritance in the United States. "The basic configuration of the plantation, in terms of its physical layout and the social relations it created," Martin Munro and Cecilia Britton point out, "was largely the same in the Caribbean and the American South."[3] But the ways we make meaning from the embodied inheritances of the plantation differ, particularly with respect to the meanings and politics of race. Rather than considering the United States as part of the Caribbean rim, scholars of race and performance have tended to embrace a U.S.-centric approach that attributes postblack formations to the new millennium.[4] The educational performances examined here, in contrast, took Caribbean paradigms as their starting point.

Even more than in the Ubu productions, these two educational performances at U.S. universities encouraged creolized and creolizing knowledge—that is, learning based on cultural and epistemological encounters, points of tension, adaptation, re-creation, reinvention, and reciprocal exchange. Students producing the plays cultivated embodied knowledge inasmuch as they learned experientially, by participating in the collaborative act of meaning making. A study of these productions illuminates how U.S.-based teachers and students can learn from Caribbean plays by creating new performances aimed at fostering creolized and creolizing literacy and premised on a meticulous study of the play and its sociohistorical context. Within these culturally conscious educational performances, social signifiers took on syncretic meanings. Teaching material that students likely perceived as historically or culturally distant or unfamiliar, the educators creolized knowledge: they negotiated between the opposing poles of sameness and difference, mobility and fixity, continuity and change in order to facilitate meaningful learning.

Educational Stagings

The university setting enabled artists to privilege education and knowledge production. Acted by students and directed (as well as translated) by professors who are my own mentors and colleagues, the university productions of Césaire's and Condé's plays encouraged critical reflection and dialogue relating to slavery's legacy and its embodied inheritance as creolization. Expanding upon the playwrights' dramaturgies of creolization, these productions found innovative, performative ways to problematize the question of cultural literacy and the contingency of social signifiers, namely race, gender, and Caribbeanness. In addition to consulting traces of the performances in personal archives and conducting personal interviews with the directors, I have viewed both of these performances on video.[5] Aesthetically Judith Miller's production of *L'Enfant des passages* used a presentational, storybook style. Lively Caribbean music punctuated the transitions, particularly as Ti-Jean and his brother walked from one world to another. In contrast with the premiere performance, actors were costumed as anthropomorphized animals. Freda Scott Giles's production of *In the Time of Revolution* similarly deployed a carnivalesque aesthetic, with several of the actors wearing masks that recalled both Commedia dell'arte and Noh theater. Projected images served to educate audiences about the history and to make links to the present day. In contrast with the postmodern approach to the costumes in the premiere, Giles's production used brightly colored period costumes. The storyteller Zéphyr's multicolored, multilayered robes evoked Yoruba Egungun costumes.

Combined with larger university events and activities, the plays were framed as opportunities for learning. Césaire's *L'Enfant des passages* was the culminating event of Miller's split-level undergraduate and graduate course on francophone Caribbean theater. Condé's *In the Time of Revolution* was translated by two UGA professors, Doris Kadish and Jean-Pierre Piriou, and staged in conjunction with an academic conference on slavery in the francophone world as well as an annual meeting of the Nineteenth-Century French Studies Colloquium. Directors, actors, and other collaborators were interested in the plays as dramatic writing but also in the academic investigations that informed them: Césaire's ethnological research on Caribbean folklore and Condé's exploration of the complex histories surrounding the French and Haitian revolutions.

Both directors researched, taught, and staged the cultural and critical literacy demanded by Césaire's and Condé's texts. These two directors wear multiple hats as artists, scholars, and devoted teachers. Giles was invited by Kadish to direct the new translation, and she prepared by studying the histories and cultures of the francophone Caribbean as well as Condé's rich oeuvre. Reading Condé's novels, Giles was particularly inspired by the treatment of history in *I Tituba, Black Witch of Salem*. Her production of *In the Time of Revolution* in 1997 stressed the way the past inhabits the present. This theme of past as present in black diasporic theater and contemporary life continues to permeate Giles's creative and scholarly work.[6] At the time she directed *L'Enfant des passages* in 1994, Miller had already begun her study of Césaire and had translated *Island Memories* and *Fire's Daughters*. She was especially interested in Césaire's work on folktales, and she would go on to adapt Césaire's creative folktale *Lettre d'affranchissement* for the stage in 1996. In subsequent years teaching this same francophone theater course, Miller would stage several francophone African plays.[7]

Insofar as the productions self-reflexively addressed identity and difference, personal, cultural positioning was an important factor in both productions. Though the two productions (in terms of both the process and the final product) were quite similar, initially the directors situated themselves differently vis-à-vis the material. As became relevant to the discussion in chapter 4, Miller is a white woman and a specialist in French-language theater with a particular interest in women-authored plays. Giles is a black woman and a specialist in African American and African theater and directing. Self-reflexively, the university productions addressed cultural positioning as a factor contributing to how we learn and produce knowledge. The artistic teams aimed to recognize the cultural and political positions of the directors, the actors, and the university while also teaching the necessary cultural and critical literacies to comprehend and make meaning from the plays.

Teaching Cultural and Critical Literacy

The university productions sought to teach cultural literacy, that is, the ability to understand the plays from an informed perspective. Diaspora literacy, according to VèVè Clark, "demands a knowledge of historical, social, cultural and political development generated by lived and textual experience." What Clark calls "marasa consciousness," in reference to the vodou sign for the divine twins, reflects the creolization of knowledge insofar as it "depends largely on our capacities to read the sign as a cyclical, spiral relationship."[8] In the cases of Césaire's and Condé's plays, an informed reader or spectator might become familiar with ethnology and history, respectively, and must be able to grasp the spiral interplay between the drama and these two academic fields. Miller and Giles worked with their actors and production teams to effectively present the plays to their audiences and to learn about the French Caribbean, the play, and the playwright. Students in Miller's class (who made up the bulk of the actors) read Césaire's ethnological article "La triade humaine dans le conte antillais" and studied French Caribbean theater, folktales, and cultural production.[9] Giles's actors worked with the dramaturge and cotranslator Jean-Pierre Piriou, a French professor specializing in the Caribbean, who was present at almost all of the rehearsals, to learn the history dramatized in the play and to become familiar with the cultures of the French Caribbean.

Both directors made an effort to reinvent what is commonly considered in the academy to be legitimate knowledge. Whereas the academy generally privileges theory over practice, text over performance, and disembodied, so-called rational knowledges over performance-based ways of knowing, the directors positioned Caribbean dance, music, and cultural practices as sources of knowledge. Student actors cultivated creolized knowledges akin to the vodou concept of *konesans*, that is, knowledge based in both experience and wisdom.[10] Students combined experiential learning with the study of texts, history, and ethnology. They avoiding driving down what Dwight Conquergood calls the "one-way street[s]" of false, ethnocentric, binary divisions in epistemology, and instead "turn[ed], and return[ed], insistently, to the crossroads." "We challenge the hegemony of the text best," writes Conquergood, "by reconfiguring texts and performances in horizontal, metonymic tensions, not by replacing one hierarchy with another, the romance of performance for the authority of the text."[11]

While Césaire's and Condé's diligent engagement with ethnology and history deepened students' learning, it also posed artistic challenges to the directors. Condé's complex text was made more accessible by Kadish's meticulous footnotes, which informed the reader of various French and Creole terms as well as the historical context. Yet since spectators are not privy to textual footnotes, Giles needed to act as a mediator. "I then asked myself, how would those footnotes be translated into theatrical action and metaphor for the audience," she wrote in an essay on the experience.[12] She effectively had to decide which historical details she believed were necessary to cultivate desired literacies. The program concisely introduces the play as "by Maryse Condé. About the slave revolts in Haiti and Guadeloupe during the French Revolution."[13] Anecdotal evidence suggests that spectators equipped with knowledge of the histories took more from the performance than those unfamiliar with the history of French slavery and the French and Haitian revolutions. Kadish remembered that those familiar with the history, particularly the scholars attending the conference Slavery in the Francophone World, appreciated the play immensely. However, other spectators reported to her that they had some difficulty following the dense historical references.[14]

Miller's team addressed a comparable challenge, in terms of both Caribbean cultural literacy and language competence. Offering an educational performance, they chose to initiate some of their spectators into Caribbean literacies prior to viewing the production. Miller had good contact with local high school French teachers, many of whom were alumni of the UW program in French education. This outreach to high schools was one of the primary reasons the play reached so many spectators. Though it was performed in French, a language many residents of Madison did not know, close to a thousand spectators attended its open dress rehearsal and four-night run.[15]

To prepare the high school teachers, Miller's team distributed an educational packet including a note "about the author and the play," a map of Columbus's voyages to the Americas, and an annotated play text.[16] These meticulous annotations described Caribbean folklore and archetypical folktale characters as well as references to local cuisine. Anticipating the high school students' intermediate language skills, Miller's team provided in-text glosses of terms and expressions in both French and Creole.[17] (Such glossing was not necessary during the UGA production since the play was performed in Standard English, though the translators and director did choose to keep certain expressions and songs in the original Creole.) The production team also cultivated historical literacy; Miller's annotations explain Césaire's subtle reference to the Tonton Macoute, the Haitian paramilitary force of the dictator "Papa Doc" François Duvalier. To give a look into Césaire's creative work as playwright, Miller specified which characters the playwright invented (such as the fireflies Tèt Zéklè and Zétoil filé), as opposed to those she took from her study of Caribbean folklore.

Embodied knowledge helped to foster necessary cultural literacy, for both performers and spectators. Dance was an integral element of both performances, as well as the rehearsal processes. At UGA choreographer Ellen Bleier, who had studied vodou dance and other forms of African diaspora dance in Santa Fe, New York, and Haiti, taught Haitian dance as well as songs in Creole to the ensemble.[18] After reading through the script with Giles, Bleier created original choreographies incorporating Haitian traditional dance and vodou liturgy. Bleier and her group of drummers played live Haitian rhythms during the performance to accompany the choreography and songs. Giles also worked with Laura Mason, a professor in the history department, to teach period songs from the French Revolution, including "La Carmagnole," "Ah! Ça Ira!," and "Daignez m'épargnez le reste" (a song that told the plight of the black slaves). While Giles relied on period music and traditional Haitian songs, Miller selected contemporary pan-Caribbean music, including the French Caribbean group Kassav, the Haitian singer Toto Bissainthe, and the Brazilian singer-songwriter Milton Nascimento. Much like Giles, Miller stressed the importance of dance throughout the rehearsal process. Her choreographer, Akua Sarr (then Akua Brath), drew from African diasporic dances to create original choreographies.[19] Live musicians were also part of Miller's performance; they were costumed and played from the stage.

In addition to cultural and historical competence, both directors fostered the critical literacy required for understanding slavery's inheritance. In line with Césaire's ethnological writings, Miller's class and production team understood Ti-Jean's behavior as a trickster response to the histories of slavery and colonialism. As Miller explained in her program note, Ti-Jean's "acts of violence . . . can only be understood as inevitable reactions to centuries of servitude."[20] With her students Miller discussed Caribbean folktales' impact on the unconscious, stressing that the Ti-Jean tale helped to keep Caribbeans psychically lucid in situations of intense oppression.[21] Giles emphasized Condé's creative connection of past and present in her production. Taking her cue from Condé's text, she wished not only to revisit history but also, she recalled, "to comment on contemporary life."[22] By projecting images behind the actors onstage, Giles brought the audience closer to the historical past as well as its political reverberations in the present. Some of the images projected were period paintings, such as a portrait of the *mulâtresse* Solitude and the painting *L'abolition de l'esclavage dans les colonies françaises en 1848* by François-Auguste Biard, which appeared on the flyer and program. Giles also projected contemporary images, including a photograph of the Duvalier father-son dictators and an image of Abner Louima.

Crossing Race and Gender

How does "race" signify when a black diasporic play is staged in the U.S. university setting? Sandra Richards writes of her experience directing

Nigerian playwright Femi Osofisan's *Farewell to Cannibal Rage* at Stanford University in 1987, where, Richards points out, fewer than 10 percent of students were in a racial minority. In this context, a study of theater as "cultural translation" (a concept developed by Gershon Shaked) must meticulously acknowledge the uneven power hierarchies and structures of domination in which the theatrical, cultural encounter occurs. Shaked argues that plays staged out of context can bridge cultural and linguistic gaps, though these productions always involve a "productive area of misunderstanding."[23] Yet, as Richards contends, staging an African play at Stanford should not be theorized simply in terms of bridging and reaffirming cultural differences (tensions between unity and difference). In contrast, her staging "confronts the politics of cultural translation in situations where 'race' is an additional, highly charged signifier, the manipulation of which reaffirms or challenges relations of dominance in the society at large." Richards's onstage syncretic mix of various theatrical signifiers (music, vibrant colors, dances, music, non-Western conventions of realism) served as a "challenge to conventional American readings of race."[24]

Similarly Giles and Miller used onstage theatrical signifiers in a syncretic way and thus crafted a creolized understanding of race. The plays depict race as a signifier in motion, defined by a series of politically inflected encounters, transgressions, and "crossings." Carine Mardorossian has argued that contemporary Caribbean women writers depict race as crossing: "Racial crossing in their novels serves as a figuration for the transgression of class and gender boundaries so much so that the notion of race itself has to be reinscribed as a complex set of crossing categories."[25] Even more saliently than at Ubu, where different understandings of race and gender came into contact and conflict, these education productions reinvented meanings surrounding "race" and "gender" transnationally, mirroring the plays themselves.

Whereas Ubu often cast African American actors in Caribbean roles, thus calling upon African Americans to enact a sort of kinesthetic black diaspora, the two university professors cast both white and black U.S. actors in Caribbean roles. Attempting to stage the instability of race, gender, and other cultural signifiers, the directors took the playwrights' cultural crossings to the next level. To be sure, these material productions necessarily reinscribed race, gender, and Caribbeanness onto real bodies onstage. Nonetheless the productions harnessed theater's material codes in ways meant to destabilize their spectators' expectations and thus to embody critical, dynamic crossings of race, gender, culture, nationality, and (to a lesser extent) class. These embodied crossings were also, of course, influenced by the director's own positioning in the racialized and gendered hierarchies of the U.S. academy at the end of the twentieth century.

Both performances challenged conventional readings of race as a fixed social signifier through casting choices. Partially due to the practical constraints of the casting pool, Giles and Miller deployed nontraditional casting. In the production of *In the Time of Revolution*, a black male actor played King Louis XVI of France. As Giles recounted to me, she had begun with a more traditional choice of a white man in the role, but it became clear to her and the ensemble during the rehearsal process that they wanted to make a change. The use of cross-racial casting corresponded with Giles's key directorial concept focused on Caribbean Carnival. According to her vision, the "theatrical use of masks and costumes would give us the freedom to play with constructions of history, race, and gender, keeping Condé's underlying themes at the forefront of the represented actions."[26] White masks of varying sizes, which evoked both Noh theater and Commedia dell'arte, were used in places where Giles found them appropriate. Since they were often given to actors playing French royalty or plantation masters, the masks, as in the casting of a black actor in the role of the French king, served to defamiliarize whiteness.

Racial crossings were less conspicuous in Miller's production since so many of the characters are anthropomorphized animals. However, while audiences would probably expect Ti-Jean, the trickster boy hero, to be played by a young black man, Miller cast four different white women in this role. This choice introduced a critical disconnect between the representation onstage and the audience's expectations, which were facilitated by the production team's own publicity. Onstage Ti-Jean is a college-age white woman, while the publicity for the play showed a sketch of the traditional Ti-Jean, a young black boy. Such moments of critical juxtaposition render strange what Brandi Wilkins Catanese calls the "the conflicting impulses of recognition and disavowal that race in performance introduces."[27] The team used theater's material realities to reproduce and expand the playwrights' textual treatment of race as an unstable, creolized social signifier and thus reignite the creolizing impulse.

Both directors additionally made choices that challenged an implied spectator's expectations relating to gender. Giles cast a woman in the role of Guadeloupe's historical hero, Louis Delgrès, which reinforced what Giles interpreted as Condé's efforts to "amend history to include [women]."²⁸ This choice was acceptable at UGA, but it probably would have not been well received in Guadeloupe, where Condé was criticized for her irreverent portrayal of Delgrès. During a roundtable discussion, José Jernidier, who had created the role of Toussaint Louverture in Guadeloupe, noted that a woman in the role of Delgrès would have seemed odd in Guadeloupe.²⁹ In Miller's production, cross-gender casting served to emphasize the playwright's subtle challenge to the folktale's traditional gender roles. As Césaire has pointed out in her ethnological writings, women in Creole folktales are reduced to a few unflattering roles: mothers whose sole purpose is to give birth before dying; sorceresses (wicked witches, stepmothers, or she-devils); nymphomaniacs; or helpless, featherbrained beauties.³⁰ Princess Bebelle, the beautiful and vapid "prize" Ti-Jean wins for slaying the Seven-Headed Beast, belongs to the last category. In casting a man, who acted in an exaggerated fashion, Miller defamiliarized the princess's performance of femininity. This choice also reinforced what she described in the program as the "ironic happy ending" (in which Ti-Jean becomes successor to the king, who may also be the plantation owner). "The hand of the dimwitted princess is his paradoxical reward for perpetrating the reigning hierarchy," Miller wrote in her director's note.³¹

It seems that the apparent cultural distance between the source (French Caribbean) and target (U.S.) cultures enabled the directors to make these critical, creolizing staging choices. Each in its own way, the performances taught about French Caribbean culture and history even as they used theater's material realities to stage critical juxtapositions that reframed and rendered strange U.S.-inflected readings of race and gender. The directors took their cue from the plays to expand upon the aesthetics of creolizations scripted by the playwrights. Yet they also had their audiences in mind, for, as Richards points out, directors act as "microaudiences who mediate [a play's] eventual reception by a general public."³²

A note from the assistant director, Carrie Sandahl, of the UW production explains that the artistic team's provocative choices partially stemmed from their desire to avoid "cultural colonialism," that is, theater productions that, despite good intentions, "fuel ethnocentric attitudes, and posit first-world audiences as able consumers of all cultures." Identifying the UW artistic team as "mostly white middle-class university students," Sandahl reveals the team's wish to disavow claims to Caribbean authenticity. Without presuming to be able to play race or Caribbeanness, the team wished to tell their own adaptation—"our version"—of Ti-Jean's struggle against oppression. They accomplished this goal, she explains, partly through the highly presentational style and the Brechtian aesthetic, that is, by showing theater's artificiality and construction. Though cognizant of cultural differences and the inevitability of misunderstanding, the UW team could nonetheless "tell the story of a resistance to oppressive power and present the possibility of change, or [what Césaire would call] 'un monde régénéré' [a restored world]."[33]

How can a performance simultaneously teach about the French Caribbean and be a new version of the play, designed to make meaning in the context of the particular university and to defamiliarize U.S.-based notions of race and gender? The result was a creolized performance that—like the plays—contained oppositional cultural and epistemological impulses. Tellingly Miller and her team gave the Seven-Headed Beast seven different guises, which spanned time periods and cultures. Each head was a paper drawing of a recognizable face, including Banania (the racist caricature of the smiling Senegalese infantryman used to sell cereal in France), Columbus, De Gaulle, Elvis, and George W. Bush. The name of each figure was written on the back of the paper cutout, which was turned around to reveal each identity (to spectators who did not recognize the face) after it was slain.

As in the Ubu productions, this creolized aesthetic also provoked misrecognitions. For example, Condé, who was present at the UGA performance, misapprehended the meaning of the final dance with which Giles chose to close the production. Bleier choreographed a dance, based in the traditional Haitian Pètwo rhythms, which was, in her words, "the revolt of the slaves against the masters (or oppressors) dance, a sort of 'ghost dance' meant to inspire Haitian slaves for battle."[34] But Condé identified this dance as the only moment in which the production appeared African American as opposed to Guadeloupean. To the author's mind, the dance was in the style of Michael Jackson.[35] In other words, Condé interpreted the production team's efforts to perform traditional Haitian dance as a representation of (black) American pop culture.

Yet due to the educational setting and ethical commitment of collaborators, when such oppositional impulses converged, deeper meanings could emerge. Interpretive tensions reiterated and exceeded meanings written into the play as text. To give an example, at the end of *In the Time of Revolution*, Guadeloupeans escape to Haiti, where they are welcomed with warmth. As the play draws to a close, Zéphyr (the storyteller character) invites the audience to ponder the extent to which we have achieved equality and justice today, whether the promises from the time of revolution have been kept. In this moment, Giles chose to project a photograph of Abner Louima, a Haitian man who was brutally beaten and sexually assaulted by police officers in Brooklyn in 1997. Thus Giles effectively made a link between Haiti and the United States that paralleled Condé's connection between Haiti and Guadeloupe. This moment revealed the larger geographical scope of slavery's legacy as portrayed in Condé's text. In other words, the pan-Caribbean reach of slavery's legacy extends to Brooklyn. Giles implicates not only the southern states (traditionally associated with American slavery) but also the North and big cities like New York, which are (ostensibly) liberal and tolerant. "For me, the suffering of Mr. Louima symbolizes how far we actually are from the promise of tomorrow," Giles wrote.[36]

U.S.-based students and scholars have much to learn from the Caribbean. Educational stagings of diverse, global plays encourage U.S. professors, students, and audiences to act as cofacilitators in the creolization of their education. The UW and UGA productions succeeded in educating student artistic teams and audiences in circum-Caribbean cultures and fostering cultural and critical literacy. The productions enacted creolizing meanings in motion by crossing social signifiers and defamiliarizing U.S.-based notions of race and gender. Provocative casting choices "paradoxically provided the most productive ground on which to disentangle the knotty web of blackness and identity," as E. Patrick Johnson finds in the study of his own classroom.[37] At the same time, collaborators were taught to be mindful of larger geopolitical and historical considerations. Knowledge production at U.S. universities and in the academy at large takes place on a power-inflected, uneven terrain. Violet Eudine Barriteau warns of the dangers of appropriating creolized knowledges without recognizing the inequities and hierarchies involved: "We cannot continue to use the Caribbean as a field in a plantation typology of knowledge production."[38] To forestall such imprudent appropriation of the Caribbean play, the UGA and UW teams engaged in a performance-based "ethics of borrowing *and* accepting to be transformed, affected by the other."[39]

The university rehearsal processes and performances also retained creolization's political consciousness. "Creolization *always* entails inequality, hierarchization, issues of domination and subalterneity, mastery and servitude, control and resistance," writes Hall. "Questions of *power*, as well as issues of *entanglement*, are always at stake. It is essential to keep these contradictory tendencies together, rather than singling out their celebratory aspects."⁴⁰ Mindful of power and positionality, the university productions sought to engage participants and attendees in creolizing ways of knowing, to rearrange our epistemological systems, to defamiliarize our ready-made cultural paradigms, and to foster dialogue surrounding the uneven politics of our shared, transatlantic pasts, presents, and futures.

Notes

Introduction

1. Césaire, *Island Memories*, 52.
2. Césaire quoted in Kourilsky, *Ubu Repertory Theater*, 38–39.
3. Though the production histories of a number of these plays extend into the twenty-first century, I will limit my analysis to the premieres and U.S. premieres. Ina Césaire's *Mémoires d'Isles* was produced in 1998 under Jean-Camille Sormain's direction, with Firmine Richard as Hermance and Jenny Alpha as Aure, at the Petit Hébertot theatre in Batignolles, France. In 2008 José Exélis directed a production in Martinique with Catherine Césaire and Suzy Singa. Simone Schwarz-Bart's *Ton beau capitaine* is the most widely restaged of this corpus; it was even staged in Dutch in the Netherlands in 2013. Noël Jovignot directed a production with Ruddy Sylaire and the voice of Yna Boulangé that toured the Caribbean in 2004–5. At the Festival Cap Excellence in Guadeloupe in the summer of 2014, Jean-Erns Marie-Louise directed the play, also acting opposite the voice of Martine Maximin. In 2003 Maryse Condé's *The Tropical Breeze Hotel* (in English) was produced in New Orleans, directed by Akin (Femi) Euba, with Troi Bechet (Emma) and Don J. Guillory (Ishmael).
4. Balme, *Decolonizing the Stage*, 2.
5. Bérard, *Theater of the French Caribbean*, 298.
6. Ruprecht, "Performance transculturelle," 313–25; Ruprecht, "Le théâtre de Maryse Condé," 147.
7. Conteh-Morgan and Thomas, *New Francophone African and Caribbean Theaters*.
8. Ibid., xi–xii, 2–3.
9. Makward, "Staging Her People's Voice." Makward has compiled an anthology of Ina Césaire's plays: Césaire, *Rosanie Soleil*. For another introduction to Césaire's theatre, see Makward, "Introduction."
10. For a complete bibliography of Condé's plays and their international production history, see Sahakian and Makward, "Théâtraographie de Maryse Condé."

11. Sahakian, "Le théâtre de Maryse Condé."
12. Bérard, "Percussion et repercussion des voix dans le théâtre de Gerty Dambury"; Makward, "Pressentir l'autre."
13. Les Éditions du Manguier, http://www.leseditionsdumanguier.com/.
14. Hall, "Cultural Identity and Diaspora," 228.
15. Jones, "Theatre and Resistance?," 83.
16. Condé, *The Journey of a Caribbean Writer*, 213.
17. Makward, "Haiti on Stage."
18. Condé, "Order, Disorder, Freedom, and the West Indian Writer," 129–30; Condé, "Chercher nos vérités," 305–10.
19. Condé, "*Créolité* without Creole language?," 106.
20. See Bernabé et al., *Eloge de la créolité*; Chamoiseau and Confiant, *Lettres créoles*. For a closer discussion of creolization and the Martinican Créolists, see Knepper, "Colonization, Creolization, and Globalization." Knepper persuasively positions the Créolists as attuned to the dynamic and unstable process of creolization yet overly insistent on its positive, affirmative results and dismissive of the ways creolization inevitably involves loss.
21. Arnold, "The Gendering of Créolité"; Arnold, "From the Problematic Maroon to a Woman-Centered Creole Project in the Literature of the French West Indies."
22. Benítez-Rojo, *The Repeating Island*, 2.
23. McKay, *Maryse Condé et le théâtre antillais*, 27–28; Makward, "Reading Maryse Condé's Theatre," 681.
24. Edwards, *Les Dramaturges antillaises*.
25. Makward, "Filles du soleil noir"; Makward, "De bouche à oreille à bouche."
26. Miller, "Caribbean Women Playwrights."
27. Mardorossian, *Reclaiming Difference*, 8–9.
28. The original text of this play in French is unpublished and has been lost. The English translation by Richard Philcox is available in the Ubu Repertory Theater Collection, Fales Special Collections, New York University.
29. This play is unpublished, but a video by Jean-Pierre Sturm is available in certain university libraries.
30. Bérard discusses U.S. audience responses to this production in "The Migration of Caribbean Theater to the North American Stage," 111–3.
31. Bérard, "The Migration of Caribbean Theater to the North American Stage," 108, 114.
32. Hill and Hatch, *A History of African American Theatre*, 273–306, 273.
33. Césaire, *Notebook of a Return to the Native Land*, 16; Césaire, *Cahier d'un retour au pays natal*, 25.
34. Hall, "Cultural Identity and Diaspora," 226.
35. Ibid., 228.
36. Glissant, *The Poetics of Relation*, 89, 32.

37. "Hall "Creolization, Diaspora, and Hybridity in the Context of Globalization," 186.
38. Ibid., 6.
39. Taylor, *The Archive and the Repertoire*, 19.
40. Vergès, "Kiltir Kreol," 180, 182.
41. Drewal, *Yoruba Ritual*, 27.
42. Daniel, *Dancing Wisdom*, 61.
43. Walcott, "The Antilles."
44. Knepper, "Colonization, Creolization, and Globalization," 73.
45. Ortiz, "The Human Factors of Cubanidad."
46. Olmos and Paravisini-Gebert, *Creole Religions of the Caribbean*, 4.
47. Hall, "Créolité and the Process of Creolization," 32.
48. Glissant, *The Poetics of Relation*, 189–94, 190, 189, 194.
49. Roach, *Cities of the Dead*, 2, xi.
50. Glissant, "Theater, Consciousness of the People," 200, 196, 203.
51. Ibid., 205, 213, 214.
52. Hill, "Perspectives in Caribbean Theatre," 6–7.
53. As a theater artist myself, I have attended rehearsals and conducted participant observation with several contemporary French Caribbean directors and performers, including Lénablou, Gilbert Laumord, Gerty Dambury, and José Exélis.
54. See Christopher Balme's discussion, based on Dietrich Steinbeck's work, of "direct" and "indirect" sources (*The Cambridge Introduction to Theatre Studies*, 98).
55. Ibid., 105–6.
56. Kim, "Finding History from the Living Archives," 201.
57. See also Ruprecht's discussion of the challenges of French Caribbean theater history in "Les pratiques scéniques et textuelles de la région caribéenne francophone et créolophone," 11.
58. Personal email correspondence with Syto Cavé, October 9, 2014.
59. Bérard, *Théâtre des Antilles*, 7.
60. Clark, "Developing Diaspora Literacy and *Marasa* Consciousness," 11.
61. Zarrilli, "For Whom Is the King a King?," 16.
62. See Glissant, *Traité du Tout-Monde*; Glissant, "The Unforeseeable Diversity of the World."

Chapter 1

1. Condé, *Heremakhonon*, 17.
2. Pfaff, *Conversations with Maryse Condé*, 41. Condé may have taken this from the Haitian historian Jean Fouchard. A similar announcement—without the name Marilisse—is quoted from a newspaper in Fouchard, *Les marrons de la liberté*, 15.
3. The Marilisse is also the accusation Veronica's family charges against her for loving a light-skinned mulatto man, and a name she herself conjures when

she sees a black woman at a powerful man's side. In choosing the name Marilisse, Condé may be imaginatively gesturing toward the Latin American archetype of the Malinche, the treacherous native woman who became the mistress of the Spanish conquistador Hernán Cortés. Like Condé's Marilisse, the Malinche is commonly accused of complicity in colonialism and of improving her own situation through sex with a powerful white man. For more on the Malinche, see Cypess, *La Malinche in Mexican Literature from History to Myth*.

4. Condé, *La Parole des femmes*, 4.
5. Collins, *Black Feminist Thought*, 70–78.
6. Philip, "Dis Place—The Space Between," 77.
7. Ibid.
8. I studied the plays in both the original French/Creole and the English translation, which I quote out of convenience for English-language readers. Although it was first produced in Martinique in 1992, *Rosanie Soleil* was not published in French until 2011. I also consulted an earlier, unpublished version of this play, which Christiane Makward graciously shared with me.
9. Simone Schwarz-Bart's *Ton beau capitaine*, which I analyze in chapter 3, takes on similar themes relating to love and slavery's sexual legacy, but in this play the woman character's body is absent from the stage.
10. Young, *Embodying Black Experience*, 7.
11. Fanon, *Black Skin, White Masks*, 91; Young, *Embodying Black Experience*, 10.
12. Hartman, *Scenes of Subjection*, 87.
13. Garraway, *The Libertine Colony*, 194–239.
14. Edwards, *Les Dramaturges antillaises*, 165. "Les femmes se sont servies de leur corps pour gagner la liberté, pour que leurs enfants soient affranchis; et les homes réduits à l'état d'esclaves regardaient cela. Donc il y a une sorte de contentieux qui n'a pas été réglé entre les hommes et les femmes aux Antilles." All unattributed translations are mine.
15. Cottias, "Free but Minor," 190.
16. See, for example, the documentary *La fièvre tout le temps*, dir. Pascal Bensoussan (Canal Antilles and Samarka Productions, 2003).
17. Murray, "Homosexuality, Society, and the State," 252.
18. Arnold, "The Gendering of Créolité."
19. Thomas, *Breadfruit or Chestnut?*, 8.
20. On the precarious role of the father in French Caribbean literature, see Loichot, "Negations and Subversions of Paternal Authorities in Glissant's Fictional Works." For a sociological perspective, see Giraud, "Une construction coloniale de la sexualité," 49.
21. Thomas, *Breadfruit or Chestnut?*, 12, 47, 8.
22. As historian Arlette Gautier points out in her study of Martinique and Guadeloupe, though women were freed three times more frequently than men at the end of the eighteenth century (and twice as often in the nineteenth), before

1830 these numbers were nevertheless small: approximately 2.8 percent of female concubines in 1776 Martinique were freed (*Les Sœurs de Solitude*, 161).

23. Cottias, "La séduction coloniale," 125.
24. See, for example, Jacobs, *Incidents in the Life of a Slave Girl*.
25. Roach, *Cities of the Dead*, 4, 2.
26. Césaire, "A Word from the Author," in *Fire's Daughters*, 4.
27. Makward, "De bouche à oreille à bouche," 137.
28. Krakovitch, "Le rôle des femmes dans l'insurrection du Sud de la Martinique en Septembre 1870," 36, 37; Nicolas, "L'insurrection du Sud" (consulted at the Bibliothèque Nationale de France).
29. Césaire, *Fire's Daughters*, 6, 7.
30. Krakovitch, "Le rôle des femmes dans l'insurrection du Sud de la Martinique en Septembre 1870," 39–41.
31. Césaire, "A Word from the Author," 4.
32. Césaire, *Fire's Daughters*, 30–36.
33. Ibid., 31.
34. Ibid., 41.
35. Césaire, "A Word from the Author," 4; Césaire, *Rosanie Soleil*, 97.
36. Césaire, "A Word from the Author," 4.
37. Makward, "Filles du soleil noir"; Miller, "Caribbean Women Playwrights."
38. Césaire, "A Word from the Author," 5; Césaire, *Rosanie Soleil*, 97.
39. Césaire, "A Word from the Author," 5.
40. Césaire, *Fire's Daughters*, 27–30.
41. Ibid., 40.
42. Roach, *Cities of the Dead*, 2.
43. Fanon, *Black Skin, White Masks*, 28.
44. Césaire, *Fire's Daughters*, 38, 39.
45. Hine, "Rape and the Inner Lives of Black Women in the Middle West", 344, 345.
46. Césaire, *Fire's Daughters*, 15.
47. Ibid.
48. Hartman, *Scenes of Subjection*, 85.
49. Gautier, *Les Sœurs de Solitude*, 139.
50. Césaire, *Fire's Daughters*, 25.
51. Césaire, "A Word from the Author," 5; Césaire, *Rosanie Soleil*, 98.
52. Bada, "Slavery and Silence in Ina Césaire's 'Mémoires d'Isles' and Denis Scott's 'Echo in the Bone,'" 89.
53. Césaire, *Island Memories*, 58–9. As I discuss in chapter 2, this scene was cut from Césaire's 2011 French edition.
54. Césaire, *Fire's Daughters*, 37.
55. Krakovitch, "Le rôle des femmes dans l'insurrection du Sud de la Martinique en Septembre 1870," 44, 41–43.

56. On Caribbean writers' portrayal of the female maroon, see De Souza, "Demystifying Female Marooning."
57. Césaire, *Fire's Daughters*, 45.
58. Clark, "Developing Diaspora Literacy and *Marasa* Consciousness," 12.
59. Césaire, *Fire's Daughters*, 44; Césaire, *Rosanie Soleil*, 127.
60. Césaire, *Fire's Daughters*, 44.
61. See Desrivières, "Entretien avec Syto Cavé."
62. Personal email correspondence with Syto Cavé, May 3, 2014.
63. Personal email correspondence with Syto Cavé, October 9, 2014.
64. Ruprecht, "Le théâtre de Maryse Condé," 149.
65. Young, *Embodying Black Experience*, 14.
66. Condé, *The Tropical Breeze Hotel*, 139, 156.
67. Ibid., 119–20, 124, 134, 123.
68. Ibid., 119, 138, 162, 119.
69. Pfaff, *Conversations with Maryse Condé*, 85, 84.
70. Hewitt, "Condé's Critical Seesaw," 641.
71. Fulton, *Signs of Dissent*, 49.
72. Quoted in Lewis, "No Silence," 545.
73. Condé, *The Tropical Breeze Hotel*, 127.
74. Ibid., 120.
75. Fanon, *Black Skin, White Masks*, 95.
76. Condé, *The Tropical Breeze Hotel*, 158, 151.
77. Makward, "Reading Maryse Condé's Theatre," 685.
78. Ibid. Condé, *The Tropical Breeze Hotel*, 142, 120, 127.
79. Ibid., 120, 143. For more on Saartjie (Sara) Baartman, see Crais and Scully, *Sara Baartman and the Hottentot Venus*.
80. Condé, *The Tropical Breeze Hotel*, 119, 127.
81. See Jules-Rosette, *Josephine Baker in Art and Life*; Lahs-Gonzales, *Josephine Baker*.
82. Condé, *The Tropical Breeze Hotel*, 119.
83. Ibid., 120.
84. Ibid., 119.
85. Makward, "Reading Maryse Condé's Theatre," 685; Edwards, *Les Dramaturges antillaises*, 92.
86. McKay, *Maryse Condé et le théâtre antillais*, 105.
87. Condé, *The Tropical Breeze Hotel*, 153, 137, 162.
88. Ibid., 159.
89. Ibid., 164. This line about the false eyelashes, repeated at the start and end of the play, was inspired by Lisette Malidor's real words spoken to Condé (see Pfaff, *Conversations with Maryse Condé*, 85). Malidor is a Martinican dancer and singer, who (like Emma) has been called the new Josephine Baker.
90. Makward, "Reading Maryse Condé's Theatre," 685; Makward, "Haiti on Stage," 133; Edwards, *Les Dramaturges antillaises*, 92.

91. Several performance scholars have theorized that Brechtian alienation effects make audiences critically aware of the everyday performance of race and gender. See Brooks, *Bodies in Dissent*, 4–5; Diamond, *Unmaking Mimesis*, xiv; McAllister, *Whiting Up*, 158.

92. Personal interview with Sonia Emmanuel, Paris, April 2, 2014; personal interview with Jacques Martial, Paris, April 1, 2014.

93. Condé, *The Tropical Breeze Hotel*, 119.

94. Pfaff, *Conversations with Maryse Condé*, 86.

95. Ruprecht, "Le théâtre de Maryse Condé," 153–54.

96. Gilbert and Tompkins, *Post-Colonial Drama*, 204.

Chapter 2

1. Hartman, *Scenes of Subjection*.

2. On the history of this rhetoric, see Schor, "The Crisis of French Universalism."

3. Nesbitt, *Caribbean Critique*, 1.

4. Burton, "The Idea of Difference in Contemporary French West Indian Thought."

5. Bernabé et al., *Eloge de la Créolité*, 87.

6. Hall, "Cultural Identity and Diaspora."

7. See Pavis, "Introduction."

8. Recent scholarship has sought to trouble these definitions and to recuperate the political possibilities of intercultural theater. See Fischer-Lichte et al., *The Politics of Interweaving Performance Cultures*; Farfan and Knowles, "Rethinking Intercultural Performance."

9. Gilbert and Tompkins, *Post-Colonial Drama*, 9.

10. Knowles, *Theatre and Interculturalism*, 21–30.

11. Bharucha, "Peter Brook's *Mahabharata*," 70, 84.

12. Brook, "The Culture of Links," 63–66.

13. Gilbert and Tompkins, *Post-Colonial Drama*, 2.

14. Balme, *Decolonizing the Stage*.

15. Ibid., 5.

16. The video contains the second act, "1794," and the second half of the third, "1802." At times the audience is visible in this recording. My sincere thanks to José Jernidier for tracking down and sharing this rare treasure.

17. Ruprecht, "Le théâtre de Maryse Condé," 154.

18. "Devait conduire à la réflexion dynamique sur le présent" (Condé, "Autour d'An Tan Revolisyon," 165).

19. Condé, *In the Time of Revolution*, 465.

20. For more on Jernidier and his troupe, see Naudillon, "Le théâtre populaire de José Jernidier."

21. For example, the scene in which Justin, Narcisse, and Pierrot conspire against their white governors, though written and published in French, was

performed in Creole (Condé, *An tan revolisyon*, 25–27; Condé, *In the Time of Revolution*, 474–76).

22. Ruprecht, "Le théâtre de Maryse Condé," 154.
23. Gaensbauer, "Protean Truths," 1141.
24. Miller, *Ariane Mnouchkine*, 65.
25. Condé, *In the Time of Revolution*, 489.
26. Ibid., 486.
27. Ibid., 471
28. Ibid., 475, 466.
29. Reinhardt, *Claims to Memory*, 108.
30. Condé, *In the Time of Revolution*, 460.
31. Ibid., 462, 463, translation modified.
32. Ibid., 469, 471.
33. Personal interview with Sonia Emmanuel, Paris, April 2, 2014.
34. Christiane Makward, "Pour une petite histoire de *An tan revolisyon, elle court, elle court la liberté* (1989) de Maryse Condé," paper presented at the symposium Théâtre Caraïbe: Le Répertoire, Paris, November 9, 2013, Christiane Makward's personal archives.
35. "Conçue pour provoquer" (Condé, "Autour d'An Tan Revolisyon," 169).
36. Personal interview with Gilbert Laumord, Paris, April 6, 2014.
37. Nesbitt, *Voicing Memory*, 201.
38. Condé, *In the Time of Revolution*, 473.
39. Personal interview with José Jernidier, Avignon, July 21, 2014.
40. "Dépeint Toussaint Louverture sous les traits d'un dictateur" (Nesbitt, "Revolution in Discourse," 244).
41. Condé, *In the Time of Revolution*, 465.
42. Ibid., 485, 486.
43. Ibid, 465.
44. Ibid., 473.
45. "Se propose de démontrer que la Révolution Française est d'abord un phénomène purement métropolitain." "La Pièce," program, *An tan Revolisyon*, Christiane Makward's personal archives.
46. For more on the *abiku* and *ogbanje*, see Ogunyemi, *Africa Wo/Man Palava*, 61–74; Ogunyemi, "An Abiku-Ogbanje Atlas."
47. Ogunyemi, *Africa Wo/Man Palava*, 61–74.
48. See Richards, "Who Is This Ancestor?"
49. Ogunyemi, *Africa Wo/Man Palava*, 62.
50. Condé, *In the Time of Revolution*, 466.
51. Ibid., 489.
52. Ibid.
53. "Un très grand succès populaire [même si je ne sais pas] si les gens ont senti le côté contestataire que nous avions essayé de faire passer" (Nesbitt, "Revolution in Discourse," 242).

54. "Avec une profonde amertume." Laure Rémy, "Œil critique sur An tan revolisyon: Amertume et sentiment de révolte d'un lecteur," *Sept Magazine*, November 23–29, 1989, 20. Reviews consulted in Christiane Makward's personal archives.

55. "Pas d'humour, mais de la dérision . . . qu'aux yeux de Maryse Condé nous n'avons que des héros de pacotille" (ibid.).

56. Nesbitt, "Revolution in Discourse," 244.

57. Houyoux, "Un Entretien avec Ina Césaire," 353.

58. Césaire, *Island Memories*, 56n8, 61–62, 62n9, 71–72.

59. Ibid., 56–57, 63.

60. Makward and Miller, "Ina Césaire," in *Plays by French and Francophone Women*, 47.

61. Césaire, *Island Memories*, 49, 53.

62. Makward, "De bouche à oreille à bouche," 141.

63. Césaire, *Island Memories*, 66, 67.

64. See Adell, "Word/Song and Nommo Force in Two Black Francophone Plays"; Bada, "Slavery and Silence in Ina Césaire's 'Mémoires d'Isles' and Denis Scott's 'Echo in the Bone'"; Edwards, *Les Dramaturges antillaises*, 114–20; Miyasaki, "Writing the Landscape of Memory."

65. "Textes recueillis et adaptés par Ina Césaire, Myrrha Donzenac et Mariann Mathéus." *Mémoires d'Isles*, unpublished script, Mariann Mathéus's personal archives.

66. I consulted the final script that the actresses used in performance, shared by Mariann Mathéus from her personal archives. I additionally consulted various similar iterations of the script in the archival collections of the Théâtre du Campagnol, Département des Arts du spectacle, Bibliothèque nationale de France (BnF).

67. Personal interview with Mariann Mathéus, Paris, April 4, 2014

68. Césaire, *Island Memories*, 57.

69. Ibid., 62.

70. *Mémoires d'Isles*, unpublished script, 4, 3, Mariann Mathéus's personal archives.

71. Césaire, *Island Memories*, 58.

72. Césaire, *Mémoires d'Isles*, 51; Césaire, *Island Memories*, 58–9.

73. Césaire, *Island Memories*, 59.

74. "Il s'agit d'accepter notre passé, il ne s'agit pas d'en avoir honte, il ne s'agit plus d'en pleurer. Nous avons acquis le droit de ne plus pleurer sur notre passé, nous devons l'assumer et pouvoir le dépasser. Se référer à notre passé, c'est montrer aujourd'hui notre pouvoir de l'assumer, malgré les vicissitudes de notre histoire. Le simple fait que ces femmes aient survécu, le courage, la force, ainsi que leur désir de faire progresser leurs enfants, pour moi fait partie d'un élan de vie qui prend des aspects libératoires." Césaire quoted in Ruben Gachy, "Les mémoires d'Isles: Maman N et maman F," *POCO*, October 1983, 33.

75. Césaire, *Island Memories*, 52.

76. "Je me suis inspirée de l'occasion de sortir l'ethnologie de son ghetto de spécialistes et de le restituer à ceux qui sont les premiers concernés" (Césaire quoted in Gachy, "Les mémoires d'Isles," 32–33).

77. Personal interview with Mathéus.

78. Makward, "De bouche à oreille à bouche," 134; personal interview with Mathéus.

79. *Berthilia*, dir. Luc Ponette (Cinéma du Réel, 1981). For more on the artistic team's use of this documentary, see Mathéus, "De l'oralité au théâtre."

80. "A cela s'ajoute le jeu des comédiennes qui sont elles-même antillaises, et qui m'ont aidée en apportant leurs vécus, leurs souvenirs, enrichissant le texte, elles ont retrouvé des gestes naturellement, la recherché a été dépassée par la vie, et aussi la mise en scène de Jean-Claude Penchenat qui connaît, il est vrai, très peu les Antilles" (Césaire quoted in Gachy, "Les mémoires d'Isles," 33).

81. "Le mécanisme de la mémoire, quelque chose qui m'est cher!" Penchenat quoted in Mireille Lespinasse, "Les Violons du Bal," *Avant Scène*, collection of the Théâtre du Campagnol, Département des Arts du spectacle, 4-Col-87/17, BnF.

82. "La mémoire des peuples et de cultures" (Césaire quoted in Gachy, "Les mémoires d'Isles," 32).

83. Jones, "Two Plays by Ina Césaire," 228.

84. Clark, "Developing Diaspora Literacy and *Marasa* Consciousness," 12.

85. "On n'en est plus au niveau de 'Qui sommes-nous?' . . . 'Quelle est notre identité?' L'identité, elle *est*. Moi, personnellement je ne me pose plus la question de l'identité, je la ressens très profondément, sans complexe, sans amertume. . . . On ne peut pas assimiler cela! Quand je lis Dostoïevsky je ne suis pas Russe, or je peux entrer dans la peau des personnages et *Les Frères Karamazov*, ça me passionne! J'aime Tchekov! Donc je crois que n'importe qui peut comprendre l'âme d'un Antillais s'il prend la peine de (se) pénétrer lui-même" (quoted in Makward and John, "Faire son théâtre en Martinique," 116).

86. "Pointillieux, on l'imagine, sur les plans politique, linguistique, et cutané." "Libéral sans doute, mais modeste, mal informé des réalités antillaises et éventuellement, à la fibre patriotique sensible." Makward, "De bouche à oreille à bouche," 138.

87. It is possible that some of the French audience members had seen performances of certain plays written by French Caribbean authors. Those few spectators familiar with this repertoire most likely had seen performances of Césaire's father's trilogy, directed by the widely respected Jean-Marie Serreau, which was written in French and relied heavily on European theatrical traditions, often referencing Shakespeare. It is also possible that a (smaller) minority had seen productions of plays such as Daniel Boukman's *Les Négriers*, written in French and performed in 1972 at the Théâtre Daniel Sorano in Paris, or of Édouard Glissant's *Monsieur Toussaint*, which was performed in 1977 at the

Cité Universitaire de Paris and made use of some Creole, though it was written mostly in French.

88. See Balme's theorization of the semiotics of postcolonial drama ("Syncretic Theatre," 227).

89. Balme, *Decolonizing the Stage*, 5.

90. Aching, *Masking and Power*, 6.

91. For a discussion of Carnival in the play, see De Souza, "Discours carnavalesque chez Ina Césaire."

92. "Inverser symboliquement la pyramide ethno-sociale" (ibid., 128).

93. See Aching, *Masking and Power*, 7.

94. Bérard, "Creole ou/et Français," 123.

95. Césaire, *Island Memories*, 70; Césaire, *Mémoires d'Isles*, 75–76.

96. Bérard, "Creole ou/et Français," 127, 124.

97. Ibid., 125–127.

98. Césaire, *Mémoires d'Isles*, 40–41.

99. Césaire, *Island Memories*, 54.

100. "Dénoncent avec humour la société coloniale dans laquelle les enfants apprennent à chanter 'Tombe la neige.'" P.M., "'*Mémoires d'Iles,* Maman N. et Maman F.' par le Théâtre du Campagnol," *Lutte Ouvrière*, January 21, 1984, collection of the Théâtre du Campagnol, Département des Arts du spectacle, 4-Col-87/17, BnF.

101. "'A l'école on nous faisait chanter la neige tombe sur Paris,' se souvient non sans sourire l'ancienne institutrice. Deux vies dessinées sur toile de fond colonial et ce n'est évidemment pas pour rien qu'au prologue, dans ces costumes où s'opposent le noir et le blanc, on évoque Christophe Colomb et ses caravelles." "Mémoires d'Isles 'Maman N et Maman F,'" *Révolution*, January 20, 1984, collection of the Théâtre du Campagnol, Département des Arts du spectacle, 4-Col-87/17, BnF.

102. "La Martinique, la Guadeloupe, qu'importe. Françaises en tout cas." J.M., "Maman N et Maman F: Mémoire des Antilles," *Le Nouveau Journal*, January 14, 1984. This review is a response to a reprise of the same production at Théâtre 18 in 1984.

103. "Il ne s'agit pas de pleurer, de s'apitoyer, de se faire plaindre, d'invoquer la pitié. Il s'agit seulement de 'dire.'" D.M., "Rue Cases—Nègres sur scène," *Témoignage Chrétien*, undated newspaper clipping, collection of the Théâtre du Campagnol, Département des Arts du spectacle, 4-Col-87/17, BnF.

104. Hall, "Cultural Identity and Diaspora," 222–37.

105. Dambury, *Crosscurrents*, 88; see also 93, 103, 130.

106. For a cultural history of creolization in Réunion, see Médea, "Creolization and Globalization in Réunion."

107. Dambury, *Crosscurrents*, 87; Dambury, *Lettres indiennes*, 7.

108. Dambury, *Crosscurrents*, 97, 154.

109. Ibid., 159, 161.

110. Ibid., 101, 105, 97–98.

111. Ibid., 117.

112. Richards, "In the Kitchen, Cooking Up Diaspora Possibilities," 159.

113. Dambury, *Crosscurrents*, 104, 125; Dambury, *Lettres indiennes*, 25, 47.

114. Dambury, *Crosscurrents*, 126, 152.

115. Though Fructueuse is neither Indian nor from their island, Paul's mother hopes they are a couple (ibid., 139–40). Paul's father also seems to approve of Fructueuse; several times before dying he tells his son to marry her (150, 158, 160).

116. Ibid., 161.

117. Dambury, *Lettres indiennes*, 6.

118. "J'avais en face de moi des enfants qui se bagarraient tout le temps entre la honte d'être ce qu'ils étaient, parce que les autres se moquaient d'eux, et en même temps le désir d'affirmer leur culture. J'ai finalement essayé de comparer, de rapprocher ce que je pouvais avoir entrevu à la Réunion de ce qui se passait effectivement en Guadeloupe et auquel j'étais véritablement confrontée puisque je travaillais à Moule. . . . Donc, je me suis retrouvée en train de travailler sur quelque chose qui finalement avait un peu nourri mon inconscient pendant que j'étais à la Réunion et qui, dans mon enfance, avait été présent, parce que j'étais allée à des cérémonies." Dambury quoted in Bérard, "Gerty Dambury, 'Mon cheval de bataille est l'intime' (Entretien)."

119. "Ils m'ont répondu qu'ils vivent dans la société guadeloupéenne, qu'ils sont guadeloupéens, que cette société a évolué, qu'elle ne les rejette plus comme avant. Et que, plus ils avaient le sentiment d'être rejetés, plus ils cherchaient à s'intégrer, à se marier en dehors de leur communauté—avec des blancs ou des noirs—pour être mieux acceptés. " Dambury quoted in Houyoux, "Entretien avec Gerty Dambury," 275.

120. Bernabé et al., *Eloge de la créolité*, 75. See Arnold, "The Gendering of Créolité"; Arnold, "From the Problematic Maroon to a Woman-Centered Creole Project in the Literature of the French West Indies."

121. Dambury, *Crosscurrents*, 112–13.

122. See Bérard, "Gerty Dambury, 'Mon cheval de bataille est l'intime' (Entretien)."

123. "Je voulais savoir s'il y aurait le même désir de retour en Inde, comme nous l'avons connu par rapport à l'Afrique" (ibid.).

124. "Donc en fait, il y a un espèce de travail, d'interrogation permanente sur ce qui part de l'Inde, ce qui arrive chez nous, ce qui demeure, ce qui se perd, ce qui se bat avec le reste de la société, ce qui veut s'affirmer, mais ne sait pas comment s'affirmer" (ibid.).

125. "Mais je n'ai pas parlé des Indiens de la Guadeloupe, ni des Indiens de la Réunion, parce que je me suis intéressée à la culture indienne en général" (ibid.).

126. Singaravélou, "Indians in the French Overseas Departments," 75; Swami, "Les Cultes indiens en Martinique et en Guadeloupe," 1175, 1182.

127. Swami, "Les Cultes indiens en Martinique et en Guadeloupe," 1181–82.

128. Ramakrishnan and Smith, *Interplay of Cultural Narratives in Martinique*, 151; Singaravélou, "Indians in the French Overseas Departments," 52.

129. "Une sorte de lieu vide à l'intérieur de nous." Dambury in Bérard, "Gerty Dambury, 'Mon cheval de bataille est l'intime' (Entretien)."

130. "Éprouvé les mêmes sentiments qu'un Guadeloupeén moyen" (ibid.).

131. See Cixous, *L'Indiade ou L'Inde de leurs rêves et quelques écrits sur le théâtre*.

132. "D'ici et d'ailleurs, "universels" dans leur inconfort de vivre et leur besoin de communiquer et d'aimer" (Makward, "Pressentir l'autre," 79).

133. Lowe, "The Intimacies of Four Continents," 192.

134. Bérard, "Percussion et repercussion des voix dans le théâtre de Gerty Dambury."

135. See Tinker, *A New System of Slavery*.

136. Ramakrishnan and Scott, *Interplay of Cultural Narratives in Martinique*, 151.

137. Singaravélou, "Indians in the French Overseas Departments," 82–83.

138. Swami, "Les Cultes indiens en Martinique et en Guadeloupe," 1176–77.

139. Dambury, *Crosscurrents*, 90–91.

140. Ibid., 94–95.

141. Ibid., 95, 153.

142. Ibid., 128.

143. Ramakrishnan and Scott, *Interplay of Cultural Narratives in Martinique*, 181.

144. Dambury, *Crosscurrents*, 128.

145. Ibid., 151.

146. Ibid., 151, 146, 147.

147. Glissant, *The Poetics of Relation*, 5–8.

148. "Author's Note," in *Crosscurrents*, trans. Richard Philcox, 1997, unpublished, Ubu Repertory Theater Collections, Fales Special Collections, New York University Bobst Library, 5. Original note, in French, program, in *Lettres Indiennes*, Création 1996, Théâtre des Halles, Dambury's personal archives.

149. "Cela pourrait se passer n'importe où." Marline Brès, "Une femme à la recherche de l'espace intérieur," *Midi Libre*, July 29, 1996, Gerty Dambury's personal archives and Ubu Repertory Theater Collections, Département des Arts du spectacle, 4-COL-61/36, BnF.

150. Personal interview with Gilbert Laumord.

151. Personal interview with Mathéus.

152. "Pulsion qui traduit le mouvement intérieur du personnage." "L'enivrante odeur de la vie," *L'Humanité*, undated newspaper clipping, Revue de Presse, Théâtre des Halles, Gerty Dambury's personal archives.

153. "Souffrance intérieure." Personal interview with Laumord.

154. "Je n'ai pas envie d'être enfermée dans l'oralité. J'en ai ras-le-bol que chaque fois qu'un écrivain antillais ou africain écrive quelque chose, on le revoie

à l'oralité, parce que vous êtes une civilisation orale, et patati et patata. Ca ne m'intéresse pas. Donc je n'écris jamais de conte. C'est pourquoi j'ai été extrêment vexée lorsque la fable dans *Lettres indiennes* a été transformée en 'yé krik . . . yé krak' par le metteur en scène Alain Timar. Je déteste les "yé krik . . . yé krak," je le dis vraiment violemment, parce que j'en ai assez d'entendre ça et je sais qu'on nous renvoie à ça." Bérard, "Gerty Dambury, 'Mon cheval de bataille est l'intime' (Entretien)."

155. Dambury, *Crosscurrents*, 119–22.

156. "Fils et filles rebelles de Césaire." "Rencontres d'Auteurs," *La Caraibe*, program, Ubu Repertory Theater Collection, Département des Arts du spectacle, 4-Col-61/36, BnF.

157. "Lettres 'indiennes'? Oui, de l'Inde de Christophe Colomb, c'est-à-dire des Antilles." G.C., "Lettres indiennes," *Politis*, July 18, 1996, Revue de Presse, Gerty Dambury's personal archives.

158. "Il n'y a pas d'Indiens . . . ça parle de la Guadeloupe." Personal interview with Mathéus.

159. Brès, "Une femme à la recherche de l'espace intérieur."

160. Danièle Carraz, "Timar aventurier de l'extrême," *Le Méridional*, July 12, 1996, Revue de presse, Dambury's personal archives.

161. Cited in *Lettres Indiennes*, Création 1996, Théâtre des Halles, Dambury's personal archives.

162. Glissant, *The Poetics of Relation*, 144.

163. Hall, "Cultural Identity and Diaspora," 228.

Chapter 3

1. Browne, "Creole Economics and the *Débrouillard*," 381–84.

2. I owe much of my understanding of *bigidi* to Léna Blou's fantastic dance technique and pedagogy. Léna Blou, "Le concepte du bigidi: Réponse d'une interculturalité forcée," talk given at the University of Georgia, September 30, 2013. See Léna Blou, "Le bigidi . . . Plus qu'un déséquilibre permanent," http://fr.lenablou.fr/fr/Lenablou/le-bigidi.html; for English, see Léna Blou, "The Bigidi . . . More than a Permanent Imbalance," http://fr.lenablou.fr/en/Lenablou/the-bigidi.html, accessed April 16, 2014.

3. In Martinique, the common proverb is *Bité pas tonbé* (To stumble is not to fall). See Pinalie, *Dictionnaire de Proverbes Créoles*, 52.

4. Erskine, *Plantation Church*, 13.

5. Olmos and Paravisini-Gebert, *Creole Religions of the Caribbean*, 3.

6. Balme, *Decolonizing the Stage*.

7. Cabranes-Grant, "From Scenario to Networks," 519.

8. Gerstin, "Tangled Roots," 27.

9. Césaire, *La Faim, la ruse, la révolte*, 13.

10. Dayan, "Vodoun, or the Voice of the Gods," 26.

11. See especially Bernabé et al., *Eloge de la créolité*; Chamoiseau and Confiant, *Lettres créoles*.

12. Beriss, *Black Skin, French Voices*, 109–13.

13. Browne, *Creole Economics*, 148–49.

14. Tarica, "Patrick Chamoiseau's Creole *Conteur* and the Ethics of Survival," 40–41.

15. On the complex social history of missionaries in Martinique and Guadeloupe, see Peabody, "A Nation Born to Slavery"; Peabody, "A Dangerous Zeal."

16. Apter, "Herskovits's Heritage," 254.

17. The majority of enslaved people in Martinique and Guadeloupe embraced Catholicism, unlike in Saint-Domingue, where few converted (see Peabody, "A Dangerous Zeal," 56). While the enslaved likely understood their conversion to Catholicism as religious syncretism, not unlike the malleability of African religions, the French missionaries saw Catholicism and African religions as mutually exclusive.

18. Gerstin, "Tangled Roots," 13–14.

19. Labat labeled the dance an African-associated *calenda* (*kalenda*), but according to the dance scholar Julian Gerstin, it may have been a *mabelo* of the *lalinklè* genre, that is, enslaved blacks' adaptation of a Parisian contredanse (ibid., 14).

20. Césaire, *La faim, la ruse, la révolte*, 13.

21. Walcott, *Ti-Jean and His Brothers*, 81–166. *Cric crac blogodo* (Saint-Éloy, premiere in Paris 1989) and *Un ladja de paroles* (Pennot, premiere in Fort-de-France, 1992). Saint-Éloy is the director of the Théâtre de l'Air Nouveau in France, and Pennot is the former director of the foundational Théâtre de la Soif Nouvelle in Martinique. For more on these storytelling-inspired productions, see Bérard, *Théâtre des Antilles*, 106–12. For Ti-Jean's presence outside of the theater, see, for instance, Schwarz-Bart, *Ti-Jean l'horizon*; Chamoiseau, *Écrire en pays dominé*, 170.

22. Houyoux, "Entretien avec Ina Césaire," 351; Césaire and Laurent, *Contes de mort et de vie aux Antilles*.

23. Césaire, "La Triade humaine dans le conte antillais," 152.

24. Glissant, "Theater, Consciousness of the People."

25. Chamoiseau, "Ti-Jean en Psychanalyse," 23–24.

26. Césaire, "Proposition pour une analyse du conte antillais," 11; Césaire, "L'idéologie de la débrouillardise," 41–48. Though Césaire also evokes the same proverb in this essay (48), she uses the French term *débrouillardise* to articulate her main, academic concept. I choose to use the Creole term *débouya* in order to acknowledge that the concept acquires specific (trickster) significance in the Caribbean.

27. Bérard, "Entretien avec Ina Césaire," 112.

28. "Un résumé formidable de l'histoire de la Martinique" (ibid.).

29. "L'aîné obéit au cadet, le cadet n'obéit pas à l'aîné" (Césaire, *L'Enfant des passages*, 15).

30. Césaire, *La faim, la ruse, la révolte*, 6.

31. "Pas de rhum ici, ti bolôm! Ici, c'est un lieu chrétien!" (Césaire, *L'Enfant des passages*, 43).

32. Ibid., 49.

33. "Je ne vais pas dévorer mon sauveur!" (ibid., 55).

34. Ibid., 105, 109.

35. During the particular "Enfant terrible" tale that Césaire transcribed, the Guadeloupean storyteller likewise did not use *Cric! Crac!* See Césaire and Laurent, *Contes de mort et de vie aux Antilles*, 214–23; see also Césaire, "Ti-Zèb/Petit Zèbre (ou l'enfant terrible)."

36. Césaire, *L'Enfant des passages*, 9, 11.

37. Césaire, "La Triade humaine dans le conte antillais"; Césaire, *La faim, la ruse, la révolte*, 8–10.

38. Bérard, *Théâtre des Antilles*, 114.

39. Césaire, *L'Enfant des passages*, 45, 31, 79.

40. Bérard, "Entretien avec Ina Césaire," 110.

41. Césaire quoted in Ruben Gachy, "Les mémoires d'Isles: Maman N et maman F," *POCO*, October 1983, 32–33.

42. Bérard, *Théâtre des Antilles*, 113.

43. Bérard, "Entretien avec Ina Césaire," 111.

44. "Miroir déformant, non en ce sens qu'il ne dit pas la vérité mais parce qu'il renvoie à une image sarcastique de la vérité" (Césaire quoted in Houyoux, "Un Entretien avec Ina Césaire," 352).

45. See my discussion of the *abiku* and *ogbanje* in Condé's *An tan revolisyon*. See also Ogunyemi, "An Abiku-Ogbanje Atlas."

46. Miller, "Ina Césaire," 159. Having studied and transcribed multiple versions of several Ti-Jean tales, Césaire concludes that Ti-Jean is the hero of a "true epic lyric": "Véritable chanson de geste" (*La faim, la ruse, la révolte*, 12).

47. Miller, "Ina Césaire," 162.

48. Jones, "Two Plays by Ina Césaire," 230.

49. Césaire, "Application de la méthode au conte," 24; Bérard, "Entretien avec Ina Césaire," 112.

50. Césaire, *L'Enfant des passages*, 63.

51. "Il y a des pays ou l'on vit différemment!" (ibid.).

52. Ibid., 10.

53. Miller, "Ina Césaire," 166.

54. See Berrian, *Awakening Spaces*, 200–201.

55. "Tête en bas, pieds en haut" (Césaire, *L'Enfant des passages*, 65).

56. See Miller, *The French Atlantic Triangle*, 51–52.

57. "La mémoire, la tradition et l'histoire oubliée" (Césaire, *L'Enfant des passages*, 11).

58. Ibid., 79.
59. Houyoux, "Un Entretien avec Ina Césaire," 349.
60. Bérard, "Entretien avec Ina Césaire," 111, 112.
61. A similar character, also named Ti-Jean, appears in folktales across the Americas. See Voldeng, *Les Mémoires de Ti-Jean*. Ti-Jean is also a character in a Breton tale. As Césaire notes, the creole folktale is influenced by both Indo-European and African folklore (*La faim, la ruse, la révolte*, 4).
62. Richards, "Under the 'Trickster's' Sign," 69.
63. For more on Esu, see Igboin, "Esu and the Problem of Evil."
64. Robert D. Pelton quoted in Richards, "Under the 'Trickster's' Sign," 69.
65. Césaire, *L'Enfant des passages*, 10.
66. Ibid., 79, 11, 71.
67. Césaire, *La faim, la ruse, la révolte*, 5.
68. "Aujourd'hui, je suis fêté et admiré mais vous m'avez sans doute reconnu: je m'appelle Ti-Jean Lorizon. Je suis un nègre oublieux et, vous le savez sans doute aussi, rien ne s'oublie plus vite que le malheur. Alors c'est à vous, à vous tous, que je demande, en notre nom à tous, de ne pas oublier. Buvons!" (ibid., 113–15).
69. See Chamoiseau, "Ti-Jean Horizon."
70. Jones, "Two Plays by Ina Césaire," 230–31.
71. Personal email interview with Annick Justin-Joseph, October 10, 2014.
72. Justin-Joseph explained, "L'esthétique du jeu . . . laissait peu de champ à l'apitoiement, mais au contraire, dans son expression très physique, tournait en dérision, ironisait les effets d'un ordre sociétal déshumanisant."
73. "Dans le cœur de notre peuple." Serge Médeuf, "Ti-Jean dans Notre Horizon," *Antilla*, July 23, 1987, 22–23.
74. "Notre réconciliation avec nous-mêmes passe par une reconnaissance de notre héros" (ibid., 23).
75. Chamoiseau, "Ti-Jean en Psychanalyse," 24.
76. "Une découverte attardée de la psychanalyse"; "Souligner et re-souligner l'incompréhensible cruauté insolente de Ti-Jean" (ibid.).
77. "Le message du vrai Ti-Jean est celui de l'amoralité pas de l'im-moralité" (ibid.).
78. Ibid., 23.
79. See Chamoiseau, "Ti-Jean Horizon," 93–100.
80. Césaire and Laurent, *Contes de mort et de vie aux Antilles*, 214–23; Césaire, "Ti-Zèb/Petit Zèbre (ou l'enfant terrible)."
81. See Chamoiseau, *Solibo Magnificent*.
82. "Décadents, aliénés" (Chamoiseau, "Ti-Jean en Psychanalyse," 24).
83. Ibid.
84. Jones, "Two Plays by Ina Césaire," 229; Médeuf, "Ti-Jean dans Notre Horizon," 22.
85. Schwarz-Bart, *Your Handsome Captain*, 238.
86. Ibid.

87. See Adell, "Word/Song and Nommo Force in Two Black Francophone Plays"; Bérard, *Théâtre des Antilles*, 172–74; Gyssels, "'I Talked to Zombie'"; Montantin, "*Ton beau capitaine / An tan revolisyon*, à bâtons rompus"; Weagel, "The Creole Quadrille in Simone Schwarz-Bart's *Ton beau capitaine*"; Ruprecht, "Performance transculturelle"; Bérard, "Au nom des loa"; see also Bérard, *Théâtre des Antilles*, 185–88.

88. Schwarz-Bart, *Your Handsome Captain*, 229.

89. Ibid., 239–43, 248–49; Bérard, *Théâtre des Antilles*, 173.

90. Schwarz-Bart, *Your Handsome Captain*, 248, 234, 249.

91. Ibid., 229.

92. Schwarz-Bart, *Ton beau capitaine*, 8.

93. Schwarz-Bart, *Your Handsome Captain*, 239.

94. Ruprecht, "Performance transculturelle," 319.

95. Schwarz-Bart, *Your Handsome Captain*, 243.

96. Bérard, *Théâtre des Antilles*, 174.

97. Schwarz-Bart, *Your Handsome Captain*, 244.

98. Cyrille, "Ca Ki Ta Nou," 228.

99. Schwarz-Bart, *Your Handsome Captain*, 234, 231, 233, 246.

100. Ruprecht, "Performance transculturelle," 318.

101. Léna Blou, "Le bigidi."

102. Schwarz-Bart, *Your Handsome Captain*, 246–47.

103. Michel, "Of Worlds Unseen," 37.

104. Schwarz-Bart, *Your Handsome Captain*, 229.

105. "'Chez nous, la gestuelle est aussi importante que le dit,' explique Simone Schwarz-Bart," *France-Antilles*, April 27, 1987, Mariann Mathéus's personal archives.

106. Unpublished text by Simone Schwarz-Bart concerning *Ton beau capitaine*, read by Mariann Mathéus, "Théâtre Caraïbe Le Répertoire" conference, November 9, 2013, Paris, Mariann Mathéus's personal archives.

107. Schwarz-Bart, *Your Handsome Captain*, 229.

108. Ruprecht, "Performance transculturelle," 320.

109. Gyssels, "'I Talked to Zombie,'" 228.

110. "Chez nous, la gestuelle se substitute souvent au textuel, la gestuelle est aussi importante que le dit, elle l'accompagne" ("'Chez nous, la gestuelle est aussi importante que le dit,' explique Simone Schwarz-Bart").

111. Alvina Ruprecht, unpublished interview with Syto Cavé, Paris, July 2011, Alvina Ruprecht's personal archives.

112. Untitled and unpublished text by Simone Schwarz-Bart concerning *Ton beau capitaine*, read by Mariann Mathéus; "Haïti sur scène," interview with Simone Schwarz-Bart, Antipodes radio program, France Culture, hosted by Daniel Maximin, January 20, 1988, Inathèque, BnF.

113. Untitled and unpublished text by Simone Schwarz-Bart concerning *Ton beau capitaine*, read by Mariann Mathéus.

114. In 2003 Paul Brodwin estimated approximately 24,000 Haitian migrants in Guadeloupe, out of a population of just 300,000. Quoted in Conteh-Morgan and Thomas, *New Francophone African and Caribbean Theaters*, 144. For a reading of the play in the context of the broader plight of Haitian migrant workers in Guadeloupe, see Kendall, "Schwarz-Bart's 'Ton Beau Capitaine.'"

115. Schwarz-Bart, *Your Handsome Captain*, 242; Schwarz-Bart, *Ton beau capitaine*, 40.

116. Schwarz-Bart, *Your Handsome Captain*, 242, 247.

117. Ibid., 234; Miller, "Simone Schwarz-Bart," 155; Miller, "Caribbean Women Playwrights," 229.

118. Adell, "Word/Song and Nommo Force in Two Black Francophone Plays," 66.

119. Schwarz-Bart, *Your Handsome Captain*, 234, 232.

120. Ibid., 241, 245, 234, 232, 229.

121. Miller, "Simone Schwarz-Bart," 153.

122. Schwarz-Bart, *Your Handsome Captain*, 234.

123. Miller, "Simone Schwarz-Bart," 152.

124. Conteh-Morgan and Thomas, *New Francophone African and Caribbean Theaters*, 152.

125. Schwarz-Bart, *Your Handsome Captain*, 237.

126. Ibid., 237–38.

127. Ibid., 237.

128. Jones, "Theatre and Resistance?," 99.

129. Miller, "Simone Schwarz-Bart," 152.

130. Schwarz-Bart, *Your Handsome Captain*, 245.

131. Ibid., 246, 240.

132. See Montantin, "*Ton beau capitaine / An tan revolisyon*, à bâtons rompus," 185.

133. "Une tension entre le visible et l'invisible" (Ruprecht, "Performance transculturelle," 313).

134. "Sans les rêves, la vie serait impossible dans les îles. Le réel est constamment compensé par les rêves." Thierry Bayle, "Théâtre Chaillot: En compagnie Créole," *Le Quotidien*, July 12, 1988, Ubu Repertory Theater Collections, Département des Arts du spectacle, 4-Col-61/102, BnF.

135. See Desrivières, "Entretien avec Syto Cavé."

136. Alvina Ruprecht, unpublished interview with Syto Cavé.

137. Ibid.

138. "Je m'adressais à l'image que j'avais de lui." Personal interview with Mariann Mathéus, Paris, 4 April, 2014.

139. Alvina Ruprecht, unpublished interview with Syto Cavé.

140. Ruprecht, "Performance transculturelle," 315.

141. Montantin, "*Ton beau capitaine / An tan revolisyon*, à bâtons rompus," 185.

142. Personal interview with Mathéus.

143. "La mise en scène peut éventuellement revêtir la voix féminine d'un corps" (Montantin, *"Ton beau capitaine / An tan revolisyon*, à bâtons rompus," 186).

144. Gyssels, "'I Talked to a Zombie,'" 228.

145. For further discussion of this production, see Bérard, "Au nom des loa," 64. Bérard views this staging choice as perfectly respecting the play's tensions between absence and presence, reality and imaginary.

146. Alvina Ruprecht, unpublished interview with Syto Cavé.

147. Reviews consulted from Mariann Mathéus's personal archives as well as Ubu Repertory Theater Collections, Département des Arts du spectacle, 4-Col-61/102, BnF.

148. "Une histoire d'amour plus forte que l'absence." Caroline Jurgenson, "Une histoire d'amour: 'Ton Beau Capitaine' est la première pièce de la romancière Simone Schwarz-Bart. Un drame d'éloignement," *Le Figaro*, September 12, 1988, 4-Col-61/102, BnF. "Simone Schwarz-Bart a su donner une dimension de totale dignité aux Haïtiens trop souvent méprisés en Guadeloupe." Caroline Bourgine, "Limoges: Rideau sur un dragon, un capitaine et une tortue," *Libération*, October 14, 1987, personal archives of Mariann Mathéus.

Chapter 4

1. In addition to the five plays I analyze in this and the subsequent chapter, Ubu also produced Condé's *The Hills of Massabielle* (*Le Morne de Massabielle*, unpublished) and Michèle Césaire's *La Nef*. Condé's *The Hills of Massabielle* (trans. Richard Philcox) was directed by Cynthia Belgrave in 1991. Michèle Césaire's *The Ship* (trans. Richard Miller) was given a staged reading under Saundra McClain's direction in 1993.

2. Shaked, "The Play"; Richards, "The Challenges of Cultural Translation."

3. These manuscripts are housed in the Fales Special Collections of the Bobst Library at New York University.

4. Judith Aita, "African Plays Find a New Audience," *Topic* 173 (1988): 38.

5. Hall, "Cultural Identity and Diaspora," 235.

6. Gilroy, *The Black Atlantic*.

7. Edwards, *The Practice of Diaspora*.

8. Harrison, "Mother Word," xii.

9. Richards, "African Diaspora Drama," 233.

10. Bharucha, "Dimensions of Conflict in Globalization and Cultural Practice."

11. Appadurai, *Modernity at Large*, 27–47.

12. Césaire quoted in Kourilsky, *Ubu Repertory Theater*, 38.

13. Ibid., 38–9.

14. Hall, "Cultural Identity and Diaspora," 228.

Notes to Chapter 4

15. Notes, Ubu Repertory Theater Collections, Département des Arts du spectacle, 4-Col-61/155, BnF.

16. Personal interview with Ronnie Scharfman, New York, May 27, 2009.

17. Césaire in Kourilsky, *Ubu Repertory Theater*, 38.

18. In addition to the Florence Gould Foundation, funds for this festival came from the cultural services of the French Embassy as well as from the Martinique Tourist Office and the Regional Agency for Tourism Development in Martinique.

19. "A Word from the Artistic Director," West Indies Festival Program, 1991, Ubu Repertory Theater Collections, Département des Arts du spectacle, 4-Col-61/652, BnF.

20. Joan Ungaro, "West Indies Festival," *Theater Week*, November 25, 1991.

21. I owe much of my knowledge of the performance to the notes and promptbook of the stage manager Elise-Ann Konstantin, which include blocking and choreography as well as meticulous documentation of sound and lighting cues, and costume changes. Sketches of the set design are archived alongside these notes. Ubu Repertory Theater Collections, Département des Arts du spectacle, 4-Col-61/155, BnF.

22. Makward and Miller, *Plays by French and Francophone Women*.

23. See Kirksey-Floyd's director's notes to the actors, February 11, 1991, Ubu Repertory Theater Collections, Département des Arts du spectacle, 4-Col-61/155, BnF. Kirksey-Floyd reiterated her emphasis on the two women's relationship during a phone conversation with me on March 23, 2014.

24. Email correspondence with Dianne Kirksey-Floyd, December 17, 2014.

25. Ade Johnson, "The 1991 West Indies Festival," *Black Ivory*, 28, undated clipping, Ubu Repertory Theater Collections, Département des Arts du spectacle, Fol-Col-61/4, BnF.

26. Ungaro, "West Indies Festival."

27. Press release, Ubu Repertory Theater Collections, Département des Arts du spectacle, 4-Col-61/652, BnF. It seems likely that Ubu rewrote this language in later press releases, but it was taken up in an article and announcement in *Black Arts New York* 5, no. 1 (1991).

28. Program, West Indies Festival, Ubu Repertory Theater Collections, Département des Arts du spectacle, 4-Col-61/652, BnF.

29. Email correspondence with Kirksey-Floyd.

30. These dances and sound cues are documented in the stage manager's script and notes, Ubu Repertory Theater Collections, Département des Arts du spectacle, 4-Col-61/155, BnF.

31. Program, West Indies Festival.

32. Phone conversation with Kirksey-Floyd.

33. Césaire, *Island Memories*, 52.

34. Notes, Ubu Repertory Theater Collections, Département des Arts du spectacle, 4-Col-61/652, BnF.

35. Shaked, "The Play," 8.
36. McClain was the assistant director to Shange for Césaire's *Rosanie Soleil*. She also played the leading role in Ubu's staged reading of Condé's *Pension les Alizés* and directed a staged reading of Michèle Césaire's *La Nef*.
37. Césaire, *Rosanie Soleil*, 118.
38. Césaire, *Fire's Daughters*, 33.
39. Ibid., 4–5.
40. Harold A. Waters, "Review of *New French-Language Plays*," *World Literature Today*, Summer 1994, Ubu Repertory Theater Collections, Département des Arts du spectacle, Fol-Col-61/8, BnF.
41. Program, Ubu Repertory Theater Collections, Département des Arts du spectacle, 4-Col-61/678, BnF.
42. See Rosette C. Lamont, "The Ubu Rep Season," *Theater Week*, September 6–12, 1993, 23–25; Annie Artignan, "Créations françaises: Ubu, ou le théâtre roi," *France-Amérique*, September 25–October 1, 1993.
43. Program and flyers, Ubu Repertory Theater Collections, Département des Arts du spectacle, 4-Col-61/678, BnF.
44. Personal interview with Françoise Kourilsky, New York, April 3, 2009.
45. "Community Affairs Calendar: October 6–12, 1993," compiled by Annette Walker, *New York Amsterdam News*, October 9, 1993, courtesy of ProQuest Historical Newspapers, New York *Amsterdam News*, Northwestern University Electronic Resources; "Spotlight on Black Art," *Black Masks*, August–September 1993, Ubu Repertory Theater Collections, Département des Arts du spectacle, Fol-Col-61/6, BnF.
46. See Shange, "Porque Tu No M'entrende?"
47. Program, Ubu Repertory Theater Collections, Département des Arts du spectacle, 4-Col-61/678, BnF.
48. Miller expressed her agreement with this choice in a personal interview, New York, August 29, 2008.
49. Shange cited in Davida Singer, "Their House Is a 'Battlefield,'" *Villager*, September 29, 1993, 30.
50. Personal interview with Watoku Ueno, New York, August 25, 2008.
51. Personal interview with Carol Ann Pelletier, New York, August 23, 2008.
52. Personal interview with Greg MacPherson, New York, August 25, 2008.
53. Bérard, "Entretien avec Ina Césaire," 117.
54. Glissant, "Theater, Consciousness of the People."
55. Personal interview with Kourilsky.
56. Notes, Ubu Repertory Theater Collections, Département des Arts du spectacle, 4-Col-61/26, BnF.
57. Rosette C. Lamont, "*Talk about Love* and *Fire's Daughters*," *Theater Week*, December 6, 1993, Ubu Repertory Theater Collections, Département des Arts du spectacle, 4-Col-61/678, BnF.

58. Anthea Kraut persuasively argues that these African American women represented black diaspora through dance. See "Between Primitivism and Diaspora."

59. Lamont, "*Talk about Love* and *Fire's Daughters*."

60. Shange quoted in Singer, "Their House Is a 'Battlefield.'"

61. Makward, "Filles du soleil noir," 335; D. J. R. Bruckner, "Theater in Review: From Martinique, a Meditation on Freedom," *New York Times*, October 20, 1993.

62. Lamont, "*Talk about Love* and *Fire's Daughters*."

63. Lamont, "The Ubu Rep Season," 24.

64. "Le rapport de domination de l'homme sur la femme semble être l'une des rares données universelles; ne s'agirait-il pas d'une super-structure ?" Ina Césaire quoted in Makward, "De bouche à oreille à bouche," 143.

65. Personal interview with Judith Miller.

66. Manning, *Modern Dance, Negro Dance*, xvi, xix.

67. See the 1992 "Digest of Education Statistics" table offered by the National Center for Education Statistics and U.S. Department of Education, http://nces.ed.gov/programs/digest/d99/d99t236.asp, accessed December 1, 2010. The table is broken into five categories of ethnicity (White non-Hispanic; Black non-Hispanic; Hispanic; Asian/Pacific Islander; American Indian/Alaskan Native) and divided along male-female gender lines. The 2.4 percent represents 12,941 black women instructional faculty and staff in all institutions.

68. Phone interview with Saundra McClain, May 24, 2009; personal interview with casting agent Stephanie Klapper, New York, August 21, 2008.

69. Personal interview with Françoise Kourilsky, Paris, June 3, 2008. I know from my discussion with Catherine Temerson that Ubu's team did try to match African American translators with black Francophone plays if possible. Personal interview with Catherine Temerson, New York, August 28, 2008.

70. Anthropologist David Beriss summarizes, "Racism in France is not principally defined by attention to color or by the deployment of racial stereotypes (although it can be). Instead racism is understood primarily as an incorrect or unjust invocation of culture" (*Black Skin, French Voices*, 38).

71. Personal interview with Kourilsky, April 3, 2009.

72. "Avoir respecté le tissue social présenté ici, mais d'avoir dépassé un naturalisme étroite." Rosette Lamont, "Sur la scene new-yorkaise: Du festival d'Avignon à Ubu Repertory," *France-Amérique*, March 8–14, 1997.

73. See my discussion of *Lettres indiennes* in chapter 2. See also Singaravélou, "Indians in the French Overseas Departments," 82–83.

74. Melinda Given Guttman, "Swept Away by 'Crosscurrents,'" *New York Theatre Wire*, March 14, 1997, Ubu Repertory Theater Collections, Département des Arts du spectacle, 4-Col-61/164, BnF.

75. Audience responses, Ubu Repertory Theater Collections, Département des Arts du spectacle, 4-Col-61/164, BnF.

76. Rosette C. Lamont, "Personal Statement," in Kourilsky, *Ubu Repertory Theater*, 42.
77. Personal interview with Kourilsky, April 3, 2009.
78. Phone interview with La Tonya Borsay, September 8, 2009.
79. Phone interview with Kavi Ladnier, May 19, 2009.
80. Personal interview with Gerty Dambury, Montreuil, June 2, 2008.
81. Phone interview with La Tonya Borsay.
82. When I asked Kourilsky about what genres of cultural music Ito drew from, she responded that he was a "world musician": he drew from the traditions of all cultures.
83. D. R. J. Bruckner, "A Prodigal Son and Parents," *New York Times*, March 12, 1997, Ubu Repertory Theater Collections, Département des Arts du spectacle, 4-Col-61/164, BnF.
84. Guttman, "Swept Away by 'Crosscurrents.'"
85. "Play Looks at Race and the Diaspora," *News India-Times*, March 7, 1997.
86. Personal interview with Stephanie Klapper, New York, August 21, 2008.
87. Aasif Mandvi, *No Land's Man* (San Francisco: Chronicle Books, 2014).
88. Personal interview with Kourilsky, April 3, 2009.
89. Personal interview with Pelletier. See also costume notes, Ubu Repertory Theater Collections, Département des Arts du spectacle, 4-Col-61/161, BnF.
90. Phone interview with Ladnier. Ladnier was never trained professionally in Bharatha Natyam—not because she didn't want to learn it but because there weren't any teachers in her neighborhood. Because she is a dancer, however, she picked up traditional Indian dance and has used it multiple times in her work as an actress.
91. "Juste . . . honnête." Personal interview with Dambury.
92. Audience responses, Ubu Repertory Theater Collections, Département des Arts du spectacle, 4-Col-61/164, BnF.
93. Bruckner, "A Prodigal Son and Parents."
94. "Mais je n'ai pas parlé des Indiens de la Guadeloupe, ni des Indiens de la Réunion, parce que je me suis intéressée à la culture indienne en général." Dambury quoted in Bérard, "Gerty Dambury, 'Mon cheval de bataille est l'intime' (Entretien)."
95. Alice Richardson, "'Crosscurrents' about Sugar Workers Opens at Ubu Repertory," *Amsterdam News*, March 22, 1997, Ubu Repertory Theater Collections, Département des Arts du spectacle, 4-Col-61/164, BnF.
96. Ibid.

Chapter 5

1. McMahon, *Recasting Transnationalism through Performance*, 8–10.
2. Collins, *Black Feminist Thought*, 164–65, 161, 168.

3. "Théâtre et oralité," hosted by Daniel Maximin, Antipodes, a France Culture program, June 11, 1985, Inathèque, BnF.
4. Condé, "Order, Disorder, Freedom, and the West Indian Writer," 131.
5. Jones, "Theatre in the French West Indies," 51.
6. Makward, "Reading Maryse Condé's Theatre," 685.
7. "La structure sociale d'un pays dominé, l'exploitation dont les Nègres sont victimes qui ne permettent pas le bonheur des êtres, et détruisent les couples" (Condé, *La Parole des femmes*, 35).
8. Much of the information presented in the following paragraphs was taken from a personal interview with Françoise Kourilsky, New York, April 3, 2009.
9. Département des Arts du spectacle, NUMAV-049429, BnF.
10. Condé is nonetheless incredulous of this notion of the "spirit of the Creole language" (*The Journey of a Caribbean Writer*, 210).
11. "Il y a bien sûr la couche créole, la couche française, la couche créole-française et ensuite le produit, le nouveau terme, la nouvelle langue" (Gauvin, "La Belle au bois dormant," 122).
12. Kanhai-Brunton, "How Handsome Can the Captain Be?," 48.
13. Schwarz-Bart, *Ton beau capitaine*, 25.
14. Schwarz-Bart, *Your Handsome Captain*, 236.
15. Kanhai-Brunton, "How Handsome Can the Captain Be?," 50.
16. Schwarz-Bart, *Ton beau capitaine*, 41.
17. Schwarz-Bart, *Your Handsome Captain*, 242.
18. Kanhai-Brunton, "How Handsome Can the Captain Be?," 49.
19. Personal interview with Kourilsky.
20. Personal interview with Catherine Temerson, New York, August 28, 2008.
21. "Parfaitement bilingue," Ubu Repertory Theater Collections, Département des Arts du spectacle, 4-Col-61/540, BnF.
22. "Director's Notes," Program, *Your Fine Captain*, Rites and Reason Theatre, directed by George Houston Bass, November 12–14, 1988, Brown University. Ubu Repertory Theater Collections, Département des Arts du spectacle, 4-Col-61/646, BnF.
23. Kim Ives, "From Haiti, Love in Exile," *Guardian*, November 15 1989. "N'a pas été vue dans les meilleures conditions linguistiques." "La femme sur bande magnétique," *Haiti Progress*, November 7, 1989.
24. Personal interview with Kourilsky.
25. Notes and publicity report, Ubu Repertory Theater Collections, Département des Arts du spectacle, 4-Col-61/208 and 4-Col-61/636, BnF.
26. Personal interview with Kourilsky. For an account, see Ruprecht, "Françoise Kourilsky."
27. "Notre propos n'était pas de copier un rituel, mais d'en inventer un" (Ruprecht, "Françoise Kourilsky").

28. Personal interview with Kourilsky.
29. Département des Arts du spectacle, NUMAV-049429, BnF.
30. Letter from Francoise Kourilsky to Denzel Washington, May 31, 1989, Ubu Repertory Theater Collections, Département des Arts du spectacle, 4-Col-61/646, BnF.
31. "*Ton Beau Capitaine*," *Black Arts New York*, September 1988.
32. Townsend Brewster, "A World on Plays," *Big Red News*, December 2, 1989.
33. Proposal to tour the play on college campuses, spring 1990, Ubu Repertory Theater Collections, Département des Arts du spectacle, 4-Col-61/646, BnF.
34. Student reactions, University at Albany, 1990, Ubu Repertory Theater Collections, Département des Arts du spectacle, 4-Col-61/212, BnF.
35. "The play develops the universal idea of exile." Kourilsky quoted in Ariane Kamp, "Handsome Captain Sails into PAC," *Albany Student Press*, March 9, 1990, 14.
36. See Ruprecht, "Françoise Kourilsky."
37. Letters from Kourilsky to Slade, Ubu Repertory Theater Collections, Département des Arts du spectacle, 4-Col-61/208, BnF.
38. Barbara Brewster Lewis, "'Your Handsome Captain': Modern Nativity story," *Amsterdam News*, November 25, 1989.
39. Ibid.
40. Brewster, "A World on Plays."
41. Miller, "Simone Schwarz-Bart," 152.
42. Ruprecht, "Performance transculturelle," 313; Gyssels, "'I Talked to Zombie,'" 228, 247; Montantin, "*Ton beau capitaine / An tan revolisyon*, à bâtons rompus," 186. As mentioned in chapter 3, Mathéus also told me that Schwarz-Bart realized in the end that Cavé's instincts were correct.
43. Personal interview with Ronnie Scharfman.
44. See Scharfman, "Exiled from the Shoah," 250–63.
45. Video, Département des Arts du spectacle, NUMAV-049429, BnF.
46. Condé, *The Journey of a Caribbean Writer*, 149.
47. Personal interview with Kourilsky, New York, April 3, 2009.
48. See Condé, *The Journey of a Caribbean Writer*, 18–31. See also, for example, Apter, "Crossover Texts/Creole Tongues," 92.
49. Personal interview with Maryse Condé, Paris, May 30, 2008.
50. Lewis, "No Silence," 543.
51. Since then, she has also cotranslated Glissant's *Faulkner, Mississippi*.
52. Personal interview with Catherine Temerson, New York, August 28, 2008.
53. Condé, *The Tropical Breeze Hotel*, 110–64.
54. Phone interview with Barbara Lewis, July 10, 2014.
55. Temerson explained that she had not had this same concern with *Your Handsome Captain* because she and Harris knew each other outside of Ubu. Personal interview with Temerson.

56. Lewis, "No Silence," 545, 550.
57. See especially Fulton, *Signs of Dissent*.
58. See Bernabé, *Fond-natal*.
59. See, for example, Knepper, *Patrick Chamoiseau*, 64–66.
60. Condé, *The Journey of a Caribbean Writer*, 32, translation modified. "J'aime à répéter que je n'écris ni en français ni en créole. Mais en Maryse Condé" (Condé, "Liaison dangereuse," 205).
61. "Très ésotérique . . . faire travailler le lecteur" (quoted in Kadish and Massardier-Kenney, "Traduire Maryse Condé," 751).
62. Philcox, "Fidelity, Infidelity, and the Adulterous Translator," 30.
63. Philcox, "Translating Maryse Condé," 33.
64. Philcox, "Fidelity, Infidelity, and the Adulterous Translator," 34.
65. Spivak, "The Politics of Translation," 370.
66. See Philcox, "Translating Maryse Condé," 282; Kadish and Massardier-Kenney, "Traduire Maryse Condé," 750–51.
67. See Okawa, "Translating Maryse Condé's *Célanire cou coupé*."
68. Ruprecht, "Le théâtre de Maryse Condé," 153.
69. Condé, *Pension les Alizés*, 13.
70. Condé, *The Tropical Breeze Hotel*, 120.
71. Phone interview with Shauneille Perry, May 22, 2009.
72. Personal interview with Kourilsky, New York, April 3, 2009.
73. Watoku Ueno, Carol Ann Pelletier, and Greg Macpherson generously explained their designs from their personal collections, which made this assessment possible. Personal interview with Carol Ann Pelletier, New York, August 23, 2008; personal interview with Greg MacPherson, New York, August 25, 2008; personal interview with Watoku Ueno, New York, August 25, 2008.
74. Program with actor bios, Ubu Repertory Theater Collections, Département des Arts du spectacle, Fol-Col-61/8, BnF.
75. Personal interview with Pelletier; personal interview with Kourilsky, April 3, 2009; phone interview with Perry.
76. Personal interview with Maryse Condé, Paris, May 30, 2008. See also Ruprecht, "Le théâtre de Maryse Condé," 153.
77. Phone interview with Barbara Lewis.
78. "Il y a eu aussi un problème de mélange de tons auquel le metteur en scène n'a pas été très sensible, le passage entre des moments d'ironie et de tendresse" (Ruprecht, "Le théâtre de Maryse Condé," 153).
79. See Ruprecht, "Le théâtre de Maryse Condé," 149; "Maryse Condé Teatral," *La Ventana*, November 18, 2010, http://laventana.casa.cult.cu/modules.php?name=News&file=article&sid=5810, accessed November 15, 2013.
80. Email correspondence with Carol Ann Pelletier, January 3, 2014.
81. Rosette C. Lamont, "Beyond Broadway: *The Tropical Breeze Hotel*," April 17, 1995, Ubu Repertory Theater Collections, Département des Arts du

Spectacles, Fol-COL-61/8, BnF. The play referenced is a critique of greed that finds its hero in a Parisian madwoman.

82. Press releases and publicity, Ubu Repertory Theater Collections, Département des Arts du spectacle, Fol-Col-61/7 and Fol-Col-61/8, BnF.

83. Invitation, Ubu Repertory Theater Collections, Département des Arts du spectacle, Fol-Col-61/8, BnF.

84. Stage manager notes, Ubu Repertory Theater Collections, Département des Arts du spectacle, 4-Col-61/159, BnF.

85. Phone interview with Perry.

86. Condé, *The Tropical Breeze Hotel*, 144.

87. This suburb had a significant French American population, according to Kapp. Personal interview with Chris Kapp, New York, May 29, 2009.

88. I would like to express my gratitude to Beth Turner for looking up her listings and to Jonathan Slaff for printing selections for me from a meticulously organized database detailing by production all of the press requests made on behalf of Ubu.

89. D. J. R. Bruckner, "Wisdom's Sad, Empty Promise in Matters of the Heart: 'The Tropical Breeze Hotel,'" *New York Times*, February 22, 1995.

90. See Ruprecht, "Françoise Kourilsky."

91. Personal interview with Kourilsky, New York, April 3, 2009.

92. Phone interview with Perry.

93. This is White's characterization of her experience in her bio in the program, Ubu Repertory Theater Collections, Département des Arts du spectacle, Fol-Col-61/8, BnF.

94. Phone interview with Saundra McClain.

95. Pfaff, *Conversations with Maryse Condé*, 84.

96. Condé insisted in 1993 that literature should give rise to thinking rather than slogans (*La Parole des femmes*, 76). See also more recent pieces; for example, Condé, "Sketching a Literature," 213.

97. Condé, *The Journey of a Caribbean Writer*, 61.

98. For more on Walter White, see Janken, *Walter White*.

99. My sincere thanks to Barbara Lewis for alerting me to White's family history.

100. Quoted in Paul Vitello, "Jane White, Actress and Singer Who Found Racial Attitudes to be an Obstacle, Dies at 88," *New York Times*, August 7, 2011, http://www.nytimes.com/2011/08/08/arts/jane-white-actress-and-singer-who-rebelled-against-racial-straitjacketing-dies-at-88.html?_r=0, consulted September 14, 2014.

101. Schwarz-Bart, *Your Handsome Captain*, 234.

102. Ruprecht, "Les pratiques scéniques et textuelles de la région caribéenne francophone et créolophone," 16.

103. Shih and Lionnet, introduction, in *The Creolization of Theory*, 28.

104. Richards, "Writing the Absent Potential," 157–58.

105. Benítez-Rojo, *The Repeating Island*, 2.

106. For an overview of these debates, see Cohen and Toninato, introduction, in *The Creolization Reader*, 14–18. For an influential critique of this trend of conflating creolization and globalization, see Palmié, "Creolization and Its Discontents."

107. Shih and Lionnet, *The Creolization of Theory*, 24.

Coda

1. Vergès, "Kiltir Kreol," 184.

2. Condé, *The Journey of a Caribbean Writer*, 59.

3. Munro and Britton, introduction, in *American Creoles*, 3.

4. See also, for example, Lowe, "'Calypso Magnolia.'" For summaries of these scholarly trends, see Cabranes-Grant, "An Essay on Racial Understanding"; Young "Black Performance Studies in the New Millennium."

5. A VHS of *L'enfant des passages* is held by several universities; I consulted the tape via interlibrary loan. A video of *In the Time of Revolution* can be downloaded from *Francophone Slavery*, http://slavery.uga.edu/francophonie/pics.htm.

6. Giles recently directed Rita Dove's *The Darker Face of the Earth* at the University of Georgia (November 2012) and presented a paper about how the past is present in this play at the National Black Theatre Festival International Symposium, 2013.

7. Miller has written an article about this pedagogical experience. See "Some Thoughts on Producing African Theatre in French with American Students."

8. Clark, "Developing Diaspora Literacy and *Marasa* Consciousness," 11, 12.

9. Césaire, "La Triade humaine dans le conte antillais."

10. See Michel, "Of Worlds Unseen," 37n19.

11. Conquergood, "Performance Studies," 43, 40–41.

12. Freda Scott Giles, "A Matter of Translation: Staging *An Tan Revolisyon* at the University of Georgia," 2. I quote from the original, unpublished English-language essay, in Giles's personal archives. A translation of this essay in French was published as "Traduire et mettre en scène *An tan revolisyon* en Amérique."

13. Program, *In the Time of Revolution*, October 15–18, 1997, University of Georgia, Freda Scott Giles's personal archives.

14. Email correspondence with Doris Kadish, September 30, 2014.

15. Phone interview with Judith Miller, October 25, 2013.

16. Educational packet, "L'enfant des Passages ou La Geste de Ti-Jean d'Ina Césaire," personal archives of Judith Miller.

17. High school students were in years 3 to 5 of their French education (personal interview with Miller). Creole expressions are marked in the text with an asterisk.

18. Personal interview with Ellen Bleier, Athens, Georgia, October 22, 2013.

19. Phone interview with Miller.
20. "About the Author and the Play," director's note, *L'enfant des passages ou La Geste de Ti-Jean*, program, April 27–30, 1994, Madison, Wisconsin, personal archives of Judith Miller.
21. Phone interview with Miller.
22. Personal interview with Freda Scott Giles, Athens, Georgia, October 22, 2013.
23. Shaked, "The Play," 13.
24. Richards, "The Challenges of Cultural Translation," 164, 182.
25. Mardorossian, *Reclaiming Difference*, 16.
26. Giles, "A Matter of Translation," 8.
27. Catanese, *The Problem of the Color[blind]*, 10.
28. Giles, "A Matter of Translation," 6
29. McKay, *Maryse Condé et le théâtre antillais*, 60.
30. Césaire, "La Triade humaine dans le conte antillais"; Césaire, *La Faim, la ruse, la révolte*, 8–10.
31. "About the Author and the Play," Educational packet.
32. Richards, "The Challenges of Cultural Translation," 163.
33. "About the Production," *L'enfant des passages ou La Geste de Ti-Jean*, program, April 27–30, 1994, Madison, Wisconsin, personal archives of Judith Miller.
34. Personal interview with Bleier.
35. Ruprecht, "Le théâtre de Maryse Condé," 158.
36. Giles, "A Matter of Translation," 14
37. Johnson, *Appropriating Blackness*, 234.
38. Barriteau, "Contesting Paradigms of Development."
39. Vergès, "Kiltir Kreol," 184, my emphasis.
40. Hall, "Créolité and the Process of Creolization," 31.

Bibliography

Aching, Gerard. *Masking and Power: Carnival and Popular Culture in the Caribbean.* Minneapolis: University of Minnesota Press, 2002.
Adell, Sandra. "Word/Song and Nommo Force in Two Black Francophone Plays: Simone Schwarz-Bart's *Ton beau capitaine* and Ina Césaire's *Mémoires d'isles.*" *Journal of Caribbean Studies* 8, nos. 1–2 (1990–91): 61–69.
Appadurai, Arjun. *Modernity at Large: Cultural Dimensions of Globalization.* Minneapolis: University of Minnesota Press, 1996.
Apter, Andrew. "Herskovits's Heritage: Rethinking Syncretism in the African Diaspora." *Diaspora: A Journal of Transnational Studies* 1, no. 3 (1991): 235–60.
Apter, Emily. "Crossover Texts/Creole Tongues: A Conversation with Maryse Condé." *Public Culture* 13, no. 1 (2001): 89–96.
Arnold, A. James. "From the Problematic Maroon to a Woman-Centered Creole Project in the Literature of the French West Indies." In *Slavery in the Caribbean Francophone World: Distant Voices, Forgotten Acts, Forged Identities*, ed. Doris Y. Kadish. Athens: University of Georgia Press, 2000.
———. "The Gendering of Créolité: The Erotics of Colonialism." In *Penser la créolité*, ed. Maryse Condé and Madeleine Cottenet-Hage. Paris: Karthala, 1995.
Bada, Valérie. "Slavery and Silence in Ina Césaire's 'Mémoires d'Isles' and Denis Scott's 'Echo in the Bone.'" *Journal of the Midwest Modern Language Association* 33/34, no. 3/1 (2000–2001): 86–93.
Balme, Christopher B. *The Cambridge Introduction to Theatre Studies.* Cambridge, UK: Cambridge University Press, 2008.
———. *Decolonizing the Stage: Theatrical Syncretism and Post-Colonial Drama.* Oxford: Oxford University Press, 1999.
———. "Syncretic Theatre: The Semiotics of Postcolonial Drama and Wole Soyinka's *Death and the King's Horseman.*" In *New Theatre in Francophone and Anglophone Africa*, ed. Anne Fuchs. Amsterdam: Rodopi, 1999.
Barriteau, Violet Eudine. "Contesting Paradigms of Development: Creating

Coalitions of the Committed." *Caribbean Studies Newsletter* 44, no. 1 (2014): 8–13.
Benítez-Rojo, Antonio. *The Repeating Island: The Caribbean and the Postmodern Perspective.* 1992. Durham, NC: Duke University Press, 1996.
Bérard, Stéphanie. "Au nom des loa: Vaudou et théâtre dans *Ton beau capitaine* de Simone Schwarz-Bart." *MaComère* 9 (2007): 97–104.
———. "Creole ou/et Français: Le multilinguisme dans *Mémoires d'Isles* d'Ina Césaire." *Glottopol* 3 (2004): 122–30.
———. "Entretien avec Ina Césaire, 13 Janvier 2006 en Martinique." *Women in French Studies* 15 (2007): 110–20.
———. "Gerty Dambury, 'Mon cheval de bataille est l'intime' (Entretien)." *Île en île*, March 2003. Accessed June 1, 2005. http://www.lehman.cuny.edu/ile.en.ile/paroles/dambury_entretien.html.
———. "The Migration of Caribbean Theater to the North American Stage." *Contemporary French and Francophone Studies* 15, no. 1 (2011): 106–17.
———. "Percussion et repercussion des voix dans le théâtre de Gerty Dambury." *L'Esprit Créateur* 48, no. 3 (2008): 76–88.
———. *Theater of the French Caribbean: Traditions and Contemporary Stages.* Trans. Tessa Thiery and Jonathan S. Skinner. Pompano Beach, FL: Caribbean Studies Press, 2014.
———. *Théâtres des Antilles: Traditions et scènes contemporaines.* Paris: L'Harmattan, 2009.
Beriss, David. *Black Skin, French Voices: Caribbean Ethnicity and Activism in Urban France.* Boulder, CO: Westview Press, 2004.
Bernabé, Jean. *Fond-natal: Grammaire basilectale approchée des créoles guadéloupéen et Martiniquais.* Paris: Harmattan, 1983.
Bernabé, Jean, Patrick Chamoiseau, and Raphael Confiant. *Eloge de la Créolité / In Praise of Creoleness.* Trans. Mohamed B. Taleb-Khyar. Paris: Gallimard, 1993.
Berrian, Brenda F. *Awakening Spaces: French Caribbean Popular Songs, Music, and Culture.* Chicago: University of Chicago Press, 2000.
Bharucha, Rustom. "Dimensions of Conflict in Globalization and Cultural Practice: A Critical Perspective." In *Conflicts and Tensions*, ed. Helmut K. Anheier and Raj Isar. Los Angeles: Sage, 2007.
———. "Peter Brook's *Mahabharata*: A View from India." In *Theatre and the World: Essays on Performance and the Politics of Culture*, ed. Rustom Bharucha. London: Routledge, 1993.
Brecht, Bertolt. *Mother Courage and Her Children.* Trans. Eric Bentley. New York: Grove Press, 1955.
Brook, Peter. "The Culture of Links." In *The Intercultural Performance Reader*, ed. Patrice Pavis. London: Routledge, 1996.
Brooks, Daphne A. *Bodies in Dissent: Spectacular Performances of Race and Freedom, 1850–1910.* Durham, NC: Duke University Press, 2006.

Browne, Katherine E. "Creole Economics and the *Débrouillard*: From Slave-Based Adaptations to the Informal Economy in Martinique." *Ethnohistory* 49, no. 2 (2002): 373–403.

———. *Creole Economics: Caribbean Cunning under the French Flag.* Austin: University of Texas Press, 2004.

Burton, Richard D. E. "Debrouya Pa Peche, or, Il y a Toujours Moyen de Moyenner: Patterns of Opposition in the Fiction of Patrick Chamoiseau." *Callaloo* 16, no. 2 (1993): 466–81.

———. "The Idea of Difference in Contemporary French West Indian Thought: Négritude, Antillanité, Créolité." In *French and West Indian: Martinique, Guadeloupe, and French Guiana Today*, ed. Richard D. E. Burton and Fred Reno. Charlottesville: University of Virginia Press, 1995.

Cabranes-Grant, Leo. "An Essay on Racial Understanding: Toward a Post-Obama State of Mind." *Theatre Survey* 55, no. 2 (2014): 249–57.

———. "From Scenario to Networks: Performing the Intercultural in Colonial Mexico." *Theatre Journal* 63, no. 4 (2011): 499–520.

Catanese, Brandi Wilkins. *The Problem of the Color[blind]: Racial Transgression and the Politics of Black Performance.* Ann Arbor: University of Michigan Press, 2011.

Césaire, Aimé. *Cahier d'un retour au pays natal.* Paris: Présence africaine, 1983.

———. *Notebook of a Return to the Native Land.* Ed. and trans. Clayton Eshleman and Annette Smith. Middletown, CT: Wesleyan University Press, 2001.

———. *The Tragedy of King Christophe.* Trans. Paul Breslin and Rachel Ney. Evanston, IL: Northwestern University Press, 2015.

Césaire, Ina. "Application de la méthode au conte." *Espace créole* 3 (1978): 21–25.

———. *Fire's Daughters.* Trans. Judith Miller. In *New French-Language Plays: Martinique, Quebec, Ivory Coast, Belgium.* New York: Ubu Repertory Theater Publications, 1993.

———. *Island Memories.* In *Plays by French and Francophone Women: A Critical Anthology*, ed. and trans. Christiane P. Makward and Judith G. Miller. Ann Arbor: University of Michigan Press, 1994.

———. *La Faim, la ruse, la révolte: Essai d'analyse anthropologique au Conte Antillais.* Fort-de-France, Martinique: Service des musées regionaux, [2005].

———. "La Triade humaine dans le conte antillais." *Présence africaine* 121–22 (1982): 142–53.

———. *L'Enfant des passages, ou La Geste de Ti-Jean.* Paris: Editions Caribéennes, 1987.

———. "L'idéologie de la débrouillardise dans le conte antillais." *Espace créole* 3 (1978): 41–48.

———. *Mémoires d'île.* In *Rosanie Soleil et autres textes dramatiques*, ed. Christiane Makward. Paris: Karthala, 2011.

———. *Mémoires d'Isles: À Manman N. et Manman F.* Paris: Editions Caribéennes, 1985.

———. "Proposition pour une analyse du conte antillais." *Espace créole* 3 (1978): 9–25.

———. *Rosanie Soleil*. In *Rosanie Soleil et autres textes dramatiques*, ed. Christiane Makward. Paris: Karthala, 2011.

———. "Ti-Zèb/Petit Zèbre (ou l'enfant terrible)." *Espace créole* 3 (1978): 12–20.

Césaire, Ina, and Joëlle Laurent, eds. *Contes de mort et de vie aux Antilles*. Paris: Nubia, 1976.

Césaire, Ina, and Joëlle Laurent. *Contes de nuits et de jours aux Antilles*. Paris: Editions Caribéennes, 1989.

Césaire, Michèle. *La Nef*. Paris: Éditions théâtrales, 1992.

———. "The Ship." Trans. Richard Miller. In *New French-Language Plays: Martinique, Quebec, Ivory Coast, Belgium*. New York: Ubu Repertory Theater Publications, 1993.

Chamoiseau, Patrick. *Creole Folktales*. Trans. Linda Coverdale. New York: New Press, 1994.

———. *Écrire en pays dominé*. Paris: Gallimard, 1997.

———. "Red Hot Peppers." Trans. Barbara Lewis. In *Rhythm and Revolt: Tales of the Antilles*, ed. Marcela Breton. New York: Penguin, 1995.

———. *Solibo Magnificent*. Trans. Rose-Myriam Réjouis and Val Vinokurov. New York: Pantheon Books, 1997.

———. "Ti-Jean en Psychanalyse." *Antilla*, July 23, 1987, 22–24.

———. "Ti-Jean Horizon." In *Creole Folktales*, trans. Linda Coverdale. New York: New Press, 1994.

Chamoiseau, Patrick, and Raphael Confiant. *Lettres créoles: Tracées antillaises et continentales de la littérature, 1635–1975*. Paris: Hatier, 1991.

Cixous, Hélène. *L'Indiade ou L'Inde de leurs rêves et quelques écrits sur le théâtre*. Paris: Théâtre du Soleil, 1987.

Clark, VèVè. "Developing Diaspora Literacy and *Marasa* Consciousness." *Theatre Survey* 50, no. 1 (2009): 9–18.

Cohen, Robin, and Paola Toninato, eds. *The Creolization Reader: Studies in Mixed Identities and Cultures*. London: Routledge, 2010.

Collins, Patricia Hill. *Black Feminist Thought: Knowledge, Consciousness, and the Politics of Empowerment*. New York: Routledge, 1991.

Condé, Maryse. *An tan revolisyon: Elle court, elle court la liberté*. Pointe-à-Pitre: Conseil Régional de la Guadeloupe, 1989.

———. Autour d'An Tan Revolisyon." *Etudes Guadeloupéennes* 1, nos. 2–3 (1990): 164–71.

———. "Chercher nos vérités." In *Penser la créolité*, ed. Maryse Condé and Madeleine Cottenet-Hage. Paris: Karthala, 1995.

———. *Comme deux frères*. Carnières-Morlanwelz, Belgium: Lansman, 2007.

———. "*Créolité* without Creole language?" In *Caribbean Creolization: Reflections on the Cultural Dynamics of Language, Literature, and Identity*, ed.

Kathleen M. Balutansky and Marie-Agnès Sourieau. Gainesville: University Press of Florida, 1998.

———. *Desirada*. Trans. Richard Philcox. New York: Soho, 2000.

———. *Heremakhonon*. Trans. Richard Philcox. Washington, DC: Three Continents Press, 1982.

———. *In the Time of Revolution*. Trans. Doris Y. Kadish and Jean-Pierre Piriou. *Callaloo* 25, no. 2 (2002): 454–93.

———. *I, Tituba, Black Witch of Salem*. Trans. Richard Philcox. Charlottesville: University of Virginia Press, 1992.

———. *The Journey of a Caribbean Writer*. Trans. Richard Philcox. London: Seagull Books, 2014.

———. *La Parole des femmes*. Paris: l'Harmattan, 1993.

———. *La vie sans fards*. Paris: J. C. Lattès, 2012.

———. "Liason dangereuse." In *Pour une littérature-monde*, ed. Michel Le Bris and Jean Rouaud. Paris: Gallimard, 2007.

———. "Order, Disorder, Freedom, and the West Indian Writer." *Yale French Studies* 83, no. 2 (1993): 121–35.

———. *Pension les Alizés*. Paris: Mercure de France, 1988.

———. "Sketching a Literature." In *The Journey of a Caribbean Writer*. Trans. Richard Philcox. London: Seagull Books, 2014.

———. *The Tropical Breeze Hotel*. Trans. Barbara Brewster Lewis and Catherine Temerson. In *Plays by Women, Book Two: An International Anthology*. New York: Ubu Repertory Theater Publications, 1994.

Conquergood, Dwight. "Performance Studies: Interventions and Radical Research." In *Cultural Struggles: Performance, Ethnography, Praxis*, ed. E. Patrick Johnson. Ann Arbor: University of Michigan Press, 2013.

Conteh-Morgan, John, with Dominic Thomas. *New Francophone African and Caribbean Theaters*. Bloomington: Indiana University Press, 2010.

Cottias, Myriam. "Free but Minor: Slave Women, Citizenship, Respectability, and Social Antagonism in the French Antilles, 1830–90." In *Women and Slavery: The Modern Atlantic*. Vol. 2, ed. Gwyn Campbell, Suzanne Miers, and Joseph Calder Miller. Athens: Ohio University Press, 2008.

———. "La séduction coloniale: Damnation et stratégies. Les Antilles, XVIIème–XIXème siècles." In *Séductions et sociétés, approches historiques*, ed. Cécile Dauphin and Arlette Farge. Paris: Seuil, 2000.

Crais, Clifton C., and Pamela Scully. *Sara Baartman and the Hottentot Venus: A Ghost Story and a Biography*. Princeton, NJ: Princeton University Press, 2009.

Cusset, Jean-Michel. *1802 ou Le dernier jour*. Paris: Ibis, 2002.

Cypess, Sandra Messinger. *La Malinche in Mexican Literature from History to Myth*. Austin: University of Texas Press, 1991.

Cyrille, Dominique. "Ca Ki Ta Nou (This Belongs to Us): Creole Dances of the French Caribbean." In *Caribbean Dance from Abakuá to Zouk: How*

Movement Shapes Identity, ed. Susanna Sloat. Gainesville: University Press of Florida.
Dambury, Gerty. *Lettres indiennes / Crosscurrents*. Trans. Richard Philcox. Paris: Les Éditions du Manguier, 2014.
Daniel, Yvonne. *Dancing Wisdom: Embodied Knowledge in Haitian Vodou, Cuban Yoruba, and Bahian Candomblé*. Chicago: University of Illinois Press, 2005.
Dayan, Joan. "Vodoun, or the Voice of the Gods." In *Sacred Possessions: Vodou, Santería, Obeah, and the Caribbean*, ed. Margarite Fernández Olmos and Lizabeth Paravisini-Gebert. New Brunswick, NJ: Rutgers University Press, 1997.
De Souza, Pascale. "Demystifying Female Marooning: Oppositional Strategies and the Writing of Testimonios in the French Caribbean." *International Journal of Francophone Studies* 3, no. 3 (2000): 141–50.
———. "Discours carnavalesque chez Ina Césaire: Déferler les *Mémoires d'Iles*." *Œuvres et Critiques* 26, no. 1 (2001): 122–33.
Desrivières, Jean-Durosier. "Entretien avec Syto Cavé: Quand le théâtre créole émane du vaudou." *Potomitan*, April 5, 2012. Accessed June 4, 2014. http://www.potomitan.info/ayiti/desrivieres/cave.php.
Diamond, Elin. *Unmaking Mimesis: Essays on Feminism and Theater*. London: Routledge, 1997.
Dracius, Suzanne. *Lumina Sophie dite Surprise*. Fort-de-France, Martinique: Desnel, 2005.
Drewal, Margaret Thompson. *Yoruba Ritual: Performers, Play, Agency*. Bloomington: Indiana University Press, 1992.
Edwards, Brent Hayes. *The Practice of Diaspora: Literature, Translation, and the Rise of Black Internationalism*. Cambridge, MA: Harvard University Press, 2003.
Edwards, Carole. *Les Dramaturges antillaises: Cruauté, créolité, conscience féminine*. Paris: L'Harmattan, 2008.
Enwezor, Okwui, Carlos Basualdo, Ute Meta Bauer, Susanne Ghez, Sarat Maharaj, Mark Nash, and Octavio Zaya, eds. *Créolité and Creolization*. Documenta 11_Platorm3. Kassel, Germany: Hatje Cantz, 2003.
Erskine, Noel Leo. *Plantation Church: How African American Religion Was Born in Caribbean Slavery*. Oxford: Oxford University Press, 2014.
Fanon, Frantz. *Black Skin, White Masks*. Trans. Richard Philcox. New York: Grove Press, 2008.
Farfan, Penny, and Ric Knowles, eds. "Rethinking Intercultural Performance." Special issue of *Theatre Journal* 63, no. 4 (2011).
Fischer-Lichte, Erika, Torsten Jost, and Saskya Iris Jain, eds. *The Politics of Interweaving Performance Cultures: Beyond Postcolonialism*. New York: Routledge, 2014.
Fouchard, Jean. *Les marrons de la liberté*. Paris: Editions de l'école, 1972.

Fulton, Dawn. *Signs of Dissent: Maryse Condé and Postcolonial Criticism.* Charlottesville: University of Virginia Press, 2008.
Gaensbauer, Deborah B. "Protean Truths: History as Performance in Maryse Condé's *An Tan Revolisyon.*" *French Review* 76, no. 6 (2003): 1139–50.
Garraway, Doris. *The Libertine Colony: Creolization in the Early French Caribbean.* Durham, NC: Duke University Press, 2005.
Garrigus, John D. *Before Haiti: Race and Citizenship in French Saint-Domingue.* New York: Palgrave Macmillan, 2006.
Gautier, Arlette. *Les Sœurs de Solitude: Femmes et l'esclavage aux Antilles du XVIIe au XIXe siècle.* Rennes: Presses Universitaires de Rennes, 2010.
Gauvin, Lise. "La Belle au bois dormant." Interview with Simone Schwarz-Bart. In *L'écrivain francophone à la croisée des langues: Entretiens.* Paris: Karthala, 1997.
Gerstin, Julian. "Tangled Roots: Kalenda and Other Neo-African Dances in Circum-Caribbean." In *Making Caribbean Dance: Continuity and Creativity in Island Cultures,* ed. Susanna Sloat. Gainesville: University Press of Florida, 2010.
Gilbert, Helen, and Joanne Tompkins. *Post-Colonial Drama: Theory, Practice, Politics.* London: Routledge, 1996.
Giles, Freda Scott. "Traduire et mettre en scène *An tan revolisyon* en Amérique." In *Les théâtres francophones et créolophones de la Caraïbe,* ed. Alvina Ruprecht. Paris: L'Harmattan, 2003.
Gilroy, Paul. *The Black Atlantic: Modernity and Double Consciousness.* Cambridge, MA: Harvard University Press, 1993.
Giraud, Michel. "Une construction coloniale de la sexualité." *Actes de la recherche en sciences sociales* 128 (1999): 45–55.
Glissant, Édouard. *Caribbean Discourse.* Trans. J. Michael Dash. Charlottesville: University of Virginia Press, 1989.
———. *Faulkner, Mississippi.* Trans. Barbara Lewis and Thomas Spear. Chicago: University of Chicago Press, 2000.
———. *Le discours antillais.* Paris: Gallimard, 1981.
———. *Mémoires des esclavages: La fondation d'un centre national pour la mémoire des esclavages et de leurs abolitions.* Paris: Gallimard, 2007.
———. *Monsieur Toussaint: A Play.* Trans. J. Michael Dash. Washington, DC: Three Continents Press, 2005.
———. *The Poetics of Relation.* Trans. Betsy Wing. Ann Arbor: University of Michigan Press, 1997.
———. "Theater, Consciousness of the People." In *Caribbean Discourse.* Trans. J. Michael Dash. Charlottesville: University of Virginia Press, 1989.
———. *Traité du Tout-Monde.* Paris: Gallimard, 1997.
———. "The Unforeseeable Diversity of the World." Trans. Haun Saussy. In *Beyond Dichotomies: Histories, Identities, Cultures, and the Challenge of Globalization,* ed. Elizabeth Mudimbe-Boyi. Albany: State University of New York, 2002.

Gyssels, Kathleen. "'I Talked to Zombie': Displacement and Distance in Simone Schwarz-Bart's *Ton beau capitaine*." In *Ici-Là: Place and Displacement in Caribbean Writing in French*, ed. Mary Gallagher. Amsterdam: Rodopi, 2003.

Hall, Stuart. "Créolité and the Process of Creolization." In *Créolité and Creolization*, ed. Okwui Enwezor, Carlos Basualdo, Ute Meta Bauer, Susanne Ghez, Sarat Maharaj, Mark Nash, and Octavio Zaya. Documenta 11_Platorm3. Kassel, Germany: Hatje Cantz, 2003.

———. "Creolization, Diaspora, and Hybridity in the Context of Globalization." In *Créolité and Creolization*, ed. Okwui Enwezor, Carlos Basualdo, Ute Meta Bauer, Susanne Ghez, Sarat Maharaj, Mark Nash, and Octavio Zaya. Documenta 11_Platorm3. Kassel, Germany: Hatje Cantz, 2003.

———. "Cultural Identity and Diaspora." In *Identity: Community, Culture, Difference*, ed. Jonathan Rutherford. London: Lawrence and Wishart, 1990.

Harrison, Paul Carter. "Mother Word: Black Theatre in the African Continuum. Word/Song as Method." In *Totem Voices: Plays from the Black World Repertory*, ed. Paul Carter Harrison. New York: Grove Press, 1989.

Hartman, Saidiya V. *Scenes of Subjection: Terror, Slavery, and Self-Making in Nineteenth-Century America*. New York: Oxford University Press, 1997.

Hewitt, Leah D. "Condé's Critical Seesaw." *Callaloo* 18, no. 3 (1995): 641–51.

Hill, Errol. "Perspectives in Caribbean Theatre: Ritual, Festival, and Drama." Sir Philip Sherlock Lectures. Special issue of *Caribbean Quarterly* 46, nos. 3–4 (2000): 1–11.

Hill, Errol G., and James V. Hatch. *A History of African American Theatre*. Cambridge, UK: Cambridge University Press, 2003.

Hine, Darlene Clark. "Rape and the Inner Lives of Black Women in the Middle West: Preliminary Thoughts on the Culture of Dissemblance." In *Unequal Sisters: A Multicultural Reader in U.S. Women's History*, ed. Vicki L. Ruiz and Ellen Carol DuBois. New York: Routledge, 1990.

Holland, Peter, and Hanna Scolnicov, eds. *The Play out of Context*. Cambridge, UK: Cambridge University Press, 1989.

Houyoux, Suzanne. "Entretien avec Gerty Dambury, Point-à-Pitre, Juin 1991." In *Elles écrivent des Antilles*, ed. Suzanne Rinne and Joëlle Vitiello. Paris: L'Harmattan, 1997.

———. "Un Entretien avec Ina Césaire, Fort-de-France, Martinique, 5 juin 1990." In *Elles écrivent des Antilles*, ed. Suzanne Rinne and Joëlle Vitiello. Paris: L'Harmattan, 1997.

Igboin, Benson Ohihon. "Esu and the Problem of Evil." In *Esu: Yoruba God, Power, and the Imaginative Frontiers*, ed. Toyin Falola. Durham, NC: Carolina Academic Press, 2013.

Jacobs, Harriet. *Incidents in the Life of a Slave Girl*. New York: Penguin, 2013.

Janken, Kenneth Robert. *Walter White: Mr. NAACP*. Chapel Hill: University of North Carolina Press, 2006.

Johnson, E. Patrick. *Appropriating Blackness*. Durham, NC: Duke University Press, 2003.
Jones, Bridget. "Theatre and Resistance? An Introduction to Some French Caribbean Plays." In *An Introduction to Caribbean Francophone Writing: Guadeloupe and Martinique*, ed. Sam Haigh. Oxford: Berg, 1999.
———. "Theatre in the French West Indies." *Carib* 4 (1986): 35–54.
———. "Two Plays by Ina Césaire: Mémoires d'Isles and L'enfant des Passages." *Theatre Research International* 15, no. 3 (1990): 223–33.
Jules-Rosette, Bennetta. *Josephine Baker in Art and Life: The Icon and the Image*. Urbana: University of Illinois Press, 2007.
Kadish, Doris Y., and Françoise Massardier-Kenney, "Traduire Maryse Condé: Entretien avec Richard Philcox." *French Review* 69, no. 5 (1996): 749–61.
Kanhai-Brunton, Rosanne. "How Handsome Can the Captain Be? Translation (of Simone Schwarz-Bart's *Ton beau capitaine*) within the Postcolonial Context." *Translation Review* 46 (1994): 46–51.
Kendall, Michelle. "Schwarz-Bart's 'Ton Beau Capitaine': Understanding Haitian Migrant Workers in the Caribbean." *Journal of Haitian Studies* 17, no. 2 (2011): 156–66.
Kim, Suk-Young. "Finding History from the Living Archives: Inscribing Interviews and Interventions." In *Theater Historiography: Critical Interventions*, ed. Henry Bial and Scott Magelssen. Ann Arbor: University of Michigan Press, 2010.
Knepper, Wendy. "Colonization, Creolization, and Globalization: The Art and Ruses of *Bricolage*." *Small Axe* 21 (October 2006): 70–86.
———. *Patrick Chamoiseau: A Critical Introduction*. Jackson: University Press of Mississippi, 2012.
Knowles, Ric. *Theatre and Interculturalism*. New York: Palgrave Macmillan, 2010.
Kourilsky, Françoise, ed. *Ubu Repertory Theater, 1982–1992*. New York: Ubu Repertory Theater Publications, 1992.
Krakovitch, Odile. "Le rôle des femmes dans l'insurrection du Sud de la Martinique en Septembre 1870." *Nouvelles Questions Féministes* 9–10 (1985): 35–51.
Kraut, Anthea. "Between Primitivism and Diaspora: The Dance Performances of Josephine Baker, Zora Neale Hurston, and Katherine Dunham." *Theatre Journal* 55, no. 3 (2003): 433–50.
Lahs-Gonzales, Olivia, ed. *Josephine Baker: Image and Icon*. St. Louis, MO: Reedy Press, 2006.
Lewis, Barbara Brewster. "No Silence: An Interview with Maryse Condé." *Callaloo* 18, no. 3 (1995): 543–50.
Lionnet, Françoise, and Shu-mei Shih, eds. *The Creolization of Theory*. Durham, NC: Duke University Press, 2011.
Loichot, Valérie. "Negations and Subversions of Paternal Authorities in

Glissant's Fictional Works." In *Naming the Father: Legacies, Genealogies, and Explorations of Fatherhood in Modern and Contemporary Literature*, ed. Eva Paulino Bueno, Terry Caesar, and William Hummel. Lanham, MD: Lexington Books, 2000.

Lowe, John. "'Calypso Magnolia': The Caribbean Side of the South." *South Central Review* 22, no. 1 (2005): 54–80.

Lowe, Lisa. "The Intimacies of Four Continents." In *Haunted by Empire: Geographies of Intimacy in North American History*, ed. Ann Laura Stoler. Durham, NC: Duke University Press, 2006.

Makward, Christiane P. "De bouche à oreille à bouche: Ethno-dramaturgie d'Ina Césaire." In *L'Héritage de Caliban*, ed. Maryse Condé. Pointe-à-Pitre, Guadeloupe: Éditions Jasor, 1992.

———. "Enraciné profond: Le théâtre d'Ina Cesaire." *Africultures*, March 17, 2010. Accessed June 30, 2014. http://www.africultures.com/php/index.php?nav=article&no=9347.

———. "Filles du soleil noir: Sur deux pièces d'Ina Césaire et de Michèle Césaire." In *Elles écrivent des Antilles: Haiti, Guadeloupe, Martinique*, ed. Suzanne Rinne and Joëlle Vitiello. Paris: L'Harmattan, 1997.

———. "Haiti on Stage: Franco-Caribbean Women Remind (On Three Plays by Ina Césaire, Maryse Condé, and Simone Schwarz-Bart)." *Contemporary French and Francophone Studies* 4, no. 1 (2000): 129–37.

———. "Introduction. Ensouché fond. Le petit théâtre d'Ina Césaire." In *Rosanie Soleil et autres textes dramatiques*, ed. Christiane Makward. Paris: Karthala, 2011.

———. "Pressentir l'autre: Gerty Dambury, dramaturge poétique guadeloupéenne." *L'Annuaire Théâtral* 28 (2000): 73–87.

———. "Reading Maryse Condé's Theatre." *Callaloo* 18, no. 3 (1995): 681–89.

———. "Staging Her People's Voice: Ina Césaire." Special issue of *Women in French Studies* 5 (2014): 173–82.

Makward, Christiane, and Adam John. "Faire son théâtre en Martinique: Ina Césaire et Michèle Césaire." *Oeuvres et Critiques* 26, no. 1 (2001): 110–21.

Makward, Christiane, and Judith G. Miller, eds. *Plays by French and Francophone Women: A Critical Anthology*. Ann Arbor: University of Michigan Press, 1994.

Manning, Susan. *Modern Dance, Negro Dance: Race in Motion*. Minneapolis: University of Minnesota Press, 2004

Mardorossian, Carine M. *Reclaiming Difference: Caribbean Women Rewrite Postcolonialism*. Charlottesville: University of Virginia Press, 2005.

Mathéus, Mariann. "De l'oralité au théâtre: L'exemple de Berthilia pour le personnage d'Hermance dans *Mémoires d'Isles* d'Ina Césaire." *Africultures*, September 11, 2014. Accessed November 30, 2014. http://www.africultures.com/php/index.php?nav=article&no=12419.

McAllister, Marvin Edward. *Whiting Up: Whiteface Minstrels and Stage*

Europeans in African American Performance. Chapel Hill: University of North Carolina Press, 2011.
McKay, Melissa. *Maryse Condé et le théâtre antillais*. New York, Peter Lang, 2002.
McMahon, Christina S. *Recasting Transnationalism through Performance: Theatre Festivals in Cape Verde, Mozambique, and Brazil*. New York: Palgrave, 2014.
Médea, Laurent. "Creolization and Globalization in Réunion." In *The Creolization Reader: Studies in Mixed Identities and Cultures*, ed. Robin Cohen and Paola Toninato. London: Routledge, 2010.
Michel, Claudine. "Of Worlds Unseen: The Educational Character of Haitian Vodou." In *Haitian Vodou: Spirit, Myth, and Reality*, ed. Patrick Bellegarde-Smith and Claudine Michel. Bloomington: Indiana University Press, 2006.
Miller, Christopher L. *The French Atlantic Triangle: Literature and Culture of the Slave Trade*. Durham, NC: Duke University Press, 2008.
Miller, Judith. *Ariane Mnouchkine*. London: Routledge, 2007.
———. "Caribbean Women Playwrights: Madness, Memory, but Not Melancholia." *Theatre Research International* 23, no. 3 (1998): 225–32.
———. "Ina Césaire: Telling Theatricalized Tales." In *Beyond Survival: African Literature and the Search for New Life*, ed. Kofi Anyidoho, Abena P. A. Busia, and Anne V. Adams. Trenton, NJ: Africa World Press, 1999.
———. "Simone Schwarz-Bart: Re-figuring Heroics, Dis-figuring Conventions." In *Theatre and Feminist Aesthetics*, ed. Karen Louise Laughlin and Catherine Schuler. Madison, NJ: Farleigh Dickinson University Press, 1995.
———. "Some Thoughts on Producing African Theatre in French with American Students." *Women's Studies Quarterly* 25, nos. 3–4 (1997): 150–58.
Miyasaki, June. "Writing the Landscape of Memory: Ina Césaire's *Mémoires d'Isles*." *Journal of Caribbean Literatures* 6, no. 1 (2009): 31–46.
Montantin, Michèle. "*Ton beau capitaine / An tan revolisyon*, à bâtons rompus." In *Les théâtres francophones et créolophones de la Caraïbe: Haïti, Guadeloupe, Guyane, Martinique, Sainte-Lucie*, ed. Alvina Ruprecht. Paris: L'Harmattan, 2003.
Munro, Martin, and Cecilia Britton, eds. *American Creoles: The Francophone Caribbean and the American South*. Liverpool, UK: Liverpool University Press, 2012.
Murray, David A. B. "Homosexuality, Society, and the State: An Ethnography of Sublime Resistance in Martinique." In *Perspectives on the Caribbean*, ed. Philip W. Scher. West Sussex, UK: Wiley-Blackwell, 2010.
Naudillon, Françoise. "Le théâtre populaire de José Jernidier." *Africultures*, March 17, 2010. Accessed July 30, 2014. http://www.africultures.com/php/?nav=article&no=9340.
Nesbitt, Frank Thompson, III. "Revolution in Discourse: Writing History in French Antillean Literature." PhD dissertation, Harvard University, 1997.

Nesbitt, Nick. *Caribbean Critique: Antillean Critical Theory from Toussaint to Glissant*. Liverpool, UK: Liverpool University Press, 2013.

———. *Voicing Memory: History and Subjectivity in French Caribbean Literature*. Charlottesville: University of Virginia Press, 2003.

Nicolas, Armand. "L'insurrection du Sud à la Martinique (Septembre 1870)." *Action: Revue théorique et politique du Parti Communiste Martiniquais*, no. 19 suppl. (December 1970).

Octavia, Gael. *Congre et Homard*. Carnières-Morlanweltz, Belgium: Lansman, 2012.

Ogunyemi, Chikwenye Okonjo. "An Abiku-Ogbanje Atlas: A Pre-Text for Rereading Soyinka's 'Aké' and Morrison's 'Beloved.'" *African American Review* 36, no. 4 (2002): 663–78.

———. *Africa Wo/Man Palava: The Nigerian Novel by Women*. Chicago: University of Chicago Press, 1996.

Okawa, Rachelle. "Translating Maryse Condé's *Célanire cou-coupé*: Dislocations of the Caribbean Self in Richard Philcox's *Who Slashed Celanire's Throat? A Fantastical Tale*." *French Literature Series* 36 (2009): 161–78.

Olmos, Margarite Fernández, and Lizabeth Paravisini-Gebert. *Creole Religions of the Caribbean: An Introduction from Vodou and Santeria to Obeah and Espiritismo*. New York: New York University Press, 2003.

Ortiz, Fernando. "The Human Factors of Cubanidad." Trans. João Felipe Gonçalves and Gregory Duff Morton. *Journal of Ethnographic Theory* 4, no. 3 (2014). Accessed June 15, 2016. http://www.haujournal.org/index.php/hau/article/view/hau4.3.031/1723.

Pago, Gilbert. *Lumina Sophie dite "Surprise," 1848–1879 Insurgée et gagnarde*. Matoury, French Guiana: Ibis, 2008.

Palmié, Stephan. "Creolization and Its Discontents." In *The Creolization Reader: Studies in Mixed Identities and Cultures*, ed. Robin Cohen and Paola Toninato. London: Routledge, 2010.

Patrice Pavis, "Introduction: Towards a Theory of Interculturalism in Theatre?" In *The Intercultural Performance Reader*, ed. Patrice Pavis. London: Routledge, 1996.

Peabody, Sue. "'A Dangerous Zeal': Catholic Missions to Slaves in the French Antilles, 1635–1800." *French Historical Studies* 25, no. 1 (2002): 53–90.

———. "'A Nation Born to Slavery': Missionaries and Racial Discourse in Seventeenth-Century French Antilles." *Journal of Social History* 38, no. 1 (2004): 113–26.

Pfaff, Françoise. *Conversations with Maryse Condé*. Lincoln: University of Nebraska Press, 1996.

Philcox, Richard. "Fidelity, Infidelity, and the Adulterous Translator." *Australian Journal of French Studies* 47, no. 1 (2010): 29–35.

———. "Translating Maryse Condé: A Personal Itinerary." *Sites* 5, no. 3 (2001): 277–82.

Philip, Marlene NourbeSe. "Dis Place—The Space Between." In *A Genealogy of Resistance: And Other Essays*. Toronto: Mercury Press, 1997.

Pinalie, Pierre. *Dictionnaire de Proverbes Créoles*. Fort-de-France, Martinique: Editions Désormeaux, 1994.

Placoly, Vincent. *Dessalines ou la passion de l'Indépendance*. Havana, Cuba: Ediciones Casa de las Americas, 1983.

Ramakrishnan, Mahadevi, and R. Scott Smith. *Interplay of Cultural Narratives in Martinique: French, African and Indian Journey toward a Pluralistic Society*. Coconut Creek, FL: Caribbean Studies Press, 2015.

Reinhardt, Catherine A. *Claims to Memory: Beyond Slavery and Emancipation in the French Caribbean*. Oxford: Berghahn Books, 2006.

Richards, Sandra L. "African Diaspora Drama." In *The Cambridge Companion to African American Theatre*, ed. Harvey Young. Cambridge, UK: Cambridge University Press, 2013.

———. "The Challenges of Cultural Translation: Directing *Farewell to a Cannibal Rage* for an American Audience." In *Ancient Songs Set Ablaze: The Theatre of Femi Osofisan*. Washington, DC: Howard University Press, 1996.

———. "In the Kitchen, Cooking Up Diaspora Possibilities: Bailey and Lewis's *Sistahs*." *Theatre Research International* 35, no. 2 (2010): 152–63.

———. "Under the 'Trickster's' Sign: Toward a Reading of Ntozake Shange and Femi Osofisan." In *Critical Theory and Performance*, ed. Janelle G. Reinelt and Joseph R. Roach. Ann Arbor: University of Michigan Press, 1992.

———. "Who Is This Ancestor? Performing Memory in Ghana's Slave Castle-Dungeons." In *The Sage Handbook of Performance Studies*, ed. D. Soyini Madison and Judith Hamera. Los Angeles: Sage, 2006.

———. "Writing the Absent Potential: Drama, Performance and the Canon of African-American Literature." In *The Routledge Reader in Gender and Performance*, ed. Lizbeth Goodman with Jane de Gay. London: Routledge, 1998.

Roach, Joseph. *Cities of the Dead: Circum-Atlantic Performance*. New York: Columbia University Press, 1996.

Ruprecht, Alvina. "Françoise Kourilsky." *Franco-Théâtres*, February 1, 1999. Accessed December 20, 2014. http://www3.carleton.ca/francotheatres/entretiens_F_Kourilsky.html.

———. "Les pratiques scéniques et textuelles de la région caribéenne francophone et créolophone: Mise au point." In *Les théâtres francophones et créolophones de la Caraïbe*, ed. Alvina Ruprecht. Paris: L'Harmattan, 2003.

———. "Le théâtre de Maryse Condé: Entretien de Maryse Condé avec le Professeur Alvina Ruprecht." *L'Arbre à Palabres* 18 (2006): 147–58. Reprinted from *International Journal of Francophone Studies* 2, no. 1 (1999): 51–61.

———. "Performance transculturelle: Une poétique de l'interthéâtralité chez Simone Schwarz-Bart." In *Poétiques et Imaginaires: Francopolyphonie litteraire des Amériques*, ed. P. Laurette and H. G. Ruprecht. Paris: L'Harmattan, 1995.

Sahakian, Emily. "Le théâtre de Maryse Condé: Une dramaturgie de la provocation du spectateur." In *Amour, sexe, genre et trauma dans la Caraïbe francophone*, ed. Gladys M. Francis. Paris: L'Harmattan, 2016.

Sahakian, Emily, and Christiane Makward. "Théâtraographie de Maryse Condé." In *Amour, sexe, genre et trauma dans la Caraïbe francophone*, ed. Gladys M. Francis. Paris: L'Harmattan, 2016.

Scharfman, Ronnie. "Exiled from the Shoah: André and Simone Schwarz-Bart's *Un plat de porc aux bananes vertes*." In *Auschwitz and After: Race, Culture, and "the Jewish Question" in France*, ed. Lawrence D. Kritzman. New York: Routledge, 1995.

Schnepel, Ellen M. "The Other Tongue, the Other Voice: Language and Gender in the French Caribbean." In *Language and Social Identity*, ed. Richard K. Blot. Westport, CT: Praeger, 2003.

Schor, Naomi. "The Crisis of French Universalism." *Yale French Studies* 100 (2001): 43–64.

Shaked, Gershon. "The Play: Gateway to Cultural Dialogue." In *The Play out of Context*, ed. Peter Holland and Hanna Scolnicov. Cambridge, UK: Cambridge University Press, 1989.

Shange, Ntozake. *For Colored Girls Who Have Considered Suicide When the Rainbow Is Enuf*. New York: Scribner Poetry, 1975.

———. "Porque Tu No M'entrende? Whatcha Mean You Can't Understand Me?" In *Black Theatre: Ritual Performance in the African Diaspora*, ed. Paul Carter Harrison, Victor Leo Walker II, and Gus Edwards. Philadelphia: Temple University Press, 2002.

Singaravélou, Pierre. "Indians in the French Overseas Departments: Guadeloupe, Martinique, Réunion." In *South Asians Overseas: Migration and Ethnicity*, ed. Colin Clarke, Ceri Peach, and Steven Vertovec. Cambridge, UK: Cambridge University Press, 1990.

Schwarz-Bart, Simone. *Ti-Jean l'horizon: Roman*. Paris: Seuil, 1979.

———. *Ton beau capitaine*. Paris: Seuil, 1987.

———. *Your Handsome Captain*. Trans. Jessica Harris and Catherine Temerson. In *Plays by Women: An International Anthology*. New York: Ubu Repertory Theater Publications, 1988.

Shields, Tanya L. *Bodies and Bones: Feminist Rehearsal and Imagining Caribbean Belonging*. Charlottesville: University of Virginia Press, 2014.

Spivak, Gayatri Chakravorty. "The Politics of Translation." In *The Translation Studies Reader*, ed. Lawrence Venuti. New York: Routledge, 2004.

Swami, Sita. "Les Cultes indiens en Martinique et en Guadeloupe." *French Review* 76, no. 6 (2003): 1174–83.

Tarica, Estelle. "Patrick Chamoiseau's Creole *Conteur* and the Ethics of Survival." *International Journal of Francophone Studies* 13, no. 1 (2010): 39–56.

Taylor, Diana. *The Archive and the Repertoire: Performing Cultural Memory in the Americas*. Durham, NC: Duke University Press, 2003.
Thomas, Bonnie. *Breadfruit or Chestnut? Gender Construction in the French Caribbean Novel*. Lanham, MD: Lexington Books, 2006.
———. "Edouard Glissant and the Art of Memory." *Small Axe* 30 (2009): 25–36.
Tinker, Hugh. *A New System of Slavery: The Export of Indian Labour Overseas, 1830–1920*. London: Oxford University Press, 1974.
Vergès, Françoise. "Kiltir Kreol: Processes and Practices of Créolité and Creolization." In *Créolité and Creolization*, ed. Okwui Enwezor, Carlos Basualdo, Ute Meta Bauer, Susanne Ghez, Sarat Maharaj, Mark Nash, and Octavio Zaya. Documenta 11_Platorm3. Kassel, Germany: Hatje Cantz, 2003.
Voldeng, Évelyne. *Les Mémoires de Ti-Jean: Espace Intercontinental du héros des contes Francoontariens*. Vanier, Canada: Les Éditions L'Interligne, 1994.
Walcott, Derek. "The Antilles: Fragments of Epic Memory." Nobel Lecture, December 7, 1992. Accessed May 11, 2016. http://www.nobelprize.org/nobel_prizes/literature/laureates/1992/walcott-lecture.html.
———. *Ti-Jean and His Brothers*. In *Dream on Monkey Mountain and Other Plays*. New York: Farrar, Straus and Giroux, 1970.
Weagel, Deborah. "The Creole Quadrille in Simone Schwarz-Bart's *Ton beau capitaine*: A Postcolonial Perspective." *Journal of Comparative Literature and Aesthetics* 32, nos. 1–2 (2009): 13–23.
Young, Harvey. "Black Performance Studies in the New Millennium." *Theatre Journal* 65, no. 2 (2013): 289–94.
———. *Embodying Black Experience: Stillness, Critical Memory, and the Black Body*. Ann Arbor: University of Michigan Press, 2010.
Zarrilli, Phillip B. "For Whom Is the King a King? Issues of Intercultural Production, Perception, and Reception in a *Kathakali King Lear*." In *Critical Theory and Performance*, ed. Janelle G. Reinelt and Joseph R. Roach. Ann Arbor: University of Michigan Press, 1992.

Index

Note: Page numbers in *italics* indicate a photograph.

Abatucci, Serge, 94, *95*
abiku child concept, 64–65, 110–11
Aching, Gerard, 78
Act French New York, 9
Adell, Sandra, 125
African-derived rituals, practices, and concepts in Caribbean: *abiku*/ogbanje child, 64–65, 110–11; dance, 12–13, 100, 104–5, 154–55, 233n19; diaspora experience and, 136–37, 149–51, 154–56, 179; displacement and, 110–11, 179–80; epistemology, 112; folktales, 100, 102, 105–18, 124, 211; Négritude movement and, 88; Quimbois, 108, 117, 175; transformation and, 12, 100–101, 104–5; Yoruba, 12, 64, 104, 110–11, 113, 207
ajiaco stew, creolization compared with, 13–14
Alliance française (New York), 176–77
Alpha, Jenny, 219n3
Anglophone Caribbean theater, diaspora performances of, 9–10
An tan revolisyon (Condé), 55–67, *57*, *60*; anachronisms in, 61–62; collective memory in, 52, 98; French and Creole languages in, 56; historical treatment in, 55–56, 58–62; larger message, 56–57, 66–67; production history, 4, 205–17; reception of, 66; storytelling in, 52, 56, 58, 62, 66, 96; theatrical approach, 56, 57–58, 67; unborn revolution image in, 63–67; universalist ideals questioned in, 58, 60–61, 67. *See also In the Time of Revolution*

Antillanité, 52
Appadurai, Arjun, 137
Arnold, A. James, 7, 27, 87
asé concept, 12–13, 14
Association of the Friends of India (Guadeloupe), 87, 88
Avignon Theatre Festival, 4, 83, 94, 96, 159, 165

Baartman, Saartjie, 43, 44
Bada, Valérie, 35–36
Baker, Josephine, 43–44, 194, *195*
Balme, Christopher, 4–5, 54, 77, 102
Baraka, Amiri, 146
Barba, Eugenio, 53
Baron Samedi, 62, 78, 81, 144
Barrault, Jean-Louis, 123
Barriteau, Violet Eudine, 216
Barthelemy, Mimi, 96
Bechet, Troi, 219n3
Belgrave, Cynthia, 184, 238n1
Benítez-Rojo, Antonio, 8, 202
Bérard, Stéphanie: on Césaire's *L'Enfant des passages*, 107, 109, 110; on Césaire's *Mémoire d'Isles*, 79; on Dambury's *Lettres indiennes*, 86–87, 88, 89, 96; on French Caribbean theater, 5, 9, 18; on Schwarz-Bart's *Ton beau capitaine*, 119, 120, 121; on Ubu production of Césaire's *Fire's Daughters*, 153
Beriss, David, 103–4, 241n70
Bernabé, Jean, 52, 187
Berryhill, Frederick D., 177
Bharucha, Rustom, 54, 137

266 Index

Biard, François-Auguste: *L'abolition de l'esclavage dans les colonies français en 1848*, 211
bigidi, concept of, 100–101, 102, 103, 120–21, 122, 128, 130, 131, 232n2
Bissainthe, Toto, 38, 154, 211
black identity: Césaire on, 2; gender relations and, 186–87; overdetermination of, 42; phenomenal blackness concept, 26; politics of, 135, 143, 146, 147, 149–51, 156–61, 172, 178, 183–84, 193–97; in the U.S., 10
Bleier, Ellen, 210–11, 215
Bois Caiman ceremony (1791), 31, 38
Bonaparte, Napoleon, 59, 61
Borsay, La Tonya, 161, 163, *164, 165*
Bouchard, Michel Marc: *The Orphan Muses*, 149
Boukman, Daniel: *Les Négriers*, 228n87
Boulangé, Yna, 130, 219n3
Brechtian theater: alienation effect, 39–40, 46, 47, 50, 56, 62, 109, 110–11, 191, 225n91; conventions of, 103, 106, 110–11, 215; *gestus*, 46, 49, 111
Brewster, Townsend, 181
bricolage, concept of, 13, 14, 17, 202
Britton, Cecilia, 206
Brodwin, Paul, 237n114
Brook, Peter, 53, 77, 88, 89, 151; *The Ik*, 75; *Mahabharata* production, 54
Brooks, Marie, 139, 143, 155
Bruckner, D. J. R., 155, 164, 167, 197
Burton, Richard, 52

Cabranes-Grant, Leo, 102
Calodat, Philippe, 94, *95*, 96
candomblé rituals, 12–13
Capécia, Mayotte, 34
Caribbean performance practices: in Cavé's production of Schwarz-Bart's *Ton beau capitaine*, 129–31; Césaire influenced by, 30, 31, 39, 71, 115–16, 153; creolization and, 3, 9, 11–12, 15; subversive messages in, 104–5; as syncretic, 100–105, 118, 134, 177–78, 200–201; in Timar's production of Dambury's *Lettres indiennes*, 94, *95*–96. *See also* storytelling; vodou
Catanese, Brandi Wilkins, 213
Cathey, Reg E., 178, *179*

Cavé, Syto, 18, 38, 119, 128, 129–31, 172, 181
Centre des Arts (Pointe-à-Pitre, Guadeloupe), 128
Centre Dramatique Régional (Martinique), 115
Césaire, Aimé: on connection between American South and Caribbean, 10, 27; Négritude movement and, 2, 52, 88; plays of, 184, 228n87; *A Tempest*, 141; theatrical contributions of, 5
Césaire, Catherine, 219n3
Césaire, Ina: career and works of, 5–6; *Contes de mort et de vie aux Antilles*, 105; as cultural authority, 141, 144; ethnological research, 1, 5–6, 67–69, 105–6, 109–10, 112–13, 208; folklore as viewed by, 16, 153–54; intercultural theater and, 54; *Lettre d'affranchissement*, 208; on recovering her black identity, 2, 11, 139, 146; staging of creolization, 3; "La triade humaine dans le conte antillais," 209; on Ubu production of *Fire's Daughters*, 153–54, 166; on Ubu production of *Island Memories*, 2, 138–40. *See also L'Enfant des passages*; *Mémoires d'Isles*; *Rosanie Soleil*
Césaire, Michèle, 8; *La Nef (The Ship)*, 9, 149, 238n1
Chaillot National Theatre (Paris), 130
Chamoiseau, Patrick, 28; Césaire's *L'Enfant des passages* criticized by, 107, 116–17; Créolité movement and, 7, 52, 97, 103, 187; moral codes viewed by, 104; "Red Hot Peppers," 185
"Chestnut" stereotype, 24, 98; Césaire's use of, 26, 28, 29, 32, 33–34, 50; Condé's use of, 39–40, 42–43, 45–46, 49, 50
Christopher, King, 7
Cixous, Hélène, 89
Clark, VèVè, 18, 76, 208
Code de l'indigénat (1887), 51
collective memory, performance and, 14–15, 52, 67, 68–69
Collins, Patricia Hill, 24, 171
Condé, Maryse: career and works of, 6; *Comédie d'amour*, 9; *Comme deux frères*, 9; on Haiti, 6–7; *Heremakhonon*, 23; intercultural theater and, 54; *I*

Tituba, Black Witch of Salem, 208; *Le Morne de Massabielle (The Hills of Massabielle)*, 9, 141, 184, 185, 238n1; "Order, Disorder, Freedom, and the West Indian Writer," 7, 171; organic knowledge production as viewed by, 16; *La Parole des femmes*, 23–24, 171; Philcox and, 159; on Schwarz-Bart's use of Creole language, 173–74; staging of creolization, 3, 206; Thomas's interview with, 28; White and, 199. *See also An tan revolisyon; Pension les Alizes*
Confiant, Raphaël, 7, 28, 52, 97, 103, 187
Conquergood, Dwight, 209
Conteh-Morgan, John, 5, 127
contresens, 185
Cortés, Hernán, 222n3
Cottias, Myriam, 28
Creole folklore: as distorting mirror, 110; moral codes in, 100–101, 112; split figures and double meanings in, 103, 105, 117; Tigre in, 107–8; Ti-Jean in, 100, 102, 105–18, 211; used by French Caribbean playwrights, 15–16, 100–132, 153–54
Creole identity: "chabine" phenotypic category, 33; folklorization and, 15; Indians and, 91–93; language and, 186–88; miscegenation and, 26–27; multiraciality of, 2, 34–37, 60, 69, 71, 99, 211–13; syncretic performance practices and, 102–5
Creole proverbs, 100–101, 115, 120–21, 232n3
Créolité movement, 7–8, 27, 52, 87, 97, 187
creolization: aesthetics of, 97–99; ajiaco stew comparison, 13–14; cultural literacy and, 18–19; gender and, 8, 44–46, 49–50; generalization beyond Caribbean, 202–3; opacity and, 14, 19; as performance, 3, 4–5, 8, 200–203; politics of performing in the U.S., 203, 205–17; power and entanglement questions, 216–17; as process, 11, 164, 205; of slavery's memory, 29; surprises of, 13; syncretic performance as moral repossession, 102–5; as term, 2–3; transformation and, 11–16, 101, 104–5, 131–32, 136–37, 205
Crosscurrents (translation of Dambury's *lettres indiennes*), 162, 164, 165; costume design, 161, 166; music and dance in, 163; performing Indianness in, 165–66; reception, 160–61, 164, 167; Réunion Island traditions in, 160, 161, 163–64, 167; set design, 163; textual translation, 159, 161; Ubu production, 4, 133–34, 159–68; universalist readings of, 163–64
"culture of dissemblance," 34–35

Dambury, Gerty, 221n53; career and works of, 6; criticism of Théâtre des Halles's staging, 96–97; intercultural theater and, 54, 161, 163–64; organic knowledge production as viewed by, 16; staging of creolization, 3; on Ubu production of *Crosscurrents*, 166. *See also Lettres indiennes*
Damico, Micheline, 61
Daniel, Yvonne, 12–13
Dawson, Alene, 150, *151*, 152
débouya, concept of, 100–101, 102, 103, 104, 106, 107–9, 112, 113–15, 117–18, 131, 233n26
débrouillardise, 100, 107, 233n26
Declaration of the Rights of Man and of the Citizen (1789), 55–56, 57, 61
De Lavallade, Carmen, 2, 138–39, *139*, 145
Deren, Maya, 152
Dessalines, Jean-Jacques, 56, 65–66
diaspora, experience of, 52–53, 82–83, 87–89, 136–38, 171–72
diaspora literacy, concept of, 18, 37, 208
Donzenac, Myrrha, 68, *69*, 71, 73–76, 144
Dove, Rita: *The Darker Face of the Earth*, 247n6
Dracius, Suzanne, 8; *Lumina Sophie dite Surprise*, 9
Drewal, Margaret, 12
Dunham, Katherine, 152, 154
Durand, Laurence, 38

Edwards, Brent Hayes, 136–37
Edwards, Carole, 8, 27
Emmanuel, Sonia, 41, 46–47, 48, 55, 61, 192
Emond, Paul: *Talk about Love!*, 149
Enéléda, Sylviane, 107, 116

Erskine, Noel, 101
Euba, Akim (Femi), 219n3
Exélis, José, 219n3, 221n53

Fanon, Frantz, 26, 27, 42; *Black Skin, White Masks*, 34
Fire's Daughters (translation of Césaire's *Rosanie Soleil*), 151; Africanist dances in, 154–55, 158; costume design, 152–53; Creole language in, 150, 158, 159; "Eyou Marassa" song in, 154; identity politics and, 147, 149–51, 156–59, 195; intercultural elements, 151–54; music in, 154; performing diaspora unity, 154–56; reception of, 156–57, 158; set design, 151–52, *152*, 153, *153*; textual translation, 147–49, 150, 158; Ubu production, 4, 133–34, 147–59, 168
Fort-de-France Festival (Martinique), 4, 38, 107
Fort Fleur d'Epée (Guadeloupe), 57, 59
Fouchard, Jean, 221n2
Foy, Harriet D., 150, *151*, *152*, 154
Frankétienne, 97
French Caribbean plantation culture: abolition of slavery (1794), 56, 57; in Césaire's *Rosanie Soleil*, 29–39; Christianity and, 103–5; Creole proverbs, 100–101, 115, 120–21, 232n3; female historical stereotypes, 23–25, 34–36; French Revolution and, 55–56, 57; male historical stereotypes, 27–28; reinstitution of slavery (1802), 56, 57; religion and moral codes, 100–101, 103, 104, 112, 233n17; sexual exploitation and power in, 24–25, 26–29, 34–37, 49–50, 64–65; similarities with American South, 206; slavery's aftereffects on love, 170–72; subversive messages in performance practices, 104–5; three-tier racial caste system, 59–60
French-Caribbean theater: American university productions, 205–17; cultural literacy and, 18–19; diaspora performances, 9–11, 133–68; folklore as basis in, 15–16, 100–101; fragility of archives, 18, 38–39; Haiti dramatized in, 7; intercultural and postcolonial approaches, 53–55; "love and trouble" narratives, 171–72, 181–82, 183, 186, 198–200; prix Carbet de la Caraïbe winners, 6; race and gender signifying in U.S. university productions, 211–15, 216; reassembling production history, 16–18; rewriting of postcolonialism, 8–9; role in transmitting and reinventing culture, 14–16; syncretic performance practices and, 102–5; syncretism in, 4–5, 102–5, 110–11, 115–18, 123–24, 132; teaching cultural and critical literacy through, 208–11; women playwrights, 5–11, 16, 168. *See also specific authors and subjects*
French Revolution (1789), 55–56, 57–58, 63–67
Fulton, Dawn, 41

Gaensbauer, Deborah, 58
Garraway, Doris, 26
Gautier, Arlette, 28, 222–23n22
Gerstin, Julian, 233n19
Gibbs, Sheila, 178
Gilbert, Helen, 50, 53, 54
Giles, Freda Scott, 207–17, 247n6
Gilroy, Paul, 11, 136
Giraudoux, Jean: *The Madwoman of Chaillot*, 193
Glissant, Édouard: Antillanité, 52; creoleness and creolization distinguished by, 11; *Faulkner, Mississippi*, 244n51; *Monsieur Toussaint*, 228n87; opacity notion, 14, 19; *Poetics of Relation*, 93, 99; relational identity concept, 112; "Theater, Consciousness of the People," 15, 16, 106, 153–54
globalization, effects of, 89–90, 91–92, 137, 185–86, 205
Grayson, Darlene Bel, 150, *151*, *152*
Guadeloupe: Catholicism among enslaved population, 103–4, 233n17; Creole proverbs, 100–101; as department of France, 6, 51, 90; dream of solidarity with Haiti, 65–66; failed independence of, 56, 63–64; final abolition of, 56, 59; French Revolution and aftermath in, 55–67; Haitian immigrants in, 237n114; Haitian migrant workers in, 124, 125–26; identity issues for, 6–7, 51–53; Indians' social struggle in, 89–93; *léwoz* dance, 100, 109; Réunion Island and, 82–83, 86–89, 160, 161, 163–64, 167;

slavery's echoes and reverberations in, 124–28
Guillory, Don J., 219n3
gwo-ka dance and drumming, 15, 66, 94, 96, 100, 120–21
Gyssels, Kathleen, 123, 130, 181

Haiti: 2010 earthquake, 18, 38–39; contemporary realities of, 7; Duvalier regime in, 7, 125, 210, 211; elements in Ubu production of Schwarz-Bart's *Your Handsome Captain*, 177–80, 183; failed dreams of, 65–66; Guadeloupe and Martinique compared with, 6–7, 37–38, 65–66; independence of, 7, 56
Haitian Revolution, 7, 31, 37–38, 56, 65–66
Hall, Stuart, 6, 53, 99, 136, 216–17; "Cultural Identity and Diaspora," 11, 14
Hansberry, Lorraine: *Raisin in the Sun*, 2
Harris, Jessica, 170, 175–77, 178, 185
Harrison, Paul Carter: *Totem Voices*, 137
Harrison, Stanley Earl, 178
Harshaw, Cee-Cee, 150, *151*
Hartman, Saidiya, 26, 35, 51; *Scenes of Subjection*, 11–12
Hatch, James, 9–10
Hewitt, Leah, 41
Hicks, Bryan, *164*
Hill, Errol, 9–10; "Perspectives in Caribbean Theatre," 15–16
Hine, Darlene Clark, 34
Holder, Laurence, 146
Houyoux, Suzanne, 87
Hughes, Victor, 57, 59, 61
Hugo, Victor, 61
Hurston, Zora Neale, 154; *Tell My Horse*, 152

identity issues: Caribbeanness, 11, 51–53, 76–77, 82–99, 104, 140–41, 143–44, 146–47, 212–13; changing perspectives, 2, 3, 168; French Caribbean caste system, 59–60; Frenchness, 51–52; identity politics and ownership, 135, 143, 146, 147, 149–51, 156–59, 160–61, 165–66, 172, 178, 183–84, 193–97; Indian diaspora and, 82–99, 159–68; for Martinique and Guadeloupe, 6–7; postcolonialism and, 54–55; racial hybridity in the U.S., 10; relational, 99; religion and, 104, 233n17. *See also* black identity; Creole identity; creolization
Indian diaspora in Caribbean: assimilation of, 87–89; caste system's disappearance in, 88; difference from U.S. experience, 160; historical experience of, 53, 82–99, 159; indentured servitude and, 89–93, 160, 167; religion and, 88–89
intercultural theater: Caribbean playwrights, 54–55, 102–3, 119, 123–24, 197, 207–17; critiques of, 53–54; culture of links and, 88, 89; definition of, 53; French audience familiarity with, 77–78; multiple viewpoints and, 75–77; recasting and, 169–71, 197–200; Ubu Repertory Theater and, 135–36, 151–54, 155–56, 161, 163–64, 199–200; world feminism and, 155–56, 157. *See also specific plays, playwrights, directors, and companies*
International Francophone Cultural Festival (Limoges), 130, 172
In the Time of Revolution (translation of Condé's *An tan revolisyon*), 205–17; dance in, 210–11, 215; embodied knowledge in Georgia production, 209–10, 215–16; nontraditional casting in Georgia production, 213–14, 216; slavery's inheritance in, 211
Island Memories (translation of Césaire's *Mémoires d'Isles*), 139, *145*; authenticity claims, 143–44, 146–47; "Bouch nou oxydé" song, 144; class and complexion issues in, 142–43; Martinican dances in, 139, 143, 155; production tone, 144; reception of, 140, 146–47; sentiments of black diaspora unity in, 138–41; songs performed in, 144; tensions and misrecognitions in Ubu production, 141–42; translators, 140–41; Ubu production, 1–2, 4, 133–34, 138–47, 168
Ito, Genji, 163, 242n82

Jackson, Ernestine, 2, 138–39, *139*, 144, *145*
Jean-Julien, Joelle, 38
Jernidier, José, 56, 62, 214
Johnson, E. Patrick, 216

Jones, Bridget, 6, 76, 111, 115, 171
Jovignot, Noël, 130, 219n3
Justin-Joseph, Annick, 107, 115–18

Kadish, Doris, 207–8, 209, 210
Kanhai-Brunton, Rosanne, 174–75, 176
Kapp, Chris, 196
Kassav, 211
Kenol, Max, 124, 128, 129–31
Kim, Suk-Young, 17
Kirksey-Floyd, Dianne, 133, 139, 140, 142, 143, 144
Klapper, Stephanie, 165
Knepper, Wendy, 13
Knowles, Ric, 54
konesans (vodou concept), 209
Konstantin, Elise-Ann, 239n21
Kourilsky, Françoise, 130, 133; as director, 159–61, 163, 165–66, 167, 177, 181–83, 200; personal background of, 134, 179–80; stagings of Schwarz-Bart's *Ton beau capitaine*, 172, 173–83; as Ubu artistic director, 134–36, 138, 141, 149, 151, 154, 157, 158, 169, 170, 172–73, 175–76, 178, 184, 189, 195, 242n82
Krakovitch, Odile, 37
Kraut, Anthea, 241n58
Kwahulé, Koffi: *That Old Black Magic*, 149

Labat, Jean-Baptiste, 104–5, 233n19
Ladnier, Kavi, 161, *162*, 163, *164*, 165, 166, 242n90
LaMama ETC, 135, 151
Lamont, Rosette C., 154, 155, 161, 193
Laou, Julius Amédé, 184; *Another Story*, 194
Laumord, Gilbert, 57, 62, 94, *95, 95*, 96, 98, 221n53
Léna Blou, 122, 221n53, 232n2
L'Enfant des passages, ou la geste de Ti-Jean (Césaire): Creole songs and dances in, 109–10; dance in Wisconsin production, 210–11; *débouya* in, 101, 106, 107–9, 112, 113–15, 117–18, 131; ending of, 106, 114, 131; first production, 107, 115–18; as folktale adaptation, 101, 105–7, 116–17, 208; folktale mediated in, 109–15; moral codes in, 101–2, 107–9, 112; plot of, 107–8; production history, 4; slavery's inheritance in, 211; spatial organization of, 110–11; stage directions in, 109; syncretism staged in, 115–18; time in, 113–15; University of Wisconsin staging, 205–17
Lettres indiennes (Dambury), 82–99, *95*; characters in, 83–86; diaspora as key to artistic process, 86–89; diaspora experience in, 52–53, 82–99; past and present in, 89–90; plot of, 82; production history, 4; Réunion Island traditions in, 82–83, 86–89; storytelling in, 94, 95–97; theme of "home" in, 85–86. *See also Crosscurrents*
Lévi-Strauss, Claude: bricolage concept, 13
Lewis, Barbara, 170, 180–81, 184–86, 191
léwoz (Guadeloupean dance), 100, 109, 120–21, 122, 130
Libre Échange, 46–47
Lionnet, Françoise, 201, 202
Louima, Abner, 211, 216
Louis XVI, King of France, 59, 213
Louverture, Toussaint, 7, 56, 59, 62, 65
"love and trouble" tradition, 171–72, 181–82, 183, 186, 198–200
Lowe, Lisa, 89
lwa (vodou divinities), 103

MacPherson, Greg, 152, 190, 245n73
makè (*gwo-ka* soloist drummer), 122
Makward, Christiane, 6, 7, 8, 30, 43, 77, 89, 147, 171; anthology of Césaire's plays, 73–74; on Shange's staging of Césaire's *Fire's Daughters*, 155; translation of Césaire's *Mémoires d'Isles*, 69, 71, 79–81, 140, 142
male-centric Caribbean culture and literary movements, 3, 25, 27–28, 34
Malidor, Lisette, 41, 224n89
Malinche, 222n3
Mandvi, Aasif, 158, *164*, 165, *165*
Manning, Susan, 156
marasa consciousness, 37–38, 50, 76, 81, 208
Marcelin, Michelle, 178
Mardorossian, Carine, 8, 212
Marie-Louise, Jean-Erns, 219n3
"Marilisse" stereotype, 23–24, 29, 32,

221–22n3; in Césaire's *Rosanie Soleil*, 34–36, 37; in Condé's *Pension les Alizés*, 25, 26, 39–49, 50, 192, 199
Martial, Jacques, 46–47, 48
Martinique: African dance witnessed in 1724, 104–5, 233n19; Catholicism among enslaved population, 103–4, 233n17; Creole proverbs, 100–101, 232n3; as department of France, 6, 51, 90; Dissidence movement in, 68, 72; final abolition of slavery, 59; folklorization problem, 15; identity issues for, 6–7, 51–53, 143–44, 146–47; Indians' social struggle in, 89–93, 159; mayor's assassination (1935), 68; Southern Insurrection (1870), 30–31, 32–34, 37–38, 68, 148–49
Mason, Laura, 211
Mathéus, Mariann, 68, 69, 71, 72 76, 94–97, 95, 128, 129–31, 144, 167
Maximin, Daniel, 97
Maximin, Martine, 219n3
McCauley, Robbie, 141
McClain, Saundra, 147, 150, 154, 158, 197–200
McGruder, Sharon, 178, 179
McKay, Melissa, 8, 44–45
McMahon, Christiana, 170
Médeuf, Serge, 116
Mémoires d'Isles (Césaire), 67–81, 69, 71; "Bouch nou oxydé" song, 72; carnivalesque tactics in, 78–79, 81; changes in prologue, 73; collaborative performance approach of, 71–72, 75–77; collective memory in, 52, 67, 68–69, 75–76, 78–79, 98; delocalized aesthetic of, 94–97; first production, 77–81; fourth wall broken in, 79; French and Creole languages in, 78, 79–81; importance of silence in, 35–36; inspiration for, 1; intercultural modifications, 73–74, 75–77, 80–81; *L'Enfant des passages* contrasted with, 107; male infidelity and abuse in, 71; onstage transformations in, 1, 67–68; play as written, 71, 72–74, 144; production history, 3–4, 68, 219n3; rape scene in, 36, 73–74; reception of, 80–81; *Rosanie Soleil* compared with, 69; spectatorship by cultural literacy, 71, 77–81. See also Island Memories

Miller, Judith, 8, 58, 111, 125, 181; staging of Césaire's *L'Enfant des passages*, 207–17; translation of Césaire's *Mémoires d'Isles*, 69, 79–81, 140, 142, 208; translation of Césaire's *Rosanie Soleil*, 147–49, 150, 156–57, 158, 208
Miller, Richard, 238n1
Mishima, Yukio, 123
Mnouchkine, Ariane, 53, 75, 77, 151; *1789*, 57–58, 60–61, 62, 63, 67; *1793*, 58; *Indiade*, 89
Montantin, Michèle, 128, 130, 181
Morrison, Toni, 146
Mosquera, Gerardo, 13–14
Munro, Martin, 206
Murray, David, 27

Nascimento, Milton, 211
Négritude movement, 2, 52, 87, 88, 168
Negro Ensemble Company, 157
Nesbitt, Nick, 52
New Federal Theatre, 157
Nietzsche, Friedrich, 108
Noh theater, 103, 119, 123, 207
Noverca, Anna, 60

ogbanje child concept, 64–65, 110–11
Okawa, Rachelle, 187–88, 189
Olmos, Margarite Fernández, 13–14
Ortiz, Fernando, 13–14
Osofisan, Femi: *Farewell to Cannibal Rage*, 212

Palcy, Raymonde, 94
Palit, Jay, 166
Paravisini-Gebert, Lizabeth, 13–14
Peck, Raoul, 190
Pelletier, Carol Ann, 135, 144, 152–53, 161, 166, 190, 245n73
Penchenat, Jean-Claude, 68, 75, 76
Pennot, Élie, 105, 233n21
Pension les Alizés (Condé), 39–49; Baker and, 43–44; Chestnut stereotype rejected in, 39, 40, 42–43, 45–46; creolizing gender in, 49–50; double reading of Emma in, 39–40; Emma's unborn daughter in, 45, 63; failed heterosexual love, 44–46; iconic juxtapositions and exaggerations, 41–43; inspirations for Emma character, 41;

Pension les Alizés (Condé) (continued)
Marilisse stereotype reinvented in, 25, 29, 39–49, 199; modifying meanings in performance, 47–48, 49, 192, 203; original performance, 46–49; plot of, 39; production history, 4; reception, 48–49; transhistorical abstractions, 43–44; women's bodies as focus in, 26; writing style of, 186–89. *See also Tropical Breeze Hotel, The*

Pépin, Ernest, 97

Perry, Shauneille, 184, 189, 191, 194–97

Pfaff, Françoise, 198

Philcox, Richard, 159, 161, 184, 187–88, 220n28

Philip, M. NourbeSe, 24–25

Pineau, Gisèle, 27, 28

Piriou, Jean-Pierre, 207–8, 209

Piscator, Ervin, *Schweik* production of, 110–11

Ponette, Luc: *Berthilia*, 75

postcolonial theater, 53–55, 67, 77–78, 99. *See also specific plays and playwrights*

Proto, Félix, 57

Quimbois, 108, 117, 175

Quotidien, Le, 128

Rameau, Patrick, 177, 178, 179, 190–91, *191*, 194, *196*

rasé, 122

recasting, 169–71, 180–83, 197–200

Refosco, Mauro, 154

Rémy, Laure, 66

Réunion Island, 82–83, 86–89, 160, 161, 163–64, 167

Richard, Firmine, 94, *95*, 98, 219n3

Richards, Sandra L., 85, 137, 201–2, 211–12

Rites and Reason (Brown University), 176

Roach, Joseph, 29, 103; *Cities of the Dead*, 14–15

Rosanie Soleil (Césaire), 29–39; Chestnut stereotype reinvented in, 25, 29, 33–34; creolizing gender in, 49–50; drumming and vodou ritual in, 31, 37–38, 50; "Eyou Marassa" song in, 37; generalizing revolutionary women in, 32–34; importance of silence in, 33, 35; legacies of resistance, 30–32; *L'Enfant des passages* contrasted with, 107; Marilisse stereotype haunting, 34–36; *Mémoires d'Isles* compared with, 69; plot of, 29–30; production history, 4, 18, 38–39; storytelling in, 31–32, 33–34, 38–39, 50; theme of, 29; unity in the unknown, 36–39; women's bodies as focus in, 26. *See also Fire's Daughters*

Ruprecht, Alvina, 5, 39–40, 119, 121, 122, 130, 177, 181, 191, 201

St. Georges, Chevalier de, 62

Saint-Éloy, Luc, 105, 233n21

Sandahl, Carrie, 214–15

Sargeant, Michael, 143

Sarr, Akua, 211

Scharfman, Ronnie, 140, 182

Schoenberg, Arnold: *Gürrelieder*, 47

Schwarz-Bart, André, 37; *The Last of the Just*, 182

Schwarz-Bart, Simone: career and works of, 6; folklore as viewed by, 16; intercultural theater and, 119; interracial marriage of, 182; novels of, 37; *Pluie et vent sur Télumée Miracle*, 171; staging of creolization, 3; on *Ton beau capitaine* as political critique, 171. *See also Ton beau capitaine*

Scott, Seret, 147, 172–73

Serreau, Jean-Marie, 38, 228n87

Serreau, Raphaelle, 38

Shaked, Gershon, 146, 212

Shakespeare, William: *The Tempest*, 141

Shange, Ntozake: *For colored girls who have considered suicide / when the rainbow is enuf*, 147, 150, 172; as cultural mediator, 150; as director, 133, 146, 147, 149–52, 154–56, 195

Sharif, Bina, *164*, *165*, 166

Shih, Shu-mei, 201, 202

Singa, Suzy, 219n3

Slade, Catherine, 169, 178, 180, 200

slavery: *abiku* or *ogbanje* child myth under, 64–65; aftereffects of, 170–72, 198–99, 211; Catholicism imposed on enslaved Africans, 103, 104, 107, 233n17; creolization as response to, 12; diaspora concept and, 136–37; displacement and, 110–11; echoes and reverberations in Schwarz-Bart's *ton beau capitaine*, 124–28; economic exploitation in aftermath of, 90–91; emasculation and, 27–28, 125–26; female historical stereotypes, 23–24; first abolition of (1794), 56, 57; freed slaves, 28, 222–23n22; gendered relationships as legacy of, 27–28, 44–46, 49–50; Indian indentured servants as echoes of, 89–93, 159, 160, 167; legacies of, 134; Martinique rebellion (1870), 30–31, 32–34, 37–38, 68; moral codes and, 101–2, 105–18, 126–27; myths of black female body, 26–29; non-violent resistance acts, 12; racialized knowledge production as legacy of, 157, 158; reinstitution of (1802), 56, 57; second abolition of (1848), 56, 59; as system of subjection, 51; temporary escape from, 12–13

Solitude (Guadeloupean female revolutionary), 59, 63, 211
Sormain, Jean-Camille, 219n3
Spivak, Gayatri, 187
Stern, Adrienne, 150
Stewart, Ellen, 135, 151
Stewart, Jon, 165–66
storytelling, Caribbean practices: Césaire's ethnological research, 5–6, 67–69, 105–6, 109–10, 112–13; in Césaire's *L'Enfant des passages*, 101–2, 106, 108–9; in Césaire's *Rosanie Soleil*, 31–32, 33–34, 38–39; in Condé's *An tan revolisyon*, 52, 56, 58, 62, 66, 96; creolization and, 3, 9; in Dambury's *Lettres indiennes*, 94, 95–97; participation in, 15–16; in Schwarz-Bart's *Ton beau capitaine*, 121–22; as survival tool, 101; as syncretic, 102–5, 110–11; as temporary escape from slavery, 12
Sturm, Jean-Pierre, 220n29
Sylaire, Ruddy, 130, 219n3

Tarica, Estelle, 104
Taylor, Diana, 12, 15
Temerson, Catherine, 170, 175–77, 185–86
Théâtre de l'Air Nouveau, 233n21
Théâtre de la Soif Nouvelle, 115, 233n21
Théâtre des Halles, 94–99
Theatre Development Fund, 196
Théâtre du Campagnol, 68

Théâtre du Soleil, 57–58, 75, 89
Thomas, Bonnie, 28
Threadgill, Henry, 177
Timar, Alain, 94, 96–97, 159
Tompkins, Joanne, 50, 53, 54
Ton beau capitaine (Schwarz-Bart), 118–32; abandonment of ambition in, 128; *bigidi* in, 102, 118–32; Caribbean men's experiences foregrounded in, 126; Creole language usage in, 173–75; dances in, 103, 118, 119, 120–23, 125, 127–28, 129–30, 131; English translation problems of, 173–77; first production, 119, 128–32; Marie-Ange placed onstage in Cavé production, 129, 130, 172; Marie-Ange's stage absence in, 126, 130, 172; moral codes in, 101–2, 126–27, 180–81; performing unresolved tensions in, 128–32; production history, 4, 128–32, 172, 176–77, 219n3; reception, 130–31, 177; Rites and Reasons production, 176; ritualization of communication in, 121–23; set design, 128; slavery's legacies in, 124–28, 222n9; song in, 129; structure of, 121–22. *See also Your Handsome Captain*
Tournafond, Françoise, 75
translation, politics of, 187–88
trickster folktale heroes, 100–101, 102, 113–15, 211
Tropical Breeze Hotel, The (translation of Condé's *Pension les Alizés*), 191, 193; casting difficulties, 190–93, 197–200; costume design, 190; earlier translation, 184–86; French emphasis of Ubu production, 193–97; irony and psychological realism, 189–93; merengue in, 195–96, 196; production history, 219n3; recasting, 197–200; set design, 189–90, 190; staging choices, 188–89; text translation, 180, 184–89; Ubu production, 4, 169, 172, 183–200
TTC + Bakanal, 56
Turner, Beth: *Black Masks*, 150

Ubu Repertory Theater: archives, 17; "Bravo Ubu" tribute, 169, 197; cultural and pedagogical context, 134–36; diaspora performance concept and, 136–38, 140; Festival of New Plays by

Ubu Repertory Theater (continued)
Women, 194; Festival of New Plays from French-Speaking Africa and the Caribbean, 184; French Ministry of Culture funding, 186; identity politics and marketing, 135, 143–44, 146, 149–51, 156–59, 172, 178, 183–84, 193–97; importance to French Caribbean theater history, 201–2; New York's theater climate and, 157–58, 168; production of Césaire's *Fire's Daughters*, 4, 133–34, 147–59, 168; production of Césaire's *Island Memories*, 1–2, 4, 133–34, 138–47, 168; production of Condé's *Hills of Massabielle*, 9, 141, 184, 185, 238n1; production of Condé's *Tropical Breeze Hotel*, 4, 169, 172, 183–200; production of Dambury's *Crosscurrents*, 4, 133–34, 159–68; production of M. Césaire's *The Ship*, 9, 149, 238n1; productions of Schwarz-Bart's *Your Handsome Captain*, 4, 130, 169, 171–83; recasting at, 169–71, 180–83, 197–200; Ubu International Festival (1993), 149–51; West Indies Festival (1991), 141, 143–44, 146–47, 239n18

Ueno, Watoku, 135, 151–52, 153, 163, 189–90, *190*, 245n73

University of Albany, 179

University of Georgia, 4, 205–17

University of Wisconsin, Madison, 4, 205–17

Vanbercheck, Danielle, 38

Vergès, Françoise, 12, 205

vodou: in Césaire's *Mémoires d'Isles*, 78; in Césaire's *Rosanie Soleil*, 31, 37–38, 155; in Condé's *An tan revolisyon*, 62; dances, 120; Haitian Revolution and, 31, 38; *konesans* concept, 209; *marasa* divine twins, 37–38, 50, 76, 81, 154, 208; possession, 122; split figures and double meanings in, 103, 128–29, 154; transformation and, 12–13, 37–38, 101, 104–5; in Ubu production of Schwarz-Bart's *Your Handsome Captain*, 177–80, 183

Walcott, Derek, 13, 14, 105, 146

Washington, Denzel, 178

Waters, Harold A., 149

White, Jane, 169, 189, 190–93, *191*, *193*, *196*, 197–200

White, Walter, 199

Yara Arts Group, 135, 151

Young, Harvey, 26

Your Handsome Captain (translation of Schwarz-Bart's *Ton beau capitaine*), *179*; Haitian elements in Ubu production, 177–80; Marie-Ange's onstage presence or absence, 181–82; recastings of Marie-Ange role, 180–83; reception, 179, 181, 182; text translation, 170, 173–77, 185; Ubu productions, 4, 130, 169, 171–83; University of Albany performance, 179

Zarrilli, Phillip B., 18

Recent Books in the New World Studies Series

Supriya M. Nair, *Pathologies of Paradise: Caribbean Detours*

Colleen C. O'Brien, *Race, Romance, and Rebellion: Literatures of the Americas in the Nineteenth Century*

Kelly Baker Josephs, *Disturbers of the Peace: Representations of Madness in Anglophone Caribbean Literature*

Christina Kullberg, *The Poetics of Ethnography in Martinican Narratives: Exploring the Self and the Environment*

Maria Cristina Fumagalli, Bénédicte Ledent, and Roberto del Valle Alcalá, editors, *The Cross-Dressed Caribbean: Writing, Politics, Sexualities*

Philip Kaisary, *The Haitian Revolution in the Literary Imagination: Radical Horizons, Conservative Constraints*

Jason Frydman, *Sounding the Break: African American and Caribbean Routes of World Literature*

Tanya L. Shields, *Bodies and Bones: Feminist Rehearsal and Imagining Caribbean Belonging*

Stanka Radović, *Locating the Destitute: Space and Identity in Caribbean Fiction*

Nicole N. Aljoe and Ian Finseth, editors, *Journeys of the Slave Narrative in the Early Americas*

Stephen M. Park, *The Pan American Imagination: Contested Visions of the Hemisphere in Twentieth-Century Literature*

Maurice St. Pierre, *Eric Williams and the Anticolonial Tradition: The Making of a Diasporan Intellectual*

Elena Machado Sáez, *Market Aesthetics: The Purchase of the Past in Caribbean Diasporic Fiction*

Martin Munro, *Tropical Apocalypse: Haiti and the Caribbean End Times*

Jeannine Murray-Román, *Performance and Personhood in Caribbean Literature: From Alexis to the Digital Age*

Anke Birkenmaier, *The Spectre of Races: Latin American Anthropology and Literature between the Wars*

John Patrick Leary, *A Cultural History of Underdevelopment: Latin America in the U.S. Imagination*

Raphael Dalleo, *American Imperialism's Undead: The Occupation of Haiti and the Rise of Caribbean Anticolonialism*

Emily Sahakian, *Staging Creolization: Women's Theater and Performance from the French Caribbean*

www.ingramcontent.com/pod-product-compliance
Lightning Source LLC
Chambersburg PA
CBHW021820300426
44114CB00009BA/258